The Director's Prism

The Director's Prism

E. T. A. Hoffmann and the Russian Theatrical Avant-Garde

Dassia N. Posner

Northwestern University Press / Evanston, Illinois

Northwestern University Press
www.nupress.northwestern.edu

A grant from the Andrew W. Mellon Foundation supported the creation of an online resource companion to this book, which includes additional archival and multimedia materials. The companion can be accessed at http://northwestern.fulcrumscholar.org.

Printed in the United States of America

10 9 8 7 6 5 4 3 2 1

Library of Congress Cataloging-in-Publication Data

Names: Posner, Dassia N., author.
Title: The director's prism : E.T.A. Hoffmann and the Russian theatrical avant-garde / Dassia N. Posner.
Description: Evanston, Illinois : Northwestern University Press, 2016. | Includes bibliographical references and index.
Identifiers: LCCN 2016011943| ISBN 9780810133556 (pbk. : alk. paper) | ISBN 9780810133563 (cloth : alk. paper) | ISBN 9780810133570 (e-book)
Subjects: LCSH: Hoffmann, E. T. A. (Ernst Theodor Amadeus), 1776–1822—Influence. | Meĭerkhol'd, V. Ė. (Vsevolod Ėmil'evich), 1874–1940—Criticism and interpretation. | Tairov, Aleksandr I͡Akovlevich, 1885–1950—Criticism and interpretation. | Eisenstein, Sergei, 1898–1948—Criticism and interpretation. | Theater—Production and direction—Russia—History—20th century. | Russian drama—20th century—History and criticism.
Classification: LCC PN2724 .P67 2016 | DDC 792.09470904—dc23
LC record available at http://lccn.loc.gov/2016011943

For Brian

Out of the crooked timber of humanity, no straight thing was ever made.
—Immanuel Kant

The painter, the poet, the composer do not hold up a mirror to nature, however ideal, but invent.
—Isaiah Berlin

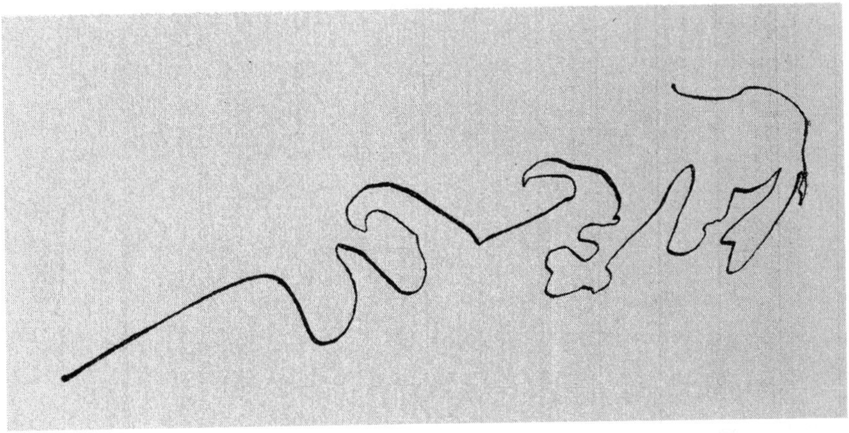

E. T. A. Hoffmann, parodic illustration (c. 1804) of the narrative structure of Laurence Sterne's novel *The Life and Opinions of Tristram Shandy, Gentleman* (1759–67). Staatsbibliothek Bamberg, L.g.o.391e/B19. Photo: Gerald Raab.

Contents

Illustrations

Note on Translation and Transliteration

Translations from the Russian are my own unless cited from secondary sources in English. Russian transliterations are based on common spellings in the text (i.e., Meyerhold rather than Meierkhol'd) and on a slightly simplified Library of Congress system for references cited in the endnotes. Years listed immediately after production titles indicate the date of premiere rather than of writing or publication. All dates are listed according to the Russian calendar at the time of the event.

Abbreviations and Acronyms

FEKS	Factory of the Eccentric Actor
GITIS	State Institute of Theatrical Art
Glavpolitprosvet	Chief Committee for Political Education
Glavrepertkom	Chief Repertory Commission
GosTIM	State Meyerhold Theatre
GVYRM (later GVYTM)	Meyerhold's State Higher Directing (later Theatre) Workshops
KhPSRO	Artistic Educational Union of Workers' Organizations
LTA	*Love for Three Oranges: The Journal of Doctor Dapertutto*
MastFor	Theatre Workshop of Nikolai Foregger (also Volmas-for)
MAT (also MXAT)	Moscow Art (State Academic) Theatre
MAT First Studio	Moscow Art Theatre First Studio
MAT Third Studio	Moscow Art Theatre Third Studio (later the Vakhtangov Theatre)
MKT	Moscow Kamerny Theatre
MAT 2	Moscow Art Theatre 2
Narkompros	Commissariat of Enlightenment
NEP	New Economic Policy
Proletkult	Proletarian Cultural and Enlightenment Organization

RGALI	Russian State Archive of Literature and Art (formerly TsGALI)
RSFSR	Russian Soviet Federative Socialist Republic
STD	Theatre Workers' Union
TEO	Theater Section of Narkompros
VTO	All-Russia Theatre Organization

Preface and Acknowledgments

FOR SEVEN YEARS I have taught History of Directing, a class in which we reconstruct and analyze theatrical productions in order to explore the artistic theories and practical work of a variety of directors. I have often observed that my brilliant and inspiring students—many of them directors in their own right—enter this class assuming certain things as theatrical givens: that realism is a norm from which other styles deviate, that a director's first responsibility is fidelity to life or to a playwright, that a choice must be made between intellectual engagement and creative inspiration, and that a director-defined theater cannot be actor- or audience-centered. They frequently are more comfortable shaping story than wielding form and assume that a production cannot dance between the representational and presentational without overtaxing the viewer's imagination.[1] Yet many are magnetically drawn to experimentation, to nonlinear dramaturgies, to site-specific theater with no fourth wall, to direct audience engagement, and to tilts of familiar conventions that propel the spectator into the realm of the unexpected. They simply don't always know which sources to mine for theatricalist devices that are immediate and fresh. This quandary is symptomatic of a broader phenomenon, a product of the fact that realism and text-centric performance have so long been the dominant modes of artistic creation in American theater.

By theatricalist devices, I mean those that unleash the theater's inherent theatricality—a word that, admittedly, as Davis and Postlewait have demonstrated, has been used in so many contexts so as to mean both everything and nothing.[2] Even Russian directors from the same era or whose work at first glance seems similar use the word to mean different things. For Konstantin Stanislavsky, who dedicated his life to spontaneous truthfulness, theatricality reeked of the showy falseness of regurgitated cliché. For others, it was the essence of true theater, an essence that was defined variously. For Alexander Tairov, it indicated the right of theater to exist as an independent form without subservience to literature, art, or moral correctives. For Sergei Eisenstein, it was linked with forcefully acting upon the senses and mind of the spectator. It is Vsevolod Meyerhold's understanding, however, with which I am concerned just now. Meyerhold celebrated a theatricality comprised of simultaneous strains of seeming incompatibilities—reality and fiction, actor and mask, content and form, truth and fantasy—that prompted artists and audiences to move beyond the reassuringly coherent world of realism, to embrace many experiences at once, and to be creatively activated by engaging with multiple truths and modes of expression.

This book examines the work of three directors, Meyerhold, Tairov, and Eisenstein, each of whom deeply mined the colliding perceptual planes of the fantastical tales of the German romantic writer E. T. A. Hoffmann in their quests to develop theater that embraced the plural, the simultaneous, and the polyphonic. Often in looking back at the history of directing, we emphasize the *Gesamtkunstwerk*, the inviolable coherence of the fictional world, and the unified vision of the director, forgetting that (to draw on this book's central metaphor) white light is actually comprised of many colors that must be refracted to be seen. These directors developed approaches to theatrical form that were comprehensive and coherent in their logic, yet were playfully infused with the worlds-within-worlds later termed metatheatre and with the wildly disparate elements of the grotesque, later to become familiar in postmodernism, the groundwork of which was laid here.

This book builds on the scholarship of Benedetti, Carnicke, Leach, Senelick, and others whose research links deeply engaged theater history with theater praxis. But while this book is meant as a creative intellectual resource for theater artists and scholars, I do not attempt to distill the innovations of these directors into a fixed method, just as Stanislavsky never intended his system to be a Method. Instead, I trace each director's philosophy of theater as it developed, as it was used with actors, and as it manifested in specific productions, some staged, others only dreamed. These explorations lay bare a new definition of theater, a theatricalist poetics. Perhaps most importantly, this book proposes that what we often view as binaries are not necessarily so, that it can be far more useful to think in terms of *and* than *or*. Directors both engage with and alter their sources. Productions can be both unified and fragmented. Theater can operate on multiple cognitive and emotional planes without diminishing audience pleasure. Intellect and art feed one another. And mining the innovations of the past can prompt the creative revolutions of the future.

One of the inspirations for this book was Clayton's *Pierrot in Petrograd: The Commedia dell'Arte/Balagan in Twentieth-Century Russian Theatre and Drama*, in which I first encountered the centrality of E. T. A. Hoffmann to Russian theater, especially in the context of his popularization in Russia of fantasy, irony, the grotesque, commedia dell'arte, the fairy-tale plays of Carlo

Gozzi, the plays-within-plays of Ludwig Tieck, and the etchings of Jacques Callot. Frequent turn-to documentary collections include Lopatin and Fomin's *Russkii krug Gofmana* (*The Russian Hoffmann Circle*) and Senelick and Ostrovsky's *The Soviet Theater: A Documentary History*. Valuable works on specific directors include Leach's *Vsevolod Meyerhold*, Braun's *Meyerhold on Theatre*, Oves's annotated edition of Meyerhold's journal *Liubov' k trem apel'sinam* (*Love for Three Oranges*), Shcherbakov's works on Meyerhold, *Columbine's Garter*, and pantomime, Worrall's *Modernism to Realism on the Soviet Stage*, Nesbet's *Savage Junctures: Sergei Eisenstein and the Shape of Thinking*, and three works on Eisenstein's early theater: Zabrodin's *Eizenshtein o Meierkhol'de* (*Eisenstein on Meyerhold*) and *Popytka teatra* (*Theater Attempt*) and the second and fourth volumes of Ivanov's *Mnemozina* (*Clouded Apollo*).

This book's sections on refraction, *Columbine's Veil, Love for Three Oranges*, and *Princess Brambilla* are developed from my previous articles: "A Theatrical Zigzag: Doctor Dapertutto, *Columbine's Veil*, and the Grotesque," *Slavic and East European Performance* 29, vol. 3 (November 2009); "Baring the Frame: Meyerhold's Refraction of Gozzi's *Love of Three Oranges*," *Theatre Survey* 56, no. 3 (September 2015); and "Performance as Polemic: Tairov's 1920 *Princess Brambilla* at the Moscow Kamerny Theatre," *Theatre Survey* 51, no. 1 (May 2010).

This book could not have been written without more than a decade of generous assistance by the staff at the Russian State Archive of Literature and Art—especially Dmitry Neustroyev, Natalya Strizhkova, Larissa Ivanova, Ksenia Demyanenko, Elena Tchougounova-Paulson, and Anna Romanenko—and the staff at the Theatre Library of the Theatre Workers' Union, the Saint Petersburg State Museum of Theatre and Music, the Harvard Theatre Collection, and the New York Public Library for the Performing Arts. Among the many dedicated Bakhrushin State Central Theatre Museum employees, I am especially indebted to Natalia Mashechkina and Natalia Zaitseva. Walter Zvonchenko at the Library of Congress gave superb archival research training. Annette Fern, former reference librarian at the Harvard Theatre Collection, provided advice and resources. Thanks to the interlibrary loan staff at Tufts University (especially Ann Marie Ferraro), Boston College, University of Connecticut, and Northwestern University. My gratitude to the late Anatoly Paniushkin, Uncle Volodia, Irina Medvedeva, and others at the Glinka Museum of Musical Culture and Chaliapin Museum who arranged for visas and lodging.

This book's creation was generously supported at Northwestern by a year-long Kaplan Institute for the Humanities Faculty Fellowship, a Faculty Research Grant, and an Undergraduate Research Assistant Grant, and elsewhere by a School of Fine Arts Dean's Grant from the University of Connecticut, a Postdoctoral Fellowship at Harvard's Davis Center for Russian and Eurasian Studies, and a Mellon Dissertation Fellowship in Original Sources from the Council on Library and Information Resources.

I am deeply obliged to the readers and editors at Northwestern University Press, especially Mike Levine and Anne Gendler, who endured a thousand questions, and to the Mellon Foundation for funding this book's online resource companion. Gratitude to the organizers and mentors of the ASTR/ATHE First Book Workshop: LeAnn Fields, E. Patrick Johnson, Ramón Rivera-Servera, Andrew Sofer, Don Wilmeth, Patricia Ybarra, and Harvey Young.

Many thanks to the brilliant scholars whose work has fed mine. Sharon Carnicke, J. Douglas Clayton, Catherine Cole, the indefatigable Caryl Emerson, Robert Leach, Julia Listengarten, Harlow Robinson, Catherine Schuler, Vadim Shcherbakov, and Nick Worrall commented on book sections, while Valleri Robinson, Colleen McQuillen, Dan Smith, Julia Vaingurt, and Ann Folino White provided forums at which to discuss them. Andrew Wachtel was on my dissertation committee and has supported me since. Warm thanks to Kevin Bartig, Jane Costlow, Robert Crane, Paul Fryer, William Gunn, Maria Ignatieva, Vladislav Ivanov, Jacob Juntunen, Sergei Korobkov and Sasha Kmelnitskaia, Andrei Malaev-Babel, Yana Meerzon, Magda Romanska, Tania Smoliarova, Sergei Tcherkasski, Manon van de Water, Vladimir Zabrodin, and the participants of the ASTR Central-Eastern European Working Session, who buoyed me with their wisdom and enthusiasm.

Among the gifted director-collaborators whose work inspires me, I am especially indebted to David Chambers, Liz Diamond, Dmitry Krymov, Yasen Peyankov, Kimberly Senior, Anna Shapiro, and Jessica Thebus.

Northwestern colleagues whose conversations shaped ideas in this book include David Catlin, Rives Collins, Marcus Doshi, Linda Gates, Cindy Gold, Nina Gurianova, Susan Manning, Hamid Naficy, Inna Naroditskaia, Michael Rohd, and, with frequency and zeal, Mary Poole, Liz Son, Harvey Young, and Tracy Davis. I am indebted to Tom Burke, Hollis Clayson, Wendy Wall, and my Kaplan Institute colleagues, who helped to magnify the volume and scope of my thinking. Supporters of this project in its early stages include Tufts graduate colleagues Emma Dassori, Eunice Ferreira, and Kyna Hamill; graduate faculty Laurence Senelick (my dissertation advisor), Claire Conceison and Tom Connolly (dissertation committee), Barbara Grossman, and Don Weingust; and Robin Kanarek, who provided office space in which to write. I am grateful for the warm support of colleagues at the University of Connecticut (Michael Bradford, Gary English, Adrienne Macki Braconi, Claire Reynolds, Bart Roccoberton), at Boston College (Stuart Hecht, John Houchin, Scott Cummings), and at the Davis Center at Harvard (Loren R. Graham, Sonia Ketchian, John Malmstad, William Mills Todd III, Hugh Truslow, and Emily Van Buskirk).

Many others supported me in myriad ways. Thanks to Natasha Bregel, who helped to translate and edit a great quantity of seemingly indecipherable Russian handwriting, and, in Moscow, to Katya Vyazova, Dima Kharazhishvilli, Alexander Gref, Masha Rastikhina, Elena Slonimskaya, and the Moscow Art Theatre School for providing homes away from home. Thanks to Jia-Yee Tang for playing through Dohnányi's *Der Schleier der Pierrette* piano score for me, to Sylvia Hernandez for verifying my circus terms, and to Ina Klinge and Su Funkhouser for their native German expertise. My gratitude to Emily Berezowsky, Liz Fancher, Fanny Gutierrez-Meyers, Eve Isenberg, Lilia Levitina, Todd Meyers, Suchitra Mumford, Karen and Ira Smith, and Vlada Tomova for their friendship and insight; to Aunt Kate and Kristin, Priscilla, and Philip Hurdle for telling me to keep going; and to John Bell, Tim Cusack, Claudia Orenstein, and Andrew and Bonnie Periale for their serenity and cheer.

Heartfelt appreciation to my students—my most inspiring teachers—especially my research assistants Jessica Hinds-Bond, who aided with Russian translations and other manuscript matters, David Calder, whose French translations appear in this book, and Julia Grigg, Liz Laurie, and Grace Overbeke, who assisted with bibliographies and proofreading. Any errors in the book are my own.

Thanks to my extended family—my siblings, parents, cousins, aunts, uncles, and in-laws—for their encouragement. Thanks to Betsy and John Posner for their years of support and child care. Thanks to my children, Sophia and Isaac, who fill my life with joy and who teach me the value of the fantasy every day.

Love and gratitude to my husband, Brian Posner, for embracing a life refracted through the prism of book writing.

Enduring thanks to Anatoly Smeliansky, who first showed me the *Orchard*, and, especially, to Laurence Senelick, for guiding me to what lay beyond.

The Director's Prism

Introduction

Hoffmann's Prism

PROLOGUE/POLEMIC: "UNNECESSARY TRUTH"

In 1902 the Russian symbolist writer Valery Briusov published a provocative polemic against the Moscow Art Theatre, calling Konstantin Stanislavsky and Vladimir Nemirovich-Danchenko's early directorial attempts to reflect life on the stage "unnecessary truth." In Briusov's view, the Moscow Art Theatre's primary error was that it had, in its first four years of existence, tried to take the historicism and Meiningenism of the late nineteenth century further:

> Modern theatres aim at the utmost verisimilitude in their depiction of life. . . . In spite of . . . this, however, there remains much that the theatre has not succeeded in counterfeiting. The Art Theatre has set itself the aim of reducing this "much." The actors there have begun to sit with their backs to the audience . . . If the play is set in winter, snow can be seen falling outside the windows. If it is windy, curtains flutter.[1]

Although Stanislavsky resented implications that his carefully layered atmospheric constructions represented an indiscriminate slice of life, and though he was later to experiment with symbolism, his early productions were typically comprised of details taken from life and the artistic shaping of production moments justified by life. Nina's dark silhouette against the lake as she performs Konstantin's play in Chekhov's *Seagull* (1898) is a powerful use of chiaroscuro, yet Stanislavsky justified the effect by having the moon rise behind her. Similarly, he crowded stage furniture surfaces with real flowers and sweets to produce the celebratory atmosphere of Irina's name-day party in *Three Sisters* (1901).

For Briusov, the Moscow Art Theatre's attempts to mimic life were contrary to the laws of theater and art: "To reproduce life faithfully on the stage is impossible. The stage is conventional by its very nature."[2] Audiences would never mistake cotton wadding for a snowstorm, painted trees for a forest, or an actor playing Hamlet for the real Prince of Denmark.[3] The

Moscow Art Theatre had simply replaced conventions that were far from daily life with new ones closer to it:

> In the Greek theatre, an actor playing someone who had just returned from foreign parts would enter from the left. At the Art Theatre, the actor is admitted to a small vestibule where he divests himself of sheepskin and galoshes as a sign that he has come from afar. But who among the audience is likely to forget that he arrived from the wings?[4]

Briusov believed that to attempt to duplicate life onstage was to deprive the theater and its audiences of the act of creation, "the only reality that exists on earth."[5] Better not to try to trick the audience into believing that what they are seeing is real and instead to help them create meanings on their own. As Vsevolod Meyerhold was to write four years later, "In the theatre the spectator's [fantasy] is able to supply that which is left unsaid. It is this mystery and the desire to solve it which draw so many people to the theatre."[6]

Briusov's proposed solution was to replace clichéd conventions that offer "no threat to the deep-rooted habits of the theatregoer"[7] with fresh ones that are "deliberately applied,"[8] in which spectators can, metaphorically speaking, see the lines of the etching or the brushstrokes of the painting. He therefore advocated for *uslovnost'*, a difficult-to-translate word that Braun renders as "stylized theatre," Hoover as "conscious theater,"[9] and which I translate as "conventionalization." Conventionalization is a conscious, overt application of theatrical conventions that are defined by each individual director or production in an eternal quest for new ways of making meaning together with an audience. Rather than being a specific style, conventionalization is a structural philosophy of theater-making that generates expectation, surprise, and thought by rejuvenating and reapplying how theatrical conventions are used.

While Briusov's proposed solution to "unnecessary truth" was to mine the conventions of ancient theater,[10] his essay prompted a much wider rethinking of theater's nature and purpose. The debate over the aesthetic language of theater that followed in Briusov's wake spawned a tremendous artistic pluralism as the newly emergent director searched for conventions that could prompt new ways of making theatrical meaning. Though many agreed with Briusov, his essay raised an essential question: if theater was to celebrate its conventionality, what should its new conventions be? Many viewed psychological realism and scenic naturalism as a return to the oppressive verisimilitude from which the German romantics had broken free a century before, mining theater of the more distant past to unearth conventions that transcended time and geography. Each director was drawn to different, often multiple forms: ancient Greek theater, especially as viewed through the lens of Nietzsche, the *theatrum mundi* metaphor of Spanish Golden Age theater, the simplicity of the Shakespearean stage, the conventionalized vocabularies of Noh and Kabuki, and popular forms previously thought too base for serious consideration: fairground entertainments, puppetry, and commedia dell'arte. Many also embraced the theatrical reforms sweeping Europe by staging plays by Maeterlinck, Ibsen, Wedekind, and others, and by engaging with the innovations of Fuchs, Appia, Jaques-Dalcroze, Wagner, Reinhardt, Duncan, and Craig.

Other art forms—music, visual art, and literature—also became inspirations for structural elements that could be transposed to the theater. Russian scenic and costume designers maintained simultaneous careers as easel painters; indeed, it often was because they were visual artists first that they were invited to design for the stage. Russian directors came to think of mise-en-scène as it developed through time in musical terms and adopted vocabularies of tempo, rhythm, melody, harmony, dissonance, and polyphony. They drew liberally from visual art to inspire theater and film composition. Literature provided practical inspiration for theater and film form, particularly works of fiction that drew attention to their own construction and encouraged the reader to participate in the making of meaning.

Among the individuals who shaped this Russian theatrical revolution, the German romantic writer Ernst Theodor Amadeus (E. T. A.) Hoffmann (1776–1822) is one of the most significant, yet one of the most understudied. A fiction writer "unequalled in displaying the sheer joy of unbridled storytelling,"[11] Hoffmann held that theater's aim was to "bear the spectator on invisible wings into the imaginary world of poesy,"[12] a belief that had profound resonance on the Russian stage and far beyond.

This book investigates Hoffmann's role in the neo-romantic counterrevolution that followed closely in the wake of the Moscow Art Theatre's early productions, focusing on how and why three directors—Vsevolod Meyerhold, Alexander Tairov, and Sergei Eisenstein—refracted Hoffmann in their theatrical experiments. Like Hoffmann, each challenged the notion that conventions must be based in fidelity to a written text or a need to mirror life. Each instead advocated for theatricalist theater—theater that celebrates itself as theater. In doing so, they avidly engaged with theatrical innovations of the past to generate a new theatricalist poetics, delighting in the subversive impudence of the act of choosing by whom to be inspired—hence these directors' well-known interest in street theater and popular entertainments, and hence, too, their interest in Hoffmann, whose fantastical tales were wildly popular with general readers, but which Goethe criticized as "the diseased works of a suffering man."[13]

On the pages that follow, I introduce Hoffmann's biography and Russian reception and analyze Hoffmannian leitmotifs and structural innovations that were especially formative to Russian theater. In the epilogue to this introduction, I define "refraction," a word I use in conventionalized fashion to illuminate the creative process of the theatricalist director, before providing a brief explanation of the book's structural logic. Directorial theories based on Hoffmannian innovations, how these theories shaped specific experiments, and the related (often heated) polemical debates over theatrical reform will be the subject of the remainder of the book.

UNDER THE SIGN OF HOFFMANN

In April 1916, a new artistic cabaret opened in the cellar of a building on Saint Petersburg's Field of Mars. Proprietor Boris Pronin intended the Players' Rest (Prival komediantov) to be a miniature underground theater, unlike his cabaret the Stray Dog, which primarily had been a meeting place for literary readings and artistic debate. From its inception, Hoffmann was a seminal figure at the Players' Rest; according to Mikhail Kuzmin,[14] the cabaret was "under the sign" of Hoffmann.[15] A few months before the opening, Pronin wrote that the premiere production was to be a pantomime dedicated to Hoffmann[16]—though this pantomime ultimately was replaced with a revival of Meyerhold's 1910 *Columbine's Veil*.

Hoffmann also inspired the cabaret's interior design. The innermost of its three low, arched rooms, each decorated by a different artist, was an intimate theatrical hall with deep blue walls, mirror fragments on the ceiling, medallions, and painted panels by Sergei Sudeikin.[17] Sudeikin dedicated this tiny theater to Hoffmann and to Count Carlo Gozzi, whose fairy-tale plays (*fiabe teatrali*) were popularized in Russia through Hoffmann's tales.[18] The painted panels that lined the windowless room depicted Venetian *baùta* in black capes and beaked white masks[19] and figures from Hoffmann's commedia novella *Princess Brambilla (Prinzessin Brambilla)*. Thus each performance in the tiny space was framed by the cabaret's underlying inspirations. In her memoirs, actress Valentina Verigina recalls seeing Sudeikin's Hoffmann room for the first time: "Here the Venice of yore, presented as though through Hoffmann's prism, could be sensed."[20] Her description of a Venice refracted through Hoffmann's prism is significant. Although Sudeikin's figures were painted in wavy lines, as though reflected back to the viewer in a distorting mirror, Hoffmann was also by then a powerful signifier in Russia for an artistically refracted view of the world.

Hoffmann has been one of the most influential foreign writers on Russian literature and the arts since his tales were published at the beginning of the nineteenth century.[21] His Russian influence took place in two major waves: the first profoundly shaped literature in the nineteenth century, and the second inspired Russian theatrical reforms in the early twentieth.[22] His mark on nineteenth-century Russian writers, especially at the height of Russian romanticism in the 1830s and '40s, was greater than that of any other German writer. Without Hoffmann, argue Lopatin and Fomin, "the whole character of Russian classical literature would be entirely different, would lose its essential traits, and, quite possibly, its most vivid colors."[23] Pushkin, Gogol, Lermontov, Turgenev, Dostoevsky, and many others engaged deeply with Hoffmann's work and artistic worldview.

Literary scholars in the mid-nineteenth century often dismissed Hoffmann, author of "The Nutcracker and the Mouse King"—the tale that loosely inspired Tchaikovsky's famous ballet—as a children's author or as "a 'madcap' writer, who composed 'amidst intoxicating coffee house fumes' and 'under the influence of wine vapors.'"[24] It was not until the turn of the twentieth century that a few began to view such a wildly fantastical writer as worthy of study. By the 1890s, studying Russian literature, especially from the romantic period, "unavoidably led scholars to the study of Hoffmann," in Zhitomirskaia's estimation, due to the indisputable breadth of his influence on so many writers.[25] This decade also saw a flurry of new translations of Hoffmann into Russian, evidence of a resurgence of interest in his tales.[26]

The first Russian monograph on Hoffmann was Sergei Ignatov's *E. T. A. Hoffmann: Man and Works* (1913).[27] Ignatov, a close colleague of Meyerhold, asserted in a lengthy chapter dedicated to Hoffmann's views on theater that Hoffmann's artistic worldview was directly aligned with Russian experimental theater, especially in its synthesis of multiple arts, its use of irony and the grotesque, its emphasis on fantasy and subjectivity, and its fascination with commedia and puppets. Ignatov linked each of these Hoffmannian motifs to contemporary Russian theater, stating, "The works of directors such as Vs[evolod] Meyerhold, F[edor] Komissarzhevsky, and N[ikolai] Evreinov have already realized to a significant degree the ideals of Hoffmann, uttered just under a century ago."[28]

Ignatov's book, Pronin's pantomime, and the hall of Hoffmann and Gozzi at the Players' Rest are but three examples of the widespread Russian theatrical fascination with Hoffmann that began in the first decade of the twentieth century and extended into the early 1920s. One historian has noted that there were more attempts in Russia to apply Hoffmann's theatrical principles and to stage his works than in any other nation.[29] Others have termed the frenzy of Russian theatrical experimentation inspired by the German writer a "cult" of Hoffmann.[30] This cult was a major inspiration for the abundant self-referential, ironic, and grotesque elements that became defining characteristics of Russian modernist theater and that together constitute a poetics that is often conflated with, yet significantly predates, Bertolt Brecht's *Verfremdungseffekt* (alienation effect).

For those under the sign of Hoffmann, Hoffmann symbolized the Russian theatricalist revolt against naturalism, the rebellion against nineteenth-century acting and production clichés at imperial and commercial theaters, and the search for conventions that would celebrate theater's inherent theatricality. The theater they developed was not the opposite of realism; nor was it simply a distortion of realism. It was, however, opposed to the calculated shapelessness of realism—the relaxed, uneven tempos of natural speech, movement derived from the lived habits of daily life—in favor of the clarity of the individually defined form found in literature, music, and other arts. Hoffmann's fantastical tales and Hoffmann's inspirations—Gozzi, visual artist Jacques Callot,[31] and Ludwig Tieck[32]—provided directors with invaluable models for redefining the theater.

Because the rise of the director and the rise of Russian theatrical "Hoffmaniana" so closely coincided, many characteristics that we have come to associate with theatricalist directors—emphasis on subjective perspective, playful manipulations of aesthetic distance, commenting on the making of theater as one makes it, and the celebration of the individual fantasy—were developed in conjunction with this Hoffmannian engagement. "Russian avant-garde artists . . . did not view artistic representation as a mirror held up to nature," Jestrovic reminds us, "they found art to be a 'crooked mirror' through which one could see more clearly."[33] So, too, these directors saw the theater more clearly through Hoffmann's distorting prism.

A Hallucinatory Visionary

Hoffmann, "the true father of magic realism,"[34] has been as variously defined as the phenomena he provoked. His life was characterized by individual and political turmoil; he lived in many places while pursuing multiple careers that, due to Napoleonic and Russian invasions, dissolved and overlapped like the shifting borders of the countries in which he lived. Born Ernst Theodor Wilhelm Hoffmann on January 24, 1776, in Königsberg, East Prussia (present-day Kaliningrad, Russia), as a young adult he changed his middle name to Amadeus in honor of Mozart. During his life he worked as a lawyer, judge, composer, music critic, theater director, music teacher, and short-story writer. Although he wrote the tales for which he is most famous only in the last few years of his life, he had a lifelong interest in music and theater. Not only did he attend performances voraciously and write music for the stage (his most famous composition, the opera *Undine*, premiered in 1816), but beginning in 1808 he served as the musical director of the Bamberg Theater, a position he held for five years. He also kept a cabinet full of marionettes and performed shadow-puppet plays for his family.[35]

It was in Bamberg that Hoffmann first received the varied theatrical experience that later informed many of his tales. He directed the theater orchestra, designed and painted sets, and performed a multitude of other tasks to stay financially afloat. Among his tales that focus on the theater are *Strange Sorrows of a Theater Manager* (*Seltsame Leiden eines Theaterdirektors*), *Princess Brambilla*, *Princess Blandina* (*Prinzessin Blandina*), and "The Compleat Stage Manager" ("Der vollkommene Machinist"), but theater also features prominently in a number of his other works, including "Signor Formica," *Master Flea* (*Meister Floh*), "Don Juan," and *The Devil's Elixirs* (*Die Elixiere des Teufels*).

Hoffmann led a dual existence for much of his life: he was a respectable member of civil society by day, but a hallucinatory, drunken, writer-musician by night. Throughout his life, he attempted to keep his two selves separate, publishing his earliest music reviews under the pseudonym Kapellmeister Johannes Kreisler, an alter ego who featured in many of his tales. This romantic notion of the division of the true creative life of the artist from the mundane philistine world is one of the most enduring features of his works. Not only do doppelgängers feature prominently in his tales, these stories also are filled with artists who encounter a fantastical reality that coexists with the physically tangible one yet is invisible to those who do not understand art. For Hoffmann, "the true world of art had an independent existence, was only loosely connected with normal reality, and certainly was not governed by the standards and tastes of the philistines of polite society."[36]

Hoffmann published his first book in 1814 and his last in 1822, the year he died at only forty-six, but he was extremely prolific during his short time as a writer. In Germany his works were reprinted numerous times, and in France a multivolume translation of his collected works appeared within a decade of his death.[37] Over the course of much of the century that followed, he gained a disproportionate reputation as a writer of horror stories. Though scholarly interest in him waned at mid-century, his popular appeal stayed strong, and his influence remained profound on writers and musicians from Poe to Wagner. Joseph Hayse notes the astonishing breadth of this influence: "Like all great inventors, he seems to have shot spores into every current that blew through his time. Dumas, Baudelaire, Poe, Hawthorne, Gogol, Dostoevsky, and even Conan Doyle are among the writers who have been cited as beneficiaries of his prodigal invention."[38] Numerous operas and ballets have been based on Hoffmann's tales, including, among many others, Delibes's *Coppélia*, based on "The Sandman" ("Der Sandmann"); Tchaikovsky's *Nutcracker*, based on Alexandre Dumas père's adaptation of "The Nutcracker and the Mouse King" ("Nußknacker und Mausekönig"); Offenbach's *Tales of Hoffmann* (*Les contes d'Hoffmann*), based on "Councilor Krespel" ("Rath Krespel"), "The Sandman," and "Tale of the Lost Reflection" ("Das verlorene

Spiegelbild"). And as Andrew Wachtel demonstrates, Stravinsky, Fokine, and Benois's ballet *Petrushka* (1911) was inspired by Hoffmannian motifs even if it did not adapt one of Hoffmann's tales.[39]

The following sections of this introduction analyze themes and structures from Hoffmann's tales that resurfaced in abundant variations in Russian theater. In Hoffmann's first and final books, *Fantasy Pieces in Callot's Manner* (1814) and *The Life and Opinions of the Tomcat Murr* (1820–22), both of which blur divisions between various selves and establish multiple perceptual planes, the writer celebrates the individual fantasy, grotesque collisions, and ironic interruptions of the fictional world—each of which I will explore in turn. These motifs and formal innovations recur and are developed in Hoffmann's theatrical tales: *Princess Blandina* (1814), *Strange Sorrows of a Theater Manager* (1818), and *Princess Brambilla* (1820). Both here and elsewhere in this book, I include brief plot summaries of Hoffmann's tales to contextualize innovations in form, which I define, for the purpose of this discussion, as the overt presence of the artist in the work and the means by which the experience of the reader is shaped.

Alter Egos and Altered Realities

Hoffmann's first published writings were music reviews penned under the pseudonym Kapellmeister Johannes Kreisler. Kreisler was not a nom de plume that the emerging writer used simply to mask his identity, however. Kreisler grew into Hoffmann's doppelgänger, a self-created alter ego that intersected with Hoffmann's life independently of his literary creations. Although Kreisler appears recurrently throughout Hoffmann's works, he is the hero of Hoffmann's first and last books: in *Fantasy Pieces in Callot's Manner*, he is featured in the "Kreisleriana," two clusters of stories based on Hoffmann's music reviews; he figures even more centrally in *The Life and Opinions of the Tomcat Murr*. Readers encounter several recurrent motifs associated with this alter ego: blurred divisions between fantasy, madness, possession, and intoxication; the eccentric artist-musician; and the conductor who provokes visual music in the minds of listeners. Several formal devices also accompany Kreisler's presence: multiple identities contained within one another, the self-referentiality of romantic irony, and nonlinear plot structure.

Hayse notes that the German word Kapellmeister, literally "chapel master," initially signified a music director at a church or chapel, but that by the eighteenth century, "*Kapellmeister* denoted a professional musician, with a stipend from a noble, whose job was to organize, perform, and direct the court's musical entertainment. Many well-known composers held such positions, often teaching music to supplement their income." By Hoffmann's day, the Kapellmeister had become "the modern orchestra conductor."[40]

Hoffmann's Kapellmeister is a composer-conductor forced for financial reasons into the role of teacher. He gives music lessons to untalented bourgeois children and plays at banal society events that Hoffmann describes in the "Kreisleriana" "to show the indignities he suffers at the hands of a culturally illiterate public."[41] In "Kapellmeister Johannes Kreisler's Musical Sufferings," Kreisler remarks sardonically that at the parties at which he plays, "music is always served up" to be "consumed by refined society with the same relish as the other offerings."[42] Kreisler's artistic disposition is incompatible with this quotidian world. The first "Kreisleriana" informs the reader that Kreisler's friends "asserted that Nature had tried a new recipe in creating him and that the experiment had gone awry, for too little phlegm had been blended with an overexcitable temperament and a devastatingly inflammable imagination."[43] The result was "a tortured musician estranged from the world and feverishly worshipping 'only what the mind produces'—his art."[44]

For readers of the "Kreisleriana," it becomes difficult to distinguish between madness brought on by intoxication—Hoffmann's tales overflow with punch and tobacco smoke—and by artistic inspiration, or, for that matter, between Kreisler as a fictional character, narrator, or his real-life creator. The insanity that "haunted the fictional Kapellmeister Kreisler," as Comini notes, "was easily ascribed in the public mind by extension to Kreisler's creator, Hoffmann, who in his habitual late-night sipping of flaming punch seemed to court derangement." In Hoffmann's most famous drawing of Kreisler, *Kapellmeister Kreisler im Wahnsinn* (*Kapellmeister Kreisler in Insanity*), "we see the gaunt, unkempt figure of the musician, his wild hair on end, holding his long-stemmed pipe aloft as he dances a bizarre jig"[45] (figure 1).

Another of Hoffmann's Kreisler (self-)portraits captures the writer's characteristic use of what Joseph Hayse calls "nested identities": Hoffmann depicts Kreisler, who refers from within the drawing back to Hoffmann (figure 2). Hayse explains, "Hoffmann seldom rests with a single doubling: the personalities proliferate, connecting the author as well as the narrator to still other personalities . . . As Hoffmann's self-portrait as Kapellmeister Kreisler with the copy of [Hoffmann's opera] *Undine* on the desk shows, the line between author, composer, artist, and the personalities each creates . . . is hard to define."[46] Hoffmann's composite and nested selves inspired Russian redefinitions of the relationship between actor and character. Meyerhold and Eisenstein each also adopted Hoffmannian alter egos: Meyerhold was Doctor Dapertutto (from "A New Year's Eve Adventure") for nearly a decade, while Eisenstein experimented with a variety of aliases, among them Peregrinus Tyss (from *Master Flea*).

Figure 1. E. T. A. Hoffmann, *Kapellmeister Kreisler in Insanity* (Berlin, February 1822). Drawing for the first edition of *The Life and Opinions of the Tomcat Murr*, volume 3. Staatsbibliothek Bamberg, Art.f.23ga. Photo: Gerald Raab.

Fantasy Pieces in Callot's Manner: Fantasy, Irony, and the Grotesque

Hoffmann's nested identities prompt a kind of double vision[47]—characters move fluidly in and out of several selves that the reader is able to hold in the mind simultaneously. This reveals larger structural techniques in the Kreisler tales and in Hoffmann's works more generally, in which boundaries between art forms are similarly blurred and easily traversed. The very title of Hoffmann's *Fantasy Pieces in Callot's Manner: Pages from the Diary of a Traveling Enthusiast* (*Fantasiestücke in Callots Manier*: *Blätter aus dem Tagebuche eines reisenden Enthusiasten*) points to Hoffmann's avid interest in the intersections of multiple arts—here visual art, music, and literature, though theater also features prominently in the tales themselves. Rather than adhering to preconceived notions of literary form, this book's "pieces" (the musical connotations of the word is intentional) vary widely in style and length, ranging from a single page to full novellas, each of which is philosophically linked to Hoffmann's view of the necessity of the fantasy, a central concern in his work and in that of his Russian enthusiasts.

Figure 2. E. T. A. Hoffmann, *Kapellmeister Johannes Kreisler in a Dressing Gown, After a Life Drawing by Erasmus Spikher* (Berlin, January/February 1815). Note the copy of Hoffmann's opera *Undine* on Kreisler's table. Original watercolor. Staatsbibliothek Bamberg, I R 65. Photo: Gerald Raab.

While the word "fantasy" in modern English is often associated with "caprice" or "whim," sometimes in a binary contrast with a pragmatic focus on reality, the German and Russian refer first and foremost to the artist's ability to create.[48] In Dal's *Explanatory Dictionary*, the primary definition of *fantaziia* is "the imagination, the mind's inventive force; the creative force of the artist, the distinctive force of creation," though, appropriately in a Hoffmannian context, the word also prompts associations with "fancy, whimsy; unrealizable delirium, unbridled thoughts," and, in music, "a free composition, based on its own caprice, without rules."[49] When Hoffmann—and Russian directors after him—refers to fantasy, he means this inventive, creative capacity.[50] In his tales, Hoffmann often emphasizes the primacy of the fantasy by having fantastical elements penetrate the real world, thus prompting artistic experiences that operate across multiple perceptual planes—hence the importance of Hoffmann-Kreisler's ability to cross from one fictional plane into another. Viewed in this context, early twentieth-century theatrical innovations such as the removal of the footlights and the intrusion of the actor into the auditorium not only broke through the fourth wall, but also drew spectators into a subjective realm of art that could invade and enliven their everyday lives.

Hoffmann wrote *Fantasy Pieces* "in the manner" of Callot as a subjective artistic response to the particular kind of creative freedom he observed in the French engraver's works. In "Jacques Callot," the book's brief preface, Hoffmann wrote: "May not a poet or writer to whom everyday life appears permeated with figures from his own romantic spirit, and who now introduces them, dressed in the glow of the strange and miraculous, apologize to this master and say he has wished to work in the manner of Callot?"[51] Hoffmann's manner of working "in the manner of," where one is deeply inspired by, yet does not directly imitate another, became foundational to the Russian view of the creative process.

In addition to being drawn to Callot's fantastical elements, Hoffmann valued the French artist's interest in the theater. Callot spent seven years early in his career "recording, in a highly animated style, court-sponsored pageants and theatrical productions" while in the employ of the Medici court in Florence. He also used theatrical perspective techniques in many etchings not set in the theater: darkly silhouetted figures often stand on the frames of his images and gaze into them, creating the impression of a living proscenium or an audience within an audience. These "repoussoir elements" increase the impression of the image's depth and guide where the etching's viewer will look.[52] Many of Callot's most famous etchings depict commedia characters—*zanni*, Pantalone, Pulcinella, and others. Hoffmann and his Russian theatrical followers also believed Callot's *Balli di Sfessania* (Dances of Sfessania, 1621–22), a series of twenty-four etchings that depict grotesque duos dancing or sword fighting (figure 3), to be Callot's documentation of actual commedia performances.[53]

In addition to these fantastical and theatrical elements, Hoffmann was drawn to Callot's use of irony, which generates simultaneous conflicting ways of perceiving a work, and the grotesque, which relies on exaggeration, collision, and bizarre fusions of humans, animals, and objects. In the preface to *Fantasy Pieces*, Hoffmann describes Callot's *The Temptation of Saint Anthony* (second version, 1635) as his ideal model for irony and the grotesque:

> To serious, penetrating viewers of Callot's grotesque man-beast figures, irony reveals all the secret meanings that lie hidden beneath the veil of farce. A devil in the "Temptation of Saint Anthony," his nose transformed into a musket aimed at the holy man, is an excellent example; the same sketch contains . . . a clarinetist using a *most* unusual organ to provide the wind for his instrument.[54]

Figure 3. Jacques Callot, *Taglia Cantoni and Fracasso*, 24th plate from *Balli di Sfessania* (c. 1621). Etching. Harvard Art Museums/Fogg Museum, Gray Collection of Engravings Fund, by exchange, S4.28.2. Photo: Imaging Department © President and Fellows of Harvard College.

Created the year of Callot's death, this etching teems with irreverent, fantastical, and nightmarish creatures that nearly swallow up the tiny Saint Anthony (figure 4).

Although the term "romantic irony" is rightly attributed to Friedrich Schlegel (1772–1829) (Hoffmann preferred the term "humor"), Russian directors and writers typically associated romantic irony with Hoffmann.[55] The term's meaning has long been debated. In the definition of romantic irony most relevant to Hoffmann and to Russian theater, the inevitable "gulf between subjective perception and reality"[56] leads to "a kind of literary self-consciousness in which an author signals his or her freedom from the limits of a given work by puncturing its fictional illusion and exposing its process of composition as a matter of authorial whim."[57] By revealing the subjective constructedness of reality, irony allows the artist, as Speight explains, "to open up the possibility of the infinity of other perspectives."[58] In many of Hoffmann's tales, most famously in "The Sandman" and *The Golden Pot*, a novella within *Fantasy Pieces*, narrators retell the story from unexpected perspectives that

Figure 4. Jacques Callot, *The Temptation of Saint Anthony* (second version, 1635). Etching. Harvard Art Museums/Fogg Museum, Gift of William Gray from the collection of Francis Calley Gray, by exchange, S3.51. Photo: Imaging Department © President and Fellows of Harvard College.

draw attention to the stories as fiction, prompting, to again use Schlegel's term, a "permanent parabasis": a "constant interruption" of the work's fictional coherence that produces "two lines of meaning that constantly challenge each other."[59] As the chorus in ancient Greek tragedy both participated in and commented on the action, so, too, romantic irony prompts the reader to perceive a work simultaneously from within and without.

Romantic irony in the theater—asides, interludes, direct audience address, play with masks, authorial interruptions, plays-within-plays, and so on—prompts a dialogue between the process of creating theater and theater itself, thus allowing audiences to mentally process conflicting perspectives. "When romantic irony is used," Jestrovic explains, "a conflicting semiotic activity takes place contributing to the effect of theatricality—the signifier and the signified are simultaneously shown as identical (through the protagonist's voice) and different (through the authorial voice)."[60] More specifically, as articulated in an article in Meyerhold's journal *Love for Three Oranges*, "The essence of irony . . . lies in *the emphasizing of the discrepancy between appearance and reality*." The article's author, Meyerhold's colleague Samuil Vermel, continues:

> Not in vain did the original word "irony" in Greek mean "pretending." . . .
>
> It is the kind of pretending that prompts an inspired actor to bring a wet handkerchief to his eyes in order to show that he is crying. Oh, drops of plain water that trickle thus down his face—you stir us more than the real salt tears of "sincerely lived-through drama!" In this there is joy, a joy that does not forsake us even when it would seem that everything has turned out so sadly.[61]

Romantic irony is closely connected to the theatrical grotesque, extreme artistic distortion that juxtaposes discordant elements or styles, the collisions of which are justified not by logic but by the artist's whim. Hoffmann's grotesque became associated in Russia with the nightmarish and with commedia,[62] especially as used by Callot, whose etchings often depict "an eccentric style of movement" and fuse animal and human elements.[63] Hoffmann additionally uses the grotesque to prompt surprise. His tales juxtapose objects and people that transform instantaneously from one thing into another; in *The Golden Pot*, real objects change into fantastical ones and back at a second glance. He also frequently collides incongruous elements: a witch is simultaneously a doorknocker and an apple wife (*The Golden Pot*), and an actor is himself, a parrot, and a puppet (*Princess Brambilla*). Eisenstein was to term these two Hoffmannian variations on the grotesque, one based on temporal, the other on spatial collisions, "successive" and "simultaneous" juxtaposition.[64]

In Russian theater, irony and the grotesque became formal devices through which to free the fantasy. Irony's self-referentiality allowed for dual emphases on the work and its creator, while the grotesque altered and commented through distortion and juxtaposition. The result, for Vermel, was theatricality, the gloriously subjective, indirect path created by the artist's fantasy:

> We define theatricality as . . . *the emancipation of a person from the life that is granted to a life that is self-created*. If life is the path of a straight line, theatricality is that same path, but taken along a line that is wavy, zigzagged, or any kind of *indirect* line. It is the eternal striving of a person toward creative work, toward the engendering of one's own world.[65]

For Vermel, intentional indirectness in any of the arts is a form of theatricality. By way of example, he notes that rhyme generates this indirect path in poetry and that cubism is "a substantiation of theatricality in painting."[66] Vermel's description of the artist's zigzag also recalls Meyerhold's earliest definition of the grotesque. Meyerhold wrote in 1911:

> Fundamental to the grotesque is a constant drawing of the spectator from one perceptual plane he has only just comprehended to another he did not expect at all . . . Thereupon each gesture, each step, each turn of the head, in short, each movement is regarded like a dance element, understood as it was understood in the ancient Japanese theater.[67]

Thus the grotesque, whether in theater, literature, music, or art, zigzags between expectation and surprise, appearance and reality, the already experienced and the yet-to-be-imagined.

Tomcat Murr: "Zig-zaggery" and the Artist-Musician

Hoffmann's final novel, *The Life and Opinions of the Tomcat Murr Together with a Fragmentary Biography of Kapellmeister Johannes Kreisler on Random Sheets of Waste Paper* (*Lebens-Ansichten des Katers Murr nebst fragmentarischer Biographie des Kapellmeisters Johannes Kreisler in zufälligen Makulaturblättern*), rightly described as "formally one of the most astonishing pieces of European fiction,"[68] is Hoffmann's most extensive experiment with the zigzagging grotesque in a single work. A foreword by a fictional editor introduces the book's extraordinary structure: a highly educated cat has decided to publish his memoirs. The editor, who "had never numbered a cat among his authors before," agrees to take the project on but makes a dismaying discovery when he reviews the proofs: "now and then Murr's story breaks off, and there are interpolations of a different nature which belong to a different book, containing the biography of Kapellmeister Johannes Kreisler!"[69] Hoffmann's editor relates his discovery that Murr had used his master's manuscript as scrap paper on which to compose memoirs and that fragments from Kreisler's biography therefore "were left in the manuscript—and were inadvertently printed too, as if they were part of it!"[70] Thus the book's structure alternates between two biographies, one of which, Kreisler's, is out of order. *Tomcat Murr*'s zigzagging between Kreisler and his cat, Hoffmann's refraction of the "zig-zaggery"[71] of Laurence Sterne's equally astonishing *The Life and Opinions of Tristram Shandy, Gentleman* (1759–67), has been aptly termed "kaleidoscopic" (figure 5).[72] As Adler notes, the kaleidoscope, which was invented just two years before Hoffmann began *Tomcat Murr*, offered a new paradigm for fragmented and subjectively reassembled artistic creations.[73]

It was not only the collisions of Kreisler's wildly incompatible worlds that prompted a Russian cult following, however, but the Kapellmeister himself, Hoffmann's idealized artist-musician. In *Fantasy Pieces*, *Tomcat Murr*, and in Hoffmann's works generally, the brilliance of Kapellmeister Kreisler's musical fantasies is unappreciated by philistine society, which perpetuates the status quo and does not understand the sublime power of art. For Hoffmann, "only a poet understands the poet. Only a Romantic disposition

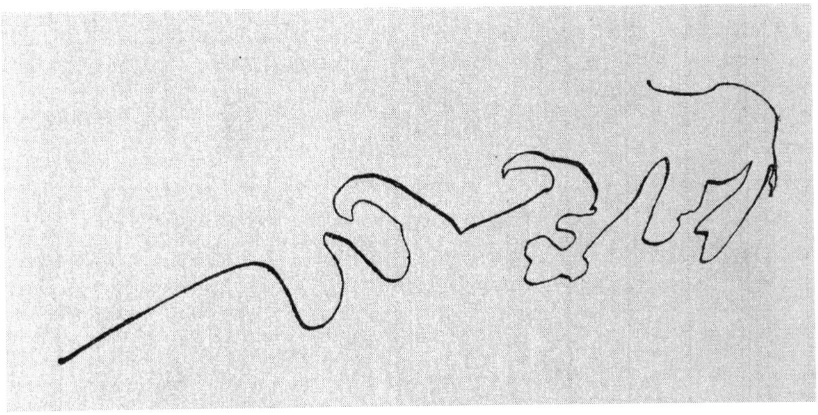

Figure 5. E. T. A. Hoffmann, parodic illustration (c. 1804) of the narrative structure of Laurence Sterne's novel *The Life and Opinions of Tristram Shandy, Gentleman* (1759–1767). Staatsbibliothek Bamberg, L.g.o.391e/B19. Photo: Gerald Raab.

can enter the Romantic."[74] Kreisler's own cat's unfeeling destruction of his master's memoirs is an ironic nod to this theme.[75]

For Kreisler, music is the artist's fantasy made tangible. Music was, for Hoffmann, the purest example of "the creative process . . . divorced from the constraints of reason."[76] In the final "Kreisleriana," an apprentice letter that Hoffmann writes to his own alter ego, it becomes impossible to distinguish between seeing and hearing music or between the creative inner world and the external quotidian one:

> The Musician—which is to say, the one in whose heart music develops to a clear, distinct awareness—is constantly surrounded by melody and harmony. It is neither empty imagery nor allegory when the musician says that colors, odors, and radiances appear to him as notes, and that he beholds a wonderful concert in their intertwining.
>
> Just as . . . hearing is an internal seeing, sight becomes an inner hearing for the musician—an awareness of music that vibrates sympathetically with his spirit, echoing everything his eye beholds.[77]

Many composers—Mahler, Beethoven, Brahms, Schumann, and others—deeply valued Hoffmann's view of music as sublime creation born of absolute freedom of the mind.[78] It is no wonder that Meyerhold, who studied to be a professional musician before turning to the theater and who treated mise-en-scène as visible music throughout his career, should view the director as a kapellmeister who conducts theatrical productions into zigzagging and kaleidoscopic wholes. Kreisler made symbolically charged cameo appearances in numerous Russian productions as a metaphor for the director-author who conducts theatrical mise-en-scène. Russian theatricalist directors valued Hoffmann's Kapellmeister most, however, for the unconstrained artistic freedom that allowed readers to encounter a new kind of fiction, and, by extension, for audiences to experience a new kind of theater.

Theatrical Reform

Hoffmann articulated in detail what this new theater should be. Though written a century earlier, nearly all his recommendations came to be implemented in early-twentieth-century Russian theater. While recurrent motifs and formal devices in Hoffmann's tales inspired similar Russian variants—multiple selves and worlds that comment on one another, the true artist versus the quotidian status quo, the director as conductor—several tales addressed theatrical reform specifically. The most influential (with dates of first publication and most significant Russian translation) were *Princess Blandina* (1814; trans. 1925), an unfinished play that experimented wildly with theatrical irony; *Strange Sorrows of a Theater Manager* (1818; trans. 1894), a comprehensive treatise on theatrical reform that celebrates Gozzi and the puppet theater; and *Princess Brambilla* (1820; trans. 1915), which advocates for reviving the commedia dell'arte as interpreted by Gozzi and Callot. *Princess Blandina* and *Strange Sorrows* have yet to appear in English translation, while *Brambilla* was first published in English a century and a half after its writing. I will therefore summarize the content and innovations of each before demonstrating each tale's relevance to Russian theater. In so doing, I move from the broad to the specific and back: from the sweeping theatrical reforms proposed in *Strange Sorrows*, to Russian interpretations of *Blandina*'s formal innovations, to *Brambilla*'s freeing approach to the creative process.

Strange Sorrows of a Theater Manager: Directing Live and Wooden Actors

Strange Sorrows of a Theater Manager is a theatrical treatise loosely disguised as a dialogue. Alexandrinsky Theatre actor Modest Pisarev,[79] who edited and introduced the 1894 Russian edition, unconditionally recommended its sweeping proposals for theatrical reform:

> Exclusively dedicated to questions of stage art, [the usefulness of] this book . . . is indubitable, as the modern Russian theater, which long ago began to stagnate in its immobility, has begun in recent years to regress perceptibly. . . . In an era of . . . such decline . . . the voice of a sober, sound critic is more than desirable—it is *necessary*.
>
> This is why this book has been translated and published.[80]

Strange Sorrows centers on two theater managers, one dressed in brown and the other in gray, who meet by chance at an inn and exchange tales of their theatrical tribulations. Brown, Hoffmann's spokesperson, leads an itinerant troupe, while Gray, the suffering manager of the tale's title, heads the local company. After listening to Gray's woes, which include a recent operatic flop featuring a dog as the lead actor, Brown seizes the opportunity to present a methodical assessment of the problems in contemporary theater, in each case proposing solutions.

Most of *Strange Sorrows* deals with the actor. Brown argues that actors must analyze each new role, embrace audience responses besides applause, play supporting as well as leading parts, and express character physically. Theater managers can cultivate talent by training actors to move beyond a single character type (*emploi*). With Brown as his spokesperson, Hoffmann also advocates for the unification of theatrical elements prompted by a single vision (a generation before Wagner's *Gesamtkunstwerk*), for scenic design that provokes the fantasy, for atmospheric lighting, for costumes that complement specific productions, and for a repertoire of plays by Shakespeare, Calderón, and Gozzi. Additional proposed reforms range from smaller audiences to well-educated critics.

Thus far, Hoffmann's advice would seem to align with the aims of the Moscow Art Theatre. However, the remainder of the tale sets up a surprise ending. Brown, who is in the process of staging Gozzi's *Love of Three Oranges*, retells the scenario, but with a number of Hoffmann-initiated changes that reframe Gozzi in a German context.[81] The two managers also ironically frame *Three Oranges* by conversing about the scenario as they retell it. Just as Brown gets to the end, Gray begs him to stop: he pictures the action vividly but thinks it impossible to stage Gozzi's *fiaba* without Antonio Sacchi's troupe,[82] the famous commedia company that originally performed it. Brown agrees that Gozzi can be staged only under specific circumstances: as opera or by *his* company. He describes the virtues of his actors: they are always kind, willing to play any part, never upstage one another, know their roles perfectly, and don't superimpose their own personalities onto the roles. When Brown leads Gray up to his room to introduce him to his troupe, he reveals that they are marionettes. Written nearly a century before Edward Gordon Craig's "The Actor and the Über-Marionette" (1907), Hoffmann's declaration of puppets as ideal actors presented a provocative new paradigm for director-actor and actor-character relationships in Russia. Brown's understanding of puppets as an ideal medium through which to revive Gozzi's plays has been especially enduring, lasting, as Tribble notes, "through the symbolist era right down to our own day."[83]

Although Hoffmann found qualities in the puppet he wished were more typical of flesh-and-blood actors, he did not want them to follow their manipulator blindly but viewed them as artists who collaborate with a singleness of purpose; Brown boasts that "complete accord and unanimity prevail in my troupe . . . they are all friendly to each other, because they all love and serve art equally."[84] Hoffmann saw puppets as performers in a wholly separate kind of theater. When asked by Grey if he might spare some performers, Brown responds: "It is as impossible for my actors to perform in your theater, my dear friend, as yours in mine."[85] For Hoffmann, because the puppet can never fully imitate reality, it frees the spectator's fantasy. Raraty explains:

> Hoffmann is suggesting that . . . the suspension of disbelief . . . must come first on the part of the spectator. Having done this, nothing will disturb his translation in the puppet theatre into the realms of poetry. This is an approach quite opposite to that normally attempted on the conventional stage, which tries to lure the spectator into an acceptance of the stage world as real by means of a dishonest counterfeit of reality—an attempt which Hoffmann . . . saw was bound to fail, simply because . . . the stage cannot truly simulate reality.[86]

Because the puppet is always a conventionalization of life rather than an actual instance of life, then, it inherently defies Briusov's "unnecessary truth."

Hoffmann's fascination with puppets and automata became a major leitmotif in his works. He juxtaposes live humans with puppet actors in several tales: *The Devil's Elixirs* includes a David and Goliath story in which the victory of a puppet David is rendered doubtful by the ominous appearance of the puppeteer's own head in Goliath's costume. "The Doubles" includes a similar device: a Pulcinella show is interrupted when the puppeteer inserts his seemingly lifeless head. *Princess Blandina* was written for the puppet theater, while the hero of *Princess Brambilla* finds his true self only after killing his puppet self in a duel.

Hoffmann's tales are similarly replete with toys-come-to-life and automata positioned uncannily between life and death. Herr Drosselmeier informs Marie in "The Nutcracker and the Mouse King" that Nutcracker used to belong to a puppeteer. "Automata" is a sinister depiction of clockwork figures that imitate life.[87] One of Hoffmann's best-known tales, "The Sandman," which inspired Jentsch's (1906) and Freud's (1919) famous discussions of the uncanny, centers on Olimpia, a beautiful but lifeless automaton, and Nathaniel, the young man beguiled into falling in love with her after viewing her though the malevolent Coppelius's magic glass.

As Tribble notes, Hoffmann's complex view of the puppet is a fusion of early German romantic interest in the marionette, in which the puppet is "a pessimistic symbol . . . a plaything of destiny on the stage of life," and later writings by Kleist, which present "a positive view" that "focus . . . on its grace, its godlikeness and above all its superiority to the human actor."[88] Because Hoffmann embraced these dissonant views rather than trying to resolve them, his understanding of the puppet could be interpreted in Russia with a great deal of variety.[89] A recurrent Hoffmann-inspired metaphor in Russian theater was the transformation of people into dolls and dolls into people; famous examples include *Petrushka* and *The Nutcracker*. Olga Glebova-Sudeikina, a habitué of the Players' Rest, engaged with this theme in reverse by creating dolls of Russian theatrical luminaries. The Bat cabaret staged parodies of Moscow Art Theatre productions, most famously *The Blue Bird* (1908), with puppets and developed what it called "living doll" numbers, such as Vakhtangov's "The Parade of the Wooden Soldiers" (1911), a staple of the Bat's repertoire in its émigré years in France and the United States.

Russian modernist artists most often interpreted the puppet in two ways: as a mechanical being devoid of life and as an idealized theatrical teacher for live actors.[90] Meyerhold, however, believed that the simplicity and precision of the puppet theater, metaphorically understood, could revive the theater of live actors. Like Hoffmann, he celebrated the puppet's inherent conventionality. In "Two Puppet Theatres," the second half of Meyerhold's seminal essay "Balagan" (1913),[91] he compares the actor of the "naturalistic school" to a puppet that has betrayed its inherent qualities; this he contrasts with the conventionalized puppet, the realm of which is a "wonderland of make-believe" in which the puppet wants "not to copy but to create." Meyerhold believed that the true calling of the live actor, to "transport the spectator to a world of make-believe,"[92] similarly could be achieved by celebrating overt "play-acting."[93]

Princess Blandina: Building and Rupturing Frames

Princess Blandina was Hoffmann's most direct experiment with theatrical play-acting. While the *Three Oranges* in *Strange Sorrows* is Hoffmann's sole extant commedia scenario, *Princess Blandina* is his sole extant play. Hoffmann wrote this play to be performed by puppets—an attempt to apply what he proposed in *Strange Sorrows* three years later. This dramatic fragment (consisting of act 1 only) is replete with authorial interruptions and framing devices inspired by the plays-within-plays of Ludwig Tieck. Tieck's *Puss in Boots* (1797), "the first manifesto of German theatrical Romanticism"[94] and a direct ancestor of Hoffmann's *Tomcat Murr*, was to become well known in theatrical Russia via its translation in Meyerhold's journal *Love for Three Oranges*.

Even more formally astonishing than *Puss* is Tieck's *Topsy-Turvy World* (1799),[95] which contains "a quadruple play-within-a-play that has yet to be outdone."[96] Its (fictional) audience interrupts the play to comment on it;

members of the audience take on roles in the play; the author, director, and stagehands appear in a play-within-a-play watched by an audience-within-an-audience; actors watch a play that shows actors watching a play (at which a member of the fictional audience cries, "What if we were fiction too?");[97] and the audience rises up in revolt to change the main play's ending. Tieck intended this constant crossing between realities to be confusing. "Romanticism is a shattering of frames," Mandel observes in his analysis of the play, "a breaking through of boundaries both outward into the universe and inward into the self's interior, and such transcendings are apt to lead to a very serious sense of infinity or inexplicability."[98]

Hoffmann used multiple frames to evoke this inexplicable infinity in *Blandina*. The outermost frame is Hoffmann's *Fantasy Pieces*, within which are two clusters of "Kreisleriana," one of which, "Johannes Kreisler's Musical-Poetic Club," frames *Blandina*. In this tale, Kreisler's friend reads the play aloud after Kreisler has been morosely pounding on the piano in a dark, smoke-filled room. Once the play begins, the reader discovers that it is framed by fictional performers (to have been played by puppets) who step in and out of their roles at will. Within these frames, which seem to multiply into infinity as in a hall of mirrors, the story that is eventually told is "a modified [*Princess*] *Turandot*,"[99] in which cruel King Killian, who would marry Blandina by force if she will not wed him, is vanquished when his head is pierced with a fork and discovered to be hollow.

Blandina opens with a comic prologue in which actors lapse in and out of character to complain about the play. There are myriad other similar interruptions that prompt permanent parabasis: a prompter who emerges from his box, the offstage voice of an enraged theater manager, and a stage manager who threatens to fine the actors, who begin shouting "down with the exposition!"[100] The play is peppered with intertextual references to Gozzi *fiabe* that lie outside its fictional frame: *Blandina*'s Tartaglia, for instance, is identified as the same scoundrel who betrayed King Deramo in *The King Stag*.

After act 1 concludes, the reader returns to the frame of the smoke-filled club. Kreisler's friend briefly summarizes the remaining action:

> Blandina does not on any account marry Amandus, [the court musician] . . . rather does the latter go to his earthly destruction at the hands of false Roderich. After his death Amandus travels through the air as a singing swan, and saves Blandina from the clutches of the devil, who had deceived her in the shape of an elemental spirit, and who had tried to lure her to ruin. Her heart breaks in the supreme bliss of song.[101]

This complete departure from Gozzi's *Turandot* marks a return to Hoffmann's characteristically fantastical plot devices. Hoffmann viewed *Blandina* as unsuccessful and had it purged from the second edition of *Fantasy Pieces*. *Blandina* was therefore probably one of the least known of Hoffmann's works until Sergei Ignatov proposed in *E. T. A. Hoffmann: Man and Works* that *Blandina* was Hoffmann's most valuable attempt to put Gozzi's principles into practice.[102]

Ignatov's interest in *Blandina*'s practical applicability led him to attempt to form a theater company that, like Sacchi's troupe, would have the audience-centered skills needed to revive Gozzi's plays. He hoped to direct *Blandina* with Meyerhold as his mentor. Though this production never came to fruition, Ignatov published a staging plan for *Blandina* in the journal *Love for Three Oranges*.[103] If *Blandina* was Hoffmann's most direct attempt to implement theatrical reform, Ignatov's staging plan is the most direct Russian attempt to translate *Blandina*'s framing devices into practical mise-en-scène. His plan focuses on the play's opening frame, for which Ignatov proposed using Callot's *repoussoir* techniques to juxtapose Hoffmann's grotesque and Gozzi's fairy-tale content[104] by placing *Blandina* physically inside the "Kreisleriana":

> On the [forestage], in different corners, the figures of Kreisler's friends are scattered in poses . . . When the reading/action begins . . . the friends freeze in their grotesque poses. Only Kreisler maintains a cloud of smoke around himself and with growing irony glances at the stage. He sits all the while at the piano with a few of his friends in armchairs, others on the low partition that divides the forestage from the stage; behind this partition are footlights and a large prompter's box. And large, silent figures look at the stage, standing at the opposite ends of the footlights.[105]

Ignatov explained that these characters were inspired by the framing figures in Callot's etchings: "These figures, frozen in their grotesque, conventionalized poses, should seem like enormous shadows on the background of a brightly illuminated stage; they should recall the foreground figures of Callot in his 'The Fan,' 'Tournament in Florence,' and 'Primo Intermedio'"[106] (figure 6).

While the prologue refracted Callot and Hoffmann, Gozzi was the inspiration for the play. Ignatov used Callot for contrast, Hoffmann for distortion, and Gozzi as a symbol of light, joy, and irony, proposing that the action on the main stage should emphasize "a very brisk tempo, use of convention in the style of the Italian comedy of masks, rhythmical movement, and keenly expressive facial expressions."[107] Ignatov maintained distinct foreground and background planes through movement, scale, color, and sound: "The small figures on the stage and the enormous ones on the forestage . . . should replicate the interrelation between Callot's two planes." The framing characters were to be costumed in dark colors and speak in "slightly muffled" tones, while the characters on the main stage were to wear "bright, fairly

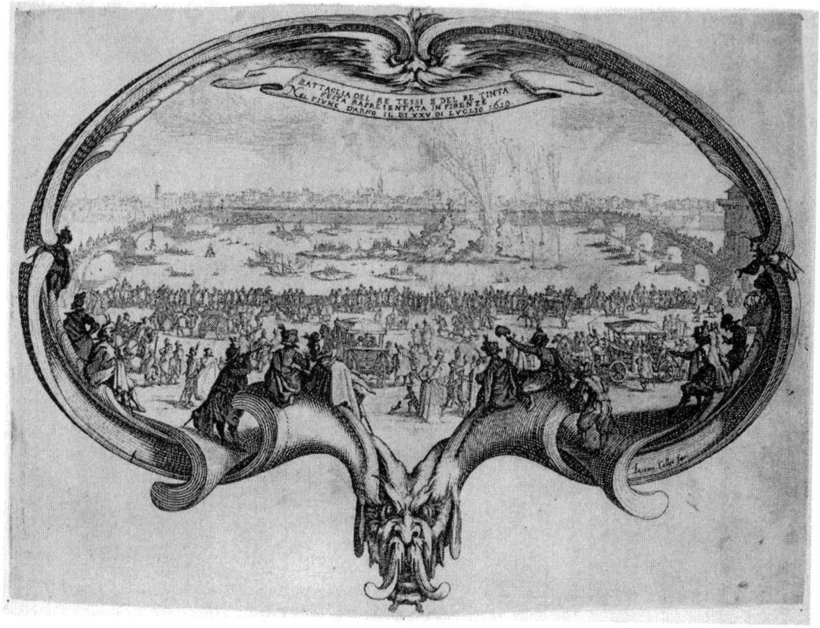

Figure 6. Jacques Callot, *The Fan* (1619). Etching and engraving. Harvard Art Museums/Fogg Museum, Gift of William Gray from the collection of Francis Calley Gray, by exchange, S3.69.1. Photo: Imaging Department © President and Fellows of Harvard College.

vivid colors" and speak in "resonant" tones inspired by "the playfulness and precision of the Italian masks."[108]

While Ignatov's staging proposal is fairly simplistic compared to Meyerhold's grotesque, Tairov's kaleidoscopic action, and Eisenstein's vertical montage, it provides important context for why each of these directors adopted similar devices—action on multiple planes, contrasting colors and sounds, framing characters, and exaggerated movement. Hoffmannian and Tieckian framing devices also recur in the plays of Alexander Blok, Nikolai Evreinov (Pirandello's artistic kindred spirit),[109] Vladimir Mayakovsky, Sergei Tretiakov,[110] and many others.

Princess Brambilla: Commedia and the Capriccio

Hoffmann continued to work in the manner of Gozzi and Callot in *Princess Brambilla: A Capriccio after Jacques Callot* (*Prinzessin Brambilla: Ein Capriccio nach Jakob Callot*). *Brambilla* conflates Callot and *carnevale*, Gozzi and the grotesque into a theatrical parable that doubles as a proposal for theatrical reform. In 1820 Hoffmann received a set of Callot's *Balli di*

Figure 7. Carl Friedrich Thiele, aquatint etching in sepia (Berlin, September 1820), after Jacques Callot's *Franca Trippa and Fritellino*, from *Balli di Sfessania* (c. 1621). Plate 4 in the first edition of Hoffmann's *Princess Brambilla: A Capriccio after Jacques Callot* (1821). Staatsbibliothek Bamberg, Sel.235a. Photo: Gerald Raab.

Sfessania as a birthday present. *Brambilla*, written later that year, was inspired by these etchings; Hoffmann used eight of the twenty-four *Balli*—numbers 12, 3, 8, 23, 17, 24, 9, and 21 respectively, one for each of *Brambilla's* eight chapters—to develop descriptions of the novella's carnival scenes and central character pairs (see figure 3). The original edition of *Brambilla* included aquatint engravings based on these *Balli*, created by Carl Friedrich Thiele, who, at Hoffmann's suggestion, removed Callot's background planes (figure 7).[111] *Brambilla* also contains numerous references to Gozzi's works and theater wars, including a hack playwright Chiari, a reference to Gozzi's real-life theatrical rival, Abbot Pietro Chiari.[112] The result is a fantastical novella that Ignatov called a dream "in the style of" Gozzi.[113] Indeed, the tale's characters, themes, and fictional planes intertwine, diverge, and reconnect in a manner that defies reason, but the plot is finally revealed to be extremely simple: two lovers find their true selves by rejecting theatrical clichés and embracing commedia dell'arte.

Brambilla is most significant in a Russian theatrical context, however, as a model for the creative process of the artist-innovator. One of the primary links between Hoffmann, Gozzi, Callot, and Tieck is that the artistic worldview of each is philosophically based on the capriccio, an Italian term that indicates a capricious work that "bursts the bonds" of previous rules and "does not correspond to the rule of imitation, that is to Aristotelian mimesis."[114] The word was initially used in the seventeenth century for overtly whimsical musical compositions and has since been adopted by composers ranging from Strauss to Stravinsky.[115]

Callot's 1617 *Capricci di varie figure di Iacopo Callot*, a series of fifty etchings the artist created in Florence, marks the "'anchoring" of the term to visual art; the capriccio has since been commonly used to describe works of art and architecture that collide real and fantastical elements.[116] Callot's *Capricci* also paired dualities in specific ways. Several feature grotesquely rendered commedia types; one presents two views of Pantalone from opposite perspectives in a single etching. Composition is also frequently based on the contrast between at least two, but as many as four, planes of action.

E. T. A. Hoffmann moored the capriccio to literature with *Princess Brambilla*. Hoffmann's capriccio "capers along freely, whimsically, arbitrarily, astonishingly," Gurewitch notes, "apparently as a pure expression of self-dissolving, self-reconstituting artistic sovereignty."[117] In the preface to *Brambilla*, Hoffmann writes:

> The kind reader . . . who may be ready and willing to put gravity aside for a few hours and abandon himself to the whimsical and audacious play of a hobgoblin, even though it may occasionally be downright impertinent, is humbly requested by the editor not to forget the basis on which the whole affair rests, Callot's fantastic caricatures, and also to consider what a musician may demand of a capriccio.[118]

Brambilla additionally linked the capriccio's whimsicality with the structure of Gozzi's polemical framing devices, which often took the form of prologues or of ironic commentary that connected his *fiabe* to the heated polemical debates that inspired and surrounded them. Thus Hoffmann's capriccio does not only advocate for freedom from rules but also for the agency to make one's own rules in defiance of others. It is both an apologia for creative freedom and a manifesto. This particular combination made the capriccio, as refracted through Hoffmann's prism, especially attractive as a model for Russian directors pioneering theatrical reform.

REFRACTION

Meyerhold, Tairov, and Eisenstein each at some point used the word "prism" or "refraction" to describe the creative process.[119] In 1907 Meyerhold called the actor "the *prism* through which the audience receives the director and the playwright."[120] In what he called "theater of the straight line," each artist—the playwright, the director, the actor—treats source material as a starting point for a cumulative artistic conversation that includes the audience. Meyerhold's very definition of theater, in his words, "assumes the existence . . . of a fourth creator, after the author, actor, and director: the spectator."[121]

Tairov used the word "refraction" to describe how virtuosic actors interpret source material. With regard to his production of *Princess Brambilla* (1920), he argued, "there are no corresponding plays in the extant dramatic literature suitable for synthesized theatrical construction, which merges elements of the Harlequinade, tragedy, operetta, pantomime, and circus, *refracted* through the modern soul of the actor."[122] For Tairov, dramatizing works of fiction by authors like Hoffmann gave actors creative freedom from the externally imposed constraints of dramatic literature, previous conventions, and fixed genres.

While in the Red Army during the Russian Civil War, Eisenstein embarked on a period of vigorous theatrical self-education that he documented in a series of notebooks. In one entry, he mused about the creative process in response to several of Meyerhold's theoretical works. Even as Eisenstein learned from them, he noted that he immediately had "the desire to make *my* meaning in refracted form."[123] In his view, any artist working "in the manner" of another inevitably and necessarily contributes something new. Indeed, throughout his career, Eisentein actively, often aggressively, refracted his sources.

The prism is one of several optical metaphors that abounded during Russia's early twentieth century: theatrical productions and reviews are filled with kaleidoscopes, magic lanterns, and phantasmagorias, while one of the era's most famous cabarets was the Distorting Mirror. Among these optical devices, the prism stands out, however, as an especially apt metaphor for the creative process of the director. On a basic level, both "direct": a prism directs light; a director directs a production. Even more significantly, in Russian modernist theater, art and *prelomlenie* (interpretation or refraction) were often treated as synonyms. While any source is inevitably redirected or made multihued when passed through the artist's fantasy, theatricalist theater was about this process.

The word *prelomlenie* is usually translated as "interpretation" in the context of art and as "refraction" in the context of light. This book's investigation of directorial interpretation *as* refraction makes it possible to explore both meanings at once. In the science of light, there are two primary ways that light can be refracted: the direction of a ray of light can be changed, or white light can be dispersed into the colors of the spectrum. The degree to which a ray of light changes direction depends on the refractive index of the medium through which it passes; because water, for instance, has a higher refractive index than glass, it bends light more. With regard to the director's refractive index, those who prioritize fidelity, authenticity, or likeness to life assume that a director should "bend" a source—a dramatic text, a historical period, observable reality—as little as possible, while those who favor subjective interpretation are more likely to alter a source's trajectory. Material dispersion, on the other hand, is the process whereby a dispersive prism refracts white light into a rainbow. If we think of the director as a dispersive prism, she or he provides a new perspective on source material by revealing aspects of it that otherwise are invisible or by taking one line of meaning—written words, for instance—and refracting it into numerous sign systems: light, sound, intonation, movement, design, audience interaction, aesthetic vocabulary, and so on.

Directors—and artists more broadly speaking—inevitably engage in both kinds of refraction, simultaneously bending and revealing the colors of the sources with which they engage. The rise of the director at the turn of the last century marked the beginning of the modern understanding of a theatrical production as a work that is simultaneously unified and refracted through the consciousness of a single artistic entity. While some of the most frequently referred-to models for the process of the director—the director-translator, the director-interpreter, the director-auteur—are commonly thought of as discrete philosophical approaches, I propose that each actually lies along a single continuum of refraction.

Viewing the director as a prism unhinges assumptions that fidelity and authenticity are necessarily measures of quality. To refract is not the same as to create sui generis, however. We might think of layering unrelated ideas atop extant material as aberration, the misdirection of light due to a fault in the optical system. Such theatrical aberrations have many possible sources: incomplete analysis, self-censorship, habit, tradition. With refraction comes the assumption that deep intellectual and artistic engagement with a source *is* a creative process, one in which a source is not imitated, but creatively transformed. As Meyerhold wrote in 1907,

> By "stylization" I do not mean reproducing precisely the style of a given era or phenomenon, as a photographer does in photographs . . . To "stylize" an era or phenomenon means . . . to renew, using every possible means of expression, the latent characteristic traits that are in the deeply latent style of any work of art.[124]

Meyerhold, who came to call himself a "production author," believed that a director becomes an author specifically through this kind of rigorous artistic response.[125]

Refraction, the artist's deep engagement with a source via the prism of untrammeled fantasy, inspires similarly free expression in others. For the actor, to refract is to play, to improvise, to make-believe rather than to live on the stage. For the audience, to refract is to generate rather than receive meaning. Refraction does not force the spectator into one of many possible "modes of seeing,"[126] but helps the audience negotiate the inevitable simultaneities of conflicting elements in art and in life. It allows for a poetics in which multiple perspectives and truths are presented simultaneously: fiction and reality, form and content, process and product. It aims to generate connotative meaning—open-ended meaning that can be interpreted variously to form new associations—rather than denotative meaning, which often assumes a single "correct" interpretation.

This view of making theater—and art more broadly—is important for several reasons: Unlike adaptation and transposition, which focus primarily on a source and its subsequent versions, refraction focuses squarely on the process of the artist.[127] Refraction allows us to think of the creative process as imaginative engagement rather than simple imitation, thus providing room for each individual who encounters a work to become a refractor of it. Thinking of borrowings, homages, and rebellions as refractions also counters common assumptions that artists should eschew engaging with outside sources for fear their work will be labeled derivative.

If we think of any artist who engages with the work of others as peering through a constellation or network of temporally and culturally positioned prisms, we discover that it is possible to look through several at once (Gogol's refraction of Hoffmann's refraction of Callot's refraction of commedia, for instance) while also looking through each independently (Gogol, Hoffmann, Callot, commedia). Thus, while this book focuses primarily on refractions of Hoffmann by Russian avant-garde directors, it also embraces his sources and nods to others that seemingly are unconnected but that Russian directors viewed as architecturally similar: Kabuki, cubism, commedia, circus, film.

As Russian directors refracted historical styles into the many colors of Harlequin and the colliding realities of the German romantics, most were far more interested in how Hoffmann's prism was made, in *how* it dispersed life into colors, than they were in mirroring the plots of his tales. This creates a unique challenge when tracing the transmission of Hoffmann's ideas: how closely these directors imitated Hoffmann cannot be assumed to be an accurate measure of how active their engagement with him was. I therefore look for Hoffmaniana in unexpected places: removed footlights, framing characters, kaleidoscopic action, the unusual angle of a movie camera, the persistence of plural points of view, and above all, the frank presence of the artist in the work.

The architecture of Russian theatricalist prisms was deeply philosophically based on the capriccio. The freedom the capriccio provided as a model for the artist's right to respond, comment, and create rather than to mirror, record, or photographically duplicate cannot be overemphasized. Russian Golden Age writers had already refracted Hoffmann's freedom of self-defined form, rejection of externally mandated rules in art-making, and celebration of the artist's individual perspective. Meyerhold, Tairov, Eisenstein, and their like-minded contemporaries viewed themselves, these earlier Russian writers, and Hoffmann, Tieck, Gozzi, and Callot as part of a shared, consciously adopted creative legacy with the potential to fundamentally redefine the theater—beginning with the elimination of "unnecessary truth."

This book uses a few unusual structural elements and conventionalized terms that warrant brief explanation. Each chapter begins with what I call a "prologue/polemic." Refraction in Russian theater is inseparable from the idea of polemic, an artistic confrontation that clarifies one's creative aims in response to others. Gozzi introduced each of his *fiabe* with a polemical prologue that framed it in the context of the reforms he proposed. Hoffmann introduced *Fantasy Pieces, Princess Brambilla*, and other works with audacious explanations of their connections to the sources he refracted. I therefore introduce Meyerhold, Tairov, and Eisenstein's work by framing it in the context of debates that surrounded it.

I discuss each director's innovations through a series of production analyses, the most detailed of which I playfully term "interludes," both to help the reader locate the book's central case studies and to link the book's structure with its thematic content. These interludes are as follows: for Meyerhold, *Columbine's Veil* and *Inspector General*; for Tairov, *Pierrette's Veil* and *Princess Brambilla*; and for Eisenstein, *Columbine's Garter.* Three of these—*Columbine's Veil, Pierrette's Veil,* and *Columbine's Garter*—are refractions of the same pantomime (see appendixes B-D) and therefore provide a unique opportunity to compare and contrast these three directors' artistic vocabularies.

Why "interludes"? Beginning with Meyerhold, many theatricalist directors believed that a play's peripheral framing characters were its most significant, that "low" popular entertainments were the most fruitful from which to draw, and that interludes, asides, and prologues were more central to audience engagement than the plays themselves. By structuring this book around interludes, I advocate for the value of ostensible interruptions that in fact allow for deeper engagement with each director's work. I also propose viewing theatrical productions—whether staged or unrealized—*as performed theory*, rather than, as often happens, placing greater weight on written theory that inspired or was inspired by productions (but was written apart from them) simply because this theory is written.

Understanding productions as polemical interventions in the theatrical status quo is particularly fruitful in the context of Russian and early

Soviet theater, namely because it focused so centrally on baring the process of creation to reveal the actor behind the mask and the artist framing the work. Within the larger context of these directors' artistic careers, this book is especially interested in the miniature, the after-hours, the provisional, the ephemeral, and the dreamed-of-but-never-performed, as these are invaluable, yet often significantly underexplored windows into their work. The book therefore analyzes several experiments that never reached the stage yet are central to these directors' development. This analysis of both staged and unrealized productions relies heavily on archival sources, most of which are unavailable in English. The plentiful quotations in the text, the documents and libretti in the appendixes, and the archival resources in the book's online resource companion provide direct access to primary sources in order to restore a fuller artistic context to creative voices repressed or distorted under Stalin.

Even now, the lingering weight of the epithets "formalism" and "art for art's sake" continue to partially eclipse the full value of this theater that fundamentally rethought, redefined, and regenerated itself by embracing theatrical creation as the lifeblood of human existence. This book also challenges a few other historical biases: that psychological realism is more truthful than other styles; that productions should faithfully transmit plays; that theatrical mise-en-scène is less intellectually substantive than spoken words; and that theater is a less fruitful medium for formal innovation than film. Another oversimplification, initially proposed by Brecht, posits that Stanislavsky and Meyerhold represent two theatrical poles, while other directors, Vakhtangov for instance, fall between them, a model that gives the impression that all Russian directors can be placed along a single continuum. I suggest that we instead view their vibrant variety as a constellation of prisms, each of which refracts its own light and the light of others in brilliantly complex ways.

Although this book traces how ideas are transmitted, it is not a book about influence. It is about the making of a creative process. Though Hoffmann's works also shaped Russian literature (the Serapion Brotherhood, for instance), playwriting (Blok and Evreinov, among others), visual art (the World of Art group and beyond), opera (including Prokofiev's *Love for Three Oranges* and Shostakovich's *The Nose*), and ballet (an example being *Petrushka*), I leave explorations of these refractions by writers, painters, composers, and choreographers to future studies so that I may more fully examine the poetics of Russian theatricalist directors and their art that, in Hoffmann's words, "surpasses the rules."[128] If, as Adler notes, Hoffmann "rewrote serious fiction's contract with the reading public,"[129] so, too, Meyerhold, Tairov, and Eisenstein rewrote the definition of theater for and with their audiences. In turning to Hoffmann, each embraced a paradox: the past was a vital foundation upon which to build something wholly new.

Chapter One

Meyerhold-Dapertutto: Framing the Grotesque

PROLOGUE/POLEMIC: "*THE CRICKET ON THE HEARTH*, OR, AT THE KEYHOLE"

In 1915 "Doctor Dapertutto" published a scathing review of the Moscow Art Theatre First Studio's intimate production of Charles Dickens's *The Cricket on the Hearth*.[1] What was unusual about the article was that it was more a review of the spectators than it was of the production. "*The Cricket on the Hearth*, or, At the Keyhole" characterized the proscenium opening, the location of the imaginary fourth wall in representational theater, as a keyhole and the spectators as voyeurs who gaze unabashedly and passively through it into a private world. Dapertutto posited that each of us "is subject to an incurable illness in consequence of which he is irrepressibly drawn to the keyhole;" it is this illness that leads us "to eavesdrop on another's conversations, to peep from the sidewalk into the windows of lower floors . . . to peer at sheets of paper across the shoulder of those writing." The primary purpose of fourth-wall theater, argued Dapertutto, is to feed this voyeuristic instinct:

> When spectators forget that they are in the theater, when they forget that it is only a performance, when it seems to them that this is life itself, oh, then! . . . See how the spectators of this kind of theater conduct themselves . . . [A] soft armchair is placed near the keyhole, "the theater is immersed in the darkest darkness," and it is possible to stare without blushing as someone gets dressed.[2]

Doctor Dapertutto was, of course, none other than Vsevolod Emilevich Meyerhold (1874–1940). Meyerhold had been following the activities of Stanislavsky's First Studio since it opened three years before, and although he unflaggingly admired his former mentor, he believed that to mirror life while placing audiences in a passive position on the other side of the fourth wall was a misunderstanding of theater that stifled its potential. For him, theater is only theater insofar as it is an act of audience-actor cocreation.

Although Meyerhold officially operated under the pseudonym Doctor Dapertutto for nearly a decade (1910–18), he penned only two articles in his journal, *Love for Three Oranges: The Journal of Doctor Dapertutto* (1914–16), as his alter ego. In the second, "Doctor Dapertutto's Glosses on Iu. Aikhenvald's 'A Denial of the Theater,'" a controversial essay that challenged theater's value as an art form, Dapertutto again advocates for creative engagement rather than passive mirroring, this time on the part of actors. "Don't repeat life in the theater," he writes, "and you will see, dear actors, how little by little your theater will become art."[3] For Dapertutto, the actor must never be reduced to a talking being that simply repeats the words of a playwright, for "the 'talking head' is the same as the gramophone. As records are placed on the gramophone, text is placed on the lips of the actor. . . . Changing only the wigs and costumes, the actor talks and talks and talks, just talks one text or another. Down with the theater of the actor-gramophone!"[4]

Meyerhold did not believe that theater should hold a mirror to life. In fact, he called mimesis "the lowest rung on the ladder—imitation with no creative input."[5] He therefore mined history for theatrical forms that shift attention away from a single focus on the fictional world and onto the perpetual co-presence of the real (the actors' and spectators' bodies and experiences in space and time) and the fictional (the world being presented). Actors are always both themselves and their characters; productions make meaning through content and form; and spectators are aware of the fiction they are watching even as they are imaginatively immersed in it. Bert O. States has called this perpetual duality, from the audience's point of view, a kind of "binocular vision" in which "one eye enables us to see the world phenomenally [and] the other . . . to see it significatively."[6] This understanding of theater as consisting of colliding perceptual planes lies at the heart of Meyerhold's creative poetics (figure 8).

Before Newton, Europeans assumed that prisms were devices whereby white light was physically transformed into the colors of the rainbow. Newton discovered that colors in white light are always there; we simply don't have the ability to see them until they are refracted. Similarly, Meyerhold believed that the theater's colors remain invisible in productions that imitate life. His aim as a director was to discover how to refract this plural experience most effectively. In this context, it becomes clear why Meyerhold-Dapertutto criticized the First Studio. Peering through a keyhole can only be done with one eye (i.e., binocular vision is impossible), and it is one-sided: the actor is blind to the spectator.

In opposition to the keyhole theater, Meyerhold structured his productions around the colliding juxtapositions of the grotesque. He stated in 1922, the year he first publicly demonstrated biomechanics:

Figure 8. Photo portrait of Vsevolod Meyerhold by Alexei Temerin (1929). КП 180170/477. © A. A. Bakhrushin State Central Theatre Museum, Moscow.

> The theater, an unnatural combination of natural, temporal, spatial, and numerical phenomena that necessarily contradicts our daily experience, is, in its very essence, an example of the grotesque. Arising from the grotesque of the ritual masquerade, [theater] is inevitably destroyed by any kind of attempt to remove the grotesque from it by basing it on everyday reality.[7]

Meyerhold's grotesque ranged from staging sharply conflicting emotions to prompting abrupt rhythmical changes to dropping a mask to show the actor behind. Such juxtapositions were achieved in two primary ways: by presenting incongruous perceptual planes in a single image, or by "oscillating" between them,[8] thus shaping the spectator's own mental and emotional oscillation. In "Balagan" ("The Fairground Booth"), Meyerhold's most famous essay on the grotesque, he quotes Andrei Bely's assessment of these two kinds of juxtaposition: "Art dismantles reality, depicting it now spatially, now temporally. For this reason, art consists either in images or in the alternation of images: the first yields the spatial forms of art, the second—the temporal forms.'"[9] Visual art often inspired Meyerhold's spatial forms—the composition of his stage pictures—while musical principles inspired his temporal forms—mise-en-scène as it develops through time.

For Meyerhold, as for Hoffmann, the grotesque was not simply a style, but "the expression of a comprehensive view of existence."[10] To understand Meyerhold's grotesque—what we now, in the wake of Lionel Abel's pioneering work, often place under the umbrella term "metatheatre"[11]—we must consider Meyerhold's framing of character, space, and other elements of the make-believe theatrical world and how he engaged audiences by confronting them with multiple planes, provoking the audience's fantasy by allowing the make-believe world to spill out beyond the proscenium divide. Meyerhold used a variety of techniques, many of them in Hoffmann's manner, to shift attention onto plural perspectives of many kinds. Hoffmann, who used self-referential framing devices to shift attention away from content alone and onto both form and content, provided Meyerhold with a valuable model for such simultaneities. In the words of one scholar of German romanticism, the literature of Hoffmann's day is "neither mere 'literature' . . . nor simply a 'theory of literature.' . . . Rather, it is *theory itself as literature* or, in other words, literature producing itself as it produces its own theory."[12] I cannot think of a more apt description for Meyerhold's work: that of *theater* producing itself as it produces its own theory.

Meyerhold's sources for creating this new theater were expansive, kaleidoscopic, a product of his deep artistic engagement with historical and contemporary innovations that resonated with his own. Among others, he drew inspiration from Baudelaire, Nietzsche, Poe, Maeterlinck, Chekhov, Stanislavsky, Craig, Ivanov, and Briusov. He was well versed in theater history (especially Kabuki and Noh, Spanish Golden Age theater, Molière, ancient Greek staging conventions, Shakespeare, commedia dell'arte) and visual art (Callot, Goya, Daumier, and others). Recurrent postrevolutionary inspirations included film, circus, music hall, Taylorism, and Eccentrism. However, as Clayton notes, most scholars have not fully recognized the German-speaking director's intense engagement with German theater and literature,[13] ranging from the romantics to historical playwrights and musicians to contemporary innovators like Wagner, Fuchs, Appia, and Reinhardt. It is clear from Meyerhold's productions, theoretical writings, and lectures that Hoffmann was at the forefront of these inspirations. Meyerhold refracted Hoffmann in a quest to reinvent the theater as it had come to be practiced—not in terms of content, but in terms of how artfully wielded form might produce a more cognitively complex, creatively engaged experience for artist and audience alike.

This chapter analyzes the seminal place of Hoffmann in the formation of Meyerhold's theatrical poetics. Many theater historians have referred to Meyerhold's Hoffmannian alter ego, to the dedicated Hoffmann column in *Love for Three Oranges: The Journal of Doctor Dapertutto*, and to Meyerhold's development of a nightmarish Hoffmannian grotesque. None, however, has treated Meyerhold's refractions of Hoffmann, especially in the decade leading up to the 1917 Revolution, in detail. Returning to this book's metaphor of the prism, I contend that Hoffmann's centrality to the formation of Meyerhold's theatrical poetics has never been fully seen. This chapter's aim is to make its multihued significance manifest.

In the first portion of this chapter, I examine Meyerhold's pseudonym, several prerevolutionary theatrical experiments, and the Hoffmann-inspired theory recorded in *Love for Three Oranges: The Journal of Doctor Dapertutto*. Brief analyses of *Balaganchik* (*The Little Fairground Booth*) (1906) and *Dom Juan* (1910) contextualize consistent devices that are examined in more depth in the chapter's longer production analyses (its "interludes"): *Columbine's Veil* (1910), Meyerhold's first experiment with the theatrical grotesque, and a published but never staged refraction of Gozzi's *Love of Three Oranges* (1914), which pioneered new modes of framing and fragmentation. The chapter concludes with a third interlude: an analysis of Meyerhold's continued development of pre-revolutionary innovations in his post-revolutionary *Inspector General* (1926), a turning point in Meyerhold's life and work.

ENTER DOCTOR DAPERTUTTO

In 1908, shortly after star actress Vera Komissarzhevskaia dismissed Meyerhold from his position as director at her theater, he was hired as a director and actor at the Saint Petersburg Imperial Theatres, a position he kept until 1918. He led a dual existence from the outset: a director of veteran actors in some of the nation's most tradition-bound theaters by day and a controversial leader of cabarets and theater-studios by night. In 1910 Teliakovsky, the head of the Imperial Theatres, informed Meyerhold that his after-hours experiments constituted a contractual breach, recommending he take a pseudonym to avoid "mutual embarrassment."[14] At the suggestion of Mikhail Kuzmin, Meyerhold adopted the name Doctor Dapertutto (from Italian, *dappertutto*, "everywhere") for experiments undertaken outside the Imperial Theatres. For the next eight years he directed, taught, performed, and wrote as Dapertutto, the magician from E. T. A. Hoffmann's "The Tale of the Lost Reflection," a story within "A New Year's Eve Adventure" ("Die Abenteuer der Silvester-Nacht," 1814).

In "The Tale of the Lost Reflection," the ominous Doctor Dapertutto conspires to steal the reflection of the tale's hero, Erasmus. For Meyerhold, who aimed to create a theater that did not simply reflect life, the choice of pseudonym could not have been more apt. The first time Erasmus encounters Dapertutto, the latter is described as "a tall, thin man with a pointed hawk's nose, sparkling eyes, and a maliciously twisted mouth, wearing a fiery red coat with gleaming steel buttons."[15] This physical description certainly fit Meyerhold, whose ample nose was frequently exaggerated in caricature. On a more literal note, Meyerhold must have seemed like he was everywhere: he had numerous theatrical projects running simultaneously. Meyerhold's sinister side was, of course, not as diabolical as the original Dapertutto, but adopting this pseudonym allowed him to play with his controversial reputation as a theatrical revolutionary and as a director who sometimes was accused of manipulating actors as Dapertutto did Erasmus. Most importantly, Dapertutto's appearance invariably signaled Erasmus's entrance into a separate, parallel realm. In assuming the fiery mantle of Dapertutto, Meyerhold entered a world of experimentation that circumvented the constraints placed on him at the Imperial Theatres.

Meyerhold delighted in playing Dapertutto as an actor does a role. This somewhat unusual use of a pseudonym illuminates how Meyerhold viewed the relationship of actor to character. Dapertutto wrote and published polemical articles such as those with which this chapter began, but Meyerhold also sometimes appeared publicly as Dapertutto, donning his second self before an audience in debates about theatrical reform. In the recollection of one of Meyerhold's actors,

> one part of the audience would applaud violently, while the other just as violently booed, whistled, and even broke chairs . . . Meyerhold went into raptures over this. . . . During such scandals, Meyerhold took his jacket off backstage and leapt out before the public in just his vest, considering this more theatrical; thus he entered into the bitter fray, and if he managed to come out of it the victor, which he often did by the most fantastical means, the battle concluded with a distinctive dialogue that Meyerhold led with the public, performing as Doctor Dapertutto or as the fantastical Meister Johannes Kreisler from Hoffmann's tales.[16]

Meyerhold used Dapertutto as a physical manifestation of the coexistence of an actor's self and character, of those theatrical moments when reality and fiction collide as an actor dons a mask to become a character or drops it to show the self that lies behind. Dapertutto thus also symbolized Meyerhold's proposed reforms. Verigina recalls that Meyerhold, "like Hoffmann's 'Godfather Drosselmeier,'"[17] "was able to free actors from spells, to wake them from the dreams into which, as he said, they had been plunged by the malevolent fairy of 'routine.' . . . Poisoned arrows rained down on the director-innovator and his actors, but he walked merrily forward, not growing spiteful or indignant at his enemies."[18] Meyerhold, Hoffmann's Russian theatrical doppelgänger, was associated with multiple Hoffmannian selves—Dapertutto,

Kreisler, Drosselmeier—and, after his 1906 performance in Blok's *Balaganchik* (*Little Fairground Booth*), with the wistful dreamer Pierrot.

It is often assumed that Meyerhold's link to Dapertutto was nominal, born of professional necessity, but Dapertutto was as indivisible from Meyerhold the director as Kreisler was from Hoffmann the writer and musician. In Hoffmann's tales, the double is "a refraction of the narrator's inner world,"[19] a prism into the artist's creative soul that allows the artist to observe her or his own creation, to maintain an omniscience that the creation itself cannot have. For Meyerhold, who was so centrally concerned with the duality of creating and observing, Dapertutto was, in Braun's words, "a real-life manifestation of the mask."[20]

Even before Meyerhold's formal doubling as Dapertutto, events in the changing world around him fed his fascination with plural perspective. The turmoil of the extended war period—the failed Revolution of 1905, World War I (1914–18), the October Revolution (1917), and the Russian Civil War (1918–21)—during which his artistic credo was formed, prompted inevitable dissonances between the world as it had been and the world as it had come to be. It is no accident that Hoffmann's tales were written during similarly tumultuous times prompted by the Napoleonic Wars. And as most scholars of Russian modernism have noted, the early twentieth century was a period of rapid technological and scientific advances, from airplanes to moving pictures, that changed the speed and point of view from which humans viewed their place in the world.

On a more personal note, Meyerhold's "angular" acting style had been at odds with the Moscow Art Theatre's early productions.[21] It is fitting that Meyerhold's first Chekhov role at the Moscow Art Theatre was *The Seagull*'s Konstantin, the young playwright eager to pioneer "new forms" (act 1). Meyerhold was enthralled with Chekhov's dramatic dissonances. When Meyerhold staged *The Cherry Orchard* in 1904, he wrote to Chekhov: "In the third act, against a background of 'stamping' . . . entirely unnoticed by anyone, Horror enters: 'The cherry orchard has been sold.' They dance. 'Sold.' They dance. . . . Merriment in which one can hear the sounds of death. In this act there is something Maeterlinckian, something terrifying."[22] This merry ball into which "Horror enters" became a recurrent Meyerholdian leitmotif, from the emotional collisions of *Columbine's Veil* to the malevolent Harlequins who steal Nina's bracelet at the swirling ball of *Masquerade* (1917), to the wild prancing of actors through the audience in *Inspector General* (1926).

As the ominous Dapertutto, Meyerhold was at the epicenter of the Russian theatrical cult of Hoffmann. He surrounded himself with others who were similarly passionate about the writer, something that helped these theatrical collaborators to forge a common artistic vocabulary. Although Meyer-

Figure 9. Mstislav Dobuzhinsky, illustration for *Balaganchik: Lyrical Scenes by Alexander Blok*, published in the journal *Torches* (*Fakely*) 1 (1906): 197.

hold's "Dapertutto" period officially ended after the 1917 Revolution, many continued to associate him with his pseudonym for the remainder of his life. Thus Doctor Everywhere became indivisible from the theatrical revolution he spawned.

Balaganchik (1906)

Although Meyerhold's first overt experiment with the Hoffmannian grotesque was not until 1910, his 1906 production of Alexander Blok's *Balaganchik* (*Little Fairground Booth*)[23] at the Vera Komissarzhevskaia Theatre was a major inciting incident for this work (figure 9). Because this seminal production has been discussed in most Meyerhold studies, here I simply note its connections to later experiments. Mikhail Kuzmin, who composed *Balaganchik*'s music, and Nikolai Nikolaevich Sapunov (1880–1912), who designed its costumes and scenery, were the same collaborators with whom Meyerhold later made his debut as Doctor Dapertutto. And to a degree that has not been fully appreciated, Blok's poetic form refracted German romanticism. In a 1908 prologue to three of his "lyrical dramas" (*Balaganchik, The*

King on the Square, and *The Incognita*), Blok wrote, "all these dramas are united by a mocking tone which perhaps makes them akin to *Romanticism*, to that 'transcendental irony' of which the Romantics spoke."[24]

Blok's play is infused with devices reminiscent of Tieck, including authorial interruptions, direct audience address, and overt acknowledgment of theatrical conventions. Meyerhold and Sapunov also added a physical theater-within-a-theater, a "little show-booth with the prompter and all the scenery exposed,"[25] one of several devices aimed at drawing attention to the production's simultaneous construction and performance. In Meyerhold's description, "the flies, together with all the ropes and wires, are visible to the audience" so that "when the entire set is hauled aloft in the booth, the audience in the actual theater sees the whole process." The area downstage of this show-booth became a *de facto* forestage, a physical place for direct audience interaction, where the "'Author' appears to serve as an intermediary between the public and the events enacted within the booth."[26]

For Meyerhold, the forestage was the physical threshold between the real and the fictional. It was where Molière had presented prologues and asides, where Shakespeare had performed within touching distance of the groundlings, where Venice's brilliant Truffaldino, Antonio Sacchi, had delivered Gozzi's polemical barbs. Meyerhold first used a deep forestage in 1906 for a production of Ibsen's *Ghosts* in Poltava, Ukraine,[27] boarding over the orchestra pit to create a bridge from stage to audience. Inspired by the writings of Georg Fuchs about the significance of the forestage to audience engagement, Meyerhold experimented with mise-en-scène in bas relief (*Sister Beatrice*, 1906) and with limiting actors to a narrow strip of stage that forced their conventionalized (through movement and costuming) bodies up to the edge of the audience's real space, an edge that was still, at that point, marked with a row of footlights (*Hedda Gabler*, 1906).

Meyerhold's three most significant early experiments with the forestage were *Balaganchik*, *Columbine's Veil*, and *Dom Juan*. As he wrote in the preface to his book-length theoretical work *On Theatre* (1913):

> Since the staging of these three plays, a particular concern of mine has been how to solve theatrical questions related to the *forestage*.
>
> Despite the fact that not one of the articles presented here has the forestage as its comprehensive theme, the reader will easily note that the question of the forestage is what draws all the threads of the book's various themes together.[28]

In *Balaganchik*, Meyerhold explored the forestage, "the area where contact between performer and spectator [is] at its most unpredictable,"[29] as a place where romantic irony can be physicalized. According to Verigina, the production's most powerful moment was the end, when Pierrot (played by Meyerhold) turned directly to the audience from the forestage:

> He stood staring at them, and it was as though Pierrot was looking into the eyes of every single person . . . Then Pierrot looked away, took his pipe from his pocket and began to play the tune of a rejected and unappreciated heart. That moment was the most powerful in his whole performance.[30]

Braun has argued that this production of *Balaganchik* "furnish[ed] the basis for [Meyerhold's] entire style, a style that in a word can be called 'grotesque.'"[31] I would modify this slightly: *Balaganchik* sparked Meyerhold's interest in deeply studying, understanding, and utilizing the formal elements that he developed into a poetics. *Balaganchik* whet his appetite, but other experiments helped him to hone the necessary techniques. One of the most significant in this vein was *Columbine's Veil.*

Interlude: *Columbine's Veil* (1910)

In October 1910 Meyerhold, Kuzmin and Sapunov opened the "House of Interludes" in Saint Petersburg.[32] The name of this theater-cabaret is symbolically significant: Meyerhold was increasingly experimenting with the interlude, the interruption, and the aside as vital opportunities for direct audience contact. The House of Interludes, Meyerhold's second cabaret attempt,[33] provided his first major opportunity to experiment with the grotesque since beginning his post at the Imperial Theatres. The cabaret's intimate space allowed him to play with close physical proximity to the audience and to eliminate physical barriers between performer and spectator: he removed the footlights, used shallow stairs to connect the stage and the auditorium, had performers enter and exit through the audience, and invited spectators to eat and drink while sitting around small tables. The evening began with "a light-hearted and celebratory parade"[34]—a performed introduction of the actors and their characters to the audience.

Though the House of Interludes was short-lived,[35] its opening bill included one of Meyerhold's most significant experiments: *Columbine's Veil.*[36] The program was introduced by Kuzmin's dramatic prologue, *The Reformed Eccentric*, the first Russian dramatic refraction of Hoffmann's "The Sandman." Kuzmin's prologue played on the popular Hoffmannian motif of puppets transforming into people. According to Sergei Auslender, Kuzmin's nephew, this prologue captured

> the style of Hoffmann's fantastic quality, the style of the mocking grotesque, a puppet drama of refined eccentricities. In it were the classic Coppelius, the

> transformation of puppets into live actors, the appearance of characters from the audience, and a wooden Schnitzler and Dohnányi, whose pantomime, *Columbine's Veil*, is the highlight of the first cycle.[37]

Meyerhold described his refraction of Arthur Schnitzler's *The Veil of Pierrette* (*Der Schleier der Pierrette*), with music by Ernő Dohnányi, as "a model for the theatrical grotesque in the manner of Callot and in the style of Hoffmann."[38] The evening also marked the director's official debut as Doctor Dapertutto.

Columbine's Veil by "Schnitzler-Dapertutto" was not Meyerhold's first Schnitzler production, but it was the first he claimed to have coauthored.[39] To accompany the performance, the House of Interludes published a libretto of the pantomime's action (see appendix B).[40] Though eyewitness accounts reveal that this libretto omits some performance details, it provides a valuable window into how Meyerhold-Dapertutto refracted this pantomime. His changes to Schnitzler's text center around two principles: creating distilled action in which the clutter of everyday life has been removed, and maximizing the grotesque's variety and extreme implementation. As Meyerhold prepared *Columbine's Veil*, his restructurings of setting and plot drew attention to the constructed nature of theatrical illusion. As Znosko-Borovsky recalls, Meyerhold reminded actors during rehearsals, "you need to tell the public openly and clearly that all that is taking place before them is a play, that all that is being shown is not real."[41]

Meyerhold also staged disorienting shifts of focus; heightened juxtapositions of contrasting emotions; musical rhythm as a shaper of mood; and visual, emotional, and temporal dissonance. Hoffmann's grotesque often places the absurd alongside the realistic using two basic methods, called "successive juxtaposition" and "simultaneous juxtaposition" by Eisenstein.[42] In the "temporal forms" of successive juxtaposition (juxtapositions that are constructed over time), Hoffmann's objects and people either transform sequentially from one thing into another or quotidian objects become fantastical and then ordinary again at a second glance. In the "spatial forms" of simultaneous juxtaposition (juxtapositions within a single spatial composition), Hoffmann fuses incongruous elements from humans, animals, and machines into a single being.[43] Meyerhold structured *Columbine's Veil* around similar successions and simultaneities.

Schnitzler's libretto, written in dialogue but intended for pantomime, centers on a love triangle: the Bohemian lovers Pierrot and Pierrette and Pierrette's wealthy fiancé Harlequin.[44] Jovial friends try unsuccessfully to cheer up Pierrot, who is pining over Pierrette's marriage to Harlequin. Left alone, Pierrot ponders suicide when a distraught Pierrette in wedding gown and veil appears and produces a vial of poison for them to drink. They share final moments; he imbibes; she wavers; and he knocks her glass to the floor before dying. Frantically, she tries to drink, but the poison has spilled. She flees, forgetting her veil. At the wedding ball, Pierrette's parents argue over her absence while the Dance Master induces guests to dance. When Harlequin discovers Pierrette's absence, he breaks the musicians' instruments, which they nevertheless continue to play in a superbly jarring example of musical dissonance. Pierrette returns, convinces Harlequin that she has never been missing, and they dance until Pierrot's ghost appears to her. Pierrette recoils, and Harlequin, suspicious, inquires after her missing veil. Pierrette flees, inadvertently leading Harlequin to Pierrot's room, where Harlequin locks Pierrette in with her dead lover. Her terror metamorphoses into a dance of death. Just after she expires, Pierrot's friends break in merrily, only to recoil in horror at finding the two corpses.

Meyerhold-Dapertutto fragmented Schnitzler's pantomime into fourteen brief episodes. Additional changes included heightening contrast, making Pierrot's surroundings more sinister, eliminating Schnitzler's local color, and restructuring the piece around successive and simultaneous juxtapositions, interpreted here as sequences of interrupted actions and concurrent collisions of moods, styles, and colors. Meyerhold framed these collisions by augmenting two minor characters, the Dance Master and the Kapellmeister/Pianist,[45] who observed and participated in the action. Dohnányi's music is a virtuosic display of shifting rhythms and styles. Meyerhold therefore took a score that was already full of contrasts and heightened them. A similar intensification of the grotesque is reflected in Nikolai Sapunov's designs and in the production libretto.

In his experiments with the theatrical grotesque, Meyerhold found a ready partner in "coauthor" Sapunov.[46] Sapunov used color to prompt visual dissonance, contrasting Pierrot's white costume with the garish attire of the guests and crowding the ball with clashing colors that were "striking in their strange combination of insolent bad taste and nervous excitement."[47] Inspired by the grotesque "ornamentation" of Renaissance architecture and by the etchings of Callot, Sapunov also juxtaposed animal and human elements,[48] most notably in the costume of Gigolo, the Dance Master. Matskin describes the effect of Sapunov's design as a whole:

> We can learn a great deal from this composition—about the range of colours, resolved by the theatre in motley, canary, mainly lemony-yellow and smoky-orange tones; about the rhythms of the action, which were angular, fragmented, emphatically eccentric and had nothing in common with the slow, smooth-flowing preciosity of the traditionally stylized pantomime; about the asymmetry that was the basic device in the portrayal of these mummers that were half-doll, half-person; about the sinister, fantastic, sometimes, for example, bird-like masks (the dance-leader Gigolo was made up as a parrot) that seemed to be borrowed from Goya's capriccios[49] and in which the essence of the characters could be glimpsed.[50]

Figure 10. Nikolai Sapunov, costume design for Gigolo, the Dance Master, in Schnitzler/Dohnányi/Dapertutto's pantomime *Columbine's Veil*, dir. Vsevolod Meyerhold, House of Interludes, Saint Petersburg (Premiere: October 12, 1910). Paper, graphite pencil, watercolor, 30.8 × 22.2 cm. ГИК 5199/291, ОР 10883. © Saint Petersburg State Museum of Theatre and Music.

Meyerhold described Sapunov's human-bird fusion in the context of the grotesque: "For the sake of a grotesque effect, Sapunov transformed Gigolo into a parrot by combing his wig from back to front to resemble feathers, and by arranging the tails of his frock-coat in the form of a real tail"[51] (figure 10). Although Sapunov's untimely drowning in a boating accident in 1912 cut his collaboration with Meyerhold tragically short, his vivid, motley designs had an indelible effect on the director.

Meyerhold's simultaneous and successive juxtapositions of tempo, action, and emotion are especially clear in the House of Interludes libretto. Meyerhold staged the opening scene (act 1, scene 1) around Pierrot's relationship to a few objects, signifiers of Pierrot's futile love. He replaced the specific Vienna locale with a broader artist-versus-philistine motif, eliminating quotidian detail and changing the sympathy of Pierrot's friends to mocking (act 1, scene 2); they even drag Pierrot down the steps and into the audience to rouse him.[52] Once Pierrot is awake, they confiscate Columbine's portrait; when he tries to retrieve it, "suddenly, from all sides, long paper noses are pointed at Pierrot."[53] Meyerhold's unfeeling and opportunistic Columbine has no intention of drinking the poison (act 1, scene 3). These scenes are structured as a series of actions, each of which is abruptly, often violently interrupted as each reaches its height: Pierrot's sleep is interrupted by his friends; a waltz is interrupted by Pierrot slamming the harpsichord lid; the Pianist's attempt to beat Pierrot is interrupted by dancing sweethearts. Columbine's arrival interrupts Pierrot's first suicide attempt, while his suicide interrupts their merrymaking.

The nine brief scenes that comprise act 2, the wedding ball, are structured as successive juxtapositions in which lively dances "in full swing" alternate with private moments of fierce conflict over the missing Columbine. At the conclusion of an opening waltz,

> The Dance Master . . . having given the orchestra a downbeat at the beginning of the quadrille, suddenly notices that Harlequin has no partner. Having stopped the orchestra with difficulty, the Dance Master calls to Columbine's parents and informs them that Columbine is missing.
>
> Scene 3: The mother explains that her daughter is probably arranging her gown and goes to call her . . .
>
> Scene 4: The Dance Master, in order to quell scandal, invites the dancers to promenade in the garden to the music of a minuet.
>
> Scene 5: Harlequin and Columbine's father wait. The mother returns. She announces that Columbine is nowhere to be found. Harlequin flies into a rage. He pulls the Pianist, whose music even further underscores the horror of the deceived Harlequin, down off the stage; he beats the Pianist and his musicians.[54]

The musicians then play Dohnányi's wild *Schnellpolka* on their now broken instruments. Each time the music changes; each time it contrasts with the undercurrent of repressed emotion; and each time the inertia of stopping and starting again increases. The technique is what today we would call filmic: long shots juxtaposed with dizzying close-ups[55] (figure 11). Bonch-Tomashevsky described his experience of these juxtapositions:

> When I recall the nightmarish polka that the comic musicians played on broken instruments, under the direction of a one-eyed, diabolically unhappy Kapellmeister, when I recall that nightmarish whirlwind of brightly-coloured and loutish bodies that whirled . . . I can feel that shiver that ran up my spine as I sat in the audience . . . I understand how it is possible to laugh and at the same time to feel all the abyss of horror, all the blackness of desperation.[56]

Comic characters and situations were engineered to contrast with the tragedy of the main characters. Bonch-Tomashevsky continues:

Figure 11. Nikolai Sapunov, scene design for act 2 wedding ball, *Columbine's Veil*. The Kapellmeister/Pianist (upstage) conducts the action while the Dance Master (downstage) argues with Harlequin. КП 176534. © A. A. Bakhrushin State Central Theatre Museum, Moscow.

> The insignificant roles of the Kapellmeister, the servants, the father and mother, and the dancing master, were emphasized. All these were characters whose brilliant antics served to underline the tragedy of the graphic Pierrot and Columbine and Harlequin, who was adroit, flattering, arrogant, and hence cruel in his anger. Against the background of a brilliant, subtly coarse *commedia dell'arte*, through an overlay of unnatural, invented gestures and fantastic costumes, there emerged with striking brilliance the basic tragedy; against the laughable the inevitable was so terrible.[57]

After Columbine's belated entrance, delayed agonizingly until scene 7, the wedding guests are forced to swirl round yet again in a "furious galop" while Harlequin bombards his bride with questions. The actors embraced these rapid shifts of rhythm and mood:

> Every single pause, every arrest in the movement, was employed by the director to stress the readiness of the guests at any given moment to tear themselves from their places and surrender to the Satanic power of the music. Breathless, they preened themselves, straightening their gaudy red, green,

> orange, pink and yellow costumes; the ladies rearranged their tall hats and their outlandish coiffures. During these pauses Columbine would materialize, her expression unperturbed and entirely innocent. Then the *Kapellmeister* would again launch himself at the piano and ferociously strike the keys. At Gigolo's imperious gesture, the whole crowd of wedding guests would resume the dance, including even the terrified portly figures of Columbine's parents. The wild dance resumed, and at its head, as amicably as if they had never exchanged a cross word, there cavorted the happy couple, Harlequin and Columbine, executing the most improbable *entrechats*.[58]

When the action had built to an emotional pinnacle, a "little moor" appeared to offer drinks to the guests and to the audience, followed immediately after by the unexpected appearance of Pierrot's ghost:

> Columbine reaches out her hand to take a glass, the little moor vanishes, and in his place Pierrot's ghost appears with the veil in his hands. Columbine tries to catch hold of the veil, but Pierrot vanishes. The phantom taunts her, appearing first in one doorway, then in another.[59]

Pierrot's floating movements contrasted eerily with the preceding chaos, slowing the tempo nearly to a standstill before the pantomime leapt into action once more, culminating in Harlequin pursuing Columbine off.

Meyerhold's most effective use of emotional juxtaposition was in the final scene. Schnitzler's original is straightforward: after Pierrette dies next to Pierrot, the friends return and discover their corpses. Meyerhold delayed this discovery for as long as possible, drawing out the tension in the audience until the onstage reveal:

> Pierrot's friends and their sweethearts enter. It seems to them that Pierrot and Columbine are merged in a passionate kiss. The Pianist enters. The merry couples wish to wake up the spellbound lovers with a dance. Sprinkling them with flowers, the couples dance, but Pierrot and Columbine are motionless. One friend pushes Pierrot. The latter falls, as does Columbine. The friends see two corpses; they are paralyzed by horror. The Pianist nearly goes out of his mind.[60]

Bonch-Tomashevsky remembered this moment for many years; as he later described it, the realization of what has happened drives the Pianist mad. He hurtles through the audience, overturning tables and chairs as he flees.[61] For an audience as yet unaccustomed to the removal of the footlights, this invasion of their space must have been terrifying.

By making the Kapellmeister/Pianist both a participant and an observer, Meyerhold used him as an emotional barometer to help the audience process

Figure 12. Nikolai Sapunov, costume design for the Kapellmeister/Pianist, *Columbine's Veil*. Paper, graphite pencil, watercolor, 32.2 × 22.7 cm. ГИК 5199/290. ОР 10882. © Saint Petersburg State Museum of Theatre and Music.

the production's uncanny emotional collisions.[62] Schnitzler's pantomime has two pianists, one for the scenes in Pierrot's room and another who conducts the musicians at the ball. Meyerhold conflated the two to make the Pianist the pantomime's rhythmical and emotional center (figure 12). This diabolical Kapellmeister dictated the rhythm of the production both literally and figuratively. This is reinforced by his act 2 center-stage location, elevated above the wedding guests on a platform, a tiny theater-within-a-theater. It is his bright music played on instruments broken by Harlequin's rage that compels the unhappy couple to prance so merrily.

Meyerhold's Pianist also functions as a symbolic Hoffmann-Kreisler who conducts in a mental state between inspiration and madness. In the 1836 words of Herzen, later reproduced in Meyerhold's journal: "[Hoffmann's] fantasy knows no limits, he writes with tousled hair in a frenzy pale with fear, quivering before his own fabrications; he himself out of purity of heart believes in it all."[63] The Kapellmeister also doubled as a theatrical incarnation of Meyerhold, the conductor of the production's mise-en-scène.[64] Spectators thus viewed Meyerhold's Pianist on at least five levels: as a character, as Hoffmann, as Kreisler, as Fate, and as Meyerhold conducting the pantomime into a *Gesamtkunstwerk* structured around distortion and fragmentation. In the Russian State Archive for Literature and Art, appended to the *Columbine's Veil* libretto is a sheet of paper with the words *Columbine's Veil*, "Hoffmanade," and "balagan" in Meyerhold's hand, affirming that for him, in this production, these things were inseparable.[65]

In April 1916 Meyerhold revived *Columbine's Veil* with different actors and new music as the premiere performance at the Players' Rest cabaret. Lest the connection between the cabaret's "Hall of Gozzi and Hoffmann" and Doctor Dapertutto's production be missed on the audience, Sudeikin, who designed both the theater interior and the revival, also designed a special costume for Meyerhold, though it was never worn: "a rose satin camisole with silver buttons, a blue cloak, a three-cornered plumed hat, and a mask with a large beak—in which Doctor Dapertutto was to greet the visitors to the special hall."[66]

The restaged *Columbine's Veil* was somewhat less warmly received than the first. In Kuzmin's analysis:

> This time, *Columbine's Veil* is more dramatic, almost tragic, less motley and fragmented, and more nightmarish. The lyrical side was emphasized more than the external side, the groupings and gestures were simplified, became more plastic and more expressive . . .
>
> Into the ceiling of the auditorium there have been inserted mirrors, in which all that takes place on the stage is reflected in hazy and slightly distorted fashion; in my opinion, it is in these mirrors that the tone of the production . . . is represented most accurately.[67]

This splintered and reassembled audience perception, generated through fragmentation and juxtaposition in the first production and via Sudeikin's distorting mirrors in the second, was *Columbine*'s most enduring innovation.

Dom Juan (1910)

The "little moor" in *Columbine's Veil* introduces a second category of recurrent Meyerholdian framing characters. Meyerhold first used "forestage servants," played by child actors in blackface, in Calderón's *The Adoration of the Cross* at Ivanov's "Tower" apartment-theater in April 1910. In Znosko-Borovsky's recollection, the curtain for this intimate production "was opened not by an invisible human-machinist; rather two little moors . . . merrily parted it and closed it again while standing in front and to the side of it or hiding behind it."[68] A month after the October 1910 opening of *Columbine's Veil*, Meyerhold premiered Molière's *Dom Juan* at the Alexandrinsky. Here Meyerhold expanded the role of the forestage servants who drew the curtain in *The Adoration of the Cross* and heralded the arrival of Pierrot's ghost in *Columbine's Veil*: in *Dom Juan*, child pages in blackface and ornate red livery shaped the action as it progressed.

Meyerhold's term "forestage servants" is commonly translated "proscenium servants." The Russian word *prostsenium* (from the Greek and Latin for "in front of the skene") refers, however, to the portion of the stage downstage of the proscenium opening rather than to the proscenium arch, as the cognate does in contemporary English. In a 1934 lecture, Meyerhold explained that the forestage "is a stage that is sharply extended forward . . . where part of the audience intrudes upon the stage, as it were, and the actor who stands on the forestage is surrounded on three sides by the audience."[69] Meyerhold's "servants" are often interpreted as metaphorical servants to the stage as a whole. While this is one of their roles, understanding them in the specific context of the forestage illuminates their function as interlocutors between the fictional world that lies behind them and the world of the audience that lies before them.

In developing the forestage servants, Meyerhold refracted sources that effect similar destabilizations of character and perception. His troubling use of blackface derives not from American minstrelsy,[70] but, most likely, from a portrait tradition that used framing figures to direct the viewer's gaze.[71] Popular in the second half of the seventeenth century, these paintings used black child pages as framing devices by placing them on the margins of a "'grand-manner' portrait" to serve "as an extravagantly dressed foil to [the] owner."[72] Many of these paintings, are, in effect, double portraits: a page looks into the painting while also guiding the gaze of the viewer. These pages often reach from the frame into the field image to hold a pet, direct a mirror, or adjust a parasol for the portrait's central figure, who takes no note of them, often instead looking directly out of the painting. Although the pages are invisible to the other participants in the picture, they are a critical part of the composition. We view their world doubly: through their eyes and through our own.

Meyerhold also was inspired by the *kurogo*, the black-clad stage attendants in Kabuki and Bunraku who tend to characters or animate puppets in full view of the audience, often while being read by the spectator as invisible. In conjunction with this, Meyerhold's *Dom Juan* experiments with the romantic irony of Hoffmann and Tieck, who emphasize that the fictional world is created and can be uncreated at the will of the artist. The forestage servants also recall the foreground figures used as *repoussoir* elements in Jacques Callot's etchings, a recurrent source for Meyerhold's mise-en-scène. Commedia's masked characters, particularly the black-masked Harlequin, were a final source for Meyerhold's forestage servants. Meyerhold was doubtlessly familiar with paintings by Antoine Watteau, which feature "black servants and black-masked Harlequins,"[73] and which influenced the World of Art group, of which *Dom Juan* designer Alexander Golovin was a part. Harlequin (and the *zanni* more generally), in Meyerhold's understanding, also served both the production and the audience. Meyerhold's forestage servants later became so closely associated with commedia in Russian theater that Evgeny Vakhtangov used the term for the masked characters in his production of Gozzi's *Princess Turandot* (1922).

Braun and others have posited that Meyerhold's "little moors" were a nod to the showy extravagance of the Sun King's era. Indeed, depictions of blacks in seventeenth-century French theater and art often "aggrandize[d] Louis XIV and his empire."[74] After 1664 black children were brought in increasing numbers from the French West Indies to France, where they worked "as maids or valets or [were] offered as playthings or pets to women of high rank at court."[75] Performers of African descent or, sometimes, European actors in blackface, were employed as actors and musicians in many entertainments at Versailles.[76] Often they performed "in the humblest and most subordinate roles in relation to the divine and absolute royal power."[77] But although Meyerhold's *Dom Juan* pages envelop the action "in a mist redolent of the perfumed, gilded monarchy of Versailles,"[78] their primary theatrical purpose was to physically negotiate perceptual planes. Meyerhold implemented this by providing the audience with conflicting information as to how the forestage servants were to be read. On one hand, they were meant to be invisible as they prepared the stage—yet they defied invisibility by performing their tasks self-consciously. In Auslender's description, "Before the action begins, a merry group of liveried little moors runs out. They light the yellow candles in the chandeliers and tall candlesticks, bring out a pan of incense and announce the beginning with a little bell."[79] At other times, they tended to other characters, setting and striking their props, powdering their noses, again prompting the audience to read them as invisible, yet again they countered this invisibility by singing a song. They also drew back tapestries covering framed images of the play's settings and rang bells to announce intermissions. Like the Kapellmeister in *Columbine's Veil*, they conducted the action before the audience's eyes.

Count Sergei Volkonsky, former director of the Imperial Theatres, was intrigued by the simultaneous readings these characters prompted:

> It was as if they were constantly running out of the play into life: they are participants in the action, yet they are ushers; they set chairs and change the setting with the speed of a stage hand who apologizes for the breach of illusion, but they also carry Donna Elvira's train and fill the stage with their fright when the Commandatore appears. This constant leaping out of the poster and back in again fills the stage—yes, the stage or the audience? In any case, it fills the production with something playfully mischievous.[80]

By destabilizing the audience's reading of familiar conventions, the forestage servants prompted rereadings of the rules of the theater. They served the production and its real-time construction by creating a living frame through which the audience peered into Meyerhold's refraction of Molière's refraction of Louis XIV's era.

Volkonsky ultimately found *Dom Juan*'s oxymoronic pairings of doubled perception to be disorienting, preferring the safety of the curtain that provided a stable, familiar divider between worlds.[81] In temporal hindsight, Meyerhold's innovations have proved more enduring than Volkonsky might have wished. Few theaters today have curtains, and many use black-clad stagehands to shift scenery and set props in full view of the audience—most of them unaware that some of the ancestors to this practice are Meyerhold's "little moors."

One might say that the remainder of Meyerhold's career was dedicated to training all actors to be forestage servants. They played a prominent role in his 1917 production of Dargomyshsky's *The Stone Guest*, this time dressed as "Capuchin friars."[82] But they figured most prominently in Meyerhold's studio work. His 1915 production of Blok's *The Incognita* incorporated forestage servants (without makeup) dressed in identical costumes. Verigina recalls that they "were played by the most talented studio members," including "Meyerhold himself, hidden behind a half mask."[83] Again, they constructed the production together with the audience:

> Dressed in special unobtrusive costumes and moving rhythmically, they brought on tables, stools, a bar, and to the rear raised a green curtain on bamboo poles . . . One of the servants sat down on the floor close at hand, ready to act as prompter . . . When the scene ended there was a roll of drums and the servants who had been holding up the curtain walked forward, stretching the curtain above the actors and then lowering it to hide them from the audience . . . When a star was supposed to fall, all the chandeliers . . . were extinguished and one of the servants lit a simple sparkler on a long pole which another raised right to the ceiling and then lowered it for the first to extinguish in water . . . .
>
> The last scene . . . was enacted on the platform itself. In front of it knelt the . . . servants, holding candles to parody footlights.[84]

After the Revolution, Meyerhold continued training actors to negotiate audience experience. He developed biomechanics to give them the requisite skills. In *Magnanimous Cuckold* (1922, remounted 1928), the company was costumed identically in *prozodezhda*, utilitarian overalls that effectively turned every character into a forestage servant by treating character and space as a metaphorical mask to be negotiated by the actor. Thus Meyerhold fundamentally inverted the theater's hierarchy of character, and, with it, the status of its "servants."

Figure 13. Alexander Golovin, design for the front cover of *Love for Three Oranges: The Journal of Doctor Dapertutto* no. 1–3 (1915). André Savine Collection, Rare Book Collection, Wilson Special Collections Library (PN2007.L5 1915 no. 1/3), UNC–Chapel Hill.

DAPERTUTTO'S *THREE ORANGES*: THE SCENARIO, THE STUDIO, AND THE JOURNAL

In 1913 Meyerhold opened a studio for training a new generation of actors to negotiate character and space together with an audience. This studio, Meyerhold's first to achieve longevity after the failed Moscow Art Theatre Povarskaia Street Studio (1905) and additional smaller-scale experiments, finally allowed Meyerhold to establish a group with "the enthusiasm of Sacchi," as Meyerhold's Hoffmann-scholar friend Sergei Ignatov phrased it.[85] Meyerhold had long been interested in commedia, but with the inception of the Borodinskaia (Borodin) Street Studio (1913–17),[86] he embarked upon a period of vigorous experimentation with Gozzi and Hoffmann's refractions of the Italian comedy of masks.[87]

In conjunction with the studio, Meyerhold published *Love for Three Oranges: The Journal of Doctor Dapertutto* (1914–16) (figure 13). This journal was the public face of what was otherwise largely a private enterprise: the studio gave only one public performance in its four years of existence, though students did sometimes perform for the convalescing soldiers with whom they shared the building, a source for Meyerhold's postrevolutionary interest in reinventing the audience along with the theater. The journal's nine issues appeared irregularly, largely due to the outbreak of World War I.[88] What finally brought about its 1916 demise, however, was a massive paper shortage that made continued publication of an already financially modest enterprise prohibitively expensive.[89]

The journal's title, *Love for Three Oranges: The Journal of Doctor Dapertutto* (hereafter *LTA*), can and should be read as a manifesto. In its first half, Meyerhold advocates for the fantastical and conventionalized theater of Gozzi, who opposed Carlo Goldoni's gradual move away from the conventionalized masks, *lazzi*, and *scenarii* of commedia and toward sanitized domestic comedy grounded in quotidian reality. Unsurprisingly, given that Meyerhold positioned himself in the theatrical camp of Gozzi, several articles in the journal accused the Moscow Art Theatre and the First Studio, where Stanislavsky's nascent system was taking shape, of wrongly pursuing the aesthetic aims of Goldoni.

The second half of the journal's title can be read on multiple levels. First and foremost, it linked the studio and journal with Dapertutto's other experiments. More broadly, it revealed that the Studio was celebrating the Italian comedy of masks as refracted through Germany.[90] As the early formalist Viktor Zhirmunsky[91] wrote in an *LTA* article called "Comedy of Pure Joy" (see appendix A):

> The German romantics created the worldwide renown of Count Carlo Gozzi. It was they who first "discovered" his dramatic fairy tales, imbued a dead literary monument with a living spirit, made vital and contemporary something that could have seemed like the accidental and outdated caprice of a "strange talent," a cultural "reactionary," an enthusiast of beautiful but lifeless days of yore.[92]

Meyerhold-Dapertutto very likely had also first encountered Gozzi's *Three Oranges* as refracted in Hoffmann's *Strange Sorrows of a Theater Manager*.

The aims of Meyerhold's journal were both scientific and unabashedly subjective. *LTA* supported and commented on the studio, a theatrical laboratory. Its authors experimented with and disseminated information on the mask as an ideal distillment of character, on the grotesque, on the application of musical principles to movement and speech, and on an artistic worldview infused with irony, framing devices, and grotesque collisions. The journal laid out the theory and history for the studio's praxis, documented its discoveries, and published plays and scenarios for the studio to use in implementing its reforms. The most significant example of this is Meyerhold,

Soloviev, and Vogak's *Love for Three Oranges*, a refraction of Gozzi's first *fiaba*, published in the journal's inaugural issue.

Interlude: *Love for Three Oranges* (1914)

In 1761 Gozzi created a "reflective analysis" of an Italian fairy tale about three oranges, framing his commedia-infused scenario with polemical attacks on his theatrical rivals.[93] In 1914 Vsevolod Meyerhold and two collaborators, Konstantin Vogak and Vladimir Soloviev, published a reflective analysis of Gozzi's reflective analysis.[94] This new *Love of Three Oranges* (*Liubov k trem apel'sinam*, translated as *Love for Three Oranges*) was later to serve as the source material for Prokofiev's opera (1919; Chicago world premiere, 1921).[95] It is also one of the most illuminating, yet strangely understudied sources of information on how Meyerhold redefined the theatrical event and the role of the actor in the years immediately preceding the Revolution. This scenario-manifesto explores how a self-aware relationship between actor and character in concert with theatrical framing devices that delineate levels of fiction can actively shape the viewers' simultaneous belief and disbelief in what they see. It also provides unique insight into Meyerhold's experiments with Gozzi as refracted through Hoffmann and Tieck.

Gozzi's *Analisi riflessiva della fiaba L'amore delle tre melarance* (*Reflective Analysis of the Fairy Tale Love of Three Oranges*) documented (after the fact) the production that became the first of Gozzi's ten *fiabe teatrali* (theatrical fairy tales). Although some English versions rewrite *Love of Three Oranges* in dialogue,[96] Gozzi's scenario contains only a few scripted lines intended to render ridiculous the singsong Martellian verse often used by his theatrical competitors.[97] Gozzi directly interpolates abundant commentary into this *fiaba*, giving equal weight to the story and its polemical frame: Gozzi's theater wars against Carlo Goldoni's domestic comedies and Abbot Pietro Chiari's bombastic tragedies. The result is that dialogue, action, and topical jabs flow between each other, sometimes seamlessly, sometimes jarringly, but always without segue.

The plot of Gozzi's *Love of Three Oranges* tells the story of Prince Tartaglia, who is languishing from a fatal case of hypochondria. Truffaldino saves the prince by making him laugh. Two warring magicians, Fata Morgana (a caricature of Pietro Chiari) and Celio (a caricature of Carlo Goldoni), battle over Tartaglia's fate. After the prince is cursed by Fata Morgana, the remainder of the story details his love, pursuit, rescue of, and ultimate marriage to one of the titular oranges, a magically charmed princess.

Gozzi's polemical framing trivializes Chiari's and Goldoni's plays by using "exaggerated parody"—framed seriousness—to make their work "doubly ridiculous."[98] Similarly, he stages comic literalizations of metaphors: Chiari's beloved Martellian verse becomes an actual poison, likened to opium, that the fairy tale's villains sneak into the prince's food. Gozzi also delights in overt convention: a devil wielding a bellows blows at Tartaglia and Truffaldino to create a "wind" that transports them vast distances in an instant, thereby avoiding the need for time to pass between scenes.[99]

Gozzi's commedia characters frame the action of the ostensibly serious plot with masks, *lazzi*, and abundant asides, thus becoming negotiators between the fairy-tale world and the world of the audience. More generally, his *fiabe* destabilize boundaries between human, animal, and object with waters that dance (in *The Green Bird*), statues that speak (in *The King Stag*), and oranges that become humans (in *Love of Three Oranges*). As Clayton describes it, "the highly theatrical introduction of animal characters, and the transformation of characters into animals and back, heralds the grotesque as a new, and subsequently important, element in the *commedia* tradition."[100]

Although Vogak, the only Italian speaker of the *Three Oranges* authors, translated much of Gozzi's *fiaba* very literally in order to produce a palpable sense of translatedness, most of the topical references to Gozzi's theater wars are conspicuously absent. In response to a negative review of their scenario, Meyerhold, Soloviev, and Vogak published a wittily caustic "open letter" (see appendix A) that explained why they reworked Gozzi as they did:

> It seems to You . . . that Count Carlo Gozzi's reflective analysis of the fairy tale *Love of Three Oranges* is noteworthy only for its element of polemical parody. You absolutely ignore its specifically theatrical aesthetic aims, which, in our view, are the most valuable aspect of this scenario . . . The essence of this element, from our point of view, consists in contrasting improvised comedy with scripted comedy, the theater of masks with the theater of character.
>
> In the divertissement that we composed (after Gozzi), we . . . entirely consciously removed Gozzi's polemical satire . . . simply because Gozzi's technical methods of scenario composition are much more important than their transient combative meaning . . .
>
> The theatrical techniques of the commedia dell'arte become more clear and more distinctly valuable to us as they resonate in the scenarios of Count Carlo Gozzi.[101]

Meyerhold and his collaborators were especially attracted to Gozzi's juxtaposition techniques. The Russian scenario focuses on how commedia masks negotiate the audience's mental oscillation between perceptual planes. Meyerhold was fascinated with how Gozzi's framing devices achieved this.

At its simplest, oscillation can take place between two planes, the fictional and the phenomenological, prompting States's binocular vision. There can also, however, be multiple theatrical planes that create the impression of many levels of experience. In *Puss in Boots* and *Topsy-Turvy World*, Tieck nested multiple theaters-within-theaters—as many as five—in which real audiences watched fictional audiences watch plays within plays within plays.[102] Hoffmann's *Princess Blandina* was a play within a play within a tale within a book (four planes—five, if you include the reader). For Meyerhold, constructing and rupturing theatrical frames prompted similar perceptual multiplicities.

Meyerhold, Soloviev, and Vogak's refraction of Gozzi's *fiaba* frames a wide variety of theatrical elements: character, dramatic structure, stage space, entrances and exits, props, theatrical genres, and conventions. This framing is paired with equally varied self-referential intrusions: masks, parades, prologues, interludes, action pushed up to the edge of the forestage, framing characters who function as a living proscenium, and individually framed stage spaces.

The Russian *Three Oranges* fragments Gozzi's prologue and three acts into "A Divertissement in Twelve Scenes, a Prologue, an Epilogue, and Three Interludes,"[103] creating an episodic structure that gives actors the necessary flexibility to shift instantaneously between plot and interruption. This structure illuminates the practical thinking behind the successive juxtapositions in *Columbine's Veil* and the fragmentation that became a defining characteristic of all Meyerhold's productions.

Three Oranges frames major characters at first entrance with what Meyerhold called the "parade," a brief, presentational "sketch" that introduces characters or themes and draws in the audience, a term borrowed from fairground and circus.[104] In "Balagan," Meyerhold explained the purpose of the parade:

> The prologue and the ensuing parade, together with the direct address to the audience at the final curtain, so loved both by the Italians and Spaniards in the seventeenth century and by the French vaudevillistes, all force the spectator to recognize the actors' performance as pure playacting. And every time the actor leads the spectators too far into the land of make-believe he immediately resorts to some unexpected sally or lengthy address *a parte* [aside] to remind them that what is being performed is only *a play*.[105]

Even before the opening prologue, *Three Oranges* stages a parade in which Gozzi's theater wars are reconceived as choruses of warring theatrical genres:

> Loud trumpet and drum sounds ring out from backstage. Actors enter the stage from both sides with shouts and noise, battling each other with quills.

> Kitchen-sink comedians advance upon über-tragic tragedians, who, desperately defending themselves, gradually fall back to center stage, where a collective scuffle ensues. Three Eccentrics unexpectedly run out headlong from the center curtain onto the stage and pull apart those fighting . . .
>
> Meanwhile, behind the curtain there is some kind of commotion: backs and heads intermittently appear outlined in the curtain; the whole thing sways; and arms and legs flash out here and there from behind it . . . The same musical sounds from the opening play backstage, but mixed with squeals and loud laughter. Suddenly, one of the corners of the curtain is lifted slightly, and several hands push onto the stage a boy, who timidly and embarrassedly walks down to the forestage.[106]

This pantomimic prologue, which introduces the little boy's spoken prologue, points to Meyerhold's later concept of pre-acting, a kinetic introduction to a character's subsequently spoken words. It also introduces three eccentrics, "the masks of the authors of the divertissement"—Meyerhold, Soloviev, and Vogak—as characters in their own play.[107]

Three Oranges features a variety of additional parades: Characters traverse the forestage as a visual introduction before joining the action. Celio and Fata Morgana are introduced with "Bengal lights and fireworks typical of a lavish spectacle" and "musical accompaniment" before commencing a wizard's war (*Three Oranges,* 23). Truffaldino's parade at first entrance consists of crossing the forestage bearing "clownish props" (25), followed by an entire procession of accouterments to a royal fête. This kind of establishing shot became important to many of Meyerhold's productions. Well-known examples include *Magnanimous Cuckold*, in which actors present themselves in front of Liubov Popova's constructivist set, and *The Forest*, in which two actors playing actors take several scenes to descend a bridge that brings them incrementally closer to the audience, an example that also recalls Kabuki's *hanamichi*.

Three Oranges contains several categories of characters that double or fragment audience perception. The "fools in the towers" and "supernumeraries in the towers" (*Three Oranges,* 18) peer down onto the main action from towers that flank a false proscenium. Both comment on the action as it unfolds, the fools verbally and the supernumeraries physically. These interjections punctuate plot moments by drawing attention to them. For example, the fools repeat key points of exposition:

> THE FIRST FOOL IN THE TOWERS: The hypochondriac prince . . .
> THE SECOND: . . . Tartaglia, who is ill . . .
> THE FIRST: . . . will recover . . .
> THE SECOND: . . . if he laughs. (*Three Oranges,* 22)

Although these interruptions are rarely longer than an aside, they are spatialized by virtue of the fact that they emanate from the proscenium arch itself, thus directing the audience's gaze from stage to frame and back again.

Meyerhold and his collaborators also physicalize Gozzi's verbal debates. The competing choruses of *Three Oranges* prompt a constant unmaking and remaking of the performance—and of the rules and genres according to which theater is constructed.[108] The kitchen-sink comedians and über-tragic tragedians who battled in the opening parade reappear in the second of the scenario's three interludes to physicalize an "argument"[109] about theatrical repertoire. Clarice, Leandro, and Brighella take turns defending their favorite genres: über-tragedy, kitchen-sink comedy,[110] and commedia, respectively. The reenactment of Clarice's favorite, über-tragedy, demonstrates how the choruses physicalize her words:

> CLARICE: I love tragic performances with characters that hurl themselves out of windows and from the tops of towers out of love.
>
> BRIGHELLA: And somehow manage to stay alive without breaking their necks.
>
> *As Clarice speaks, a chorus of über-tragic tragedians performs. . . . A king does not want to give his daughter in marriage to a young knight. The latter throws himself from the tower in grief. After him, in despair, comes his bride. Finally the saddened king follows their example. The king remains alive and meets the young lovers, also alive, at the base of the tower. Collective joy.* (*Three Oranges*, 32)

After Leandro's chorus of kitchen-sink comedians performs similar parodic antics, Brighella, who advocates instead for commedia, dons a Harlequin mask and performs a *lazzo*. In this scene, which does not appear in Gozzi,[111] Harlequin laments to himself that his beloved Smeraldina is to marry a farmer. Brighella then splits Harlequin into two Harlequins who debate with one another over whether to live or die:

> BRIGHELLA: Why should you hang yourself?—Because, I want to.—You will not hang yourself.—I will hang myself.—I assure you that you won't.—I swear to you I will.—I tell you, you will not hang yourself.—Just you wait, you scoundrel, I know how to get rid of your meddling! (Harlequin takes out a stick, deals several full-weight blows onto his own back and takes off running.) Ah, finally our scamp has skedaddled! Now we can hang ourselves without interference. (*Three Oranges*, 34)

In this *lazzo* of oscillation, we witness an acrobatic quadrupling of character: an actor plays Brighella, who plays not one, but two Harlequins, framing the process whereby an actor becomes a character to celebrate virtuosic creation without need for psychological identification. This scene also physicalizes what Marvin Carlson calls "ghosting."[112] Just one year earlier Meyerhold wrote, "The mask enables the spectator to see not only the actual Arlecchino before him, but all the Arlecchinos who live in his memory."[113]

Instead of trying to pretend that the actor does not exist when the character is present, Brighella's *lazzo* of oscillation acknowledges that theatrical embodiment is a dance between at least two selves, both for the actor and for the audience. This splitting of actor and character, what Julia Vaingurt calls "bifurcation,"[114] allows the creator to observe the creation, to maintain an omniscience that the material alone—the body or the mask—cannot have. In later writings on biomechanics, Meyerhold developed a formula to articulate this process: $N = A_1 + A_2$, where N is the actor, A_1 the creator, and A_2 the creative material.[115] The actor's creation of a role was, for Meyerhold, an act of authorship, not a passive manipulation by a director or playwright. In this sense, it is more accurate to think of Meyerhold's actors as puppeteers of their bodies and characters than Meyerhold as a puppeteer depriving actors of agency, a common misunderstanding of Meyerhold's work with actors.[116]

Meyerhold and his collaborators viewed Gozzi's commedia masks as framing characters that shape audience experience through commentary. Tieck took these framing characters further by adding a fictional audience. In *Puss in Boots*, argues Zhirmunsky:

> Tieck replaces [Gozzi's] masks with real spectators. . . . [who] sit in the *parterre* [orchestra seats] and watch this fairy tale; during the intermissions they exchange remarks; they interrupt the action of the play with their own critical commentary; they applaud and hiss; conversations in the *parterre* serve as an introduction to the play and a theatrical departure from it. Thus the *parterre's* participation in the action gives Tieck the ability to develop an element of comic reflection, the bearer of which in Gozzi had been the masks.[117]

As in Gozzi's *fiabe*, Tieck "compels the actor to break character, thereby revealing the actor standing behind the guise of the play's character."[118]

In the work of the Borodinskaia Street Studio, the framing of character and the framing of space were inextricably linked. And it is this link that, for me, is this scenario's—and the studio's—most significant innovation. *Three Oranges* expands the bifurcation of the actor into a kaleidoscopic splintering of playing spaces with multiple nested frames. Meyerhold drew extensively from visual art, especially from the etchings of Callot, to inspire this mise-en-scène on multiple planes. We now know that Callot's *Balli di Sfessania* (see figures 3 and 28) aren't literal depictions of commedia players,[119] but Meyerhold and his collaborators believed they were and examined them closely for information on commedia physicality. Each etching contains multiple planes: focal figures in the foreground contrast with other characters performing, fighting, or strolling in the background, itself often divided into planes.[120] This foreground/ background divide is even more apparent in Callot's etching *The Fan*, an image identified in Meyerhold's journal as an inspiration for action on contrasting planes (see figure 6).[121] The silhouetted figures that crouch on the frame are reminiscent of a fictional audience that watches a play-within-a-play. They, too, provoke a double perspective: the viewer views the picture both directly and through the gaze of the framing figures.

Meyerhold used the forestage in the same way. *Three Oranges* calls more than a dozen times for action on the forestage, especially during interludes and parades. His published studio notes contain multiple references to training actors how to play on the forestage. Meyerhold eliminated the footlights not simply to control lighting design or to eliminate the fourth wall but to replace the fourth wall with a permeable liminal space in which the actor becomes the negotiator for the audience of the production's multiple planes.

Three Oranges also prompts plural perspective by dividing the stage into individually framed spaces. The description for the opening setting, for instance, reads as follows:

> The theater is set up as the interior of a theater building being prepared for a grand spectacle. Along the sides of a generous forestage, tall towers for the fools are set up. . . . At the bases of the towers are built-in alcoves from which actors, as they are performing, take props: at one point the king's crown, etc. Along the wings from the towers to the upstage area stretches a semicircular, opulent, two-tier facade with a great quantity of doors covered by curtains. In the middle of the facade is a large gate . . . covered with a . . . curtain, behind which lies a second stage. (*Three Oranges*, 19)

Thus there are several framed spaces: the forestage, the main stage, and the upstage stage within a stage, but also the towers flanking the proscenium, the framed areas for props, the curtained doors, and the balcony. Centuries earlier, wings began to be arranged successively to force a feeling of infinity extending from the vantage point of a single perspective. Meyerhold replaced these wings with frames that provoke a different kind of infinity: one of infinite perspectives.

In his book *Postdramatic Theatre*, Hans-Thies Lehmann argues that theatrical productions of European scripted drama have tended historically to treat ruptures of their frames as temporary interruptions:

> Even if theatre has a number of conventionalized disruptions of its closure (asides, direct audience address), the play on stage is understood as diegesis

> of a separated and "framed" reality . . . which is marked off against its environment as a separate "made up" reality. While arguably "real," the occasional disruption of the theatrical frame has traditionally been treated as an artistically and conceptually negligible aspect of theatre. . . . The artistic task consisted in integrating all this into the fictional cosmos as inconspicuously as possible, so that addressing the real audience and speaking outside the play would not be noticeable as a disturbing element. In this respect, one can draw a parallel between the drama in theatre and the "frame" of a picture that closes the picture off to the outside and at the same time creates an internal cohesion.[122]

While this may be true of many representational dramas, Meyerhold's understanding of theatrical frames and their "disruptions" is a major exception to Lehmann's claim, one that warrants more attention than it has received. In Meyerhold's view, frames are neither negligible nor inconspicuous. They are the artist's thinking made visible. Framed disruptions prevent actors from leading the audience "too far into the land" of a fictional world that envelops and lulls them,[123] instead prompting them to participate in the infinite possibilities of "mak[ing]-believe," the unbridled joy of creation. In Zhirmunsky's words, "For the romantics, Gozzi represented 'comedy of pure joy.' . . . Let art be like play—light, cheerful, fantastical, not like everyday, all-too-ordinary life!"[124]

In her analysis of Hoffmann's narrator in "The Sandman," Maria Tatar suggests that Hoffmann's "narrative intrusions . . . do not disrupt the fictional illusion, as is generally assumed, but rather *remind us that we are contemplating a world created by a mind* . . . The self-conscious narrator, through his reflections on himself and on the creative process, never lets us forget that we are in the realm of art."[125] The intended effect of this on the reader is that "the narrator's reflections . . . stimulate the reader to engage in the same kind of activity on a higher level: to reflect on a mind reflecting on itself."[126] It is easy to see how Meyerhold adapted this to the theatre. Reminding audiences that they are in a theatre does not *disrupt* illusion; it allows them to reflect on a production reflecting on itself. Meyerhold's constructed and deconstructed frames gave audiences the opportunity to create through thought. I suggest describing this theatrical technique as dissonancing—intentionally generating a conflict between a viewer's "field of expectations"[127] and what is actually presented in order to prompt reflection—rather than as distancing—moving the viewer farther away from the familiar.

For several of the Russian formalists, Viktor Shklovsky most famously, the purpose of baring the device (*obnazhenie priem*) and estrangement (*ostranenie*) was a revivification of life and art, a renewed ability to perceive and experience. For Meyerhold and his circle, who used different terms for related but not identical ideas, the purpose of irony and conventionalization was joy, an unfettering of the fantasy, a revivification of theater through shared actor-audience creation. The ideas of Shklovsky and Meyerhold converge, interestingly, in Shklovsky's musings on theater. In "The Making of *Don Quixote*," he writes:

> As far as the theater is concerned, the illusion presented on the stage ought to have a "flickering" quality to it (i.e., it should alternate with the other, more realistic element in the play). As for the spectator, he must experience within himself a shift in his perception of the action onstage from the "contrived" to the "realistic" and back.[128]

Whether we term this flickering, oscillation, binocular vision, or, after Brecht, "complex seeing,"[129] this audience experience contextualizes the cognitive effect that Meyerhold was trying to provoke. In *Three Oranges*, Meyerhold and his collaborators bared the frame that separates the theatrical world into here and there, reality and fiction, person and character, thus transforming the frame itself into a liminal space in which meaning can be generated by actors and audiences alike.

Meyerhold, Soloviev, and Vogak's *Three Oranges* prompted a broad theatrical conversation that extended far beyond its immediate practical use: providing Meyerhold's studio participants with techniques for negotiating audience experience. Plural perspective was to function similarly in numerous subsequent productions that refracted Meyerhold's innovations. Just a few examples include Sergei Sudeikin's designs for Fedor Komissarzhevsky's *Tales of Hoffmann* (1915), Prokofiev's opera *Love for Three Oranges* (1919) and its designs by Boris Anisfeld for the world premiere (1921) (figure 14), Vakhtangov's fantasy-infused *Turandot* (1922), Evreinov's metatheatrical plays of the 1910s and 1920s, the multiple levels in Tairov's American expressionist productions, collisions of framed realities in Sergei Eisenstein's films, and, years later, the defamiliarization devices of Brecht, though there is an important difference between estrangement in Meyerhold and estrangement in Brecht.

For Brecht, the activation of the spectator was something to be harnessed. Though Meyerhold's staging techniques may seem similar, for him the activation of the spectator was something to be unleashed. Brecht created dialectics of dissonant possibilities that the viewer is prompted to try to resolve outside the theater. Meyerhold created a symphony of dissonances that embrace the impossibility of resolution as the fundamental, if uncomfortable, stuff of which life is made. He believed that content and form coexist, just as a painting and its frame, fiction and reality, and character and actor coexist, and that it is by embracing dissonant simultaneities such as these that we free ourselves to create.

Figure 14. Boris Israelevich Anisfeld, Russian (1879–1973), design for Prokofiev's opera *Love for Three Oranges* (Chicago world premiere, 1921). Note Prokofiev's four competing choruses on the forestage and the observing figures in the towers. Pink Curtain #2, from *Love for Three Oranges*, n.d. Gouache and watercolor, with pen and black ink, gold metallic paint, and charcoal, over graphite, selectively varnished, on off-white laid paper, 565 × 780 mm. Friends of American Art Collection, 1922.84, The Art Institute of Chicago.

The Borodinskaia Street Studio

Although Meyerhold, Soloviev, and Vogak's *Three Oranges* was never publicly staged,[130] it publicly bared the inner workings of the Borodinskaia Street Studio. Each of its authors was closely involved in studio activities. Soloviev taught commedia history and technique. Meyerhold trained students in stage movement and the grotesque. Vogak translated several of Gozzi's critical writings for *LTA*, taught voice classes, and participated in the studio's only public performance (1915). As Meyerhold and his collaborators implemented the reforms laid out in *Three Oranges*, they trained students to develop expertise in three basic categories.

The first was the creative responsiveness of the actor's mental and physical instruments: the fantasy and the body. This included honing the ability to play (to "make-believe") through improvisation; cultivating a deep understanding of the history of theater, art, music, and "the literary balagan" (Hoffmann, Tieck, and others); and generating exercises that refracted this knowledge through a contemporary prism, trained the actor's instantaneous responsiveness, and developed playfulness and virtuosity in commedia, acrobatics, dance, and athletics. Voice classes in musical elocution taught actors to "overcome the formless, relaxed tempo of naturalism."[131]

The second was responsiveness to the material elements of performance. In his studio notes, Meyerhold writes that performing in response to "dramatis elements"—rather than to dramatis personae only—sharpens the actor's ability to interact with the material world and to punctuate a production visually.[132] This begins with understanding the actor as one part of a larger artistic cosmos. As Meyerhold mused from the imagined point of view of one of his actors:

> "Since my acting will reach the spectator simultaneously with the scenery and music, in order for the combination of all performance elements to have a *precise meaning*, acting must be one of the components of this sum of dramatis elements." Knowing . . . how the whole theatrical work came to be, the actor who goes out onto the stage transforms himself, becoming a work of art.[133]

Meyerhold describes the interaction between the actor's movement and music as polyphonic: "Music and the actor's movement . . . are brought to life simultaneously and in their progressions (music and movement, each in its own plane) form a distinctive kind of polyphony."[134] By extension, each of a production's dramatis elements might be thought of as a distinct line in a polyphonic understanding of theatrical production.

The third category, what Leach has called "the cornerstone of Meyerhold's theatre,"[135] was making the spectator a co-creator. Meyerhold's definition of theater "assumes the existence . . . of a fourth creator, after the author, actor, and director: the spectator. Conventionalized theater creates the kind of staging in which the spectator, with the imagination, creatively, has to finish drawing what a given scene hints at."[136] This finishing of the drawing cultivates creative cognitive flexibility and, in Meyerhold's view, trains spectators as makers. It is in this third category that the studio's engagement with Hoffmann, Tieck, romantic irony, and Gozzi was most central and that the connection between *Three Oranges* and studio work is most apparent. In *Three Oranges* and in studio exercises, actors learned to perform on multiple planes, to self-introduce for the benefit of the audience, and to oscillate effortlessly between fiction and reality, content and commentary.

Soloviev and Meyerhold documented their class activities in a regular *LTA* "Studio" column that provides valuable detail on specific experiments.

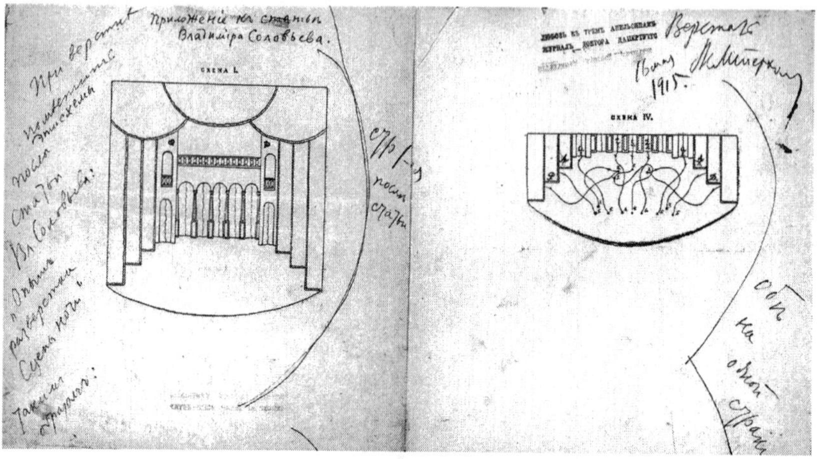

Figure 15. Proof sheet illustrations by Alexander Rykov for Vladimir Soloviev's article "Experiments with Staging the Night Scene" (with Meyerhold's comments) for the journal *Love for Three Oranges* (May 16, 1915). ГИК 17118/2, f. 44, ed. khr. 3. © Saint Petersburg State Museum of Theatre and Music.

Soloviev lectured on topics "related to the theatrical method of studying the techniques of commedia dell'arte,"[137] including "E. T. A. Hoffmann and his *Princess Brambilla* as a new understanding by the German romantics of the fate of Italian improvised comedy," the Gozzi-Goldoni-Chiari theater wars, Gozzi's *fiabe*, Atellan farce, Roman mimes, commedia in France, and Molière, all of which he viewed as part of a shared genealogy.[138] He accompanied these lectures with practical work, using "Bergamo dance" as a foundational performance technique[139] and his scenario *Harlequin the Matchmaker*[140] to introduce "the characteristic gestures and movements of the most common masks."[141] He also taught the "parade," "the role of forestage servants in performance," and "the significance of the grotesque."[142] Students experimented with commedia *lazzi*, including "night scene," "the city," and "the duel."[143] Soloviev's drawings of the stage configuration for the night scene—a comic *lazzo* based on characters not being able to see each other in the dark—are notably similar to the design of *Three Oranges*, demonstrating the studio's ongoing interest in spatial framing devices (figure 15). Studio students rehearsed the second interlude from *Three Oranges* and also refracted it into a new scene, "Three Oranges, an Astrological Telescope, or, the Lengths to Which Love for the *Metteur en Scène* Can Go," in which little of Gozzi's plot remained, but which now featured, symbolically, a telescope that makes everything in the heavens clear and everything on the ordinary earth impossible to see.[144]

Meyerhold's classes acquainted actors with the physical and rhythmical skills needed to perform in the new theater. He cultivated play and the joy of creation, "the death of psychologism," "the amalgamation of the past and the contemporary," the grotesque,[145] and a theatricalist basis for stage movement, arguing:

> In theater that reproduces life photographically (naturalistic theater), movement is considered from the perspective of its use in the business of helping the spectator understand this or that task of the playwright . . . Theater is an art, and . . . everything must be subordinate to the laws of this art. The laws of life and the laws of art differ.[146]

He developed exercises that honed the actor's interactive response to the material world, using props to train the hands, costumes as initiators of gestures, and scenery, space, and light as instruments on which to play physical music, an idea inspired in part by Adolphe Appia. Techniques included:

> The significance of the "recoil" [*otkaz*]. . . .[147] The precision and intrinsic value of gesture. The actor's self-admiration while acting. The technique of using two planes (stage and forestage) . . . The actor's costume as decorative adornment and not as utilitarian necessity. Hats as a pretext for a theatrical bow. Sticks, lances, rugs, lanterns, shawls, cloaks, weapons, flowers, masks, noses, and like instruments as material for training exercises for the hands . . . Tulle in the hands of forestage servants as distinct punctuating accents for the gestures and conversations . . . of the main dramatis personae. The parade as an essential and autonomous part of theatrical performance.[148]

Each of these exercises was supported by a clearly reasoned view of its larger purpose in developing the new actor.

After a century of using Stanislavsky-based actor training (in its many versions), we sometimes forget that Meyerhold and his studio collaborators developed their pioneering approach to actor training just when Konstantin Stanislavsky, in collaboration with Vakhtangov and Leopold Sulerzhitsky, was shaping the early System at the Moscow Art Theatre's First Studio. The Borodinskaia Street Studio focused on training actors to activate audiences creatively. As Leach has shown, "The fundamental cause for the split between Stanislavsky and Meyerhold at the very beginning of the century lay in their divergent views of the place of the audience in the theatrical event."[149] Instead of Stanislavsky's "public solitude," Dapertutto's actors presented themselves via the parade. In lieu of tracking "given circumstances," students learned to respond to their immediate artistic environment. Instead of "experiencing" a role, studio participants grew adept at oscillating between mask and self. This

Figure 16. Alexander Rykov, costume design for "Harlequin, Dealer of Slapstick Blows," Borodinskaia Street Studio (1915). Paper on cardboard, gouache, 29.9 × 23 cm. КП 180169/1536. © A. A. Bakhrushin State Central Theatre Museum, Moscow.

training was based in refracting—not imitating—historical forms with similar aims.[150] As Meyerhold stated in a 1916 lecture, "The establishment of a formal canon rests on . . . the genetic study of traditional forms,"[151] but "all inclinations toward lifeless-academic epigones are considered harmful."[152]

The Borodinskaia Street Studio gave only one public performance; in it, it placed its actor training process onstage.[153] The February 12, 1915, presentation consisted of ten études, interludes, and pantomimes (in celebration of theatrical work that is provisional, between acts, or without words) performed in the manner of the studio's sources.[154] Nearly every scene was performed in a different style—"after" Callot (figure 16),[155] as a clown act,[156] as a parody of marionette theater,[157] in the style of nineteenth-century French Harlequinades[158]—to give actors corporeal experience of devices they refracted. The performance space was arranged on two levels to allow for different kinds of play on the forestage and main stage. Instead of a "traditional" stage, there was a "fairly high platform" in front of which was "a forestage carpeted in a semi-circle with dark blue cloth." As actors performed, "they constantly had to jump from platform to 'forestage' and back again."[159] One scene was presented with "street performers" on the main platform and an internal audience on the forestage to "stir up the contemporary audience."[160]

For Meyerhold, it was far more important that audiences be stirred up than that they be universally laudatory. The 1915 no. 1–3 issue of *LTA* featured an unusual studio section, "Reviews from the Daily Press and Remarks by the Editors of the Journal of Doctor Dapertutto on the February 12, 1915 Evening of the 'Studio.'" The eighteen pages that follow are organized in two columns: on the left are reprints of reviews, beginning with the most negative; these are rebutted on the right with wit—and larger font size—by Meyerhold and his collaborators. Meyerhold reveled in controversy and, as is clear from this studio report, taught his students to do so as well. Sergei Yutkevich later recalled Meyerhold saying, "If everyone praises your production, it can be said for certain that it is worthless. If the show is met entirely with bayonets, there might be something good in it. If it splits the audience in half, then quite possibly your work is good."[161]

Once Meyerhold began to teach regularly, he did so for the remainder of his life with remarkably consistent aims in terms of developing physical agility, responsiveness to the material elements of performance, and direct audience engagement. The Borodinskaia Street Studio closed in 1917, but it was followed by Meyerhold's 1918–19 Courses on the Technique of Theatrical Productions and, in 1921, by his State Higher Theatre Workshops, where he developed biomechanics. After the Revolution, in the spirit of the studio as a necessary laboratory for experimentation, Meyerhold called his assistant directors "laboratory assistants" and simultaneously ran a school, workshop, and theater that supported and creatively fed one another.

Love for Three Oranges: The Journal of Doctor Dapertutto

Ziegler has noted with respect to the history of Hoffmann publications that "previous editors often treated the extensive frames" of Hoffmann's works "as orange peels, publishing collections of stories with no mention of the enclosing structure. This neglect has given rise to interpretive problems that consideration of the frame resolves."[162] The same might be said of *Three Oranges*, one in a series of several oranges: Giambattista Basile's "The Three Citrons" (and other tales) in the *Pentamerone* (1634–36); the Italian oral fairy tale tradition; Gozzi's scenario; German romantic refractions by Hoffmann and Tieck; Meyerhold, Soloviev, and Vogak's divertissement; Prokofiev's opera; and subsequent stage productions.

The most directly interrelated trio of oranges is Meyerhold's scenario, studio, and journal. Each framed the others in necessary ways: the journal contextualized the artistic aims of the scenario, and the scenario illuminated the thinking behind the studio's practical work, which was, in turn, documented in the journal. If Meyerhold, Soloviev, and Vogak's divertissement was a manifesto for a new theater, the journal provided context for and analysis of what that new theater should be.[163] This present chapter has referred to roughly a dozen of the journal's over 100 essays, dramatic works, and reviews. Rather than attempting to survey the remainder in this section, I will provide an overview of the journal's publication history, collaborators, content, and influence before turning to brief analyses of the "Hoffmaniana [*sic*]," the journal's dedicated Hoffmann column, and of two polemical essays that contextualize how the studio presented itself and was perceived from without.

From its inception, the journal was a project of modest means, launched with only 100 rubles and supported overwhelmingly by the fervor of its participants.[164] The main Saint Petersburg editorial address was Meyerhold's own apartment and the Moscow address—Sergei Ignatov's. Authors, many of whom were artistic colleagues or relatives, were not paid for their essays and translations. It was an amateur enterprise, fueled on enthusiasm, dedicated to supporting, defending, and disseminating information about the studio's experiments. Many of the journal's writers were experts in the studio's primary fields of study—commedia, Gozzi, fairground, German romanticism, circus, and so on. Zhirmunsky was but one of many journal collaborators associated with Russian formalism.[165]

LTA reveled in informed subjectivity; like Hoffmann, Meyerhold used source material "as a springboard into his own fantasy."[166] As the studio publication, it was aimed at a select audience of students and like-minded followers. As stated in the first issue, "In appearing before the public, we will say nothing about our goals and intentions, we will not advocate any kind of program. We will talk about ourselves and our work, sometimes about the work of others insofar as it interests us."[167] Meyerhold required that all his students read the journal, both in this prerevolutionary period and, as we learn from Eisenstein's letters, in the 1920s, when Meyerhold was developing biomechanics.[168]

Looked at as a whole, *LTA*'s particular strain of subjectivity clearly refracts the structure of Hoffmann's *Fantasy Pieces in Callot's Manner. Fantasy Pieces* contains the "Kreisleriana," unconventional music reviews in which the division between Hoffmann and his alter ego Kreisler is blurred, polemical pieces against bourgeois philistines who do not understand music, fictional letters (including a letter from Kreisler to Hoffmann), and novellas, all prefaced with a brief ode to Callot's irony and grotesque. Although this preface is the shortest piece in the book, it is arguably the most important, as it frames the work to follow.

LTA's structure is undeniably similar, though focused on theater. Individual issues often include (with variations) a "Hoffmaniana" column (essays dedicated thematically, artistically, or polemically to Hoffmann); production reviews, often ironic in tone; poetry, plays, or scenarios; historical and theoretical articles; polemical responses to theatrical "philistines;" a chronicle of studio activities; contemporary artistic news; and book reviews (often of works by studio affiliates). Most fascinating are its theater wars: external attacks on the Studio that the journal's editors republish and reframe with their own commentary interpolated, thus publically undermining their critics. Throughout the journal, Meyerhold and Vladimir Soloviev (pseud. Volmar Luscinius) delight in slipping in and out of their alter egos by penning essays and scenarios under either name or by having one "self" refer to another.

Despite the fact that *Love for Three Oranges* was Dapertutto's journal, Meyerhold wrote only a handful of its articles. Other than class descriptions that appear in the studio notes of most issues and (possibly) some of the essays signed by the editors, he co-authored two plays (including *Three Oranges*) and two theoretical essays, wrote the two Dapertutto pieces with which this chapter began, and penned a short polemical essay on Benois. The journal published many theoretical articles, however, that have largely escaped historical attention, possibly because they were written by authors with whom readers have less familiarity. The immediate framing article for the *Three Oranges* divertissement, for instance, Samuil Vermel's "Moment of Form in Art," calls for actors to elevate their art through increased attention to theatrical form.[169] Theoretical essays that directly supported the studio's praxis include Vermel's "Irony and Theatricality" (see Introduction) and Zhirmunsky's "Comedy of Pure Joy" (see appendix A), published alongside Vasily Gippius's translation of Tieck's play. Other essays are historical, their content ranging from provincial circus history to an essay on Euripides by Sergei Radlov, who also contributed a translation of Plautus's *Brothers Menachmus*. In addition to full-length plays, the journal published commedia-infused interludes and scenarios intended to feed studio experiments.

Dapertutto's journal also contains a great deal of practical material on commedia. Gozzi was almost entirely unknown in Russia at the time. Meyerhold and his collaborators set about to change this on multiple fronts. The journal bookended its run with Gozzi fiabe—*Three Oranges* in the first issue and Blokh's translation of *The Snake Woman* in the last.[170] Each issue included abundant material on Gozzi, commedia, or both. Soloviev contributed a seven-part series on commedia history and staging techniques, which he capped with an essay on his own experiments with the *lazzo* of night. Vogak translated substantial portions of Gozzi's "Ingenuous Disputation and Sincere History of the Origin of My Ten Tales for the Theater (*Ragionamento ingenuo, e storia sincera dell'origine delle mie dieci Fiabe teatrali*)," while Konstantin Miklashevsky (known in France as Constant Mic), whose seminal book on commedia was required reading for studio students,[171] contributed essays on commedia's character types and acrobatic elements. Callot became a practical, accessible source of inspiration for the studio through Miklashevsky's book, which reproduced several of Callot's *Balli* and their preliminary studies.

Direct homage to Hoffmann appeared primarily in the "Hoffmaniana" column. This title evoked associations with Hoffmann's "Kreisleriana," and, structurally speaking, served a framing function similar to the Callot preface in *Fantasy Pieces*. Most of the "Hoffmaniana" argue for Hoffmann's relevance to contemporary theatrical practice; in the words of Kniazhnin, author of the inaugural "Hoffmaniana": "You connected the past with our present . . . we once again remember You, having forgotten only briefly."[172] *LTA* also contains references to Hoffmann in published lecture notes, in a review of "living marionette" performances at the Bat,[173] and in Dapertutto's polemical pieces.

Although the "Hoffmaniana" was the journal's only dedicated column, it appeared almost as sporadically as the journal itself. The three 1914 "Hoffmaniana," published in the journal's first three issues, praised Hoffmann's work while also providing information about publications, Russian translations, and the writer's influence on Russian literature and culture. These essays cultivated the studio's almost religious zeal for Hoffmann; in Cheauré's words, "the 'Hoffmaniana' [sometimes] seem like a prayer."[174] Vladimir Kniazhnin's "Hoffmaniana I" (see appendix A) provided a bibliography of recommended Hoffmann resources in Russian for students and studio followers. "Hoffmaniana III" (1914 no. 3) excerpted laudatory appraisals of Hoffmann by nineteenth-century Russian authors, while "Hoffmaniana II" (1914 no. 2) listed nineteenth-century translations and critical writings, noting that "our Russian infatuation with Ernst Theodor Amadeus Hoffmann in the [18]30s was staggering! Where did it come from and how was it created, that general atmosphere of infatuation, like the rhythm of a dance that grasps hold of everyone?"[175]

The four 1915 "Hoffmaniana," all published in that year's no. 1 issue, are markedly different in tone: rather than demonstrating Hoffmann's value, they provide widely varying examples of contemporary Russian engagement with his works. "Hoffmaniana I," Sergei Ignatov's staging plan for *Princess Blandina* (see Introduction) proposed practical theatrical applications of the framing devices of Callot, Gozzi, and Hoffmann. "Hoffmaniana II" reprinted reviews of a 1915 translation of *Brambilla* that had prompted a debate over the value of the novella and of fantasy more broadly. "Hoffmaniana III" published two recent Moscow lectures: the first on Hoffmann's fantasy as interpreted in Russian literature, the second a close reading of Hoffmann's literary transposition of musical dissonance. "Hoffmaniana IV," to which I now turn, reprinted a lengthy criticism of the studio, reframed with Soloviev's satirical response.

Dapertutto's journal generated a climate of "red-hot polemics"[176] that its editors took pains to preserve on its pages. Such articles in *LTA* fall into two general categories: satirical defenses against attacks on the studio's work and criticisms of those with whom Meyerhold and his collaborators disagreed. One of the most common criticisms of Meyerhold's journal and studio was that their interest in theater history was "nostalgic and antiquarian,"[177] a charge also commonly leveled against Nikolai Evreinov's Theatre of Yore (Starinnyi teatr), which staged two seasons that engaged with performance traditions that pre-dated what Znosko-Borovsky called the "antitheatrical nineteenth century."[178]

In November 1915, Dmitry Filosofov, former literary editor of *World of Art* (*Mir iskusstva*), the famous journal founded in 1899 by Filosofov's cousin Sergei Diaghilev, published a scathing criticism of the intellectual foundations of the Borodinskaia Street Studio. In his attack, Filosofov described what had long made Hoffmann attractive to World of Art artists:

> It was not only Hoffmann the writer that captivated us; his multi-faceted artistic personality attracted us to him. His "musical soul," his comprehensive amateurism, his understanding of the theater. For Hoffmann, directors and Kapellmeisters were not "talented" technical specialists, but rather sovereigns over a whole world, wonder-workers who make fools of philistines and introduce a pure, naive, musical soul into a world of fantastical reality. . . . Naturally, in the "World of Art" circle, where so many successful theatrical undertakings were conceived, Hoffmann was "one of us."[179]

For Filosofov, Hoffmann represented many of the World of Art group's ideals, which included a desire to renew the arts via a fusion of past and present, a belief in the validity of the artist's self-defined reality, and a celebration of amateurism "in the original and good meaning of the word,"[180] that is, in the sense of always having been surrounded by art and therefore instinctively understanding it. Hoffmann, who dubbed Kreisler a "traveling enthusiast," similarly believed that the artist's intuitive understanding of the creative realm surpassed philistine, albeit professional skill.

Hoffmann had long been an inspiration for the World of Art group, members of which included Bakst, Benois, and Roerich, major contributors to the Ballets Russes design revolution then in progress. Benois even described Hoffmann as his "'patron' on Mount Parnassus," lauding the writer's understanding of romanticism "as a special disposition to see in everything the connections between this world and 'the next.'"[181] Filosofov, too, viewed Hoffmann as a kindred enthusiast, one who was not to be debased by simple imitation:

> Hoffmann was not a "teacher" in general, nor in essence can he be. We loved him without ceremony, without any hocus-pocus. But somewhat later, in the

> next generation perhaps, Hoffmann was turned into a teacher, into a theoretician from whom one should specifically learn. The brilliant dilettante was turned into an expert, the eternal improviser into a professor. I am referring to Meyerhold's "studio" and to the journal of "Doctor Dapertutto."[182]

Filosofov mistakenly assumed that the studio was attempting to faithfully mirror the past: "All this is very sweet, interesting, 'scrumptious' . . . But, Lord, how sad is it when this restoration 'cubed' is presented as a new, youthful trend in the theater!"[183]

Filosofov's article also condemned an incomplete Russian translation of *The Golden Pot*, which he wrongly attributed to studio cofounder Vladimir *Nikolaevich* Soloviev. It was actually a reprint of only the first half of the nineteenth-century writer Vladimir *Sergeevich* Soloviev's translation.[184] Filosofov paired what he thought to be Meyerhold's colleague Soloviev's inept *Golden Pot* translation with a negative assessment of *Princess Brambilla*, one of the studio's major inspirations, calling it a "questionable work" that Hoffmann probably wrote "only for the money."[185] Filosofov realized his mortifying attribution error almost immediately. He published a public apology to Soloviev a week after his initial attack. By then, however, he had set himself up as a target for an aggressive rebuttal.[186]

Meyerhold called the affair a "magnificent scandal"[187] and gleefully republished Filosofov's attack in *Love for Three Oranges* along with Soloviev's response to it. Soloviev responded with palpable irony that he did not understand how Filosofov, "a member of the 'World of Art' group where Hoffmann is 'one of you,'" could have made such an error, concluding:

> I am even alarmed . . . that Mr. D. Filosofov, in touching affinity with the philistine theory of German professors, considers *Princess Brambilla* "unnecessary to anyone" . . . Thus we find confirmation in our times of Hoffmann's division of humanity into two groups: musicians and just nice people.[188]

Although Meyerhold and his collaborators did not preserve Gozzi's theater wars in their refraction of his *fiaba*, like many artistic innovators of their day, they participated in theater wars of their own.

Meyerhold and Soloviev polemicized against others as jubilantly as they defended themselves from attacks. An especially illuminating example is Soloviev's *LTA* review of the first Russian production of a Gozzi play: Komissarzhevsky's 1912 *Princess Turandot* in Friedrich Schiller's adaptation (figure 17). Fedor Fedorovich Komissarzhevsky (1882–1954) was the first Russian director to stage full-length productions of works by both Gozzi and Hoffmann.[189] Three years after he premiered *Turandot*, he adapted and directed (with Vasily Sakhnovsky) a full-length dramatic adaptation of

Figure 17. Nikolai Sapunov, costume design for Gozzi's *Princess Turandot*, dir. Fedor Komissarzhevsky, Nezlobin Theatre (1912). КП 189959. © A. A. Bakhrushin State Central Theatre Museum, Moscow.

Hoffmann's *The Bride Choosing* (1915). He attempted a 1915 *Tales of Hoffmann* at the Zimin Opera Theatre, for which Sergei Sudeikin created vivid, phantasmagorical designs, one of which featured masked figures peering out of multiple internal frames at the beautiful automaton Olimpia (figure 18). Komissarzhevsky successfully staged a second *Tales* in 1919, designed by the cubist painter Aristrakh Lentulov, at the Artistic Educational Union of Workers' Organizations Theatre-Studio (KhPSRO, later the New Theatre), where he experimented with "synthesized" acting and "dynamic" design.[190] Lentulov used the actors' costumes and faces as canvases on which to paint, much as Marc Chagall was to do two years later at the Moscow Yiddish Theatre. Igor Ilinsky, who studied with Komissarzhevsky before joining Meyerhold's State Higher Theatre Workshops in the early 1920s, remembered this latter *Tales* as being "among the few theatrical events I have seen in my life that makes one wholeheartedly love the theater, the kind of theater in which one receives impressions and aesthetic enjoyment whole, as with symphonic music."[191]

Eisenstein recalled Komissarzhevsky's *Princess Turandot*, which he saw on tour in Riga, with a fondness that equaled Ilinsky's memory of *Tales*, identifying it as the first production to set him on his path "through theater

Figure 18. Sergei Sudeikin, scene design for the Olimpia act of Komissarzhevsky's unrealized production of Offenbach's *Tales of Hoffmann*, Zimin Opera Theatre (1915). КП 60434. © A. A. Bakhrushin State Central Theatre Museum, Moscow.

to cinema" and to ignite the flame of his interest in commedia and the grotesque.[192] A review by Sakhnovsky, who was to cofound the V. F. Komissarzhevskaia Theatre with Komissarzhevsky in 1914, gushed over *Turandot* "to the point of being ecstatic,"[193] praising its "decorative values,"[194] its "romantic" atmosphere, and its fusion of psychological emotionalism with gentle fantasy, concluding, "In this production there are so many refracted rays from the past, so much fantasy, so much reflection of contemporary taste and thought. In this production . . . is theatre as it should be."[195]

Soloviev's *LTA* review of the 1914 revival of Komissarzhevsky's *Turandot* was as condemnatory as Sakhnovsky's was complementary. Rather than celebrating the fact that Gozzi had finally reached the Russian stage (albeit in Schiller's adaptation), Soloviev fulminated wittily that Komissarzhevsky, with whom Meyerhold already had a history of polemicizing,[196] had not done the intellectual legwork to understand Gozzi's formal innovations. Soloviev criticized Schiller's adaptation for many of the very things that Sakhnovsky valued, objecting, for instance, that a naturalistic interlude was, "thanks to its psychologically realistic basis, precisely the sort of thing against which Gozzi fought so passionately during his lifetime."[197] Much of Soloviev's polemical analysis—it can't exactly be called a review—suggests that Komissarzhevsky reverted to the methods of the Moscow Art Theatre rather than pioneering new forms appropriate to Gozzi's plays: "The theatre, having undertaken a production of *Turandot*, evidently breathed a sigh of relief when it discovered in Schiller a psychological motivation for the unexpected scenic structure, and thus did not find the only appropriate interpretation of the play—*as exaggerated parody*."[198] Thus "Gozzi's theatre of wonders was sacrificed to verisimilitude and poetry."[199]

Soloviev's criticism of *Turandot* illuminates several formal and philosophical elements that he, Meyerhold, and their studio collaborators upheld as foundational to the new theater. Soloviev's essay calls for irony to replace psychological realism, for the mask as a device that mediates between theatrical planes, and for design as a tool with which to augment the grotesque rather than to achieve historical accuracy.[200] Soloviev also maintained that any Gozzi production required far more attention to action on the forestage than Komissarzhevsky had provided: "The masks in their banter with the public sat before dimly lit footlights; how could the director forget that the forestage is the stage space where the actor's most significant play takes place, and how could he not flood the primary theatrical playing space with rivers of light?"[201]

As these *LTA* articles demonstrate, Russian refractions of Hoffmann, Gozzi, and commedia were as varied as they were abundant. Within the Russian avant-garde there were numerous ideological fissures. Examining them reveals the tremendous variety that often exists within seeming homogeneity. These essays also illuminate how the studio refracted its sources: Meyerhold expected rigorous dramaturgical research of himself and of his contemporaries as part of the process of refracting "material from the past" through "contemporary thinking."[202] The whole purpose of the studio was to "train a new type of actor, with the help of whom to overturn theatrical culture at its very roots."[203] The year after Dapertutto's journal folded, the 1917 October Revolution overturned Russian society at its roots, giving Meyerhold a unique opportunity to fuse his theatrical revolution with the political one.

It would be difficult to overstate the influence of Meyerhold's journal. The future film director Sergei Yutkevich, who became a student at Meyerhold's State Higher Theatre Workshops in 1921, recalls that his awe for the legendary Dapertutto bordered on fanaticism:

> I had already read Hoffmann's tales, on the pages of which the legendary Doctor first appeared, but even so I wanted to find out why an already famous Russian director was masking himself with this character, a director whose name resounded on the pages of the press and was imprinted in our youthful consciousness . . .
>
> The journal of Doctor Dapertutto revealed to the reader scenes of the vicious battle between the supporters of Count Carlo Gozzi and Carlo Goldoni.

> "Jokes characteristic to the theater," born of the improvisations of the commedia dell'arte masks, came to life in detailed description, and these experiments, conducted by the mysterious Doctor and his assistant Volmar Luscinius (Vl. Soloviev) . . . teased the imagination, drew a picture of a kind of magical theatrical world.[204]

Meyerhold's creative work, his "Meyerholdiana" (not to be confused with the "Meyerholditis" of which he was later accused),[205] produced a fierce, widespread interest in the theater community of his day, particularly among those who artistically came of age with the Revolution: Radlov, Foregger, Yutkevich, the Eccentrics, Babanova, Ilinsky, Garin, Shostakovich, Prokofiev, and innumerable other figures in theater, art, music, literature, and film.

INTERLUDE: *INSPECTOR GENERAL* (1926)

In his desire to create theater that was fresh and relevant, Meyerhold consistently built upon previous experiments. While the best-known images of his work are those of the biomechanical actors in *Magnanimous Cuckold*, Meyerhold incorporated Hoffmann-infused plural perspective, framing, and the grotesque into all his productions. His efforts to engage the audience's fantasy manifested as ever-bolder attempts to transform the space between spectator and performer by reframing it—removing the footlights and curtain, having actors perform facing or among the audience, creating theaters within theaters—thus blurring divisions between theater and life. Romantic irony provided a theoretical foundation for forestage servants and other visible/invisible characters whose presence negotiated plural perspective. Hoffmann's musical grotesque contributed to Meyerhold's precise scoring of roles, sounds, and gestures and sharp changes of tempo within a role or scene.

Meyerhold's 1926 production of *Inspector General* (*Revizor*) warrants special attention for its synthesis of these elements in the twentieth century's most famous and controversial production of Gogol. As theatrical fodder for Meyerhold, it was an ideal choice. Like Hoffmann's fictional worlds, which Gogol also refracted, Gogol's settings often seem recognizable, even exaggeratedly mundane, yet he gleefully collides the impossible and the ridiculous with this carefully constructed banality. Many reviews of Meyerhold's *Inspector* noted its nested refractions: Meyerhold > Gogol > Hoffmann. Some referred to the production's Hoffmannian tone or to lead actor Erast Garin's Khlestakov as a character straight out of Hoffmann,[206] while others conflated the Gogolian and Hoffmannian, continuing a Russian tradition of associating Hoffmann's grotesque with Gogol's; some even called Hoffmann a "German Gogol."[207] Gvozdev's description was especially evocative; he called Meyerhold's *Inspector* "a theatrical symphony on themes suggested by Gogol."[208]

David Chambers, who co-staged a 1997 reconstruction of Meyerhold's *Inspector General* at Yale,[209] writes that "Meyerhold's *Revizor* contains probably the densest *mise-en-scène* ever composed onstage . . . It ricochets from egregious humor to deadly menace in a twinkling—more likely it sees no distinction between the two."[210] In the pages that follow, I will note some of the connections between Meyerhold's artful wielding of form in *Inspector General* and his earlier attempts to define form in *Columbine's Veil* and *Three Oranges* to show Meyerhold's development of consistent spectator engagement devices.

Meyerhold's audiences were very familiar with *Inspector General*, the near-century of performance tradition surrounding it, and Gogol's works more broadly. Every change Meyerhold made was a response to this tradition and to recent productions, including the 1921 Moscow Art Theatre version featuring Mikhail Chekhov as Khlestakov. Unsurprisingly, Meyerhold's changes were controversial. While rewriting this classic play and its traditional mise-en-scène, he drew from Gogol's entire oeuvre to develop a refraction of which he called himself the production author. Meyerhold originally developed this approach when refracting pantomimes and scenarios with little or no scripted dialogue, but because *Inspector* and the performance tradition that accompanied it were more widely known, each of Meyerhold's innovations had a ghosted tradition behind it of which audiences inevitably were aware.

Although some critics dismissed Meyerhold's *Inspector* as an arrogant departure from Gogol (one newspaper cartoon shows Meyerhold sitting atop Gogol and throttling him),[211] the director's creative engagement with Gogol was meticulously conceived. Meyerhold believed that much of what was accepted as traditional had more to do with what Mikhail Chekhov called "fossilized" habits than it did with Gogol's actual thinking.[212] On July 20, 1925, Meyerhold wrote to his laboratory assistant (assistant director), dramaturg, and co-adapter Mikhail Korenev requesting that the latter make a list of the play's most essential elements, taking special note of early variants and of "places that fell victim to the censors' ink or were crossed out by theater managers contemporary to Gogol that then became known as 'the traditional cuts.'"[213] For Meyerhold, this accumulated weight of censorship—self-censorship, official censorship, and artistic censorship by nineteenth-century hacks—could finally be stripped away in a postrevolutionary Russia. Korenev worked closely with Meyerhold, meticulously documenting the year-and-a-half development and rehearsal process, thus preserving an invaluable double perspective on the production and its creation. The company tried out his initial cuts and additions to the play in table readings in the fall of

1925, adding in bits from early variants and from other works by Gogol, including *Marriage, Dead Souls*, and *The Gamblers*.[214]

One of the great lingering Stalinist myths about Meyerhold is that his work with actors was dictatorial. As Leach affirms, "The myth of Meyerhold repressing actors, put about in the 1930s to justify the repression of him, is categorically denied by virtually all who worked with him."[215] Meyerhold designed the stage space and orchestrated the rhythms of *Inspector General* "to find the easiest path for the actors"[216] to find freedom of melody within the structure of his directorial harmony. For Meyerhold, the actors' artistic contribution and the director's precise orchestration were complementary forces; in his words: "I understood what the art of the stage director was when I learned to provide harmony for the melodic line of the performance—which is what acting is."[217] Meyerhold dedicated the first rehearsals of *Inspector General* to "establish[ing] a shared beginning between actors and director."[218] He did not distribute roles immediately, but, in a process made familiar more recently by Théâtre du Soleil, "the majority of the company members tried out many roles."[219] Meyerhold talked through his character interpretations to clarify how each would be different from previous clichés, reminding the actors, "I am speaking not in order to dictate, but to clarify all the circumstances that you need to take into account."[220]

Meyerhold and Korenev fragmented Gogol's five acts into a series of self-contained episodes. A month before opening, the production had nineteen. By the general rehearsal[221] (December 8, 1926) and the premiere (December 9, 1926), it had fifteen. Shortly after opening, it was compressed to fourteen,[222] inclusive of the final dumb show. By then it had become Meyerhold's practice to keep "chronometrage" reports—records of the run time of each episode in a production. For *Inspector General*, these chronometrage reports informed decisions to merge, curtail, or reorder episodes. In the spirit of Meyerhold's overt making and unmaking of productions, content and sequence were not indelibly fixed, and additional changes were made over the course of *Inspector*'s long stage life.[223]

Meyerhold's *Inspector General* created a world of uncertainty and disorientation. Tiny stages emerged from behind doors or from the flies, only to disappear again. Characters entered through furniture or disappeared through trap doors. Sequential scenes became simultaneous ones. Character itself was a fluid, shifting, and uncertain thing: actors alternated between liveness and objectness, and quick-change costumes and individual costume pieces became masks with the power to alter the personality of those who donned them. One of the production's most commented-on qualities was its absolute musical precision. Instruments, voices, and gestures were timed, but also whistles, the drumming of fingers on a table, and the sound of walking, calculated to the number of steps.[224]

Numerous devices and motifs with which Meyerhold experimented in earlier work recurred in new variations in *Inspector General*, including fragmentation, collisions of life and lifelessness, doppelgängers, successive and simultaneous juxtaposition, musical scoring of movement and action, framing, and plural perspective. I analyze instances of each in several of the production episodes with the assumption that these analyses sometimes inevitably spill out of the frames of individual episodes and into broader discussions.

The Stage Space: Fragmented Framing

Inspector General's stage composition was one of Meyerhold's most innovative attempts to make the space between performer and spectator unpredictable. Meyerhold's rewriting of Gogol into episodes was visually mirrored in a fragmented space with thirteen sets of identical double doors. These masked a larger pair of doors from which small truck stages emerged. These steeply raked mobile stages were trapezoidal, the downstage edge spanning approximately 14 feet (6 *arshins*), but the upstage edge only 9 (4 *arshins*), prompting a compressed, if not forced, perspective.[225] In some scenes the platforms were crammed with as many as thirty actors, but even smaller groupings looked overcrowded when they shared the space with the enormous mahogany furniture.[226] Due to the steep rake, actors and furniture alike were tilted visibly in the direction of the audience.[227]

For all but four episodes, a platform stage preset with tableaux of characters and furniture glided up to the audience before the scene sprang into action. At the scene's conclusion, it retreated to make way for a second platform on which the next scene was preset. If previously Meyerhold had actors approach the audience, here the entire stage approached the audience. In the context of Meyerhold's earlier work, these truck stages are essentially mobile forestages, while *Inspector*'s many doors are multiple tiny proscenium openings. The sheer quantity of these identically framed doors provoked disorientation, a sense of infinite possibility, and heightened curiosity as to how they would be used.[228]

Episodes 1 (Chmykhov's Letter) and 2 (An Unexpected Affair)

In the opening scene, the town's officials rode up to the audience on the first little stage, frozen. All held long pipes of varying lengths and were surrounded by billowing smoke that, for spectators familiar with Meyerhold's Dapertutto days, recalled the hallucinatory Hoffmann. After two characters commenced a game of checkers,[229] the scene sprang into action. Each gesticulated in riotous, choreographed response to the Mayor's announcement that an inspector general was to visit, fragmenting and echoing the word *revizor* in endless variations.[230] This physical and vocal virtuosity established the production's reliance on the rhythmical grotesque. Most extant photographs

Figure 19. Rehearsal for episode 1 of Gogol's *Inspector General*, dir. Vsevolod Meyerhold, Meyerhold Theatre (1926). Photo by Alexei Temerin. КП 180170/1046. © A. A. Bakhrushin State Central Theatre Museum, Moscow.

of this scene are of its rehearsals, from which we learn that Meyerhold had the actors rehearse in a tiny room no bigger than the truck stages, cultivating the necessary physical precision by constraining the space in which the actors developed their mise-en-scène (figure 19).

Meyerhold collided images of life and lifelessness throughout the production. Many episodes began and ended with *tableaux vivants* that prompted brief uncertainty as to whether or not the scene's figures were alive. He achieved a similar effect through disembodiment and fragmentation. Several actors wore white gloves, one function of which was to make them aware of hand movement so they could eliminate unnecessary gestures.[231] The gloves also allowed Meyerhold to isolate hands from bodies and to multiply them by mirroring them in the polished mahogany surface of the table behind which actors sat.[232] This disembodied multiplication continued in the second episode, "An Unexpected Affair," which featured Bobchinsky and Dobchinsky's retelling of their "discovery" of the inspector. Meyerhold staged this duo as one person split into two: they often interrupted each other and repeated each other's lines, a doubling that was doubled again in the reflection of their hands on the table surface.[233]

Episode 4 (After Penza)

The set for the scene at the local inn where Khlestakov first appears was the only one to be flown in, establishing this location as unique.[234] One audience member referred to this set as a "booth,"[235] evoking associations of *Balaganchik*'s theater-within-a-theater. The inn's curved staircase, which recalled the curve of a forestage, framed characters in individual parades at first entrance. The Mayor's stately descent was undermined by a "truly acrobatic circus number":[236] Dobchinsky tumbling down the stairs only to be swallowed up by a trapdoor, a stunning production moment that Eisenstein dubbed "a mise-*hors*-scène."[237]

Here and throughout the production, Meyerhold presented Khlestakov's inner workings with deliberate transparency. At first entrance, this character was physically all right angles, a bread roll hanging from his jacket pocket instead of a pocket watch. His costume and physicality contrasted with the "officer-in-transit," an invented character inspired by Gogol's *The Gamblers*. This doppelgänger accompanied Khlestakov throughout the play, according to Meyerhold, to serve as a confidant.[238] The officer-in-transit framed Khlestakov in various additional ways, however, by watching the action as member of the audience within the play, aiding Khlestakov in his transformations, and even completing Khlestakov's lines for him. Character in *Inspector* was a fluid thing that allowed multiple selves to coexist. Khlestakov used costume pieces as metaphorical masks with the power to shape how others perceived him.[239] He donned and removed items to change personality as a chameleon changes colors, resulting in an ominous unpredictability that kept the locals in constant terror.

Episodes 3 (The Unicorn) and 5 (Full of Most Tender Love)

Meyerhold echoed these successive character transformations in episode 5. This invented scene, which featured Anna Andreevna, the Mayor's wife (played by Zinaida Raikh, Meyerhold's real wife), was based on one of popular entertainment's favorite tricks: the quick change. As she prepared to meet Khlestakov, she emerged from behind a screen in dress after dress.[240] Dobchinsky watched her the entire time, simultaneously observing and participating in the stage action. He became so distracted by scene's end that he attempted to exit through Anna Andreevna's enormous wardrobe, which occupied the entire rear of the platform.[241]

"The Unicorn," a thematically linked scene (eventually conflated with episode 5), inspired by one of Gogol's early drafts, centered on Anna Andreevna's fantasies about her many suitors. Her fantasy quickly became physicalized: "Officers, officers—under the chairs, in trunks, as chairs themselves"[242] poured out of the furniture and filled the little stage. In a mise-en-scène partly inspired by a Callot etching of cupids,[243] a suitor-in-the-box popped out of the top of her cupboard and presented a bouquet of flowers, upon which the other lovers, all singing to her while strumming imaginary instruments, simultaneously collapsed, one with a gun to his chest.

Episodes 6 (The Procession) and 7 (Behind a Bottle of Tolstobriushka)

In episode 6, Khlestakov and the town officials process to the Mayor's house along a railing that split the full stage into parallel planes. Khlestakov and the officer-in-transit were downstage of this railing, while the town officials were upstage, clustered together "like a bureaucratic centipede" as they moved across the stage.[244]

In episode 7, in which the Mayor and his family entertain an already very drunk Khlestakov, the latter sat nestled next to Anna Andreevna on a sofa of ridiculously exaggerated proportions, especially in comparison to the tiny divan on which the Mayor and his daughter sat crammed. Khlestakov peppered his carefully timed movements with absurd details: lighting a cigar with a candle, eating watermelon with a knife and fork as if it were cake, and placing Anna Andreevna's little finger on a silver spoon to kiss it. In the latter part of this scene, he engaged in a drunken, yet precise dance, during which he "fell into the arms of a servant, righted himself, yelled incoherently about a 700 rouble melon, then stopped, and, raising one leg into the air almost parallel to his body, just stood there like a post."[245]

In this scene, the officer-in-transit became a visual barometer for the audience of Khlestakov's true internal state. Meyerhold staged this in counterpoint. While Khlestakov was seated in a position of honor, the officer-in-transit settled on the edge of the stage, partially obscured from the others by a table, surrounded by enough bottles to get extremely drunk. Khlestakov's intoxication imbued him with a boldness that grew until he was standing on the sofa waving a sword. Simultaneously, the officer was holding himself up, barely able to sit. Khlestakov and his alter ego concluded the episode in the same state, however: collapsed in a drunken stupor, Khlestakov stage left and the officer stage right, while the others tiptoed out en masse (Figure 20).

Episode 9 (Bribes)

The production's most effective—and most famous—use of simultaneous juxtaposition was in the episode called "Bribes." In Meyerhold's production, Gogol's sequential bribery scenes took place all at once, as if Khlestakov were playing a "simultaneous exhibition of chess games" with the town officials.[246] The episode began with the stage entirely bare except for two chairs, stage center, upon which Khlestakov and the officer-in-transit sat with the servant Osip on the floor nearby. In semidarkness, eleven hands knocked on eleven doors, which opened together to reveal eleven white gloves holding

Figure 20. End of episode 7, "Behind a Bottle of Tolstobriushka," *Inspector General*, Meyerhold Theatre (1926). Photo by Alexei Temerin. Laurence Senelick Collection.

white packets of money, thrust forward from the dark doorways (figure 21). Khlestakov's movement became increasingly automaton-like as he took these bribes, while the mechanization of bodies framed in identical proscenium doorways established an image that was critical to the effect of the production's final tableau.

Episode 15 (Universal Embarrassment) and Dumb Show

Though the production was filled with alternations of suspended and frenzied motion, the most extreme example of this was the last episode. In "Universal Embarrassment," the bedlam that ensued after the townsfolk discover that Khlestakov is an impostor was visually reinforced by the placement of the mayor into a straitjacket and the descent of Anna Andreevna into a hysterical stupor. Olga Bokshanovskaia, an attendee at the general rehearsal, described the coup de théâtre that followed:

> And suddenly all the characters pass in a row from one end of the stage to the other, in a kind of frenzied dance, then they cross, still dancing, into the aisle in front of the first row of seats, and meanwhile a canvas drop cloth with

Figure 21. Episode 9, "Bribes," *Inspector General*, Meyerhold Theatre (1926). Photo by Alexei Temerin. КП 180170/910. © A. A. Bakhrushin State Central Theatre Museum, Moscow.

> enormous letters—the gendarme's last line—reels down from above and hides the stage. The actors . . . vanish through the side doors. When the drop has curtained the whole stage, they all issue from under it and run madly along the side aisles of the parterre . . . and disappear into opposite side doors.[247]

The curtain, inscribed with the message that the true inspector had arrived, obscured the stage for long enough for all the live actors to be replaced with wax and papier-mâché effigies of themselves (figure 22). These mannequins of the play's characters were positioned in an arc in front of the doors, frozen in animated poses, marking the play's end, but leaving the audience unsettled. This eerie image accompanied by dead stillness was Meyerhold's most brilliant use of the grotesque. At one point in the planning process, he played with the idea of heightening this extreme contrast between life and death even more by inviting the audience onto the stage after the performance and charging them "a special admission fee to view the panopticon."[248]

"Panopticon" (*panoptikum*) in Russian refers to a waxworks or cabinet of curiosities. Meyerhold stated in a planning rehearsal that the production's "panopticon," Gogol's imperial-period characters, represented symbolically "that the old way of life has died along with the Revolution."[249] The word

Figure 22. Dumb show, *Inspector General*, Meyerhold Theatre (1926). Photo by Alexei Temerin. КП 180170/921. © A. A. Bakhrushin State Central Theatre Museum, Moscow.

also has a second meaning, however: it is a building designed so that all of its internal parts can be viewed simultaneously. This view of every side of an object at once, something that brings Meyerhold's productions philosophically very close to cubism, was essential to *Inspector General*.[250] Meyerhold put the audience in a unique position of omniscience that was palimpsestic as well as panoramic. Not only could they see this bygone world frozen in all its imperial-era variety, they also saw the bribes scene ghosted in the arc of similarly isolated mannequins, and the movement of live bodies, there just a minute before, frozen in these inanimate ones. Although Meyerhold justified the production's political relevance by calling it a criticism of Russian imperial-period society, it was more than this. It was a continued call by Meyerhold for new theatrical forms that defied ossification. Even though Meyerhold's *Inspector General* was populated with "dead souls," it celebrated the theater's ability to generate new life with each new production.

EPILOGUE: A WATERLESS FLOOD

Meyerhold's belief that theater must constantly reinvent itself sparked raging debates, with *Inspector General* at their center, about the role of the director-artist in the Soviet Union. Within the immense body of critical literature that grew up around this production, two articles, one by Vladimir Blium, another by Mikhail Chekhov, illustrate how the prerevolutionary culture of theatrical polemics devolved into a postrevolutionary atmosphere of artistic persecution.

Inspector General opened in 1926, three years after Lenin launched the "Back to Ostrovsky" campaign, a return to both the nineteenth-century realist playwright and to a prerevolutionary cultural past. This contributed to an upsurge in productions of nineteenth-century playwrights, Gogol included. Significantly, 1926 was also the year Stalin came to power. The year lay sandwiched between two other major shaping events in Soviet theater: three years before, in 1923, Glavrepertkom, the state theater censorship bureau, was established, and three years later, in 1929, Commissar of Enlightenment Anatoly Lunacharsky, the most powerful supporter of theatrical pluralism in the 1920s, resigned. In 1926 Meyerhold's theater still received bountiful state funding, but before *Inspector General* even officially opened, Walter Benjamin wrote that the Communist Party had "come out against the production" and that "applause in the theater was restrained . . . perhaps . . . due to the official line more than to the audience's actual reaction."[251]

A well-known face in what Benjamin called the "front against Meyerhold"[252] was Vladimir Blium.[253] In 1920, when Blium was editor of the periodical *Theatrical Herald* (*Vestnik teatra*), he and Meyerhold declared "October in the theater" in order to wage the Revolution anew on the theatrical front. In 1923 Blium became head of the theater and music division of Glavrepertkom. He continued to write, sometimes using reviews to attack productions that had been passed against Glavrepertkom's recommendations by the more artistically forbearing Lunacharsky.

In his review of *Inspector General*, Blium discredits Meyerhold's production by contending that any success it had garnered was a result of unhealthy notoriety. He wrote:

> The failure of the production seemed inevitable: the audience did not come out for this above all painfully dull performance[254]—and there was nothing, therefore, to fear that, in the development of our theater, Meyerhold's *Inspector General* would leave any trace.
>
> Then suddenly everything changed. Lunacharsky took the performance under his temperamental protection. The high, authoritative position of this critic immediately created a sort of "mighty handful" of proponents . . . The theater decided to organize an evening of "debates about *Inspector General*," marked by a scandalous and entirely unseemly appearance by Meyerhold. They created a buzz about the play—and the public is now coming out in droves . . . This is now a direct danger to our theater . . . That is why we must

> not cease to cry out against the hocus-pocus of this harmful production that is corrupting our post-October theater.[255]

In an alarming conflation of Gogol's fantasy with mental illness, Blium painted the "other world" valued by the Russian symbolists, integral to Hoffmann and Gogol, central to Meyerhold's theatrical perspective, as mentally unhealthy.[256] Fantasy was falling out of favor.

Meyerhold was passionately committed to fusing the political revolution with his artistic one. Many of his productions in the 1920s were both politically topical and engaging to audiences in brilliant and unexpected ways. In *Tarelkin's Death* (1922), he hung apples on strings above the audience for them to eat.[257] Actors and motorcycles entered through the theater aisles in *The Last Decisive* (1931) and *Earth Rampant* (1923) respectively. And, to Blium's dismay, Meyerhold staged a debate over *Inspector General*, as he had done for productions in his Dapertutto days.[258] But despite their postrevolutionary ideological content, Meyerhold's productions were never intended to lead viewers to a unified experience. Beginning in the 1920s, he had his laboratory assistants meticulously track up to twenty different audience responses—silence, noise, loud noise, reciting along, singing, coughing, stamping, fidgeting, shouting, weeping, laughing, sighing, commotion, applause, whistling, hissing, leaving the theater, standing, throwing things at the stage, and rushing the stage[259]—indicating that he thought that any of these responses were possible. In this context, the conclusion to Blium's article is enlightening as a sign of things to come: it implies that artistic predictability is a necessary indication of political commitment. Blium writes: "Political indifference, mysticism, and formalism have merged in Meyerhold's *Inspector General* in a disharmonious, incoherent, and *disorganized* din."[260] This was one of the earliest condemnatory uses of the word "formalism," accusations of which later became a death warrant for many, Meyerhold included.[261]

Mikhail Chekhov's diametrically opposed response to *Inspector General* provides insight into Meyerhold's innovations and his detractors' strategies.[262] In Chekhov's view, the production prompted such violent reactions because it shook the foundation of what it means to create:

> Nothing is more difficult than penetrating the true content of a work of art, and nothing is easier than . . . creating the illusion of novelty, breaking apart past forms . . . and assembling new arbitrary figures from their fragments. To really penetrate the content of the creative spirit of an artist, you must be an artist yourself. . . .
>
> Meyerhold . . . realized that to stage *Inspector General* and only *Inspector General* would mean to torment himself with the crippling weight of a vow of silence. *Inspector General* began to grow, swell and crack open. Out of these

> cracks gushed a flood: *Dead Souls*, "Nevsky Prospect," Podkolesin, Poprishchin, the Mayor's wife's daydreams, horrors, laughter, raptures, the screams of ladies, the fears of civil servants . . . From Meyerhold we expected *Inspector General*, but he showed us something else: he showed us a world the full content of which embraced a realm of such magnitude that *Inspector General* is only a fraction of it, only a single note in an entire melody. And we were frightened. We artists realized that Meyerhold was publicly exposing our impotence in dealing with fragments. . . .
>
> We began to look for a poison to give to the one who deprived us of peace, who troubled our artistic conscience. The poison we sought turned out to be right at hand . . . "mysticism" is freely available, a proven, fashionable poison. We knew that a few drops of it, introduced into the creative organism of the artist, placed his life under suspicion in our artistic community. And we did not hesitate to do this with Meyerhold . . . The false artists . . . shouted "mysticism in Meyerhold" instead of shouting "fog and obscurity in us."[263]

It took over a decade, but this poison, introduced by Blium and others, eventually took full effect. The 1938 "Resolution on the Liquidation of the Vs. Meyerhold Theatre" accused the theater of being

> thoroughly bourgeois and formalistic. As a result, to suit ultraleft craftiness and formalistic mannerisms, even classical works of Russian drama were presented by the theater in distorted, anti-artistic guise, with a misinterpretation of their ideological substance . . .
>
> In view of this, the Committee for Artistic Affairs under the Sovnarkom USSR has decreed: . . . the liquidation of the Meyerhold Theater as alien to Soviet art.[264]

Stanislavsky welcomed Meyerhold into his Opera Studio, where the latter worked briefly before being arrested on June 20, 1939.

In one of theater history's greatest tragic ironies, Meyerhold developed a new alter ego in the final weeks of his life, a side effect of his brutal interrogation and torture in Moscow's Lubianka prison. In a two-part appeal to Molotov in January 1940, Meyerhold wrote:

> Immediately after my arrest . . . I was plunged into the deepest depression . . . I began to convince myself that the government felt that the sins I had committed had received insufficient punishment . . . and that I should undergo further punishment, which was now being administered through the agency of the NKVD. "It serves me right," I convinced myself, and that "I" split into two. The one began to search for the "crimes" of the other, and when it failed to find them it began to make them up. In this process my in-

terrogator proved to be a well-experienced assistant, so we set about inventing things together in close collaboration.[265]

On February 2, 1940, Meyerhold was shot in the Military Collegium basement. He officially became a "nonperson" until his sentence was overturned fifteen years later.[266] A director who had so exuberantly celebrated the unquenchable complexity of the creative self suddenly had never existed.

This chapter has dealt relatively little with Meyerhold in relation to his immediate postrevolutionary productions. By no means do I intend to imply that his political fervor was less central to his work than other scholars have claimed. However, a primary focus on the *content*—the political message—of Meyerhold's early Soviet productions has sometimes confined our understanding of his artistic relevance to a specific social and political context, while Meyerhold's theatrical *form*—and with it, his freeing view of the creative process, so eloquently described by Mikhail Chekhov, remains more broadly revolutionary.

Returning briefly to the article with which this chapter began, Meyerhold was critical of spectators at the First Studio's *Cricket on the Hearth* because they were passive: they accepted the images, conventions, and content offered to them without question or thought. What is clear from Meyerhold's enthusiasm for the brouhahas at which Dapertutto made public appearances and the gleeful nose-thumbing tone of many *LTA* articles is that he ultimately wanted something very simple: for artist-makers and audience-makers to re-create the theater together with each new performance. He despised clichés—even (or especially) clichéd versions of his own conventions that sprang up like mushrooms in productions across the nation and far beyond its borders—because for him to reproduce a cliché meant not to think or make.

Even though Meyerhold's most controversial banned productions, Erdman's *The Suicide* and Tretiakov's *I Want a Baby*, featured content that complicated rather than toed the party line, for Stalin, the most dangerous problem with Meyerhold's theater was that it created makers instead of followers. Meyerhold's productions refracted audience thought into provocative colors that scattered too unpredictably. Stalin, on the other hand, preferred a return to theater as a mirror—the rose-tinted mirror of socialist realism, which reflected an ideologically conformist world that Stalin promoted as real and mandated from 1934 until his death. In act 1 of *Mystery-Bouffe* (1918 first version, 1921 second version), the first revolutionary play Meyerhold staged, Vladimir Mayakovsky describes the Revolution as a waterless flood sweeping the world. Like the Revolution, the waterless flood of Meyerhold's provocative experiments, productions, and publications—his "Meyerholdiana"—awakened the fantasy of those who encountered it in far too many ways to be contained.

Chapter Two

Tairov-Celionati: Mime-Drama and Kaleidoscopic Commedia

PROLOGUE/POLEMIC: "THE DUSK OF *THE DAWNS*"

In January 1921, Alexander Iakovlevich Tairov (né Kornblit, 1885–1950) scathingly criticized Vsevolod Meyerhold's production of Émile Verhaeren's *The Dawns*, which opened in late 1920 to commemorate the third anniversary of the October Revolution. In a lecture called "The Dusk of *The Dawns*," Tairov articulated his views on the role of theater and of the actor in postrevolutionary Russia:

> [*The Dawns*] was staged not as a theatrical presentation, but as a rally. Here the actor was deprived of the opportunity to create his own character. . . . instead of a performer [Meyerhold] should have put an agitator on the stage. This would have been only logical and twice as effective, laying bare, first of all, the theatrically reactionary essence of this pointless undertaking and eliminating the intolerable falsity that became the leitmotif of this entire quasi-theatrical production.[1]

In addition to hinting at the rift between the two directors that had intensified after their failed collaboration on Claudel's *The Exchange* in 1918,[2] Tairov's criticism of Meyerhold's production reveals the widening gap between the two directors' views on the purpose of theater in the wake of the Revolution. Meyerhold famously promoted "October in the theater" after becoming head of the Theatre Department of Narkompros (the Commissariat of Enlightenment) in the fall of 1920, after which he attempted to liquidate all the state academic theaters, of which Tairov's Moscow Kamerny Theatre was one, and to require that all theaters stage revolutionary content using the radical forms of "cubism, futurism and suprematism."[3] Although Tairov was a pioneer of theatrical cubism—Kamerny artists introduced cubism to the Russian stage—he spent his immediate postrevolutionary years defending theater as an autonomous art form that should express universal truths and experiences rather than being a vehicle for topical political content, declaring, "A propagandist theatre after a revolution is like mustard after a meal."[4]

Tairov did not oppose the political overthrow. He welcomed the opportunities it provided for creative freedom, especially in the brief but entirely censorship-free period that followed the 1917 February Revolution. Alisa Koonen, Kamerny lead actress and Tairov's future wife,[5] recalled those days "as a time of deep, free breathing and great spiritual uplift."[6] Though Tairov was largely apolitical, apart from having been in a Marxist club as a student, he believed himself to be conducting an artistic revolution that paralleled the political one. In his lecture on *The Dawns* he stated, "The Kamerny Theatre is truly revolutionary. . . . Of course it is not poster revolutionary, of course it is not agitationally revolutionary, of course it is not politically revolutionary, but it is revolutionary in its theatrical essence."[7]

In a 1917 pamphlet-manifesto, *Proclamation of an Artist*, Tairov wrote about the freedom he hoped the Revolution would provide artists to express individual creative responses to the world. For him, this included a striving toward beauty to be shared with all lovers of art. He argued that there was therefore no need for an exclusively proletarian theater:

> Since the end of March, posters have begun to appear on the streets about special performances and concerts "for the people," while a whole series of speeches have discussed the question of what kind of art the people can understand, what kind of art the people need. . . . Is art really a train with sleeper cars for the "clean" public and with heated freight cars for the people?
>
> No. . . . Art is for all those in whose souls there is either a conscious or unconscious thirst for beauty. Everything that is created with human talent, everything that bears the true stamp of creativity, all this is included in the notion of *art as such*—all this and only this is the object of the democratization of art.[8]

One of the central debates in postrevolutionary theater was how it should serve the proletariat. Within the wide variety of opinions, two main viewpoints emerged: the theatrical Left advocated a rejection of the bourgeois past in favor of proletarian-generated forms using the aesthetics of the avant-garde, while others, Lenin among them, felt that peasants and workers should be elevated to the heights of the greatest achievements of the past.

Anatoly Lunacharsky was the head of the Commissariat of Enlightenment, the Soviet organization responsible for bringing education and enlightenment (the Russian word *prosveshchenie* has both meanings) to the predominantly illiterate Russian population through schooling and the arts. He subsidized Proletkult, a proletarian arts organization comprised of hundreds of amateur groups, and the futurists, despite his doubts about their extreme artistic methods. However, he supported traditional theaters with equal vigor and larger subsidies, believing that "the proletarian theatre would be created through . . . mastery and development of traditional forms" rather than "through rejection of the past."[9] It was his hope that established theaters would eventually choose to incorporate revolutionary content into their repertoires voluntarily.

Tairov did not agree entirely with Lunacharsky or with the theatrical Left. He believed that theater freed by a revolution should remain free to develop organically and autonomously and that it therefore could not serve things external to it: literature, tradition, or politics. Theater was instead to be an art form through which human beings could express and experience the joy of creation. It could achieve this by developing virtuosity, by nurturing the central creative role of the actor-maker, by using techniques from professional popular entertainments, and by creating performances that provided spiritual sustenance for their audiences.

Several months before Meyerhold's "October in the theater" declaration intensified the ongoing debate between artistic leftists and traditionalists, Tairov staged one of the Kamerny's landmark productions, *Princess Brambilla: A Kamerny Theatre Capriccio after Hoffmann*, described by one viewer as "one of the most brilliant spectacles ever seen."[10] *Brambilla*, a theatrical refraction of E. T. A. Hoffmann's 1818 novella, premiered at the Kamerny on May 4, 1920, marking the culmination of more than a decade of intense Russian theatrical interest in the German writer and in the commedia dell'arte world his novella refracted. Tairov used Hoffmann, a writer temporally and physically distant from Russia, to clarify and comment on the Kamerny's own theatrical agenda in the context of the uncertain future of Soviet theater. This overt commentary is especially apparent in the Kamerny's *Brambilla* promptbook, which provides an invaluable window into the production's intellectual foundations.[11] Using the self-referential devices of romantic irony, this performance text placed the principles most central to the Kamerny's theatrical views on the lips of the actors as they performed their roles. As theory was introduced in the promptbook, it was physicalized in production. As the characters discussed how the theater should be revolutionized, the actors showed that revolution in progress, thus jubilantly declaring the Kamerny's vital role in defining the theater of the future.

This chapter traces the Moscow Kamerny Theatre's artistic path in its early years, focusing on refractions of Hoffmann that supported the Kamerny's artistic aims: to create a virtuosic actor-centered theater that focused on pantomime, commedia, and improvisation. This chapter's "interludes" include Tairov's pre-Kamerny production of Schnitzler's *Pierrette's Veil* (1913), which illuminates Tairov's pioneering approach to what he called "mime-drama," and a detailed analysis of *Princess Brambilla* at the Kamerny. The chapter concludes with

Figure 23. Photo portrait of Alexander Iakovlevich Tairov (né Kornblit, 1885–1950). Laurence Senelick Collection.

a look forward to the Kamerny's ongoing experiments with pantomime and self-referentiality, international influence, and continued contemporary relevance.

MIME-DRAMA AND THE NEW THEATER

Like many of his generation, Tairov (figure 23) began by studying law, but found himself irresistibly drawn to the theater. In 1906, after performing as an actor in various provincial and amateur theaters in his native Ukraine, Tairov auditioned for and was hired by Vera Komissarzhevskaia during her theater's tour to Kiev. That same year, the star actress appointed a new director: Meyerhold. Tairov played small roles in several of Meyerhold's productions, including the Masker in Blue in *Balaganchik*. He felt, however, that Meyerhold had "insufficient regard for the actor" and was "at the mercy of the scenic artist"[12] and left Komissarzhevskaia's to join the Peredvizhnoi (Itinerant) Theatre. At the Peredvizhnoi, Tairov directed his first production, *Hamlet*, and began to link music with the actor's physical expressiveness in an *Uncle Vanya* "conducted to uninterrupted musical accompaniment."[13]

In 1913, the year Tairov received his law degree, the Georgian director Konstantin Mardzhanov opened a new theater in Moscow, the Svobodny

(Free) Theatre, the aesthetic mission of which was to explore "synthesized theater" (*sinteticheskii teatr*) that would "do away with the specializing tendency which separated the functions of a singer from those of an actor and placed the dancer in a different company from the acrobat."[14] Mardzhanov was intrigued by Tairov's concept of music and movement as unique conveyers of inner truth and hired him to direct a Schnitzler pantomime, *Pierrette's Veil* (1913), the same pantomime that Meyerhold had refracted in 1910 (as *Columbine's Veil*) into a manifesto for the theatrical grotesque.

Interlude: *Pierrette's Veil* (1913, 1916)

Pierrette's Veil was Tairov's first entirely wordless theatrical production at a time when such experiments were, by all accounts, very new. In Russian/Soviet critic Pavel Markov's recollection:

> There was a great deal of talk about pantomime in those years—talk of which nothing came. Moscow did not know about Meyerhold's studio experiments. At the Svobodny Theatre, Tairov put theory into practice in his own way.
>
> At that time he protested against everyday life on the stage and accused the Moscow Art Theatre of naturalism (though the MAT's break from naturalism had become obvious). He continued to reject the laws of conventionalized theater, in the practice of which he saw impassable aesthetic contradictions. Tairov then boldly proclaimed the art of pantomime, the liberation from literature in the theater, the cultivation of the "synthesized" actor.[15]

In turning to wordless drama, Tairov embarked on a new experimental path that was distinct from both naturalism and conventionalization. With *Pierrette's Veil*, he attempted to rediscover theater's fundamental laws while refracting the pantomime's themes, the actors' internal modes of expression, and the emotional essence of gesture.

As Markov reminds us, Tairov's accusation of the Moscow Art Theatre as naturalistic did not accurately reflect that theater's experiments over the years immediately preceding *Pierrette's Veil*. Tairov was referring, as many have since, to MAT productions of Chekhov, Ibsen, Gorky, and others, which premiered between 1898 and 1904 but remained in the theater's ongoing repertoire. Stanislavsky codirected a conventionalized *Hamlet* with Edward Gordon Craig in 1911[16] but already had been experimenting with symbolism for several years.

In 1908 Stanislavsky and Leopold Sulerzhitsky staged Maeterlinck's symbolist play *The Blue Bird*. The role of Mytyl was played by a young actress, Alisa Koonen, who permanently left the MAT five years later, much to the dismay of Stanislavsky, who saw such departures as acts of personal betrayal. It was Koonen who played Pierrette in *Pierrette's Veil*. The creative collaboration between Tairov and Koonen began rather stormily, but it continued productively for the remainder of their lives: Koonen helped to found the Moscow Kamerny Theatre, became Tairov's lifelong partner in and outside the theater, and, until Stalin liquidated the theater in 1950, was the central performer around whom the Kamerny's repertoire was fundamentally shaped.[17]

Tairov initially sought to distinguish *Pierrette's Veil* from pantomime "in the sense that it is usually understood"[18] by giving it a new name: mime-drama (*mimodrama*). In an unpublished 1913 lecture to the Svobodny actors, he explained the importance of mime-drama for the new theater he was pioneering:

> Firstly, we have dissociated ourselves from pantomime . . . that is, from the kind of theatrical work in which words are replaced with gestures without any apparent necessity and in which the gesture therefore is simply an accidental replacement of the word. This kind of gesture can be called illustrative. It is not an inevitable expression of the actor's emotional experience, but only serves as an illustration of a word or thought that is not spoken out loud but is implied nonetheless . . . Mime-drama is built on entirely different principles . . . Here gesture does not serve as a substitute for the word; it is independent and of independent value. The emotional experience of the actor can be expressed with various forms: in drama it is primarily with words, in mime-drama—with gesture. . . . Correspondingly, pantomime and mime-drama make different use of the music that accompanies them. Whereas in pantomime gestures are determined by the music and are linked in this regard to ballet, in mime-drama the interdependence between music and gesture is deeper, internal.[19]

For Tairov, mime-drama had the potential to circumvent the need for words entirely in favor of making visible the invisible internal workings of the self—thought and emotion—an idea with seeds in symbolism's neo-romantic rejection of the quotidian in favor of deeper planes of existence.

Tairov also identified what he viewed as the broader creative ramifications of mime-drama: a return to actor-centered theater, exemplified by commedia, in which the actor was the "only creator" of the performance and there were "no written plays . . . only a scenario." For Tairov, "mime-drama gives the actor the ability to return to this creative work . . . to become not only the performer of the production but also its author."[20] For Meyerhold, the director was the author of the production, in which the actors were the authors of their roles. Tairov's definition of theater made the actors the central generators of a production. Four years earlier he wrote, "In every art there is one main thing without which that art would be unfathomable: in sculpture—form; in painting—paint; in literature—the word; and in theater—the person. In the actor alone lies the entire essence of theater."[21]

Although *Pierrette's Veil* is a pantomime, Schnitzler wrote it in dialogue in order to reveal the thoughts behind each character's actions. In Dohnányi's score, each line of this movement-dialogue is placed next to the corresponding musical phrase, as in opera. Tairov launched the rehearsal process with Iu. K. Baltrushaitis's Russian translation of Schnitzler's libretto. This straightforward Russian rendition of the German is preserved in Tairov's archive, as is Koonen's copy of the piano score with Russian translations for the first half of the pantomime hand-copied into it above the German.[22] According to Koonen, Tairov wrote these translations in for her before rehearsals began and used them to spark movement that then was developed collaboratively.

Meyerhold and Tairov tried in different ways to free the theater from being an "illustrator of literature."[23] As we have seen, Meyerhold rewrote or restructured most of the works he staged. In many cases, extant primary sources record how. Though abundant rehearsal notes and promptbooks for many of Tairov's productions exist, he did not always document how he developed the mise-en-scène during rehearsal. This seems to be the case with *Pierrette's Veil*, probably because Tairov proposed a process of mutual discovery rather than passed-down gesture, directorial scoring, or other working methods then in use. As he told the actors, "We will search for the movement and the gestures . . . during the working process . . . It is a sizeable and difficult task. We will search together."[24]

Tairov discouraged the actors from illustrating the pantomime's words, story, or music. In initial rehearsals with Krechetov, who played Pierrot, Tairov warned: "Under no circumstances are you to use external decorativeness."[25] Instead, they worked to translate emotional impulse into gesture—the inevitable external expression of an internal state. In Tairov's words, mime-drama requires gesture that is "concrete, universalized, and maximally expressive. A gesture should have volume to it; it should be three-dimensional, like a sculpture."[26]

This concept of mime-drama was extremely challenging for Koonen, an actor raised and nurtured at the Moscow Art Theatre, as it was so vastly different from any approach she previously had experienced.[27] Her initial frustration was compounded by the fact that she resented having left the MAT only to work with a completely unknown and relatively untried director. Several pages of her rehearsal notes preserve traces of her struggle to accustom herself to this new way of working, which focused on the emotional and the physical over the psychological. Her notes document moments where she was to convey specific emotions ("horror," "relief," "fear") and chart the sequence of her actions for the first scene in Pierrot's room, noting the corresponding measures in the musical score.[28] Her dawning realization of the potential of this working method became clear in the rehearsals for the final scene, Pierrette's death dance. Although her rehearsal notes for this scene are somewhat telegraphic, she describes the choreography in detail in her memoirs:[29]

> Harlequin, having overtaken Pierrette in Pierrot's attic, locks her in with her dead lover. In terror, Pierrette tries to escape, to break open the door. The door won't give. She throws herself toward the window, jumps up on the windowsill, holding on to its frame, beating like a bird. Then Pierrette's mad scene begins. She thinks that Pierrot is sleeping; she quietly goes up to him, tries to wake him, tenderly strokes his face, and touches his cheek with hers. The music changes. Pierrette tries to lift Pierrot from the chair, wants to dance with him, and steps in a circle, but the lifeless body falls to her feet. In terror, like one hunted, she hides in the corner and then rushes about the room. Finally, in a last surge of desperation, she throws herself onto Pierrot and dies.[30]

In Koonen's recollection, Tairov helped her refine the movement for this scene into precise, discrete moments:

> The door won't give. That's right. You raise your head. Glance at Pierrot. Horror. You freeze. Hold four beats. You hear the change in the rhythm? Rush to the window. Climb onto the windowsill. This is your last hope. A crescendo in the music. You hear it? That is your internal cry. Feel it: behind your back is the dead Pierrot. Hold on to the frame. With despairing movements. Try to pull it toward you. Your hands as tense as strings. That's right. Good.[31]

This scene became one of the most lauded in the production. It also marked an artistic turning point for Koonen. One of the most highly acclaimed actresses of the Soviet period, Koonen became famous for her monumental yet precise physical expression of profound emotional content.

To stage an experimental wordless pantomime at a theater that relied on ticket sales was also a new thing. Koonen recalls that Mardzhanov had difficulty getting financial backing for a production that did not have words, songs, or dances in a familiar, expected sense.[32] When rehearsals were far enough along, the cast performed without makeup, costumes, or sets for an invited audience that included a potential sponsor who previously had been skeptical about the potential of wordless drama. This sponsor, Sukhodolskaia, was deeply moved by their performance and agreed to fund the costumes and scenery.[33]

Each aspect of the final production, which opened on November 4, 1913, placed the actor at its center. For instance, Anatoly Arapov designed largely monochromatic scenery—gray and silver—in order to foreground the bodies of the actors. Tairov described Arapov's design as follows:

> Act 1: Pierrot's room. Stern lines of gray walls, gray fabric curtains, two simple armchairs, also gray, a table, and the only bright patch: a red tablecloth on the table. On the upstage plane is an enormous attic window. Outside the window flashes of carnival fires are reflected. Act 2: A room in the house of the wealthy Harlequin. The wedding ball. The stage is divided into two planes connected with broad steps. On the upstage plane is the orchestra . . . downstage is the crowd of guests. Columns of dark silver, sprays of silver on the rich brocade costumes of the guests. With the help of moving lights, all this should create the impression of a whirlwind, as if a malicious silver blizzard is on the stage. Act 3: Pierrot's garret again. But it should look different . . . Here an important role will be played by light, with which we will try to create the tragic atmosphere of this act.[34]

Tairov staged the action of the act 2 wedding ball on three spatial planes: the musicians were far upstage against the silver background; vividly attired wedding guests danced on the broad steps; and the wrathful Harlequin, clad in black with a checkered vest that hinted at his commedia ancestors, fumed further downstage about his absent bride.[35] This scene was highly acclaimed. In the words of one reviewer, "its brightly-multicolored brocade costumes against a background scenery of antique silver, with its intense music and striking groupings of dancers, provoke applause up until the very moment the curtain falls."[36] Audiences found Arapov's use of color to be especially effective, though theater entrepreneur Sergei Mamontov complained that it was "regrettable that the silver columns dance along with the guests," as they were "poorly attached."[37]

At the center of the actor-centered production was Koonen. If Meyerhold's *Columbine* had made Pierrot the pantomime's focus, here the production's emotional nucleus was Pierrette. This is clear from Koonen's description of her rehearsal process with Tairov, but also from a libretto summary published in the newspaper *Theater* (*Teatr*) (see appendix C), in which the ball scene description is structured around Pierrette's emotional response to the pantomime's horrific events (figure 24):

> The festivities began long ago, but Pierrette is missing. But lo, she comes, barely concealing the horror she has experienced; still with the sight of death in her eyes, she returns to the sober, humdrum world where she must live by

Figure 24. Finale of act 2 wedding ball scene in Schnitzler/Dohnányi's *Pierrette's Veil*, dir. Alexander Tairov, Moscow Kamerny Theatre (c. 1916). Russian State Archive of Literature and Art, f. 2328, op. 1, ed. khr. 342: 10.

> Harlequin's side. With difficulty she manages to mollify her groom's anger and draw him into the whirlwind of dance. But before Pierrette's stunned soul rises the shade of the dead Pierrot. Perplexed by her alarm and fear, Harlequin suddenly notices that she is not wearing a veil. In a new burst of rage, he showers Pierrette with reproaches, questions, and threats. In the now whirling crowd, the shade of Pierrot again appears to her.[38]

This focus on Pierrette is significant for two reasons: it is the only instance in this book of a woman becoming the embodying figure of the romantic conflict between the "sober, humdrum world" and the truer realm of the individual self. It also establishes a lifelong theme in the joint work of Koonen and Tairov, in which Koonen was the central figure in a repertoire chosen around strong heroines—Sakuntala, Juliet, Antigone, Phaedra, Joan of Arc, Adrienne Lecouvreur, and many others. Meyerhold referred to himself as a production author; Koonen became the author of a repertoire.

Spectators were for the most part complementary of Koonen's Pierrette, though some found her acting too psychological and "not always in time to the music."[39] One viewer argued that Chabrov (Harlequin) and Krechetov (Pierrot) were, through physical stylization, able to get closer than she "to the essence of pantomime, the aim of which is not to illustrate the word . . . but to *replace* it entirely."[40] Mamontov noted, however, that Koonen's performance had an honest emotional force to it, that she "splendidly controls her facial expressions: her naive eyes wide with terror remain in the spectator's memory for a long time."[41] Another observed, "The flash of despair and anger that seizes the bridegroom, the appearance of Pierrette . . . this forced dance and terrible vision of the phantom—the dead Pierrot—all this is played excellently,"[42] concluding that the final scene, "so terrifying, so full of despair and fear of death, is very strongly realized by Miss Koonen."[43]

Tairov's production began with a prologue in which a sibyl warns Pierrot and Pierrette of the tragic fate that is to play out in the pantomime. This prologue, written by Baltrushaitis, the pantomime's translator, was by all accounts unsuccessful. In Bonch-Tomashevsky's uncomplimentary evaluation, the pantomime as framed by this prologue "resembles a diamond sewn up in a bag of elephant hide."[44] Tairov used this introductory framing device very differently than Meyerhold, whose frames prompt disorienting, self-multiplying worlds. As Clayton notes, *Pierrette's Veil*'s prologue "has the effect of strengthening the metaphysical connotations of the play. It also has the effect of placing the events of the play, which are . . . specific as to time period and place, in a timeless context, symbolized by the ancient, mythical figure of the sibyl."[45] Many of Tairov's subsequent productions juxtaposed the universal and the specific in similar ways.

Unsurprisingly, several reviewers contrasted Tairov's *Pierrette* with Meyerhold's *Columbine*, but also with *Balaganchik*. Engel called Dohnányi's terrifying *Schnellpolka*, played on broken instruments, "nightmarish" and "Hoffmannian."[46] Bornyi contrasted the conventionalized character and emotion of *Balaganchik*, in which a clown "bleeds" cranberry juice, with this production, which converted commedia masks into "authentic people, here everything is 'for real,' everything is in earnest."[47] Another reviewer posited that Tairov's "very successful" production took a middle course between Meyerhold's *Columbine*, which was "fully permeated with the mysterious rays of mysticism" and the quotidian realism of the Viennese original.[48]

Bonch-Tomashevsky's comparative analysis of Tairov's and Meyerhold's pantomimes is the most detailed.[49] He observes that Tairov's staging "is extremely interesting, both because of the pantomime—a desired, but, alas, so infrequent guest on our stage, and because the director has attempted in it to give his original interpretation of 'drama without words.'"[50] He felt, however, that its extreme actor-centered approach resulted in the oversimplification of minor characters, that Koonen's performance played too frequently on the notes of "fear and suffering,"[51] and that the jarring collisions of Meyerhold's grotesque generated a more exciting audience experience than Tairov's "heightening of tragedy."[52]

Despite some criticisms, *Pierrette's Veil* was very well received. Bonch-Tomashevsky deigned it the most successful of the Svobodny's productions.[53] The Kamerny revived *Pierrette's Veil* in 1916, with Koonen again

Figure 25. Pierrette (Alisa Koonen) and Pierrot (Nikolai Tseretelli) in *Pierrette's Veil* (1916), dir. Alexander Tairov, Moscow Kamerny Theatre. Photograph collection of A. B. Chizhov.

playing Pierrette—this time opposite Nikolai Tseretelli as Pierrot—after the young, impoverished troupe unexpectedly had the opportunity to purchase the costumes and settings from the Svobodny's head of costuming[54] (figure 25). It became one of the Kamerny's staple productions. As Koonen recalls, "We, the actors, loved it, and so did Tairov. Audiences loved it. It ran roughly a thousand times."[55] In Worrall's analysis, *Pierrette's Veil* was Tairov's "first exploration of what was to become a permanent theme in his work—the conflict between eternal categories expressed in archetypal terms where living beings become representative carriers of eternal, abstract principles."[56]

As Tairov's first major Meyerholdian refraction, *Pierrette* helped Tairov to define his unique voice as a director. Seven years later, *Princess Brambilla*, Tairov's first production of Meyerhold's beloved Hoffmann, gave Tairov a similar opportunity to celebrate the Kamerny's earned triumphs and to demonstrate his theater's parity in the artistic community of his day. *Brambilla* became a further development of the actor-centered aims with which Tairov first experimented in *Pierrette's Veil*, the major differences being that Tairov and Koonen had since founded a theater of their own and that Tairov had had time to fully train his actors' physical expressiveness. In refracting

Hoffmann's *Brambilla*, Tairov treated well-known sources anew to define and celebrate his own theatricalist poetics.

One other pre-Kamerny production by Tairov deserves brief mention for its playful use of irony. In December 1913 Tairov premiered J. H. Benrimo and G. C. Hazleton's *The Yellow Jacket*. In this play, adapted from a Chinese folk tale, Tairov overlaid Chinese theater conventions with the contemporary Russian theater's call for conventionalization. He used objects such as stools and ladders symbolically (as roads or mountains) in ways that Brecht was not to imagine until his *Lehrstücke* of the late 1920s. As Worrall notes, *The Yellow Jacket* also used framing characters similar to Meyerhold's forestage servants:

> The props man acted as a kind of silent executant, instigating the changes and transformations and facilitating the development of the action, scattering confetti to suggest a snowstorm, holding out a stick to represent a door, creating the illusion of a boat journey and raising a lighted candle in a hoop on a stick to suggest moonlight.[57]

This production, in addition to Meyerhold's *Three Oranges*, was to be an important aesthetic source for Vakhtangov's 1922 *Princess Turandot*, which exuded a similarly playful self-referentiality.[58]

The Moscow Kamerny Theatre

In 1914 Tairov and Koonen founded the Kamerny (Chamber) Theatre in revolt against much of the theater of their day. Koonen recalls Tairov's first lecture to the company, in which the director stated: "Our platform consists of searching for new paths in the theater, of experimenting. Our program will be a struggle. A struggle with the evils that have maimed the theater and led it to a dead end."[59] The theater was active in its search for these new paths: over the course of its 35-year existence, which spanned two world wars, two revolutions, and a civil war, it staged over fifty premieres. It was one of very few theaters with prerevolutionary, theatricalist roots to survive for nearly the entire Stalinist period, though its creative lifeblood was incrementally drained away beginning in the late 1920s, a process that was accelerated after the theater's inadvertently politically disastrous production of Demian Bedny's *Epic Heroes* (*Bogatyri*, 1936).

The Kamerny's premiere production was Kalidasa's Sanskrit drama *Sakuntala*, translated by poet Konstantin Balmont; like *Pierrette's Veil, Sakuntala* provided Koonen with a strong leading role. Tairov later credited Koonen with much of the theater's success, stating that without her "crystallization of a new craft of acting in the fiery conquest of obsolete methods," his directorial ideas could never have been implemented.[60] Pavel Kuznetsov's designs for *Sakuntala* emphasized the beauty of the expressive human body in motion: the actors were "half-naked and painted with body paint."[61] In Worrall's analysis: "At a time when pessimism was very fashionable, especially in the Russian theater, Tairov strove to assert the possibility of a different, very real and glorious world in which beauty and human wisdom reigned triumphant."[62]

Another premiere two years later illuminates Tairov's experiments with framing space, but to different ends than Meyerhold had in *Three Oranges* and elsewhere. In Annensky's *Famira Kifared* (*Thamyris the Cithara Player*), a production made famous by Alexandra Exter's constructivist designs, Exter and Tairov explored "sculptural form" in costuming and the use of multiple stage levels that were, as in Adolphe Appia's work,[63] intended to provide a rhythmical keyboard upon which the actors' bodies could play.

Although the Kamerny's repertoire danced between many different playwrights, styles, genres, and nations—it was one of the most international of its day—the actor was at its center. Tairov advocated for theater that would rely not on literature or on painting but on the creativity of the master actor, "someone armed with rhythmical and musical sensibility and capable of handling all dramatic genres from tragedy to operetta and pantomime."[64] He thought of his ideal performer as an "Über-actor," partly in response to Craig but more so against Meyerhold.[65]

Tairov also continued to work toward synthesized theater, toward a visually stunning *Gesamtkunstwerk* of forms that previously had been considered separate disciplines: painting, sculpture, music, opera, literature, pantomime, commedia, and dance. Tairov achieved synthesis through a consistent emphasis on beauty and musical rhythm as unifying principles. He emphasized graceful agility to the point where Meyerhold, in the ongoing polemic between the two directors, accused the Kamerny "dandies" of excessive balletic prancing in their attempts to achieve expressive movement.[66]

Tairov divided theater into two basic genres, the harlequinade and the mystery, thus deliberately redirecting the historical focus on comedy and tragedy. These contrasting genres represented complementary theatrical poles in which "the joy of laughter is provided by the harlequinade, and the joy of transformation is provided by the mystery play."[67] He typically sought to balance this theatrical yin-yang by staging one of each genre per season. In keeping with his synthesized theater experiments, he worked increasingly with mixed genres beginning in the 1920s, but he retained an interest in complimentary binaries and theatrical joy for his entire career.

Tairov's work responded directly to the theater of his day. Not only did he frequently give speeches and publish articles about his work and artistic aims, he developed his own productions of plays that recently had been mounted elsewhere, as we have seen with *Pierrette's Veil*. The Kamerny staged Wilde's *Salomé* (1917) in partial response to Nikolai Evreinov's and Max Reinhardt's productions[68] and Ostrovsky's *The Storm* (1924) in polemical reply to Meyerhold's *Forest* (1924).[69] *Brambilla* provided a similar opportunity for Tairov to stage his theatrical views in response to others.

INTERLUDE: *PRINCESS BRAMBILLA*: A KAMERNY CAPRICCIO AFTER HOFFMANN (1920)

By 1920, *Princess Brambilla* had long been part of the Russian modernist debate over theatrical reform.[70] In the wake of the 1915 Russian translation of *Brambilla*, a fierce polemic developed between *World of Art* journal literary editor Dmitry Filosofov and the editors of Meyerhold's journal *Love for Three Oranges* over the tale's merits and appropriate ways in which to work in Hoffmann's manner. Possibly in response to this debate, Tairov commissioned a dramatic adaptation of Hoffmann's tale; this 1915 version by L. Krasovsky with a verse epilogue by P. Antokolsky became the foundation for the Kamerny's 1920 production.

For several years, Tairov delayed staging *Brambilla*, however, primarily because he felt the young and inexperienced troupe did not yet have physical skills equal to the movement demands of such a complex undertaking. As described by Tairov, he considered *Brambilla* each time the next year's season was being planned:

> *Princess Brambilla*, this long-standing dream of the Kamerny Theatre, was in the theater's works for more than five years. This does not mean that we rehearsed the play for five years . . . it means that five years ago we started planning *Princess Brambilla* . . . that for five years we did not dare to stage it, because we could not say . . . with the pure conscience of an artist, that we had found the means whereby we could create it.[71]

Many of the Kamerny productions staged during this period prepared the company for *Brambilla*. In *Famira Kifared*, as in *Pierrette's Veil*, the Kamerny attempted to "silence the incessant sound of words, so that words, both now and in the future, will give way to gesture, which has the same right to primacy in the theater as does the word."[72] The Kamerny developed this more fully in its continued experiments with pantomime, most notably in Lothar's *King Harlequin* (1917), which Tairov viewed as preparation for *Brambilla* and which similarly cultivated "gestures born of the freedom and joy of the human body."[73]

At the end of 1920, by which time the troupe had staged *Adrienne Lecouvreur*, which solidified Koonen's reputation as the premier tragedienne of the Russian stage, and *Princess Brambilla*, which demonstrated the virtuosity of the Kamerny's *corps de drame*,[74] Tairov declared that "the first period of the Kamerny Theatre, *the period of seeking its own path, has ended.*"[75] Significantly, it was at this point that Tairov published his only book-length theoretical treatise, *Notes of a Director* (1921). Hoffmann's calls in *Princess Brambilla* for theatrical rejuvenation, for the eradication of artistic mediocrity, for an actor-centered theater based on improvisation, and for theater as a prism through which to interpret the world found particular relevance in the Kamerny's celebratory production.

Hoffmann's Capriccio

Hoffmann's *Princess Brambilla: A Capriccio after Jacques Callot* (1820) comprises three artfully interwoven stories that depict allegorically how the theater should be rejuvenated. The central tale focuses on Giglio Fava, who, though he is a popular matinee idol, is a vain and uninspired tragic actor. As he searches for his doppelgänger and truer self, Prince Cornelio Chiaperri, who metaphorically represents commedia, Giglio is guided through the bewildering twists and turns of the Roman *carnevale* by the benevolent charlatan Celionati. At Celionati's prompting, Giglio wears a series of exaggerated costumes à la Callot that help him recognize his truer self. Giglio is in love with two women, a humble seamstress named Giacinta Soardi and Princess Brambilla, who turn out to be one and the same. His commedia self vanquishes his hack-actor self in a duel, the details for which are drawn from one of Callot's *Balli di Sfessania* (see figure 3). Finally, after gazing into the mirror of Urdar, a metaphor for the theater, Giglio and Giacinta realize that they have become a theatrical prince and princess, having finally discovered the true theater—commedia—and their genuine artistic selves.

Parallel to this parable of Hoffmann's vision for the theater of his day is an indirect re-creation of the battle between Carlo Gozzi and Pietro Chiari. Gozzi's other major rival, Carlo Goldoni, is not mentioned directly, but Chiari figures in the novella as a hack playwright who overstuffs Giglio's gluttonous matinee-idol belly with the indigestible roles of insipid plays, an intertextual reference by Hoffmann to *Love of Three Oranges*, in which Fata Morgana tries to poison Prince Tartaglia's food by lacing it with Chiari's Martellian verse. Gozzi is also featured indirectly in frequent mentions of his *fiabe*, which form the basis for the repertoire at Giglio and Giacinta's new theater.

As is typical of Hoffmann, the novella contains a third tale that interweaves with these parallel narratives. In it the charlatan Celionati tells a group of German students a story about the kingdom of Urdargarten. At first the account of the hopelessly unhappy King Ophioch and the disturbingly merry Queen Liris seems unrelated to the main plot. At story's end, however, the mage Hermod transforms a magical prism into the spring of Urdar, which fills the mirror-clear lake of Urdar, into which the king and queen gaze and are freed by seeing their true selves reflected for the first time. At the end of *Brambilla*, the reader realizes that Hoffmann views the theater as a mirror made by the prism of fantasy, which clarifies through distortion and without which we cannot understand ourselves or the reality that lies beyond the everyday. *Brambilla*'s narrative style is indirect, often deliberately disorienting, re-creating in the reader the confusion Giglio feels as he navigates multiple realities. In keeping with Hoffmann's description of the work as a capriccio, many of the events are stream of consciousness and improbable, such as the story of Prince Cornelio, who was born small enough to fit inside a candy box.

The charlatan Celionati—actually Prince Bastianello di Pistoja in disguise—invisibly controls the lives of Giglio, Giacinta, and their alternate selves. He is a kapellmeister, a corporeal manifestation of fate, and Giglio's puppetmaster: the tale repeatedly refers to Giglio's matinee-idol self as an empty puppet. Celionati has the power to alter the vision of characters in the story, making it possible for them to see miracles invisible to the naked eye. He sells Giglio magic spectacles to help him find his princess and seems to control the phantasmagorical appearances of Brambilla and her royal entourage. He also keeps Giglio's vision clouded until the new Giglio and Giacinta recognize themselves in the mirror of Urdar.

Hoffmann's *Brambilla* operates on multiple levels, then: as a literary refraction of Callot's etchings; as a fairy-tale allegory for Hoffmann's proposed process for theatrical reform; as a nostalgic look back to an idealized past when commedia reigned; and as a philosophical treatise on the purpose of theater and its potential. *Brambilla*'s leitmotifs—commedia as the true theater, the actor's search for a more creative approach to character, refracted and manipulated vision, the false self confronted by the true self, and the presence of omniscient forces that orchestrate the action—each were central to the Kamerny's capriccio.

The Celionati of the Kamerny

As with Meyerhold's Kapellmeister in *Columbine's Veil*, Celionati had a special symbolic significance in the Kamerny's *Brambilla*. Tairov never adopted a Hoffmannian pseudonym; Tairov was already an assumed surname that replaced the overtly Jewish "Kornblit" he inherited from his assimilated Jewish father. Yet he had much in common with *Brambilla*'s benevolent charlatan, who helps actors to discover their true selves. Sergei Ignatov, who was not involved in the original production but who joined the Kamerny literary board the year after it opened, hinted at this connection between Tairov and Celionati: "With *Princess Brambilla*, Hoffmann affirms the art of the theater as something autonomous, as a fully independent type of creative work . . . Perhaps even now we should seek out a charlatan Celionati, who would lead us . . . to this idea, to its full, conclusive affirmation."[76] Ignatov similarly noted a resemblance "between Giglio Fava and the Kamerny Theatre."[77] Tairov-Celionati was committed to Hoffmann's view of theater as an autonomous art form and to nurturing and sustaining the Kamerny actors, many of whom remained members of the theater for their entire careers.

There were significant differences between Tairov and Meyerhold that extended beyond the fierce public disagreements like the one with which this chapter began, yet both had an extensive fascination with Hoffmann. Both were drawn to Hoffmann's altered, subjective perspective, but to different ends. Meyerhold focused on self-referentiality, framing, and the grotesque. Tairov sought virtuosity, synthesis, and a resultant joy. If Meyerhold used Hoffmannian distortion to create jarring, dissonant emotional effects, Tairov used it to create unity, albeit a unity that was whirling and swift. In *Princess Brambilla*, one distortion melted into another as in a phantasmagoria, one of Tairov's favorite descriptors for the visual impression he sought. Interestingly, though *Brambilla* itself delighted in multiple frames—plays-within-plays, Celionati as a framing character, doubles that duel one another—Tairov's productions rarely crossed over into the space of the audience, preferring to enclose the fictional world generated by the Kamerny's actor-creators. Within the magical confines of the proscenium frame, *Brambilla* emphasized celebration, escape from the turmoil of the Russian Civil War (1918–21), and a joyful carnival atmosphere that contrasted sharply with life outside the theater.

The *Brambilla* Promptbook

Previous scholarship on the Kamerny's *Brambilla* has discussed the production largely in aesthetic terms. This is to be expected, given the emphasis Tairov himself placed on theater's artistic goals. Clayton, Torda, and Worrall each have vividly described the design, movement and theatrical integration of pantomime and commedia-inspired techniques.[78] *Brambilla*'s significance extends, however, beyond its ability to entertain full houses with stunning theatrical fireworks. Although many of the Kamerny's early productions, ranging from Wilde's *Salomé* to Scribe's *Adrienne Lecouvreur*, had similar aims in terms of celebrating theatrical theater, emotional gesture, and the virtuosic Über-actor, *Brambilla* was an important part of the polemic regarding the place of theater—and of the Kamerny specifically—in the new Russia. It is a fascinating example of performance as theory, a staged precursor to the publication of Tairov's *Notes of a Director* the following year.

Throughout his career, Tairov advocated repeatedly for theater as an independent art form, arguing in *Notes* that the theater has no business trying to reflect plays faithfully. He proposed that theater should move away from dramatic literature altogether, that its inherent, autonomous mission is to "create *its own, new work of art to be valued in and of itself*."[79] He therefore preferred to work with fiction rather than dramatic literature, feeling that the latter was "too confining for our scenic constructions." In this early stage in the Kamerny's life, he planned to use works by "geniuses" like Hoffmann as malleable raw material until his actors were skilled enough to create autonomously.[80] Subsequent Kamerny adaptations from literature or film include, among others, Hoffmann's *Signor Formica* (1922), Chesterton's *The Man Who Was Thursday* (1923), *Rosita* (1926, an adaptation of a Mary Pickford film), *Egyptian Nights* (1934, an adaptation of Pushkin's, Shakespeare's, and Shaw's versions of the Antony and Cleopatra story), and an unrealized *Eugene Onegin* (1936), written for the Pushkin death jubilee.[81] Although by the end of his career Tairov had staged more dramas than adaptations, each play in the largely foreign repertoire of the Kamerny's first two decades was, to some degree, a refraction, since the Kamerny commissioned its own translations.

Tairov approached *Brambilla* as a capriccio for actors. In a lecture on *Brambilla* he stated:

> There are no corresponding plays in the extant dramatic literature suitable for synthesized theatrical construction, which merges elements of the Harlequinade, tragedy, operetta, pantomime, and circus, refracted through the modern soul of the actor . . .
>
> Therefore we create them ourselves, using Hoffmann for the time being, for in his unbridled fantasticality we find a wealth of material that rhythmically corresponds to our active aspirations.
>
> But, in "distorting" Hoffmann, that is, in theatrically transforming him, we . . . create a great deal ourselves . . . This is why we have called our production of *Princess Brambilla* a Kamerny Theatre capriccio.[82]

Well into *Brambilla*'s run, one reviewer reflected on this use of the capriccio as a model for creation:

> As Hoffmann built his capriccio on the basis of Callot's drawings, interpreting [refracting] them in the context of literature, the theater built its theatri-

> cal capriccio in precisely the same way, interpreting the Hoffmann work in the context of the theater. As a result we can speak of three different works of art that may be congenerous in their basic concept but are entirely different in their realization, based on the embodying art form of each—Callot's drawings, Hoffmann's capriccio, and the capriccio of the Kamerny Theatre.[83]

In Tairov's words, "This Kamerny Theatre capriccio is a capriccio to the glory of Hoffmann, for his soul is in it . . . the soul of a phantasmagoria that we have constructed in a specifically theatrical way."[84]

Koonen, who did not perform in *Brambilla*, asserts in her memoirs that there was no script for the production, only a scenario.[85] Her misremembering most likely reflects the company's free manner of working with Krasovsky and Antokolsky's fully scripted play. There are two extant versions of this dramatic adaptation. The 1920 production promptbook (hereafter called the RGALI promptbook after its holding archive), which is heavily annotated with handwritten corrections and cues, provides an invaluable window into the production's intersections of theory and practice.[86] The second version (hereafter called the VTO text after its original holding archive) is a postproduction variant that incorporates many of the handwritten textual changes from the RGALI promptbook. While the VTO text illuminates how the text may have been simplified over the course of *Brambilla*'s rehearsals and run, it omits stage directions and provides less information about the development process. The analysis that follows therefore focuses on the RGALI promptbook. In the performance of *Brambilla*, as this working text reveals, Tairov generated a theatrical world where inspirations from Hoffmann and commedia converged with a vision of an ideal theatrical future in which actors do not only speak, but also dance and tumble; where excellence, improvisation, and theatricality are the assumed ideal; where art explores universal truths through metaphor; and where the audience is immersed in a breathlessly joyful theatrical experience.

In refracting *Brambilla*, Tairov was more interested in interacting with Hoffmann's thematic leitmotifs than in maintaining fidelity to its complex triple plot. The most serious "operation" the Kamerny performed on *Brambilla* was the elimination of the mystical portions of the story; Krasovsky's dramatic version also eliminated Gozzi's theater wars to focus on the Giglio/Giacinta story. As in Hoffmann's source text, the play's structure is cyclical: it begins in a realistic setting, shifts to a phantasmagorical realm, then returns to an improved reality redefined by commedia.[87]

The most significant feature of the RGALI promptbook is its conflation of Hoffmann's proposals for theatrical reform with the Kamerny's. Hoffmann's tale-manifesto proposed that commedia techniques and a subjectively altered view of the world together could engender true theater. In act 2, tableau 1, scene 4 of the Kamerny script, for instance, Celionati advises Giglio how best to find the elusive Brambilla:

> Don't think that you can enchant [Brambilla] with a beautiful costume. On the contrary: the more strange, the more outlandish it is, the sooner you will draw attention to yourself. But most important are the spectacles. Spectacles and a big nose to support them.[88]

This description of Giglio's costume is drawn from Hoffmann's source tale, in turn inspired by Callot's *Balli* (see figures 3, 7, 28). In the Hoffmann and Kamerny capriccios, the spectacles and exaggerated nose become a metaphor for commedia refracted through the fantasy and virtuosity of the actor.

New Ways of Seeing

The theme of distorted vision recurs frequently in *Brambilla*, but it has three major manifestations in the promptbook: Giglio's need for the altered vision the magic spectacles provide; Giglio's real and metaphorical blindness; and the clarity of vision that comes to those who peer into the mirror of Urdar, the distorting mirror of the theater. In each case, the promptbook posits that only through altering an individual's vision can she or he see clearly, that subjective artistic distortion reveals inner truth. The matinee-idol Giglio becomes a metaphor for the modern actor—a polemical statement aimed at Tairov's theatrical contemporaries—and, after his transformation, a metaphor for the actor-creator that the Kamerny cultivated.

Celionati is the first to introduce Giglio to his need for altered vision. Act 2 opens with the charlatan selling snake oil and jars of Adam's tears to the crowd. After Princess Brambilla and her entourage process across the stage, Celionati tells curious onlookers the story of Brambilla and her search for Prince Cornelio Chiaperri. He attempts to sell magic spectacles to aid those who wish to join Brambilla's search. He calls out:

> But don't think you'll be able to detect Prince Chiaperri with your bare eyes, or that you will recognize Princess Brambilla among the masks. <You must also have magic spectacles.> Any buyers? (*The throng rushes to buy the spectacles. They crowd forward and shout. A general scuffle ensues.*)[89]

At first these spectacles seem no different from the charlatan's other hoaxes. Suddenly, though, Celionati reveals himself to Giglio as an omniscient magician who inexplicably knows a great deal about him. Celionati tells him:

> You will not be able to find your dream right away. To do this the noble prince himself must kill the pitiful actor. This is difficult. . . . However take them and try. (*Gives him spectacles.*)[90]

Once Gigolo dons the magic glasses, the walls of the palace suddenly become transparent, allowing him to glimpse the princess inside. Celionati warns Giglio that this charmed vision will only last if he awakens his true artist within, and Giglio's temporary clarity fades.

Giglio is in a fog of clouded vision throughout the play, a blindness through which he experiences fleeting visions such as this one. Most significantly, Giglio is blind to his shortcomings as an actor and to his histrionic regurgitations of crowd-pleasing clichés. He complains haughtily to Celionati:

> GIGLIO: You dare to consider me a bad actor, me, the idol of all Rome?
>
> CELIONATI: . . . This is only your imagination and nothing more . . . True, you sometimes have flashes of inspiration when you have not merely played princes, but when you were acknowledged from without as a prince. An embryonic prince lives in each of us, but not everyone is able to discover it within his soul. Right now you do not play for yourself, but for success, for the crowd, for the fanfare . . . The prince in you has died.[91]

The Kamerny's embryonic prince replaces Hoffmann's candy-box-sized Cornelio, but the message remains the same: true actors cannot play only for applause.

The prism-generated mirror-lake of Urdar finally provides Giglio and Giacinta with permanent clarity. Here the magician Ruffiamonte holds up a mirror, showing them their future theatrical reflection, their potential:

> RUFFIAMONTE: To know yourself is very hard, and not many can do it. But I have a magic mirror that shows a person his real face, reveals to him his true essence. Here it is. Take off your masks and look into it.
>
> GIGLIO AND GIACINTA: (*taking off their masks and looking into the mirror*)
>
> GIGLIO: (*exclaiming joyfully*) Giacinta.
>
> GIACINTA: Giglio.
>
> GIGLIO: Oh, my beautiful dream, my princess.
>
> GIACINTA: Oh, my prince. (*They joyfully look at each other and then throw themselves into each other's arms.*)[92]

After a celebratory pantomime, Giglio and Giacinta assume their rightful roles as improvisatory commedia actors in the local theater—La Scala in the Kamerny production.

Refracted Commedia

If distorted vision allows the artist to recognize true theater, commedia exemplifies what this new theater should be. The RGALI promptbook celebrates commedia's triumph in two ways: Giglio's Callot-inspired costume replaces the matinee-idol costume that merely flatters his vanity, and Giglio is killed in a duel by his own doppelgänger, a physical embodiment of his metaphorical potential as an actor.

At Celionati's prompting, Giglio attends *carnevale* in a costume à la Callot, hoping that he will be noticed by Princess Brambilla. The prompt-book tells us he enters "wearing a long, glued-on nose and enormous spectacles . . . On his head there is a red cap with rooster feathers; at his waist is a broad wooden sword."[93] This is in stark contrast to the costume the still-vain Giglio later chooses for himself. A description in act 3 of Giglio outside Brambilla's palace reads: "In the window stands a gilded cage and in it sits Giglio. He is in a blue and gold caftan, red vest, and yellow trousers, and from a distance is reminiscent of a parrot."[94] Giglio's entrapment in a birdcage as a result of this second costume (which Giglio mistakenly hoped would make him attractive to Brambilla) allows him to realize that only the commedia mask allows him to discover his creative self. As Giglio sits in the cage, having been mistaken for a parrot, he muses:

> Why did I deck myself out in this idiotic costume? Why did I have to part with my dear masquerade costume that caused such a commotion on the Corso? . . . Oh, it's lying there, the poor thing, at home, like a hide that has lost its body. . . . My "self" is lying there without a body, and my body is sitting here deprived of its "self."[95]

Giglio finally understands that the costume, in Tairov's words, "is a means of making the whole body, the whole figure of the actor, more expressive and vibrant."[96] Tairov believed that costumes never simply decorate the actor, that they should be "a second skin" that "enrich[es] the expressiveness of the actor's gesture."[97]

In a duel scene between Giglio and his doppelgänger, Prince Chiaperri, Giglio destroys his own hack-actor self once and for all. This scene, which I reproduce at length, was widely acknowledged as the most striking in the production:

> GIGLIO: This is amazing. I am fighting my own self. . . . For I have split in two, and here my two "selves" stand facing one another. But if this first "me" (*points to himself*) is an actor and a performer, then who are you, my second "me"?
>
> DOPPELGÄNGER: (*proudly*) I am a prince. Yes, I am a prince. Let us continue.
>
> GIGLIO: I am ready, my prince.
>
> DOPPELGÄNGER: (*Thrusts the sword into Giglio's chest. The latter falls on his back. His mask falls off, and he is recognized.*)
>
> VOICES: Why that's Giglio Fava. Bravo! Giglio Fava! Bravo!

GIGLIO: Oh, I am dying. . . . (*raising himself on an elbow*) Oh, he poisoned me with his roles, that cursed Abbot Chiari. (*Shakes the rolled-up scripts out of his pockets.*) Here they are . . . look, more and more of them. . . . Oh, save me. Save me. Empty me out quickly, or I'll die of a bloated belly.

MASKS: (*guffawing*) Bravo, Giglio Fava. To hell with Abbot Chiari. Ha, ha, ha.

GIGLIO: But no, nothing can save me now. Too late. . . . I'm dying. . . . A great actor is perishing. (*Lies on his back and dies.*)

MASK IN BLACK: Signori, here before us is the body of a great player. But the prince is alive.

MASKS: Long live Prince Cornelio Chiaperri.

DOPPELGÄNGER: (*proudly*) I need no congratulations. (*Puts the sword back in its sheath and, with head raised proudly, walks through the crowd.*)

MASK IN BLACK: Now, signori, with honor let us return to the earth the body of the renowned actor, who died just as he lived: playing a role until his last gasp.[98]

Giglio's death by bad play was, of course, not simply a statement about Gozzi's rival Chiari, but about Russian theater, which, Tairov felt, valued fidelity to dramatic literature to the point of artistic stagnation. The master actor was to use the body as an expressive vessel filled not with plays but with the ego, "a creative personality who conceives and translates into reality a work of your own art."[99]

All *Brambilla*'s major themes converge in this duel scene: it unites the production's themes of commedia and seeing; it foreshadows the hero and heroine seeing themselves reflected in the mirror-lake of Urdar in act 4; and in it Giglio lets go of his false self, a puppet stuffed full of roles devoid of real art. The power of actor-generated theater is once again affirmed in the final scene as Giglio and Giacinta discuss their ability to wield their own inventive power, improvise onstage, and truly create. Like many other directors, Tairov worked to develop a radically new definition of theater. *Brambilla* gave him the opportunity to do so specifically from the point of view of actors, encouraging them to unlearn old ways of approaching their roles and to become new, virtuosic makers.

Brambilla on the Stage

In the production, Tairov transformed *Brambilla's* theoretical foundations into vivid, whirling mise-en-scène. The show's polemical elements would not have been missed on Tairov's artistic contemporaries, but its polemicizing was deliberately saturated with gaiety and color. Tairov wanted his audiences to absorb the production and its meanings primarily with their senses. His comments on *Brambilla* express the same sentiment as his later review of *The Dawns*: "Is art really a platform for philosophy? Is the stage really a lesson in logic? Absolutely not. . . . The stage is the art of theatrical action. Only thus . . . should it create an impression . . . for the whole charm of art is in the incomprehensible."[100]

Tairov retained the spirit of Hoffmann's twists and turns in the form of incessantly shifting pantomime and carnival scenes. As Abram Efros mused:

> Was there a plot in what we saw? I don't remember, maybe! Were there heroes? Probably, in the director's notes! . . . There were spinning, singing, sparkling, fleeting appearances of dozens of mask-people, cloak-people, nose-people, sword-people, banner-people, changing with unheard of tempos and lightning-fast regroupings.[101]

Tairov's goal of sensorially bombarding his audience appears to have been met: he commented with no small satisfaction that some spectators left the theater with headaches.[102] Yet each of the production motifs was backed by clear and consistent choices. The design served two main functions linked to themes from the promptbook: It captured a refracted perspective through a phantasmagorical approach to the design, as if each stage element was fragmented and multiplied through a kaleidoscope. Likewise, the script's praise of actor-based, professional popular theater was echoed in the performer-centered stage and costume design and in actor-generated solutions to technical challenges.

Tairov recurrently used specific words—fantastical, chimerical—to describe *Brambilla*'s style. Most frequently, he called it phantasmagorical: "We believe that specifically in this performance presented by the Kamerny Theatre . . . here is that spirit of phantasmagoria, that spirit of transformation, that spirit of the real mixed with the unreal, the material with the immaterial, that produces the skill of an author like Hoffmann."[103] Phantasmagorias create the impression of transformation via rapidly changing magic lantern slides. Tairov achieved a similar effect with swirling action, episodic structure, and fragmented stage space. Anticipating Tairov's productions of American expressionist plays in the 1920s and 1930s, Torda has called the Kamerny's particular style of distortion "consciously expressionistic," noting its "exaggeration," "surrealistic scenery," "boldly defined shapes," "episodic structure," and "dream-adventures . . . as if the performance of *Brambilla* took place in the mind of Giglio as refracted through the imagination of Hoffmann."[104] The main difference between Tairov's expressionism and the German variation is that Tairov's distortion and disorientation were deeply joyful.

Figure 26. Georgy Yakulov, scene design maquette for *Princess Brambilla*, dir. Alexander Tairov, Moscow Kamerny Theatre (1920). Russian State Archive of Literature and Art, f. 2328, op. 1, ed. khr. 377: 3.

Design: The Spiral and the Kaleidoscope

While *Brambilla* recalled a range of optical effects, Georgy Yakulov's design owes its greatest debt to the kaleidoscope. By fragmenting stage space and unifying disparate elements, he created an overall impression of splintered, multihued synthesis. Within this stage space, Tairov created the mise-en-scène in spirals, a defining characteristic of his blocking patterns in subsequent productions. The design and mise-en-scène for one of his most acclaimed later productions, Vishnevsky's *Optimistic Tragedy* (1933), positioned actors along spiraling curves to show the steady progress of humanity from disorder to order.[105] In *Brambilla*, such spirals reinforced the promptbook's allusions to spinning, whirlwinds, and dizziness and emphasized the theme of distorted vision.

Yakulov's fantastical scenic design evoked a sense of impermanence and theatrical magic. The set, described as "a spiral construction of Cubist-Baroque forms,"[106] was characterized by what Ignatov called "an abundance of curlicues"[107] in vivid colors reminiscent of a Roman sunset. The Pistoja Palace took the form of an abstract central column from which an undulating staircase spilled down onto the main platform (figure 26). In addition to providing actors with a rhythmical keyboard for their carnival antics, Yakulov saw this palace as conveying "the unreliability of the images of the Pistoja Palace, their fluidity and kaleidoscopic quality."[108]

Yakulov's set created the impression that the viewer could see the world of *Brambilla* from multiple perspectives. Efros called Yakulov's style a kind of "simultaneity" in which "the object appears from every side at once, in the displacements created by the rotation around an axis."[109] Ignatov commented on the "splintering" of the stage space, adding: "It was as if the artist was trying to divide . . . the very stage floor into its fine component parts. In this subdivision of parts he saw the dynamics of rhythms."[110] The large downstage center area was kept open for the actors' play, while the sides and rear of the stage each had small platforms from which characters could observe the action. Yakulov originally hoped the set could occupy much more of the stage floor, but Tairov insisted on maintaining open space in which to showcase the actors' movement.

The constantly shifting scenery and lighting design increased the impression of unified fragments. Actors manipulated screens and banners similar to the portable scenic elements in productions by other contemporary directors (Craig, Komissarzhevsky, Vakhtangov), allowing each scene to transition seamlessly into the next and to complement "emotional [and] rhythmic changes in the dramatic action."[111] Lighting became a visual extension of emotion, particularly in the duel scene. As Giglio's false self died, "a shaft of purple light was thrown upward from the prompter's box, casting enormous shadows on the backdrop. . . . The figures . . . move from the dim green of the sides into this central shaft of purple and out again."[112] In another scene, carnival dancers were "illuminated by burning torches, juggled by one of the revellers into phantasmagoric patterns."[113]

While the scene design evoked a kaleidoscopic world, it also provided a practical, rhythmically expressive performance space. The costumes served a similar dual purpose. Konstantin Derzhavin observes that they were designed to allow the actors the greatest possible range of movement and to convey the impression of a masquerade.[114] Although the whirlwind atmosphere was amplified in carnival scenes filled with whirling capes, the actors' freedom of movement was of utmost importance. Harlequin's costume, for example, "closely fitted the actor's body like a glove and provided him with the ability to physically reflect his sensations through gesture."[115]

Working in Hoffmann's manner, Yakulov refracted Callot's *Balli* in several costume designs. Nikolai Bykov, one of the *Brambilla* actors, recalled in an unpublished memoir that "Callot's drawings were brought in as models; they infected . . . Yakulov and he created wonderful sketches of carnival costumes and masks."[116] Several of Yakulov's carnival figures refract Callot in their exaggerated abandon. In some cases, Callot also inspired movement. In one produc-

Figure 27. Carnival scene, *Princess Brambilla*, Moscow Kamerny Theatre (1920). Russian State Archive of Literature and Art, f. 2328, op. 1, ed. khr. 378: 5.

tion photograph (figure 27), the physical position of the carnival masker on the far right refracts that of Franca Trippa in the etching with Fritellino (figure 28).

Another significant design element was the production's use of masks and puppets. In a unique take on the larger Russian quest to synthesize multiple art forms in the theater, Tairov intermingled puppets and live actors. The Kamerny's puppetry division, established in February 1920 and run by Vladimir Sokolov, created *Brambilla's* masks and puppets.[117] Actors were dressed as "giants, camels and ostriches,"[118] but the puppetry division likely also created the show's other fantastical figures. In a photograph of Brambilla's opening procession, a puppet horse ridden by a distorted figure is surrounded by squat, masked figures with sagging potbellies, ringed in turn by unmasked onlookers. These puppets and masks prompted multiple planes of reality. In the most realistic scenes, characters wore no masks; in carnival scenes, small black half-masks covered the eyes of revelers who responded to their environment corporeally. Giglio, his rival, and members of the main pantomime appeared in more grotesque versions of commedia masks, usually with ridiculous noses. The most fantastical masks were worn by the members of Brambilla's entourage. These juxtapositions of actors, masks, and puppets affirmed that different performance forms could be synthesized, while nodding to Hoffmann's collisions of multiple planes.

Music and Movement

For Tairov, rigorous physical training turned actors' bodies into virtuosic masks that unmasked individual creativity. Tairov understood commedia as a

Figure 28. Jacques Callot, *Franca Trippa and Fritellino*, 23rd plate from *Balli di Sfessania* (c. 1621). Etching. Harvard Art Museums/Fogg Museum, Gray Collection of Engravings Fund, by exchange, S4.29.7. Photo: Imaging Department © President and Fellows of Harvard College.

practical, actor-centered, actor-generated theater that prepared actors to use their bodies as creative instruments. Kamerny actors had complementary training in acrobatics, dance, and circus skills. It was in conjunction with this extensive physical training, first fully implemented in *Brambilla*, that Tairov began an acting school at the Kamerny, though it did not receive official status until 1923. According to Bykov, he and his fellow actors received eight months of acrobatic training in preparation for *Brambilla*, in addition to which they studied commedia history and technique, juggling, fencing, and Italian dance, focusing especially on the tarantella.[119]

Music and dance were essential to *Brambilla*'s synthetic approach; unifying rhythmic elements permeated every scene. Tairov worked closely with house composer Henri Forterre, bringing him in to rehearsals to write the music for each scene after the staging was already well along; this gave Forterre the opportunity to compose for specific dramatic needs and to complement the action, much as film scores do today.

Dance became the unifying principle behind all the movement in the production. Tairov used the tarantella to reinforce the energy of the whirlwind atmosphere and to help actors perform with physical precision. Ignatov observed that dance rhythms permeated individual scenes (the duel scene in particular) as well as the many ensemble pantomimes: "We cannot find a single movement that is not subordinated to rhythm and that does not emerge simultaneously as an element of dance or acrobatics."[120]

Acrobatic elements were similarly integrated into the movement of individual characters, that of Celionati in particular. According to Ignatov, Celionati's "every movement was subordinated to the overarching concept, and in his leaps about the whole stage and in his distorted poses there is a grotesque[121] that always impresses the crowd, never becoming a caricature. . . . He has exceptional control over his supple, brilliantly trained body."[122] This emphasis on movement is a direct application of Giglio's discovery of the power of the mask. Here, the performers submitted to their roles on one level, but to a more profound degree they submitted to the character of the collective atmosphere, manifested in the celebratory musical pulse that drove the action.

Commedia was a style the Kamerny actors studied intensely, but Tairov did not attempt to mirror the Italian comedy of masks on his Moscow stage. As Clayton has demonstrated, Russian versions of commedia were as different from the Italian comedy of masks as they were from each other. According to Derzhavin, Tairov's commedia broadly refracted "the theatrical tricks of the old itinerant *cabotinage*, which found their last refuge in circus clown routines and in the performances of conjurers and prestidigitators."[123] *Brambilla* glorified the continued relevance of commedia, however: a fresh approach to character and improvisation, a tradition that was both popular and professional, and a theater in which actors generated their own material.

Pantomime and the Master Actor

Pantomime was the most significant manifestation in *Brambilla* of this metaphorical commedia. Amiard-Chevrel identifies twenty-one scenes in *Brambilla* that contained pantomimic elements, ten of which consisted entirely of wordless action with no direct equivalent in Hoffmann's novella.[124] Tairov boasted that the pantomime scenes, in which the mime-drama experiments from *Pierrette's Veil* were bearing fruit, comprised fifty minutes of the two-and-a-half hour production. From the beginning of the rehearsal process, pantomime was the major element in the production that actors were encouraged to improvise.[125] Tairov asked the actors to create scenes collaboratively and to work out technical challenges physically instead of relying on stage machinery—no small feat in a production so steeped in theatrical magic, and, hence, technical challenges. He insisted on "transferring the entire burden of creating the performance . . . of conveying Hoffmann's phantasmagoria—and laying this entire burden on the shoulders of the actor" by reducing the use "of every possible theatrical machine to zero."[126] This conviction that the skill of the actor could and should surpass that of any machine was one of the Kamerny's founding principles.

The production's low-tech approach received its most enthusiastic accolades in the central pantomime. This pantomime, a full eighteen minutes long, takes place at the end of act 2. In the promptbook it appears to be a simple transcription of the equivalent scene in Hoffmann.[127] It is clear from contemporary accounts, however, that it was performed entirely differently. Its function was similar to the Brighella-Harlequin interlude in Meyerhold's *Love for Three Oranges* in the sense that both showcased the actor's virtuosity for the benefit of the audience. While Meyerhold's Brighella-Harlequin *lazzo* focused on the performer's ability to oscillate between self and mask, Tairov's pantomime emphasized actor-generated theatrical magic.

The final version of the pantomime centered on a recurrent plot device from nineteenth-century fairground pantomimes, introduced to Russia by the Ravels: the dissection of Harlequin. In the Kamerny production, Columbine's jilted lovers seize Harlequin when he is not looking, lay him on a table, saw him into bits, and scatter his body pieces about the stage. Columbine is disconsolate until a good fairy gives her a magic wand with which she puts the pieces together again and reunites the lovers.[128] In Koonen's recollection, the pantomime featured a finale in which actors dressed as giants, camels, and ostriches performed in wild, joyful rhythm as they "danced, tumbled, juggled flaming torches, and crossed the stage on stilts."[129]

In the description of Alexander Rumnev, who played Harlequin, Harlequin's rivals laid him on a large trunk with high wooden sides, brandishing an alarmingly large knife over him (figure 29). They threw a white cloth over Harlequin's body as they discussed the operation. While the cloth was airborne, the trunk lid swiveled, replacing the living actor with a dummy made in seven pieces. Once the cloth was removed, the audience took the dummy for the real actor, gasping as he was cut into bits. After the procedure was finished, the trunk was carried backstage and Rumnev climbed out to prepare for the second half of the trick.[130]

While Harlequin's pieces were reassembled into an upright empty silhouette, Rumnev imperceptibly replaced each of the dummy parts with a part of his own body, beginning with his legs, then his torso, his arms, and finally his head. This trick required tremendous physical flexibility. According to Tairov: "Harlequin . . . controlled his body to such a degree that he was able to fit through an aperture that nobody else could have passed through; he was able to assume poses that nobody else could hold, and he gradually revealed his body to the audience."[131] In this pantomime, Harlequin was cut into pieces and reborn. In the play that framed it, Giglio's paper-and-cardboard self was

Figure 29. Main pantomime, *Princess Brambilla*, Moscow Kamerny Theatre (1920). Russian State Archive of Literature and Art, f. 2328, op. 1, ed. khr. 378: 10.

dissected and his true self reincarnated. Both *Princess Brambilla* and its pantomimic microcosms declared that the Kamerny's years of experimentation and self-generated artistic revolution had borne rich fruit.

At the very end of the Kamerny's *Brambilla*, Giacinta compliments Giglio on a commedia performance they have just completed. Giglio replies: "Yes, that is what our Italian comedy of masks is so good at: at providing room for the creative work of the actor."[132] In the Kamerny promptbook, "our Italian comedy of masks" is crossed out and replaced with the words "our theater." This small handwritten change captures how the Kamerny's refracted its inspirations. Like Meyerhold, Tairov had no interest in reconstructing the past. Hoffmann and commedia were artistic fodder for declaring that the theater of the future—the theater of the Kamerny—would triumph.

Brambilla in Its Time

In the many reviews that praised the Kamerny's *Brambilla*, the thing critics complimented most was its timeliness. The fact that the Kamerny removed *Brambilla* from its repertoire after only two and a half years (but over a hundred performances) indicates even more strongly its appropriateness in a specific political and cultural context. Several critics described Hoffmann's tales as especially resonant in Russia's environment of theatrical experimentation; others saw Hoffmann as even more relevant than native Russian authors. As Koonen later mused: "The fantastical Romantic Hoffmann was somehow astonishingly consonant with the entire atmosphere that reigned at that time in art."[133] Markov similarly noted: "It so happens that the most fantastical and most subjective poet of Germany, a dreamer and a fairy-tale writer, has remained comprehensible and close in the years of war and revolution."[134] *Brambilla* was timely in its message of hope for the future; its declaration of the power of art and the need for art to survive despite tumultuous economic and financial times; its celebration of the Kamerny's years of experimentation and hard work; and its call to preserve the theater's professionalism and artistic autonomy precisely when debates over the Soviet repertoire were coming increasingly to the fore.

In a lecture on *Brambilla*, Tairov referred repeatedly to his attempts to create joyful theater, stating: "In both [the harlequinade] and the [mystery], joy should arise in the audience . . . for theater that leaves the audience jaded and shaken rather than renewed and joyful is not a true work of art."[135] Though Tairov's techniques differ from Meyerhold's emotional clashes, as Clayton notes, Tairov's words recall an article in *Love for Three Oranges*, "Comedy of Pure Joy" (see appendix A), in which Zhirmunsky argues that Gozzi's *fiabe* appealed to the romantics because of their love of pure play, that they evoked a "world of another order, more exalted, joyful, and resplendent than the one that surrounds us."[136] These statements parallel Tairov's description of the task of *Brambilla*: "Despite the shock that Giglio . . . undergoes, despite all this, Hoffmann wants to convey a . . . great joy, a great affirmation and acceptance of life. . . . Living laughter and living joy: this is the task of . . . *Princess Brambilla*."[137]

Like many Russian modernist artists, Tairov had a fundamental faith in the transformative power of art. As Worrall observes, Tairov believed that awakening "great love" and "creative enthusiasm" helped individuals "to overcome the insuperable."[138] The first six years of the Kamerny's existence were marked by an extended period of interlinking wars: World War I overlapped with the February and October Revolutions, followed soon after by the Russian Civil War. Widespread famine began in 1918 but peaked in 1921–22, resulting in roughly five million deaths nationwide.[139] In this context, Tairov's repeated emphasis on joyful theater can be read two ways: that the theater can and should effect positive transformation and that the theater is a place to celebrate art's contribution to life. The greater life's difficulties, the greater the need for theater that is life- and art-affirming. One reviewer concurred:

> This well-put-together artistic collective doesn't care one whit: not about our economic ruin, nor about the difficulty in obtaining necessities—in the turbu-

> lent whirlwind of carnival, the symphony of paint, silk, canvas, and admirably trained human bodies astonishes, startles, and, finally, enthralls the spectator, who knows perfectly well, incidentally, that all the brilliance and sumptuousness of the production is achieved with a minimal expenditure of resources, with a purely theatrical approach.[140]

This description succinctly captures what it was about *Brambilla* that was so appealing: the Kamerny, with a little paint and a great deal of training, infectiously conveyed the joie de vivre that sustained many who survived the difficult Civil War years. This was expressed in *Brambilla*'s prologue, which can be read as the Kamerny's manifesto of theatrical joy:

> For though in the earth's grime we drag our feet,
> Yet let our thoughts soar in the skies.
> And if we manage but for a time
> To tear you from the dull humdrum of life
> And toward the bright, azure land
> Of springtime reveries, fantasies, and fairy tales
> To carry you on the wings of dreams,
> Then our aim shall thus have been attained,
> And we shall find in this the highest reward.[141]

Brambilla was imbued with hope for the future of theater and, indirectly, for the future of revolutionary Russia: while Giglio's world is warped and confusing, it resolves into a new and better one through concentrated human effort.

The repeated emphasis on joy in *Brambilla* was also a celebration of the Kamerny's own ability to survive. Since opening shortly after the start of World War I, the new theater had struggled along with everyone else against famine and cold, but, as Koonen chronicles in her memoirs, the Kamerny had additional challenges, as they were a young and inexperienced troupe with significant financial burdens. The company was evicted from its original building and endured landlords who refused to heat the theater adequately even when there were not fuel shortages.[142] However, the troupe was dedicated to maintaining the ensemble; Koonen recalls that they voluntarily worked without pay and basic comforts in order to keep the theater afloat,[143] while Bykov recollects that he couldn't keep away from rehearsals: "Rehearsals for *Brambilla* were long and hard. I loved these rehearsals so much that I walked to them even when I wasn't in one scene or another. The word 'walked' should be interpreted literally, as the trams weren't running in Moscow during those years."[144]

The ebullient spirit of *Brambilla* celebrated the Kamerny's ability to succeed despite such difficulties. In 1919 the Kamerny gave a command performance of Wilde's *Salomé* for Lunacharsky, who was so impressed that he returned the company to their original theater at 23 Tverskoi Boulevard (from which they had been evicted), released them from the obligation to pay rent, granted them a generous state subsidy, and, by the beginning of 1920, included them in the then still comparatively autonomous group of "state academic" theaters that were not (yet) required to include revolutionary content in their repertoires.[145] This designation turned out to be both a blessing and a curse: it gave the Kamerny legitimacy and artistic independence, but it made the theater seem more old-fashioned than it was. Tairov later defended the theater's innovativeness:

> I believe that each production of a living theater, but not an academic one—the Kamerny Theatre is not an academic theater, despite the fact that its critics desperately want this to be true and insist on calling it academic—that each production . . . is a stop along the ongoing journey of what that theater wants to become.[146]

Lunacharsky also obtained funds for the Kamerny to expand the size of its chamber auditorium to eight hundred seats in order to accommodate its rapidly swelling audiences.[147] The Kamerny was one of the best-attended Soviet theaters throughout the 1920s; its appeal to the younger generation was particularly strong.

Tairov participated actively in the national debate over the future of Soviet theater, his confidence perhaps boosted by the popularity of the Kamerny, the skill of his actors, and Lunacharsky's public approval. Each of *Brambilla*'s declarations of an ideal future was related in some way to this debate. Tairov's call for an entirely actor-centered theater was a rejection of both Stanislavsky and Meyerhold, each of whom he felt limited the actor in different ways. His disdain for theatrical hacks was perhaps a subtle criticism of the Soviet repertoire, still in its infancy, and his call for virtuosity a response to the surge of amateur theaters under the umbrella of Proletkult.

Above all, Tairov defended the artistic autonomy of theater (even as he accepted state support), both in *Brambilla* and in his 1921 *Notes of a Director*. The commedia and pantomime sequences in *Brambilla* were self-generated and highly skilled, demonstrating the actor's earned right to create. Tairov believed that theater could interpret life, process life, and capture the essence of life but that it should not reproduce life. The Kamerny's work was timely, but not topical. Tairov held that the theater's autonomy should not be stilted by service to political or moral agendas that lay outside it or by subservience to other arts—a stance that later fueled accusations of irrelevant aestheticism. As he concluded in *Notes of a Director*:

A whole series of arts already have their own science, or at least some firm beginnings of it.

Now it is the theatre's turn.

But in order that this science have a suitable base for its construction and development, it is necessary that theatre art at last get an accurate picture of itself and dissociate itself from all attendant elements, it is necessary to carry out . . . completely the *theatricalization of the theatre*.

Theatre is theatre.

It is high time we learned this simple truth once and for all.[148]

EPILOGUE: AN INDEPENDENT PATH

In 1922 Tairov staged a second Hoffmann tale, *Signor Formica*, as an operetta.[149] Adapted by Vladimir Sokolov, *Formica* opened on June 13, just a few days before the hundredth jubilee of Hoffmann's death. Although it contains scenes set in the theater, *Formica* differs from *Brambilla* in that it focuses on what it means to be an artist rather than on how to reform the theater. *Formica* would seem to have been a good choice for the Kamerny, as it contains several scenes set in the theater in which doppelgängers confront one another. However, reviews of *Formica* were overwhelmingly negative. Hoffmann's supposed mysticism and individualism were increasingly coming under fire by 1922, despite the Hoffmann jubilee celebrations, but the Kamerny must also have recognized the production as unsuccessful, as it is almost entirely neglected in Kamerny publications.

Formica was, by all accounts, less whimsical and more simply drawn than its predecessor. One reviewer wrote:

> *Princess Brambilla* has one doubtless advantage: it is so convoluted that the viewer somehow is curious to follow its puzzles and charades. Something like a sporting interest awakens in him. In *Signor Formica*, on the contrary, everything is so clear and obvious that after the very first act the story becomes boring. All the seams show too much.[150]

Critics seem to have taken particular issue to a Hoffmann made unappealing by excessive realism. One reviewer strongly preferred Hoffmann's "fantastical madness" to the "naturalistic madness" of the Kamerny's production.[151] Another commented:

> In *Signor Formica* Tairov repeated *Princess Brambilla* in several places, and those places were interesting. In the remaining *horrible dictu*, A. Ia. Tairov

> showed us Hoffmann in a completely new and, admittedly for us, unexpected form. This was a Hoffmann from the everyday, from realism. It resounded like some peculiar, wild artistic dissonance. And why hide it? At times it reeked of the "famous" traditions of the "House of Shchepkin."[152]

The production designs for *Formica* have less of the capriccio, less Callot, and more angularity than their *Brambilla* counterparts, perhaps evidence that the Kamerny was attempting not to repeat *Brambilla*. But *Formica* was not a manifesto as *Brambilla* had been, and in this, perhaps, lay its greatest shortcoming. As Efros notes, "Tairov's and Yakulov's attempts to create a variation [to *Brambilla*] in *Signor Formica* two years later . . . ended in failure . . . *Formica* was *Brambilla's* epigone."[153]

The Kamerny did not perform any more Hoffmann works after 1923, when *Brambilla* was pulled from the repertoire (though not until after the production had toured successfully in Germany and France), but the theater continued to refract its own refractions in various ways. Its cubist *Romeo and Juliet* (1921), designed by Alexandra Exter, splintered the stage space into "acting stations" that were "rhythmically calculated" to feature the actors' whirling, vivid movement.[154] In 1922, the Kamerny's critically acclaimed *Phaedre* returned to *Pierrette's Veil*'s central focus on the actor via an emotionally heightened approach to tragedy, at the center of which was Koonen. That same year, the Kamerny staged *Giroflé-Girofla*, a lighthearted take on the double, in which Koonen played both of the operetta's titular twins.[155] In 1923 the Kamerny school that supported the actor training for *Brambilla* received official status. Its students studied "improvisation, make-up, dance, diction, movement, juggling, acrobatics, fencing, gymnastics," as well as puppetry and theater history.[156]

The Kamerny's production of O'Neill's *The Hairy Ape* (1926) was Tairov's first successful attempt to fuse a self-contained theatrical world with content sympathetic to the Revolution; in it, the Kamerny brilliantly merged virtuosic pantomime with a celebration of the physical might of the proletariat. *The Hairy Ape* opened at the Kamerny Theatre on January 14, 1926.[157] By all accounts, its highlight was its opening pantomime. On the lowest level of a three-tiered set that evoked the upper deck, cabins, and stokehole of an ocean liner, Yank and his fellow stokehole workers, sweating, covered in coal dust, nevertheless brimmed over with raw life and proletarian dignity. Koonen describes this scene vividly:

> The scene in the stokehole, lasting seven minutes . . . created a tremendous impression. Chained to a huge, fire-breathing furnace, the men hurl coal into the gaping crater with a powerful stroke of their shovels . . . The beauty of the bare muscles gave the sensation of the all-powerful might of human labor.

> Here, there finally appeared with immense conviction that synthetic acting mastery which Tairov preached with such unwavering persistence.[158]

Tairov juxtaposed these scenes with pantomimes that featured distorted, mechanized upper-class choruses, thereby contrasting capitalism's rigid dehumanization with the defiant humanity of the worker—a common theme in the Soviet theatre of the day.

Two years later, Tairov attempted a Soviet take on the play-within-a-play motif with the world premiere at the Kamerny of Bulgakov's *Crimson Island* (1928). This play's internal play parodied the Revolution, while a fictional audience at a fictional general rehearsal contained a comic censor who initially proposed the play be banned—a bold statement about censorship for both Bulgakov and Tairov, as the real censor, Vladimir Blium, was probably in the real audience at the real general rehearsal. The production played over sixty times before being banned.

The Kamerny's *Crimson Island* promptbook contains a distinctive kind of frame, one that appeared with increasing frequency in the Soviet 1920s—one drawn in red ink: the censor's cuts and the censor's official stamp on the front cover. Much of Tairov's artistic career was framed in the red ink of censorship. He was permitted to continue working for thirty-five years, but the Soviet press increasingly discredited him as a director with an insufficiently Soviet perspective and with too great an interest in international cultures. Pavel Markov, who wrote such a glowing review of Tairov's 1913 *Pierrette*, wrote in 1934, the year socialist realism was mandated, that Tairov "looked upon the stage as a field for conventional acting that had nothing whatever to do with real life and naturalistic imitation" and that he practiced "aestheticism . . . to the point of abstraction."[159] Ironically, the Kamerny's enormously successful *Optimistic Tragedy* (1933), which featured Koonen in the tragically optimistic role of a female Commissar who dies heroically so that socialism may flourish, provided an important model for socialist realism.

Tairov received the Order of Lenin in 1945, but accusations of "formalism" and "cosmopolitanism"—a post-World War II epithet frequently bestowed upon Soviet Jewish intellectuals—gained momentum not long after, while Soviet newspapers publicly exposed his Jewish surname by publishing it. On May 27, 1949, Order no. 408 of the Committee for Artistic Affairs of the Council of Ministries of the U.S.S.R. removed Tairov from his post as Kamerny artistic director. In addition to accusing him of not staging enough ideologically appropriate Soviet plays, this order, excerpts from which are translated into English for the first time here, stated:

> In its working methods the theater preserved elements of old formalist ways that interfered with the deep and multifaceted revelation of the contemporary

> reality and life of the Soviet people. The productions of the Kamerny Theatre were characterized by coldness and dryness; they lacked the necessary passion and party commitment characteristic to contemporary art. As a result, the majority of the productions quickly left the stage.
>
> Not having succeeded in overcoming former mistakes, Artistic Director A. Ia. Tairov in his practical work . . . has not been able to stand firmly on the path of realistic art . . .
>
> The management did not utilize the creative abilities of the collective and did not nurture the development of creative individualities; the advancement of young people had a random quality. In recent years the theater did not train or replenish itself with talented young actors.
>
> Artistic Director A. Ia. Tairov was not guided by the collective and did not take into consideration the public opinion of the theater. Single-handedly dealing with creative issues, A. Ia. Tairov isolated himself from the collective. Taking charge of all directorial staging work, A. Ia. Tairov did not allow fresh directorial forces into the theater.[160]

It is ironic that Tairov, whose entire artistic philosophy centered on developing emotionally powerful productions that nurtured the centrality of the actor, should be accused of the very opposite—and that this should be the grounds for his dismissal in the last days of his creative life.

On October 11, 1949, Order no. 867 reassigned Koonen to the Vakhtangov Theatre. Koonen and Tairov were promised work at the Vakhtangov that never came to pass. Both were forcibly retired soon after and, to their dismay, prohibited from future work.[161] The Kamerny actors were relieved, redistributed, or absorbed into the Pushkin Theatre, which opened in August 1950 in the Kamerny premises at 23 Tverskoi Boulevard, where it remains today. Tairov died the following month, on September 25, 1950, of a degenerative brain illness.

The Kamerny Theatre's influence on Russian and western theater during Tairov's lifetime was far more profound than is generally recognized; Torda observes that over 5,000 articles on the Kamerny in over twenty languages had appeared by 1935.[162] Yet, with a few notable exceptions, Tairov's innovations remain underexplored.[163] Dasha Krijanskaia cogently proposes two reasons why: "The fact that Tairov was alien to both of the mainstream traditions of Russian theatre . . . prompts scholars to view Tairov's art as a peculiar and extraneous offspring," and Tairov's "formal aesthetics" fell out of favor during the socialist realist period.[164] Both of these reasons have contributed to an erasure that is no less enduring than Meyerhold's; it is simply of a different hue.

For the first twenty years of its existence, the Kamerny was one of the most vivid and innovative theaters in the world. In Worrall's assessment, "The story of Tairov's theatre in the 1920s consists of a struggle with its critics and a courageous attempt to pursue an independent artistic course."[165] Many of the experiments Tairov conducted while pursuing this independent path remain applicable to the theater of today: training actors in multiple artistic vocabularies, an actor-centered rather than autocratic approach to directing, consistently strong roles for women, an emphasis on visual and corporeal meaning, and the conviction that theater is a joyful expression of the creative soul.

Chapter Three

Peregrinus Tyss Meets Pipifax: Eisenstein, the Grotesque, and the Attraction

PROLOGUE/POLEMIC: *TARELKIN'S DEATH*

In the fall of 1922, Sergei Mikhailovich Eisenstein (1898–1948) worked as Meyerhold's assistant director on a production of Sukhovo-Kobylin's nineteenth-century play *Tarelkin's Death*. This new production of a play Meyerhold previously directed in 1917 was infused with theatrical vocabularies in vogue in the postrevolutionary 1920s. It embraced the "circusization" and "music-hallization" of the theater promoted by the Eccentrics, Sergei Radlov, Nikolai Foregger, and Meyerhold himself. It also experimented with a new relationship between actors and objects. Earlier that year, in Meyerhold's *Magnanimous Cuckold*, the theatrical set became a playground for biomechanically trained actors. In *Tarelkin*, props and furniture pieces were defined by specific individual functions: Varvara Stepanova designed trick "acting instruments" that would startle and delight (figure 30). Braun describes their effect:

> Each concealed a trap: the table's legs gave way, the seat deposited its occupant onto the floor, the stool detonated a blank cartridge. . . . As though all this was not enough to tax the spectator's nerves and the actor's courage, an assistant director . . . seated in the front row announced the intervals by firing a pistol at the audience and shouting "Entrrr-acte!"; there were helter-skelter chases with the pursuers brandishing inflated bladders on sticks; at the end Tarelkin escaped by swinging across the stage on a trapeze. Illusion was never given a chance to intrude.[1]

Tarelkin's juxtapositions, aural and visual surprises, and circus acts had a mixed reception, in part because Stepanova's acting instruments did not always function as intended. Yet this first—and last—formal directorial collaboration between Eisenstein and Meyerhold marks a significant intersection in the crisscrossing paths of two of the twentieth century's most renowned directors. Meyerhold's prerevolutionary interest in treating objects

Figure 30. Brandakhlystova's children, played by Vladimir Liutse and E. Bengis, in Sukhovo-Kobylin's *Tarelkin's Death*, dir. Vsevolod Meyerhold, State Higher Theatre Workshops (Premiere: November 24, 1922). Negative reproduction, 11.7 × 8.7 cm. ГИК 9302/39, ОН 16024. © Saint Petersburg State Museum of Theatre and Music.

as scene partners with which the actor shapes audience response developed here into acting instruments that bombard the audience's senses.

The collaboration between Meyerhold and Eisenstein was, by all accounts, a fraught one. Eisenstein had been studying with the Master (as Meyerhold's students called him) for over a year, but he was to abandon his studies shortly after the production's opening. An anecdote by Zharov, a *Tarelkin* actor, reveals that Eisenstein sometimes redirected Meyerhold's direction during rehearsals:

> Eisenstein, this production's second director, told us explicitly during rehearsals before we went out on stage, after looking around to see if Meyerhold was coming:
>
> "Brothers, go clown it up!"
>
> And so we did.[2]

While Eisenstein agreed with many aspects of Meyerhold's theatrical revolution, from the start he also wanted to take his teacher's ideas along a more radical path of his own making.

Zharov recalls that Eisenstein stopped working at the table with Meyerhold at some point during the rehearsal process and instead sat in the auditorium scribbling in a little book, implying a possible falling-out. Zinaida Raikh, Meyerhold's wife, left Eisenstein a note shortly after the premiere that advised, "it is essential that you leave M[eyerhol]d, as M[eyerhol]d once left Stanislavsky."[3] And so Eisenstein left Meyerhold, taking a position as lead director of a Proletkult troupe and immersing himself in rehearsals for Ostrovsky's *Enough Stupidity in Every Wiseman*, about which he wrote his seminal 1923 essay, "Montage of Attractions."

After Eisenstein turned to film, especially in the second half of the 1920s, he was defensive of implications that his work in cinema was derivative of Meyerhold's in theater. As Clayton observes in response to Eisenstein's apparent need for self-preservation and autonomy:

> The problems Eisenstein had with the Oedipal complex are well known; it is therefore not surprising that he should project them upon that notoriously authoritarian figure, Meyerhold. . . . There were perhaps reasons beyond the intellectual or aesthetic ones to explain Eisenstein's departure from theatre and espousal of cinema. But it is clear that . . . the lessons absorbed in Meyerhold's theatre continued to shape Eisenstein's thinking to the end.[4]

Meyerhold's influence on Eisenstein was both profound and multifaceted, as Bordwell confirms:

> Eisenstein's belief in controlling the spectator through the performer's bodily virtuosity; his emphasis on rhythm and pantomime; his interest in Asian theatre, the circus, and the grotesque; even his 1930s attempt to create a curriculum in which film directors would undergo stringent physical and cultural training—all were initiated or strengthened by the association with Meyerhold.[5]

Often we think of influence in terms of imitation. Influence in Eisenstein's case can be more precisely understood in terms of argument. His creativity was most fully activated when staging a rebellion—or a perceived rebellion (it was often one-sided). As Kleiman observes, "Eisenstein felt as if he were constantly engaged in a tournament, and of course the medieval ideal was that the tournament was not a war but a friendly contest."[6] Eisenstein developed new forms in polemical debate with contemporary conversations about theater and its audiences. His "montage of attractions," for instance, intentionally contrasts with the "accumulation of tricks" that Grigory Kozintsev promoted in his 1922 Eccentrist manifesto.[7] It is in this context that we should understand Eisenstein's relationship to Meyerhold—and to several of Meyerhold's sources, including Hoffmann, Tieck, Gozzi, and commedia.

Eisenstein's sources of inspiration were dizzyingly voluminous; he insatiably read, listened to, and watched the works of others. His interest in popular entertainments, circus in particular, and in visual art was equally avid. Just a few of the artists refracted in his work are Daumier, El Greco, Callot, Goya, Piranesi, Gauguin, and Michelangelo.[8] In 1928 Eisenstein called James Joyce's *Ulysses* "the Bible of the new cinema";[9] he avidly read Freud; and he had a lifelong passion for Kabuki. "No understanding of the Soviet film artist can be complete," notes Perry, "which does not recognize the passion with which [Eisenstein] sought to assert himself and the multiplicity of layers upon which he lived and worked."[10]

In defining Eisenstein's theatrical inspirations, many scholars have focused on postrevolutionary forms that shaped the structure of his work: circus, Eccentrism, American and French film serials, detective novels, and so on.[11] Without disregarding these sources, I hope to position Eisenstein in a larger temporal conversation, one that did not begin with the Revolution, one that at first seems disjointed, yet, at second glance (after all, in Hoffmann, much is revealed at a second glance), has a startling degree of continuity. In examining Eisenstein's interest in Hoffmann's form, I shed new light on the thinking behind Eisenstein's formal innovations and, through this, on the poetics of Eisenstein's theater and film. Eisenstein's early innovations can be understood most precisely not in the context of the carnivalesque, of surrealism, or of expressionism, but of the theatrical grotesque.

Eisenstein's work in theater and film marked a new development in Russian Hoffmaniana. Although many Russian kindred artists had a deep interest in Hoffmann, Meyerhold was the first to use Hoffmann to reconceive theatrical form and creative audience engagement. Tairov took Hoffmannian disorientation in a new direction, making the master-actor a magician who bombarded spectators with kaleidoscopic images and elated them with virtuosic skill. Meyerhold embraced Hoffmann's nightmarish qualities, while Tairov was drawn to his phantasmagorical ones. Eisenstein was less interested in the grotesque as a style than as a way to structure art. For the most part, increasingly over the 1920s, he rejected the mystical and nightmarish content with which Hoffmann had become associated but avidly embraced the writer's architecture of form, especially his use of dissonance, juxtaposition, and plural perspective, to redefine theater and film form from the point of view of audience engagement.

Although Eisenstein moved, in his words, "through theater to cinema," his theatrical experiments provided the foundation for an artistic philosophy that supported his entire career.[12] He did not simply pass through theater en route to film; he viewed film through the prism of theater. To a degree that has not been fully appreciated, Eisenstein's early theatrical work (1917–24), including staged work but also unrealized projects, served an essential function in the development of his artistic worldview. As Ivanov and Ivanova rightly note, "it is not only 'the real theater of Eisenstein,' consisting of his productions that were staged and shown to audiences that deserves serious study, but also the 'imagined theater . . .' that appeared in his writings, reflections, sketches, etc."[13] As Perry argues, the seemingly separate aspects of Eisenstein's creative process—drawing, theory, teaching, filmmaking (and, I would add, theater)—were fundamentally interrelated, meaning that "no part can be understood without understanding the whole."[14] Yet despite the availability of several recent Russian books on Eisenstein's theatrical innovations, Eisenstein's theatre still has received comparatively little attention in English-language scholarship.[15]

Beginning in 1917, Eisenstein jotted down notes and designs for dozens of imagined theater productions, ideas from many of which resurface in his films. This "imagined theatre" provides a rare window into the formation of an artist. In them we clearly see his nascent interest in simultaneity, irony, and distortion. Sketches teem with simultaneous settings and framing devices, plays of scale and forced perspective, and fusions of animals, machines, and humans. Eisenstein experiments with the grotesque, but in a new iteration increasingly grafted with a postrevolutionary sensibility. Though he begins by exploring commedia, as Meyerhold did before the Revolution, the working-class entertainments of Eisenstein's day—circus, variety, film, and detective novels—fueled new vocabularies of juxtaposition. Eisenstein's intense theatrical exploration bears some similarities to Meyerhold-Dapertutto's studio years, though while Meyerhold had a physical theater laboratory, Eisenstein's was initially a mental one. Both experimented avidly—Meyerhold with raw, untrained students, and Eisenstein with raw drawing and writing materials. In the process, both clarified aesthetic grammars that persisted throughout their careers.

This chapter analyzes how Eisenstein's theater designs and staging plans helped him to develop and articulate a poetics of theatrical form. His theater can be divided roughly into three phases: experiments and ideas he recorded on paper as part of a vigorous self-education, often in a one-sided, private polemic with other productions; designs and staging plans for amateur and professional theater projects for the Red Army, Proletkult, and various Moscow theaters before becoming Meyerhold's student; and projects, some staged, some not, that overlapped temporally with and extended beyond his time as Meyerhold's student. Although Eisenstein intentionally worked on plays across genres from disparate periods, I will examine those that refracted Hoffmaniana most directly: his early designs for commedia and Gozzi plays (1918–19), notes on and designs for Offenbach's *Tales of Hoffmann* (1919–21), unrealized productions of Hoffmann's *The Golden Pot* (1920–1928) and *Master Martin the Cooper and His Men* (1921–22), and designs for Meyerhold's unrealized *Puss in Boots* (1921–22). These works provide a theoretical foundation for this chapter's central "interlude," Eisenstein and Sergei Yutkevich's pantomime *Columbine's Garter* (1922), a refraction of both Meyerhold's *Columbine's Veil* and Tairov's *Pierrette's Veil*. Of all Eisenstein's unstaged works, *Columbine's Garter* is the most significant: it provides a detailed perspective on how Eisenstein refracted the work of other theatricalist directors, and it was Eisenstein's first attempt to define the attraction.

This examination of the years leading up to *Wiseman*, Eisenstein's first solo directing project, reveals that Eisenstein's attraction is a refraction of the theatrical grotesque. In his analysis of the achievements of Eisenstein's films, Jean Narboni notes:

> What are outlined here are the principles of a cinema which thinks (but does not stop at that) the sequence of its images not as a continuous flow but as *alternation*, the replacement of one by the other, an iterative succession (each first of all having a value in its own right); a cinema that . . . shows up and points to the *frame* and *framing* of its shots . . . , designating its framing procedure, the delineation of its *take*, what it *holds* (as opposed to the unnoticed juncture with 'the world'). . . . This is the only cinema capable of comprehending itself as a signifying practice, aware of its materiality, detaching itself at last from the ideology of 'lived experience.'[16]

Were we to substitute the word "theater" for "cinema," this could serve as a definition for Meyerhold's grotesque. Though Eisenstein drew on a range of sources throughout his career, examining his refractions of Meyerhold and Meyerhold's sources provides distinctive clarity on the development of Eisenstein's film thinking and of the theater thinking that preceded and shaped it.

THE THEATRICAL ADVENTURES OF MR. PEREGRINUS TYSS

In his biographical writings, Eisenstein frequently recalls his overbearing architect father, Mikhail Osipovich, with whom he lived in Riga after his parents divorced in 1909. Eisenstein's father insisted that his son, who loved to draw, read, and daydream, become an engineer, and so to engineering school the young Sergei went. Moving to Saint Petersburg in 1915 to study at the Institute of Civil Engineering gave him the opportunity to live with his mother, Yulia Ivanovna. It also set him on the path that led to his rejection of engineering as a vocation.

The first theatrical production that, in Eisenstein's words, "ruined" him, that is "converted" him to the theater, was Komissarzhevsky's 1912 *Princess Turandot* (see figure 17), which he saw on its Riga tour. As he recalls:

> Especially stunning were the commedia dell'arte masks (only later, already in Petrograd, did I find out what it was and what I had seen; then, I remember, I was even a little shocked—"Pantalone" in China!) and the entirely unfamiliar treatment of the footlights, the prompter's box, the auditorium . . . I still consider this production to be decisive to my "career."[17]

When Eisenstein moved to Petrograd, he saw several of Nikolai Evreinov's productions at the Distorting Mirror and Meyerhold's *The Steadfast Prince*, *Dom Juan*, and *Masquerade* at the latter's notorious premiere on the eve of the February Revolution. Eisenstein describes the effect *Masquerade* had on him, especially in conjunction with what he was reading at the time:

> [After *Turandot*,] for 2–3 years . . . I completely lost interest in the theater. . . . But then . . . I bought Muratov by chance,[18] then Vernon Lee,[19] then Miklashevsky was published,[20] then I discovered Peretts's collection,[21] *Three Oranges, On Theatre*, etc., and ended up at *Masquerade*. This latter production I consider to be the decisive one on the path mapped out by *Turandot*. From that point forth, a definite passion for directing in the form of innumerable plans, stagings, sketches for everything I read.[22]

Eisenstein embraced theater and revolution simultaneously. Just after the February Revolution, in March 1917, he joined the Ensigns Engineering School. When it was disbanded in January 1918, he volunteered as a Civil War engineer for the Reds, for whom he constructed "transport routes and defense fortifications." His father was an engineer for the opposing Whites. In July 1920 Eisenstein became a designer for a Red Army front-line theater troupe, with which he remained until he moved to Moscow in October 1920.[23]

In November 1917, just days after the October Revolution, Eisenstein developed a libretto and designs for his first commedia-inspired pantomime, *The Millions of Pierrot*,[24] thereby initiating his prolific Civil War-period theatrical self-education. He reflected in 1920:

> Beginning in 1918—a sudden change in external circumstances: I left the Institute for army service (a good thing) and a two-year tragedy—I rode around all of Russia with the army engineer corps. Getting to Petersburg for short snatches of time, unsystematically trying to fill in the gaps of everything I didn't know: Craig, *Theater for Oneself*, Tieck, Hoffmann, Immermann, Browning.[25]

Figure 31. Sergei Eisenstein, simultaneous setting, inspired by medieval scene design conventions, for a play Eisenstein penned as Peregrinus Tyss, *A True Comedy about the Lustful Sorceress Tortellina, the Black Goat, God's Righteous Judgment, and Also about the Crafty Devils Orishel and Tortishel and Other Amusing Events as They Happened in the Good City of Madaur in Ancient Times.* Handwritten caption by Eisenstein above the drawing: "Comedy of the Black Goat: Les Mansions" (March–June 1920). Russian State Archive of Literature and Art, f. 1923, op. 1, ed. khr. 736: 12.

Eisenstein's insatiable theatrical appetite is evident in the breadth of the over 100 plays—most penned by others, a few by him—for which he created designs and staging plans, many of which responded directly to contemporary Russian theatrical experiments.[26] A number of his earliest designs are for plays with metatheatrical elements: Shakespeare's *Hamlet*; Gozzi's *The Snake Woman, The King Stag*, and *Love of Three Oranges*; and Aristophanes's *The Birds, The Clouds*, and *Lysistrata*. He also wrote additional commedia-inspired pantomimes, including *A Dozen Hours of Columbine* (1919–20).[27]

In February 1920, in Velikie Luki, near the Russian border with today's Belarus, Eisenstein directed his first production with the Eighteenth War Construction Project. Arkady Averchenko's *The Double*, in which Eisenstein also played the "Man in Spectacles," is a lighthearted piece in two acts about a tangle of events brought about by mistaken identity: a traveler, Kolesakin, is taken for a local engineer of means, Zaitsev, and takes advantage of the situation to predictable comic effect: the bewildered Zaitsev encounters a series of people who believe they have talked with him earlier that day.[28] As is clear from the production's playbill and poster, most participants doubled the play's fictional doubles by performing under pseudonyms, Eisenstein included.[29] This is the first record of Eisenstein having used the pseudonym Peregrinus Tyss, the hero of Hoffmann's *Master Flea* (figure 31).

Peregrinus Tyss was not Eisenstein's first nom du plume, nor was it to be his last. He signed many drawings, some reviews, and a few political cartoons "Sir Gay," an English pun on his given name. "R. O'Rik," another Anglicized pseudonym, was based on "Rorik," a pet name given him by his childhood nurse. Shortly after he became a student at Meyerhold's State Higher Theatre Workshops in the fall of 1921, he adopted a new alter ego; he and fellow student Sergei Yutkevich became a clown duo: Pip (Yutkevich) and Fax (Eisenstein), together "Pipifax." The last record I have found of Eisenstein using the name Tyss was in spring or early summer 1920,[30] a few months before he moved to Moscow; most likely he was concerned that to use a Hoffmannian pseudonym in the city where Meyerhold worked would be viewed as derivative of Dapertutto.

As Zabrodin notes, Eisenstein's Hoffmannian pseudonym was probably indeed inspired by Meyerhold, whom he admired wildly (albeit still from a distance) and in whose written works he was then fully immersed.[31] Eisenstein was one of many of his generation whose admiration for Meyerhold-Dapertutto bordered on fanaticism. Like Meyerhold, Eisenstein grew up speaking German and had an independent interest in Hoffmann: he had read the writer's tales as a child, at which point *The Golden Pot*'s Archivist Lindhorst became one of his favorite characters.[32] He also owned a cherished portrait of Hoffmann.[33]

Master Flea, like *The Golden Pot* and *Princess Brambilla*, is a whimsical, yet consciously constructed fantasy. Its formal elements provided fodder for Eisenstein's montage in theater and film, particularly with regard to disorienting collisions of disparate realities, selves, and truths. It opens with a little boy, Peregrinus Tyss, on the verge of opening his Christmas presents with his doting parents looking on. The narrator makes a surprising revelation several pages in, however: Tyss is not actually a little boy, but a grown man playing at being a little boy; his parents are dead; and he purchased the toys himself in a curious annual ritual. This is revealed in increments with a keen sense of the impact that each revelation will have on the reader.

This disorientation born of deliberately leading readers down one wrong expository path only to surprise them with another becomes a series of similarly disconcerting threads that run throughout the tale: characters lack stable identities; the setting of Frankfurt am Main is juxtaposed with the magical land of Famagusta; and humans are fused with animals, plants, and spirits. Tyss encounters a mysterious woman, first introduced as Aline, then as Dörtje Elwerdinck, then as Princess Gemaheh. We learn that Tyss's friend George Pepustch is also a thistle. Tyss eventually recalls (through a fog of temporal distance) that he himself is really an ancient king. The tale is structured around competing realities in which individuals are their own doppelgängers in collision with yet a third, mystical self. Characters change scale and form unexpectedly and frequently inhabit the uncanny space between life and death.

As the tale careens unapologetically through these planes, one point of stability is the story of Master Flea, who begs Tyss to protect him from slavery to Dörtje Elwerdinck and Leuwenhoek (a flea tamer and mage who, by his own admission, has been dead for nearly a century). As an expression of gratitude for Tyss's protection, Master Flea inserts a tiny microscope, no bigger than a grain of sand, into Tyss's eye. The result is that Tyss can see the true thoughts of those around him, thoughts that rarely coincide with their speaker's words. The microscope thus reveals the characteristic romantic duality between the false, quotidian world and the true, inner world. It also becomes a metaphor for the all-seeing lens of the artist, a serendipitous parallel to Eisenstein's later framing of the world through the camera lens.

Tyss's biography is at times strikingly similar to Eisenstein's own, particularly with regard to the relationship between Tyss/Eisenstein and his father:

> Dilettantes were an abomination to [Mr. Tyss], and yet Peregrinus showed every sign of becoming such a dilettante, having acquired in his own way a chaotic jumble of knowledge . . . Peregrinus cared nothing about the real world, his father knew of no other; and so it was inevitable that, as Peregrinus grew older, this should give rise to an ever-increasing conflict between father and son. This caused great sorrow to Peregrinus's mother . . . [who] was perfectly happy to tolerate his activities, little as she understood his dreams and fancies, and she could not understand why his father was so anxious to impose a specific occupation on him.[34]

Tyss drops out of university and goes on a three-year wander; serendipitously, Eisenstein similarly left engineering school to join the Red Army. More significant than biographical parallels, though, is the symbolic link between Tyss's unbounded wanderings and Eisenstein's theatrical explorations. The spirit of Hoffmann's freedom to use any and every useful source in radically new combinations infused Eisenstein's work at every stage of his career. In Russia it was well understood by then that to assume Hoffmann's mantle was to define one's own rules and to revel in the process of creation. It is in this spirit that Eisenstein-Tyss created his designs and production plans. Although Eisenstein's first commedia drawings predate his adoption of Tyss as a pseudonym, I propose that we think of 1917–20, the years that span what Ivanov and Ivanova call Eisenstein's "theatrical apprenticeship,"[35] as his Tyss period in acknowledgment of the nature, purpose, and scope of his explorations.

Figure 32. Sergei Eisenstein, costume design for *Amusements on the Water and in a Field* (c. 1917–18), "Harlequin's entrance." Signed "Sir Gay." Russian State Archive of Literature and Art, f. 1923, op. 1, ed. khr. 698: 31.

Framing Commedia (1917–19)

Eisenstein's first extant commedia experiment was not, as Leyda and Voynow mistakenly assert, based on Goldoni's *The Honest Courtesan* [*sic*] (*La putta ornorata*) (Eisenstein sympathized, of course, with Meyerhold's anti-Goldoni polemics), but on a commedia scenario by the same name: he recently had read Vladimir Peretts's collection of scenarios and interludes performed by Italian players at the court of Tsarina Anna in the eighteenth century.[36] Another of Eisenstein's commedia sources was Miklashevsky's book *La commedia dell'arte*. Because Eisenstein avidly read what issues of *Love for Three Oranges* he could and created designs for Gozzi plays that were available in Russian only in *Love for Three Oranges*, we can assume he had at least the inaugural issue with Meyerhold, Soloviev, and Vogak's *Three Oranges* and the 1916 no. 2–3 issue, which contained Gozzi's *Snake Woman*. Eisenstein's sketches for these and other commedia scenarios refract numerous Meyerholdian reforms, several of which are particularly noteworthy, as explorations begun here illuminate later work.[37]

Eisenstein experimented in several drawings with contrasting main characters and commedia masks. A design for *Amusements on the Water and in a Field* features the scenario's main characters standing in the center of the drawing in turbans and flowing robes. They are framed on both sides by grotesquely distorted masked characters. Eisenstein also constructed colliding planes by juxtaposing geographical locations (recalling Eisenstein's surprised "Pantalone in China!"). Additionally the main characters, whose

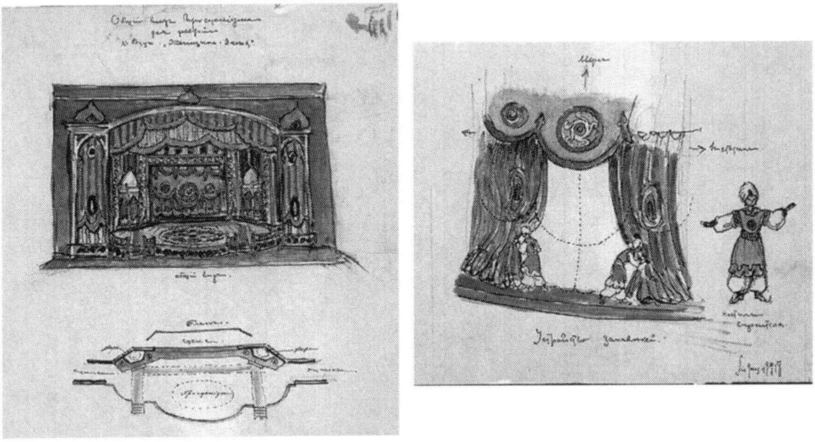

Figure 33. Sergei Eisenstein, staging designs for Gozzi's *The Snake Woman* (February 26, 1918). Left, from top to bottom: stage-within-a-stage; ground plan of forestage. Right: forestage "attendants." Russian State Archive of Literature and Art, f. 1923, op. 1, ed. khr. 698: 11.

actions are story-driven, illustrate the play's fairy-tale reality, while the *lazzo*-driven masks, who comment on the story, are infused with the grotesque (figure 32).

For *The Snake Woman*, Eisenstein experimented with Meyerholdian framing devices by clearly delineating an oval forestage and an upstage theater-within-a-theater. Eisenstein used forestage servants, or "attendants" as he retitles them, to draw back the curtain of this internal stage. Like the liveried pages in Meyerhold's *Dom Juan*, Eisenstein costumed these attendants to correspond to the world of the main story, here a fairy-tale version of Tiflis (Tbilisi, Georgia) (figure 33).

In his sketches for *The Green Bird*, Gozzi's last *fiaba*, Eisenstein plays with framing devices from Meyerhold, Soloviev, and Vogak's *Three Oranges*. Second-story windows flanking the proscenium arch contain characters peering down onto the action below. Eisenstein's design pays homage to Serlio's 1545 comedy setting in *Architettura*, but with the addition of Meyerhold's balcony characters (figure 34).[38] Onstage observers resurface in a design by Eisenstein for *Four Harlequins*, this time with the addition of two arches upstage center beyond which Venetian canals can be seen in the distance and atop which are functional playing spaces for the actors.

Eisenstein's interest in trying out the framing devices about which he was reading and had seen in Meyerhold's productions is palpable in these

Figure 34. Sergei Eisenstein, scene design for Gozzi's *The Green Bird* (c. 1917–19). Russian State Archive of Literature and Art, f. 1923, op. 1, ed. khr. 698: 28.

designs. In particular, he grapples with how to represent multiple planes of reality, contrasting physical and dramaturgical styles, and characters in relation to each other, the stage space, and the audience. His sketches investigate how the innovations about which he was reading functioned and how they might be taken further. What happens, for instance, if one combines Serlio's proscenium-based perspective design, Meyerhold's illusion-disrupting framing devices, and Gozzi's *Green Bird*?

Such intersections abound in Eisenstein's early writings. In May 1919 he began keeping a diary that systematically recorded his theatrical discoveries and polemics.[39] He continued making regular entries in notebooks until July 1920. A September 5, 1919 entry (later revised) illuminates the greater intellectual context of Eisenstein's commedia musings. In it he explores what it means to work "in the spirit of" another:

> I read a whole series of works "after" Gozzi, "after" Tieck, etc. (Luscinius, Meyerhold, Soloviev, etc.) and thought about the methods of creative work "in the spirit of," for example, commedia dell'arte, mysteries, etc. I involuntarily recalled (again, I have the desire to make *my* meaning in refracted form) the words of S[ergei] Radlov (at a session on "improvisation methods"), where he said that one must read all the classics, all the work of contemporary artists etc., etc., and . . . the "elixir," the hidden spring, the mysteries of the craft

> will come into you unnoticed through all this material. (S. Radlov, of course, would not recognize his words in such a reworking, but that is not important: the spark that gave birth to my thought came precisely from this. . . .). I think the same should be kept in mind when creating "after" or "in the spirit of."[40]

In Eisenstein's view, any artist working in response to another contributes something new, ideally in the form of a dynamic, original creative response. Long before he began his professional theater work, Eisenstein used sources "in refracted form" to spark his own creative revolutions.

Refracting *Tales of Hoffmann* (1919–21)

Eisenstein's designs and staging notes for Offenbach's 1881 *Tales of Hoffmann*, developed between 1919 and 1921, illuminate Eisenstein's unique, often aggressive approach to working in the manner of others. His preliminary notes begin with a polemical attack on a production of *Tales* by Yosef Lapitsky that Eisenstein had seen in Petrograd,[41] focusing on act 2, the Olimpia act, of this production:[42]

> To talk about the staging of this scene is very difficult, that is, to say anything new and purely original—Lapitsky's dolls are almost unavoidable. . . . As soon as you begin thinking about Olimpia, fortunately, the scenery frees itself entirely from his influence, for the dirty, two-toned rags with which he wanted to say something nightmarish . . . can hardly be considered scenery at all.[43]

Lapitsky, known for realism in other productions,[44] created a ball scene in *Tales* that was designed to startle: the guests were all automata like Olimpia—an attempt to capitalize on the then-ubiquitous marionette metaphor.[45]

Eisenstein's criticism of Lapitsky's *Tales* provided him with a starting point for his own ideas. His counter-solution to Lapitsky's dolls was to treat Olimpia as an automaton but the guests as marionettes.[46] His design for an Olimpia with unnatural, mechanical angles and a glassy expression contrasts sharply with his designs for the guests: grotesque fusions of humans, animals, and objects.[47] Both here and later in *Columbine's Garter*, Eisenstein uses marionettes metaphorically as unthinking figures wielded by outside forces and automata as vehicles for acts of malevolence against other characters. Olimpia serves this latter function in Hoffmann's original tale and in Offenbach's opera.

In preemptive anticipation of would-be skeptics, Eisenstein stages a defense of his production plan as he writes it, imagining himself in a polemic not only with Lapitsky, but with anyone who might accuse him of unoriginal thinking:

Figure 35. Sergei Eisenstein, scene design for Offenbach's *Tales of Hoffmann*, act 2 (March 12, 1920). Russian State Archive of Literature and Art, f. 1923, op. 1, ed. khr. 735: 4.

> The guests are marionettes; Olympia alone is a mech[anical] doll. "You think this is surprising?" they will say to me. "He has replaced a factory doll with a marionette and thinks this is imaginative?" But indulge me: the range of a marionette's movement differs fundamentally from the movement of a factory doll . . . The marionetteishness of the guests gives us the key to the scene design: everyone knows that marionettes hang on strings that come from above the stage. "So what?" Well, then you can't build the usual "entrance doors"—the upper jamb will be an obstacle when the figures enter, for it will catch the strings. "You mean a box without doors instead of a room?" No—I'd make a stage like in children's toy theaters, where the room is depicted not with three walls, but with successive side wings. . . . Between these "screens" (conventionalized entrances) our marionettes can freely flit in and out without catching their proposed threads.[48]

Eisenstein also used these screens to create radically forced perspective (figure 35). He writes, "The screens, as they get further from the footlights, become drastically shorter and shorter, emphasizing the perspective of the nar-

Figure 36. Sergei Eisenstein, *periaktoi* configurations for *Tales of Hoffmann*, act 2 (1920). Russian State Archive of Literature and Art, f. 1923, op. 1, ed. khr. 735: 5.

rowing (*blanc et noir*) checkerboard floor."[49] He intended to make the actors seem as if they had been brought down to the scale of toy theater. Eisenstein initially hoped that tall performers and short performers could be grouped by height, downstage and upstage respectively, to intensify the impression of forced perspective. In lieu of borders and wings, the background was to be masked "with my beloved black velvet" in order to provide "a fantastical, rather nightmarish . . . 'backdrop' in a figurative sense."[50]

Eisenstein's designs collide toy-theater wings with Greek and Renaissance *periaktoi*—three-sided, mobile scenic units that pivot to reveal a different setting on each side. In scene designs dated June 1920, almost a year after Eisenstein penned his initial staging notes, the wings are no longer fixed, and he has replaced two-dimensional screens with *periaktoi* that can be moved to any position on the stage to provide a climbing and playing space for the actors (figure 36). Over the course of a year, Eisenstein transitioned from a picture-frame perspective with conventionalized elements to a shiftable perspective that undermines an audience's spatial assumptions. The checkerboard floor reiterated Eisenstein's metaphor of the guests as marionettes played upon by unseen forces. This metaphor also informs his costume designs, dated another year later, in September 1921. One dour-looking woman has a bulbous skirt that envelops her legs entirely, making

Figure 37. Sergei Eisenstein, costume design for *Tales of Hoffmann*, act 2 (September 17, 1921). Russian State Archive of Literature and Art, f. 1923, op. 1, ed. khr. 735: 10.

her look simultaneously like a giant water jug and an enormous, unwilling pawn (figure 37).

In these designs, Eisenstein links Hoffmann with the Russian theatrical grotesque. He was particularly interested in Meyerhold's use of contrast, incongruous elements, and perspectival shifts. Many of Eisenstein's designs are also jarring amalgams of human, animal, object, and bird. Although these designs never resulted in a production of *Tales*, similar animal-human collisions resurface in his later works, most famously in his film *Strike* (1925), in which police spies are juxtaposed with animals corresponding to their personalities (see figure 45) and a police massacre of innocent strikers is intercut with the slaughter of a bull.

TYSS'S MOSCOW EXPERIMENTS

To his joy, Eisenstein was transferred from the Red Army's Construction Division to the Theatre Section in June 1920. He wrote in a letter to his mother, "Even now . . . I am afraid to believe that I will entirely belong to a theater."[51] For the remainder of the summer he traveled the countryside creating sets for agit-productions and slogans for agit-trains. In fall 1920, as the Civil War wound down, he was demobilized. From the same letter to his mother we learn that students in the Red Army were given the option of returning to their previous universities in September 1920.[52] Eisenstein did not wish to continue his engineering studies, but he did want to leave active military service. He therefore moved to Moscow in October to study Japanese at the General Staff Academy. Nearly simultaneously he was made head of design for the Proletkult First Workers' Theatre. Within months he had dropped his Japanese studies (though he maintained a lifelong interest in Japanese culture) and had immersed himself in the theater.[53]

One of Eisenstein's early recurrent collaborators was Valentin Smyshliaev, a director and actor who started out at the Moscow Art Theatre and its First Studio and was then a director at Proletkult. Shortly after Eisenstein moved to Moscow, Smyshliaev invited Eisenstein to co-design (with L. A. Nikitin) a production of Jack London's *The Mexican* (premiere March 10, 1921).[54]

During Eisenstein's first years in Moscow, he worked primarily as a designer. Yet his images and mise-en-scène ideas significantly shaped each production's meaning, use of space, approach to character, and relationship with an audience. In other words, Eisenstein directed through design. This is clear from his account of his role in *The Mexican*:

> My first move (trespassing upon the director's job, since I was there in the official capacity of designer only) was to propose that the fight be brought into view. Moreover I suggested that the scene be staged in the center of the auditorium to re-create the same circumstances under which a real boxing match takes place . . .
>
> The playing of our young worker-actors in the fight scene differed radically from their acting elsewhere in the production. In every other scene, one emotion gave rise to a further emotion (they were working in the Stanislavsky system), which in turn was used as a means to affect the audience; but in the fight scene the audience was excited directly.
>
> Our scene employed realistic, even textural means—real fighting, bodies crashing to the ring floor, panting, the shine of sweat on torsos, and finally, the unforgettable smacking of gloves against taut skin and strained muscles. Illusionary scenery gave way to a realistic ring . . .
>
> Thus my realization that I had struck new ore, an actual-materialistic element in theater.[55]

In Meyerholdian terms, Eisenstein had discovered how the grotesque can heighten theater's perpetual real/fictional duality.

Eisenstein created designs for over twenty projects in Moscow, some realized, others not, over the next three years. Among those that reached an audience are *The Mexican, Macbeth, Be Kind to Horses*, and *The Phenomenal Tragedy of Phetra* (a parody of the Kamerny's *Phaedra*). Those that did not reach an audience include *Tsar Hunger, Puss in Boots, Heartbreak House*, and Hoffmann's *Golden Pot* and *Master Martin the Cooper and His Men*. Because the prolific and startlingly innovative theater of the early 1920s was generated during war and famine, many promising projects were abandoned due to lack of funds or perceived irrelevance to the Revolution.[56] Eisenstein lamented in a letter to his mother that "due to concerns about its 'ideological side,'" work on *Tsar Hunger*, for which he had hopes of collecting a substantial and much-needed fee, was halted.[57]

Eisenstein's collaboration with Smyshliaev on *The Mexican* led to two separate, overlapping attempts to stage Hoffmann tales: *The Golden Pot* and *Master Martin*. It is not entirely clear who initiated these projects. Though Eisenstein later complained that Smyshliaev's directing style had too much of the Moscow Art Theatre in it for his taste, Cherkassky notes that Smyshliaev used Hoffmann's works as a vehicle for "synthesizing the lessons of the psychological theater (in its Vakhtangovian variant) with presentational theater, the theater of the conventionalized-metaphorical realm."[58] Smyshliaev planned to direct both Hoffmann adaptations (the first in collaboration with Arensky), while Eisenstein was to design, though for Eisenstein the border between director and designer was always blurred. Eisenstein wrote in a letter to his mother that he was working on the *Golden Pot* adaptation with Arensky[59] and in another that he was cowriting a play with Smyshliaev, likely *Master Martin*.[60]

Master Martin (1920–22)

In the unlikely event that Eisenstein proposed staging *Master Martin the Cooper and His Men* (*Meister Martin der Küfner und seine Gesellen*), one of the most quotidian of Hoffmann's tales, it would seem to be an odd choice. Its fantastical elements are few, especially when compared to *Master Flea*'s forays into fantasy. *Master Martin* relates the adventures of two young German artists in love with the same woman, Rosa, the daughter of Master Martin, a bourgeois wine-cask builder to whom both young men are apprenticed. The tale is an allegory for being true to oneself as an artist: only after one of the young men embraces his true calling as a silversmith is he able to win Rosa's love.

Eisenstein was concerned that postrevolutionary proletarian audiences might find *Master Martin* irrelevant. He wrote in his initial staging notes, "The 'tale' of *Martin* is so very colorless and 'all by itself' so trifling that a comic reinvigoration of it will give necessary sustenance to the audience."[61] It is telling that Eisenstein thought of a theatrical production in terms of nourishment. He added: "A sugary-sweet *Master Martin* is not only untheatrical but is boring even to read. Some heroic efforts are needed not only in order to interest the audience . . . until the end with this story that doesn't in any way relate to us. Which means the artificial graftings of the theater."[62] These "artificial graftings" include framing devices from Eisenstein's Tyss period juxtaposed with postrevolutionary justifications. He divides both stage space and dramatic content into two planes—action and comically framed action—by placing a working-class circus frame around the temporally, geographically, and ideologically distant bourgeois German world.

On the circus plane, a pair of fools constantly interrupts Hoffmann's story with *lazzi* and commentary in the manner of Meyerhold, Soloviev, and Vogak's *Three Oranges*—but with bolder interjections. Eisenstein imagined having the fools say at the very beginning: "Typical sugary German romanticism from the beginning of the last century. . . . Let's spice it up!"[63] This "spice" pervades the entire imagined production. Eisenstein adds: "The Sachsian Fastnachtsspiel is staged with a clownish feeling, with a prologue in a cassock that just barely covers its bell-decorated hat."[64]

Several of Eisenstein's sketches reveal that the stage was to be set up in, by now, familiar fashion: twin portals flank an ornate proscenium arch. Balconies atop the portals are connected by an inner stage with a curtain. Upstage and above this closed curtain, the rooftops of the city of Nuremberg can just be glimpsed.[65] The inner curtain is topped with a horizontal gymnast's bar on which the fools walk, fight, or sit dangling their legs into the scene below. The use of the horizontal bar as a circus-infused double proscenium frame illuminates the thinking behind the similar configuration in Eisenstein's 1923 *Wiseman*: both serve as the top frame of a stage-within-a-stage upon which characters perform (see figure 44).

Eisenstein's fools observe and comment on the action in various ways as they sit upon its frame. Much of their business is devoted to penetrating the action: they drop a basket onto the stage, steal food from characters below, and even crash through the roof.[66] In one instance, they cheekily disconcert Master Martin, blurring the line between actor and character as they do:

> Two fools: "I know something you don't know! . . . There can't be anything unexpected in a theatrical performance—it's all decided ahead of time!" "No it's not!" "Yes it is!" "Well, what if the wine casks of Master Martin were to burst!" (Down below Martin nervously checks the casks and, having assured himself that everything is in order, threatens them with his fist.) Uproarious laughter.[67]

In Meyerhold's *Three Oranges*, the fools in the towers clarified action on the main stage by commenting on it. Eisenstein gives his fools freer rein to intervene in the action and the structure of the theatrical event. They brawl over how theatrical surprise is structured, the end result of which is that both tumble down into the scene below. Eisenstein evidently enjoyed exploring the many possible variations of these juxtapositions between planes, as he added, "Later, as needed, [the fools] sit on the horizontal bar snacking on herrings."[68]

Because the fools, who speak in colloquial dialect, are the characters most closely aligned to Eisenstein's spectators, their comments allow viewers to refract Hoffmann's tale from their own point of view. Thus Meyerhold's earlier use of fools as an interrupting and refocusing device is replaced with fools as a tool for comic refraction. Story and commentary operate in a constant dialectic in which comic action impudently renders would-be serious action ironic, much as Meyerhold had done with his staged debates over theatrical genres in the second interlude of *Three Oranges*. In one scene in which Master Martin kisses a small child, the fools mimic his actions, but their "child" is a jug, presumably of wine, which they raise to their lips for other purposes. The fools also parody Martin's actions (Eisenstein does not indicate which) via an "erotic parody" with sausages.[69]

In addition to comic *lazzi*, Eisenstein's fools introduce acrobatic acts into the production, a conflation of clownish business with circus techniques:

> The roles of the fools—the correct introduction (for now in a small dose) of acrobatic elements into the drama (leaps from balconies, a scene on the horizontal bar). Maybe a scene on the rooftops of the houses that form the proscenium opening *à cheval*.[70] A figure standing on the horizontal bar against a background of town and blue sky (*rouge et orange*) would be very effective and expressive.[71]

These *lazzi* and acrobatic circus turns are a precursor to Eisenstein's attraction, though he did not yet call it by this name. *Master Martin* also demonstrates Eisenstein's intense interest in exploding notions of how theater space can be used. In *Columbine's Garter* (1922), Eisenstein and Yutkevich set some of the action in the flies high above the stage. In *Wiseman*, which opened a year later, Eisenstein took this even further: in the production's short film, "Glumov's Diary," characters even climb the outside of the building in which the production took place.

The December 6–8, 1921, issue of *Ekran* (*The Screen*) announced that *Master Martin* was to open imminently at Proletkult.[72] Cherkassky informs us that by the following spring the production had been fully rehearsed and was ready to open, upon which it was banned. Despite the fact that 1922 was Hoffmann's jubilee year, Hoffmann's works, especially at a proletarian theater, were increasingly considered insufficiently supportive of postrevolutionary political ideologies.

The Golden Pot (1920–28)

Attempting to trace Eisenstein's work on *The Golden Pot* in any detail is more difficult. There are nearly a hundred extant designs and sketches from *The Mexican* and over a dozen pencil sketches for *Master Martin*. For *The Golden Pot*, RGALI holds one design and one accompanying sketch.[73] When Eisenstein first embarked on the adaptation in December 1920, he wrote in a letter to his mother, "For Monday, [P. A.] Arensky and I are intensely 'molding' Hoffmann's 'Golden Pot.'"[74] The following week he added: "Regarding my dramatization with Arensky (my part is the entire theatrical-staging plan and the entire production concept and 15 designs) of Hoffmann's *Golden Pot*, it has been deemed . . . stageworthy; they are afraid only of staging complications. . . . We will try to get it staged at the Moscow Art Theatre Studio."[75]

Despite the lack of additional production detail, *The Golden Pot* warrants some discussion because of Eisenstein's deep artistic connection to the tale and recurrent use of examples from it to articulate his understanding of the grotesque. Nikitin writes that Eisenstein was drawn specifically to "the phantasmagorical nature of the situations in the creative work of the German writer, the unending metamorphoses of the material world, [and] the suddenly dropped mask of decorum from behind which something completely opposite from what the reader had expected peers out."[76]

Hoffmann's *Golden Pot* is famous for its dizzyingly free approach to the fantasy. In a tale with abundant twists, turns, and false starts, the student Anselmus is caught between a mundane world and a truer realm in which the Archivist Lindhorst is really a fire salamander and Anselmus's beloved, Serpentina, Lindhorst's daughter, is really a little green-gold snake. Anselmus becomes caught between these worlds, as a result of which most think him mad. When Lindhorst's enemy, a witch (the daughter of a dragon's quill and a beet), tries to bring about Anselmus's destruction, it seems the student will lose the ability to believe in the fantasy world: he becomes trapped in a crystal bottle, a metaphor for those willingly ensnared in the everyday. After he vanquishes his attachment to the quotidian, he and Serpentina live happily in Atlantis, the kingdom of poesy.

As in many of Hoffmann's tales, wine and tobacco are gateways into another world. Anselmus first sees Serpentina after smoking "health tobacco." Quickly, however, he is able to see the fantastical after a second glance at the everyday. The story is filled with instantaneous transformations, nearly all of which happen at a second glance. Absurd juxtapositions are related matter-of-factly and without segue. Anselmus looks at an ordinary doorknocker and sees that it is a witch. Romantic irony is also used to grotesque effect. The tale takes the form of eleven vigils told from different perspectives—sometimes in third person, sometimes from a character's point of view, sometimes addressed directly to the reader. One vigil launches into a mystical story unrelated to anything thus far, though the reader eventually learns that it is Lindhorst's fantastical autobiography.

After a temporal gap for which we lack explanation, *The Golden Pot* went into rehearsals at the MAT Second Studio in 1924. It was designed, cast, placed on the production calendar, and rehearsed, upon which Glavrepertkom banned it, "alleging its 'difficulty.'"[77] A series of petitions from the second Moscow Art Theatre, where Mikhail Chekhov was artistic director, followed; these continued, to no avail, until 1928, the year Chekhov emigrated.[78] The production was first banned in 1925. In 1926 the Directorate of the State Academic Theatres of Moscow and Leningrad permitted rehearsals as long as no money was spent. When the MAT 2 renewed its petition in 1928, they were asked to turn over "the original manuscript of the text and the production designs, after which they disappeared,"[79] never to reemerge from Glavrepertkom's bowels.[80]

Eisenstein often used *The Golden Pot* to explain the architecture of the grotesque. In 1935 he gave a talk on contrasting trends in Russian theater. He argued that Vakhtangov's style was not a synthesis of Stanislavsky and Meyerhold, as is often thought, but a collision of the two. When asked to define the grotesque, he used an example from *The Golden Pot*—the same example Meyerhold used in "Balagan" ("The Fairground Booth") in 1913—to clarify:

> It is as if it is reality, but, at the same time, it isn't. If you look at Hoffmann's writings, in *The Golden Pot* the apple seller is also simultaneously a witch. Lindhorst in *The Golden Pot* is both an elderly archivist and, at night, a fire salamander; what's more, this is not in the order of normal transformations. Lindhorst, when he is an archivist, wears a robe with a hint of fire salamander, and when he is a fire salamander, there remain in him some elements of the archivist . . .
>
> It is precisely the absence of synthesis that is a sign of the grotesque. Elements that are supposed to be synthesized into a whole are present, not blending together, because if they blended together we would have a different order of creation . . . The fantastical plane and the real one, the material plane and the immaterial one are present not as a kind of unity in which either one side or the other turns to face you; rather in the grotesque we have the infiltration of one plane into another and an emphatic collision between the real and unreal.[81]

Eisenstein explains how such collisions apply to the theater: "On one hand we try to create a theatrical illusion, but at some point the theatrical mask is dropped and the actor winks at the audience, that is to say, breaks the frame of theatrical illusion."[82] This "winking," which collides the real and the fictional, is precisely what Eisenstein was trying to achieve when he placed a real boxing match inside the fictional world of *The Mexican*. Later, in *Wiseman*, he juxtaposed the prerecorded medium of film with the liveness of acrobatic stunts, producing an effect remarkably similar to seeing an actor's face emerge from behind a mask.

This definition of the grotesque illuminates why it is that Eisenstein experimented so frequently with framing devices. He was ever fascinated with the effect on a viewer of radical perspective shifts, with the infiltration of disparate selves into a single character, and with images that prompt viewers to generate new meanings. Eisenstein's profound understanding of the architecture of disorientation is probably the most significant reason *Battleship Potemkin*'s (1926) scene on the Odessa steps has become so famous. The juxtapositions of close-ups and long shots, the ways in which time is manipulated by having soldiers descend the steps again and again (not unlike Hoffmann's narrators, who begin their stories again and again): all these techniques were fundamental to Eisenstein's grotesque.

At Meyerhold's Workshops

In September 1921 Eisenstein had his first opportunity to study directly with Meyerhold. Not long after Theatre RSFSR 1 folded, leaving Meyerhold without a theater of his own, he opened the State Higher Directing Workshops (GVYRM). According to Yutkevich, Meyerhold founded his workshops in response to the tempestuous 1920/21 season at RSFSR 1, where he had provoked wild controversy with his declaration of "October in the theater" and with his agit-productions of Verhaeren's *The Dawns* and Mayakovsky's *Mystery-Bouffe*. After the local authorities forcibly closed RSFSR 1 due to (unfounded) accusations that it was not "financially lucrative and [that] its troupe of actors was haphazard," Meyerhold opened the workshops to "prepare an army of young people for a new offensive against the ramparts of the academic theaters."[83]

The State Higher Directing Workshops soon changed names to the State Higher Theatre Workshops (GVYTM) in acknowledgment of its two training programs: directing and acting, though Meyerhold required that students study both.[84] Directing students also developed designs and staging plans, often for productions Meyerhold hoped to mount. All students studied biomechanics, then in the process of development, along with supplementary physical training: gymnastics, boxing, fencing, acrobatics, *barre*, dance, and rhythmic gymnastics.[85] Meyerhold shared the building with film montage pioneer Lev Kuleshov, a cohabitation that allowed for cross-pollination between Meyerhold's fragmented theatrical forms and Kuleshov's belief that "the core of the meaning" of a film lay in its montage.[86] During the winter of 1921–22 Meyerhold added a "Free Workshop" for advanced students with previous theater experience; *Magnanimous Cuckold* grew out of this group's after-hours rehearsals.[87]

In August 1921, two Sergeis, Eisenstein and Yutkevich,[88] both future filmmakers, passed the entrance examination to GVYTM. Their directing studies began the following month. With his workshops, Meyerhold returned to the experimental spirit of his prerevolutionary studio work. Yutkevich provides a vivid firsthand account of the formation of the workshops and of his first days there as a student:

> In the fall of 1921, we found ourselves in a small auditorium of a three-story mansion on Novinsky Boulevard that previously had housed a high school. Meyerhold himself lived there with his family on the third floor in a small apartment. From there one went down a narrow, creaky, wooden staircase that abutted a small classroom space filled with ordinary school desks. The entire premises of GVYTM consisted of this room and the small auditorium . . .[89]
>
> At the first lesson, Eisenstein and I perched on the desk right next to the teacher's table. Behind it appeared Meyerhold. He looked at us sharply, piercingly, and announced that we would study two subjects: directing and biomechanics. Thus for the first time we heard this strange word that meant a new system of expressive stage movement . . .
>
> Meyerhold began to teach directing just as singularly . . . He got very excited and improvised on the spot, creating an image of a kind of ideal director who, in his opinion, should always conduct his own production . . . The director should, according to Meyerhold, "listen closely to the reaction of the audience and through a complex signaling process change the rhythms of the production based on the viewers' reaction."[90]

Yutkevich recalls that even then Eisenstein was impatient, that he wanted "to shake Meyerhold up and discover the true recipe [lit.: "kitchen"] of his creative work." Meyerhold was willingly pulled into conversation:

> That year Meyerhold was not doing anything in the theater and devoted all his time to us . . . We asked him to tell us about specific productions. We were interested in how the plan originated for the staging of Blok's *Balaganchik* at the Komissarzhevskaia Theatre, and how he worked with Ida Rubinstein on D'Annunzio's *La Pisanelle* in Paris, and much more . . . Our curiosity usually warmed Meyerhold up; he lit up and began to tell us amazing things frankly and in detail.[91]

Eisenstein's recollection of his time at Meyerhold's is far more ambivalent than Yutkevich's. Although he studied Meyerhold for almost five years before studying *with* Meyerhold and had already read many of the books Meyerhold assigned,[92] he hoped to gain much more as Meyerhold's student. He recalled having learned more from three days of observing Meyerhold rehearse *Nora* (*A Doll's House*, 1920) than he had in all his other creative life experiences to date. What Eisenstein hoped Meyerhold would provide was a directorial method. What he got instead was a director who was not seeking to codify a method, but to test and retest a definition of theater. In 1921, Meyerhold's primary concern was with experimenting in a new political and artistic environment in which he did not, at the time, have his own theater. The spring after Eisenstein joined Meyerhold's workshops, *Magnanimous Cuckold* opened. We now look back on it as a landmark production, but at the time it was simply a public demonstration of a provocative experiment. Eisenstein embraced such experiments, but was frustrated by the perceived elusiveness of their methods.

One of the most enlightening accounts of Eisenstein's simultaneous homage to and rebellion against Meyerhold is recorded in an autobiography that Eisenstein wrote in 1946, seven years after Meyerhold's arrest (when it was dangerous to write about Meyerhold at all) and two years before Eisenstein's death. "Wie sag' ich's meinem Kinde? (How do I tell my child?)" provides unique insight, albeit in hindsight, into Eisenstein's ambivalence. He wrote of Meyerhold's lecture-conversations at GVYTM:

> Meyerhold was directing with his hands.
> A flashing eye.
> Holding a puppet from Java.
> The master's deft fingers moved the gilt arms of the doll.
> The white face with slanting eyes spun from left to right.
> The doll had come to life like Ida Rubinstein; we remember her pose from a painting by Serov.
> And it was not a puppet in Meyerhold's hands,
> but Ida Rubenstein in *Pisonella*.
> And—flinging his hands upwards—Meyerhold directed the cascades of flashing fabrics which fly up in the scene of the market on the shore, on the stage of the Grand Opéra, in Paris.
> His hands froze in mid-air . . .
> And we had a preview of the "dead scene" in *The Government Inspector*.
> The dolls stood inanimate; and those, which sparkled on stage all evening in their image, danced past them wildly.
> The incomparable master stood like Gogol in silhouette.
> Then he lowered his arms . . .

Figure 38. Meyerhold in his study with portrait of Zinaida Raikh (as Anna Andreevna in *Inspector General*) behind him and *wayang golek* puppet profile just visible on the far right. This is the only known photograph of Meyerhold with this puppet. КП 319555/2. © A. A. Bakhrushin State Central Theatre Museum, Moscow.

> You could just hear the faintest ripple of applause; kidskin gloves marking the guests' approval, after Nina's romance[93] in *Masquerade* on the stage of the Alexandrinka, the day before the February Revolution in 1917.
> The sorcerer suddenly snapped the cord of enchantment.
> He held gold-painted wooden sticks and a piece of coloured cloth.
> The king of the elves had vanished.
> At the small table sat Lindhorst, the lacklustre archivist.
> His lectures were mirages and dreams.
> Notes were frantically jotted down.
> And on awaking, one's notebooks were covered in "goodness only knows."[94]

Eisenstein's description pairs Hoffmann's shifting characters in *The Golden Pot* with a similarly elusive Meyerhold. Indeed, Eisenstein juxtaposes multiple Meyerholds: the revered teacher, the Hoffmannian mage who wields actual puppets (figure 38), human puppets (in *La Pisanelle*), and puppet humans (in *Inspector General*) in contrast with *The Golden Pot*'s Archivist Lindhorst, who oscillates between fantastical and quotidian selves. Elsewhere in the same sketch, Eisenstein transforms Meyerhold into Eisenstein's own father and into *Balaganchik*'s Pierrot, all the while narrating from the point of view of the student Anselmus, who is ushered through dizzying, unstable worlds, subject, against will and reason, to Meyerhold's lectures, which hypnotize him into a glorious madness. In addition to revealing a great deal about Eisenstein's attitude toward Meyerhold, this essay is a brilliant example of the radical new definition of character that imbues much of Eisenstein's theatrical work: if multiple selves—and, by extension, multiple realities—can coexist, then the purpose of art is not to aim at a single truth, but to grapple with the collisions of multiple truths. By refracting a Hoffmannian–Meyerholdian notion of character as an accumulation of selves rather than as something to be psychologically revealed, Eisenstein introduces larger questions about how artists process the associations that shape their creative identities.

This sketch of Meyerhold is also a brilliant exploration in metaphor of Eisenstein's rejection of a single theatrical style in favor of investigating theatrical form. In *Master Martin* he abandoned the "sugary" romantic vocabulary that predated the 1917 Revolution in its origins but lingered into the Soviet 1920s in its implementation. Yet Eisenstein embraced the *form* of Hoffmann, Tieck, Gozzi, and Meyerhold. Like Meyerhold, Eisenstein's theater was based on aggressive juxtaposition; he actively wielded framing devices; and he never neglected the impact of a work on its audience. Characteristically, given his interest in colliding disparate sources, Eisenstein had no difficulty embracing the grotesque of Hoffmann and the dialectics of Marx.

Puss in Boots (1921–22)

Eisenstein generated his most direct Hoffmannian/Meyerholdian experiments between 1919 and 1922, with the greatest burst taking place during the year he was Meyerhold's student. He developed *The Golden Pot, Master Martin*, and *Columbine's Garter*, each time with a collaborator, outside Meyerhold's workshops. At Meyerhold's workshops, his most significant projects were *Tarelkin's Death*, Shaw's *Heartbreak House*, and Tieck's *Puss in Boots*.

Just a few days after Eisenstein completed scene designs for *Puss in Boots*, Meyerhold wrote a letter to Narkompros (the Commissariat for Enlightenment, of which Lunacharsky was head) and Glavpolitprosvet (the Chief Committee for Political Education)[95] to petition for a new theater of which Meyerhold would be artistic director, proposing that it be "supported with state funding by Glavpolitprosvet" and located "in the premises of the former Theatre RSFSR 1."[96] Meyerhold appended a list of eleven proposed plays that could form the new theater's initial repertoire. Most deal in some way with a revolutionary uprising: Wagner's *Rienzi*, Jirásek's *Dogheads*,

Esenin's *Pugachev*, and Mérimée's *Jacquerie* are at the top of the list, followed by Lunacharsky's *Don Quixote Liberated*.

The remaining plays primarily represent works or authors with which Meyerhold had experimented in his Borodinskaia Street Studio days. Crommelynck's *Magnanimous Cuckold* is followed by *Puss in Boots* "after" Tieck, Shakespeare's *Hamlet*, Gozzi's *King Stag*, and Aristophanes's *The Assembly Women*.[97] Though this second group of plays at first seems less directly revolutionary than the first, each deals in some way with a revolt: in *Magnanimous Cuckold* a wife rebels against a jealous husband, in *Hamlet* and *King Stag* evil usurper kings are defeated, in *Puss in Boots* a cat helps his peasant master acquire a kingdom, and Aristophanes's assembly women institute a new egalitarian government. Each also draws attention to theatrical illusion through self-referencing, plays-within-plays, and direct audience address. Thus Meyerhold hoped to pair revolutionary content with revolutionary innovations in form.

Before submitting this list, Meyerhold had his students begin developing plans for several of its plays. For the winter 1921–22 exams, Meyerhold asked Vladimir Liutse[98] to work up designs for *Magnanimous Cuckold*, Yutkevich for *The King Stag*, and Eisenstein for *Puss in Boots*.[99] Meyerhold had made several attempts to mount a production of *Puss* since publishing Gippius's translation of the play in *LTA* and in a single edition (1916). This postrevolutionary *Puss* was to be rewritten, however. Eisenstein wrote to his mother in early 1922, "I'm working for [Meyerhold] on the scenery and costumes for *Puss in Boots* . . . Incidentally, not a single letter remains from the text—we are reworking it together."[100]

Though Tieck's play conveniently celebrates the triumph of the peasant, Tieck's content was less important to Meyerhold than his form. A decade later, when Meyerhold increasingly was being accused of formalism, he defended Tieck's usefulness in a lecture. After reminding listeners that Blok's closeness to Tieck had first attracted Meyerhold to *Balaganchik*, he added:

> The entire worldview of Tieck I could throw in one room and lock up there, but . . . I would take his play *Puss in Boots* into in any acting studio today . . . because the play offers the kind of devices for bringing the audience closer to the stage that provide the ability to construct a new kind of production . . . In music, it rightly happens that some very modern author or other gets ready to write a very revolutionary piece . . . Do you think that he . . . doesn't look over, in the quiet of his study, a fugue by Bach or some wonderful thing by Mozart or Beethoven? You see, he uses the technical devices that teach him how to construct a fugue.[101]

Meyerhold initially had P. Dementiev, a directing student from the Free Workshop, develop a staging plan for *Puss*; Dementiev's plan choreographs (on paper) interactions between the stage action, the authorial/directorial interruptions, the internal audience, and the real audience for each scene of Gippius's translation. This proposed production was designed for a traditional proscenium theater, likely the Zon, as Dementiev's notes indicate the need for a curtain, footlights, proscenium arch, and prompter's box. The most innovative aspect of Dementiev's plan is the staging of the production's fictional spectators. He proposed to seat "the musicians and Kapellmeister . . . in an audience balcony" and to have "the play's audience enter through the [real] auditorium" before sitting along the outer edge of the forestage, high enough so that their heads would jut above it, ringing it like footlights. Dementiev adds, "The lights in the footlights and on the sides . . . are lit during the prologue, interludes and epilogue; thus the 'public' is lit and the stage is 'beautified' during the scene changes."[102] Dementiev presented his plan in a lecture at Meyerhold's workshops on December 22. Eisenstein, who began his designs for *Puss* that same day, would certainly have attended.

Meyerhold's assignment for Eisenstein proposed a different internal audience configuration. He wrote in a note: "Confidentially: my plan for staging: the [false] audience faces us as do the conductor of the orchestra and the prompter; beneath the stage: the playwright, technicians, and workers, return immediately."[103] The quick design sketch on this note, made either by Eisenstein or Meyerhold,[104] and Eisenstein's subsequent December 28–29 designs[105] propose that Tieck's planes of fiction be layered vertically: upstage figures are physically higher than downstage ones in a series of tiers. Far upstage on the highest level is the play's internal audience, facing the real audience. Below this are the orchestra and conductor, next the prompter, and finally the stage. Stairs lead down both sides of the stage into the real audience but also to a fully visible area under the stage. The real audience therefore views the production as if they themselves are backstage watching the layered vertical construction-in-progress of Tieck's fictions. In Yutkevich's recollection, the result was that:

> Tieck's characters always in effect led a dual existence: they appeared as actors on the stage of this little theater, sometimes addressing the imaginary audience, at other times stepping down off the stage to come to the backstage that was visible to us. With this device Eisenstein superbly emphasized the ironic intonation inherent to German romantic creative work.[106]

Yutkevich adds that Eisenstein later developed a similar simultaneous on/offstage in his designs for *Heartbreak House*, which incorporated fully visible sofas for the actors to sit on when they were not performing: "Thus here, as in Tieck's play, the backstage was revealed, and, obviously, according to the director's concept, the irony, also inherent in Shaw, was to be theatrically

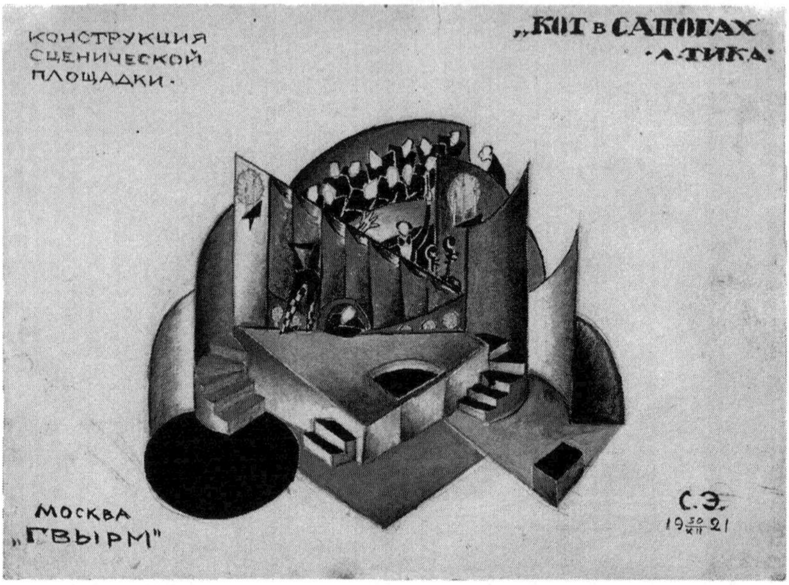

Figure 39. Sergei Eisenstein, scene design for Tieck's *Puss in Boots*, State Higher Theatre Workshops (December 30, 1921). Russian State Archive of Literature and Art, f. 1923, op. 2, ed. khr. 1627: 2.

incarnated in the two-plane behavior of the actors."[107] This design was also vertical: a constructivist assemblage of ladders and geometrical shapes rested atop the "offstage" seating for actors.

In *Love for Three Oranges*, Meyerhold framed discrete portions of the stage—the forestage, the proscenium towers—as loci for self-referential commentary. In *Puss in Boots* and in subsequent projects, Eisenstein divides the stage into vertical layers with two noteworthy results. Commentary on the action, whether it frames the action from above or below, is established visually as more important than the action itself. If one of the major innovations of cubism was that it showed multiple sides of an object simultaneously, through vertical montage, Eisenstein provoked an experience of different simultaneous perspectives.

In later *Puss* design variations (dated December 30 and January 3), Eisenstein retained the backstage perspective and vertical staging but abandoned the proscenium theater, fragmented the layered stage into angular, irregular planes, and made the onstage figures—the audience, conductor, orchestra, and prompter—integral elements of the design rather than simple inhabitants of it (figure 39). Meyerhold's proposed production appears, based on these design changes, to have changed venues. In Fevralsky's recollection,

"*Puss in Boots* was conceived as a mass spectacle with numerous interludes on contemporary themes; it was supposed to be played in an arena."[108] To Eisenstein's frustration, Meyerhold abandoned both *Puss in Boots* and *Heartbreak House* before opening. *Tarelkin's Death* was to be Eisenstein's only major collaboration with Meyerhold to reach the stage.

INTERLUDE: PIPIFAX'S PANTOMIME: *COLUMBINE'S GARTER* (1922)

While Eisenstein was working on *Puss in Boots*, he adopted a new alter ego. Yutkevich had been using a Hoffmannian name; he signed a letter to Eisenstein, "Your incorrigible phantast . . . Maestro Nutcracker."[109] That winter, inspired by the virtuosity and freedom of their biomechanical training, the two began performing short sketches as a clown duo; Yutkevich was a "white" clown called Pip and Eisenstein a "redheaded" clown called Fax.[110] By late January, the pair was writing to each other as "Pipifax,"[111] a German word that implies tomfoolery but is also the name of a game that requires coordination to pass a ball atop a baton,[112] an appropriate confluence of meanings for two clowns in the process of honing their physical agility.

It was as Pipifax (lit.: Pip *and* Fax) that Eisenstein and Yutkevich struck up a correspondence about a pantomime the two planned to create independently of Meyerhold's workshops. They hoped to supplement their "meager" student rations by getting it staged at MastFor (Foregger's Theatre Workshop), where both Sergeis had worked previously as designers.[113] MastFor, founded in 1921 by Nikolai Foregger von Greifenturn and Vladimir Mass, celebrated the circusization of the theater and the human as machine; it was most famous for its machine ballets and its parodies of many shows of the day. Eisenstein and Yutkevich's first design project at MastFor spoofed Vesnin's cubist designs for the Kamerny's *The Tidings Brought to Mary*, after which the two designed Foregger's *Be Kind to Horses*, a work largely consisting of topical jokes and music-hall parodies.[114]

Eisenstein and Yutkevich's pantomime, initially called *Columbine's Wedding Veil* (*Fata Kolombiny*), was to be a radical refraction of Schnitzler's *Pierrette's Veil*. By late summer 1922, when the coauthored libretto was completed, they had changed the title to *Columbine's Garter* (*Podviazka Kolombiny*, or *The Columbian Girl's Garter* in its appended English title). Nowhere was their simultaneous homage to and rebellion against Meyerhold more direct than in this pantomime. Eisenstein and Yutkevich's shift away from Hoffmannian pseudonyms to clown alter egos is symptomatic of a broader desire to refract the forms of Meyerhold using the artistic vocabularies of their generation. Before the Revolution, Meyerhold drew from popular entertainments that were temporally and geographically distant from him. Eisenstein and Yutkevich, partly inspired by Meyerhold, Radlov, Foregger, and the Eccentrics, refracted those that surrounded them: circus, music hall, detective stories, and Charlie Chaplin. *Columbine's Garter* was Eisenstein's first theatrical use of another popular entertainment—film—and thus marks a crucial nexus between Eisenstein's theater and his life in film that followed.

Schnitzler's pantomime was ideal material for these young clown-director-designers "to make *my* meaning in refracted form."[115] Its previous two manifestations as an experiment-manifesto were well known: Meyerhold's *Columbine's Veil* was the first Russian production to apply Hoffmann's grotesque to the theater, while *Pierrette's Veil* was Tairov's inaugural experiment with mime-drama. Eisenstein and Yutkevich did not see Meyerhold's 1910 production at the House of Interludes or its 1916 Players' Rest revival, but they were inspired by the colors and composition of Sapunov's act 2 designs (see figure 11),[116] had heard Meyerhold lecture on the production, and had conversed about it with audience members.[117] They expressed their deep admiration for *Columbine* and its creator by dedicating their pantomime to Meyerhold: "to the Master of *The Veil*, from the novices of *The Garter*."[118] Eisenstein and Yutkevich had, however, seen Tairov's *Pierrette's Veil* (1913, rev. 1916) at the Moscow Kamerny Theatre, though several years into its long run. Yutkevich's recollections of it are decidedly uncomplimentary: "Tairov's version we categorically rejected, considering it tasteless and archaic. In accordance with our views at the time, we decided to 'urbanize' and 'modernize' it."[119]

With a youthful audacity that imbues every aspect of this project, *Columbine's Garter* refracted both productions, thus preserving an uncommonly direct response both to Meyerhold's innovations in theatrical form and to Tairov's postrevolutionary reception by the theatrical Left. Meyerhold's production was not parodied, exactly, but its content and form were taken to new extremes. Eisenstein and Yutkevich did, however, lampoon Tairov's *Pierrette*, joining a long Russian tradition of theatrical parody that includes the cabbage-parties at the MAT and Bat cabaret, works by Evreinov at the Distorting Mirror, and, during the New Economic Policy (NEP), irreverent lampoons by Foregger and by the Eccentrics.

An Eccentric *Columbine*

In spring 1922 Yutkevich went to Petrograd to join the Eccentrics at their newly established Factory of the Eccentric Actor (FEKS), leaving Eisenstein in Moscow to begin drafting the pantomime. The term "eccentric" originally denoted absurd, unexpected elements in circus and music hall performance. Eccentrism as a theatrical movement celebrated the "electrification," and "Americanization" of the theater and prompted jarring juxtapositions of circus, music hall, new technologies, Charlie Chaplin, and American detective novels. Joyful and exuberantly youthful (all but one of its founders were teenagers), they also embraced the grotesque collisions of Hoffmann and Gogol, Italian futurism, silent film, jazz, and the nonlinear construction of the Russian folk show *Tsar Maximillian*.[120] Eccentrism in theatre was short-lived but influential: most of its members transitioned to film after 1924 and became some of the Soviet era's leading directors.

In 1921 Grigory Kozintsev, Georgy Kryzhitsky, and Leonid Trauberg gave the first public reading of their Eccentrist manifestos, an event the scandal of which likely paralleled the futurists' "Slap in the Face of Public Taste" nine years before. The following year, they published their manifestos in a cheap paperback edition by a made-up press, "Eccentropolis," and opened FEKS, their actor training school. Yutkevich did not deliver a manifesto at the 1921 gathering, but he joined their ranks shortly after and published a manifesto in their 1922 collection.

While Yutkevich was in Petrograd, Eisenstein conceived the basic elements of what was by then called *Columbine's Wedding Veil*: an old man Pierrot; a huge, arched garret window that doubles as a vertical playing space; and a Columbine who comes to Pierrot expressly to kill him (by nursing him on poison from a spoon, or, in a variant note, from an enormous breast marked with a skull and crossbones). Other notable elements from this early draft include a parody of the balletic movement style of Nikolai Tseretelli, the Pierrot in the Kamerny's *Pierrette* (see figure 25). Most significant is Eisenstein's exploration of a Hoffmannian definition of character based on layering multiple conflicting selves; in describing Pierrot's four friends, Eisenstein writes, for instance, that they "could be a consultation of doctors, could be funeral parlor agents,"[121] embracing the possibility of disparate traits by infusing them with ambiguous traces of each.

Notably absent from this draft (of act 1 only) is the Eccentric vocabulary of the final version, meaning either that Yutkevich was the driving force behind the Eccentric insertions or that the duo made these additions when Eisenstein joined Yutkevich in Petrograd at the end of June. Yet both were probably thinking of the project in terms of Eccentrism. One of Eisenstein's student projects, evaluated by Meyerhold in June 1922, was to create designs for Shaw's *Heartbreak House* in the manner of the Eccentrics.[122] Eisenstein's design, an arched vertical structure on which characters climb, is likely the closest we will get to knowing what Pierrot's window in *Columbine* might have looked like (figure 40).

By late summer, the pantomime libretto was complete. Like its predecessors, *Columbine's Garter* focuses on a tragic love triangle—Columbine,

Figure 40. Sergei Eisenstein, Eccentric scene design for Shaw's *Heartbreak House*, State Higher Theatre Workshops. Appended is a handwritten note by Meyerhold, dated June 19, 1922: "S. M. Eisenstein's scene and costume designs for a play requiring an Eccentric treatment are accepted as having fulfilled the given assignment—and brilliantly so." Paper, applique, ink, 34.7 × 48.5 cm. КП 62005. © A. A. Bakhrushin State Central Theatre Museum, Moscow.

Pierrot, and Harlequin—but *how* this story is told is new. The libretto is dense with collisions of music hall, circus, film, and commedia and is teeming with topical nods to productions running at other theaters, to individuals, and to specific films.[123] Act 1 opens with an aged, morphine-injecting Pierrot (to be played by a woman in male drag) positioned on the huge vertical window of his garret, longing for his lover Columbine, a *café-chantant* star. After a short film that displays Columbine in semi-undress, she arrives and pretends to make love to Pierrot, then strangles him with the red steel garter Harlequin has given her as a wedding present. At the act 2 wedding reception for Harlequin and Columbine at the Metropolitan Hotel, guests are entertained with topical songs and jazz. Harlequin, a lithe, mysterious circus performer and a capitalist garter manufacturer, sits on a trapeze above the audience, scanning the crowd below for Columbine. He is furious that his bride is missing, and, in his anger, beats her parents (with a boxing match) and smashes the jazz band instruments (a stunt with trick drums). Once Columbine arrives, Harlequin admonishes her (with a trapeze act) after she is distracted by Pierrot's ghost, played by two marionettes. In act 3, an American detective, Ned Rocker, uses an electric chair to reanimate the dead Pierrot. Now an electric automaton zombie, Pierrot pursues and strangles Columbine in "the steel embrace of her electric lover" (*Columbine's Garter*, 20). In a surprise metamorphosis, Rocker reveals that he is Harlequin incognito. The finale reprises a song by the jazz band and a dance between the dead Pierrot and Columbine.

There are enough direct parallels between Kozintsev's "A. B. Parade of the Eccentric," the opening manifesto in the Eccentrist collection, and *Columbine's Garter* that Eisenstein and Yutkevich's pantomime may have been intended to be a staged Eccentrist manifesto: its premiere, which never occurred, was to have predated what became the inaugural FEKS production, *Marriage* "after" Gogol. Specific images from Kozintsev's manifesto that recur in *Columbine's Garter* fall into two categories: those of an outmoded past—"bald pates," Barons, art with a "fig leaf"—and positive images of an Eccentrist future—film, circus, boxing, parades (in a Meyerholdian sense), whistles and sirens, detectives, electricity, police nightsticks, jazz, music hall, "a clown's blinking nose," "red wigs standing on end," the "crackling cinema," American advertisements, and references to films, including *The Mysteries of New York* and *The Laughing Mask*.[124] One important difference is that Kozintsev referred to a play as "a piling up of tricks at a tempo of 1,000 horse power,"[125] while Eisenstein instead called for a montage of attractions. For Eisenstein and Yutkevich, the Eccentrics' accumulated audience shocks were insufficient; very much Meyerhold's students, Pip and Fax believed that theater must also provoke creative thought.

The Birth of the Attraction

In *Columbine's Garter*, Eisenstein and Yutkevich describe their work for the first time with a new term, "the attraction," to be theorized in Eisenstein's "Montage of Attractions for *Enough Stupidity in Every Wiseman*" the following year. Zabrodin posits that Eisenstein probably first encountered the term "attraction" in relation to theater in Meyerhold's 1913 essay "Balagan," which Eisenstein read and annotated multiple times during his Civil War travels.[126] In his essay, Meyerhold argued that the principles of the *balagan* (fairground booth) are also central elements in cabaret, music-hall, and variety, and that "namely in these little theatres and in a third of 'attractions' there is more art than in the so-called serious theaters, which feed themselves on literary exercises."[127] The word resurfaces in Eisenstein's notes from a May 16, 1922, lecture by Meyerhold on how images are juxtaposed and synthesized by audiences into meaning:

> The combination of two concrete material concepts (moon, frying pan) into one that is not concrete—the Imaginist[128] image "the frying pan of the moon."
>
> Stella's first scene [in *The Magnanimous Cuckold*]. Its construction. Cage and flowers. Distillation: I do love you, Bruno.
>
> (A work of art is a form of violence.) The attraction. The "images" of the Eccentrics. Simple counterpoint. [129]

Though Eisenstein's notes are telegraphic, Meyerhold's thoughts on how an audience synthesizes disparate images in *Magnanimous Cuckold* ("cage and flowers") to distill a third ("I do love you, Bruno") are similar to Eisenstein's later use of disparate images in *October* (1928) (Tsar and toppled monument) to distill a new idea (the Tsar's regime being toppled). This technique also bears the mark of GVYTM neighbor Lev Kuleshov, who believed that meaning in film "emerged in the combination of shots more than in the intrinsic characteristics of given shots."[130]

In Yutkevich's recollection, Eisenstein first suggested the attraction as a theatrical term in response to their love of roller coasters:

> We rode on them tirelessly, feeling a boyish pleasure from the breathtaking drops and takeoffs. In the roar of roller coaster cars we shouted out verses from our favorite Mayakovsky poems, dreaming aloud of the new theater we would create. . . . You could say that all the theories of Eccentricity were born on these American mountains.
>
> One day after one of these visits, I came to Eisenstein . . . so flushed and excited that he asked what was the matter. When I said that I had been on my favorite attraction again, he exclaimed: "Listen, there's an idea! What if we call our work a 'theatrical attraction?' After all, don't we also want to jolt our spectators with almost the same physical force with which they are jolted by an attraction?"
>
> And above the dedication on the front cover of *Columbine's Garter* appeared: "Invention of Theatrical Attractions by Sergei Eisenstein and Sergei Yutkevich."[131]

From these three sources—Meyerhold's essay, Eisenstein's lecture notes, and Yutkevich's memoirs—we learn that the attraction is immediate, affective, audience-centered, viscerally jolting, draws from popular forms, and uses juxtapositions that prompt active mental synthesis. The word also implies a shift away from theatrical meaning that is denotative (psychologically and/or visually representational) to meaning that is connotative (self-contained units and literalized metaphors).

Columbine's Garter provides a vital link between Eisenstein's earlier Hoffmaniana and this nascent notion of the attraction. Similarly to the "acting instruments" in *Tarelkin*, literalized metaphors in *Columbine's Garter* were calculated to provoke "jolts," in Yutkevich's description. Emotion and conflict were not to be psychologically revealed but performed as film interludes, circus acts, stunts, or songs. These attractions were organized in sequences of juxtapositions that form the artistic "zigzag"[132] that now is so strongly associated with Eisenstein's film montage.

Perry, among others, describes Eisenstein's film work in terms of "polyphony," "simultaneous attractions," "fugue," and "counterpoint of sound and image."[133] He uses the structure of Eisenstein's *Ivan the Terrible* (part 1, 1944) as an example of where "Eisenstein called for three voice lines to be woven into a polyphonic tapestry of sound and image,"[134] adding:

> He was not interested in polyphony as a structural device but rather in the effect that polyphony had upon the viewer. . . . Eisenstein's materialist conception required that the spectator be drawn into a creative act when experiencing the work. . . . Polyphonic construction, or montage in all of its meanings, became the formal device for overcoming the representational nature of the intransigent shots, making it possible for the viewer to create new thoughts and feelings.[135]

Columbine's Garter uses precisely this kind of structure, creating a polyphonic tapestry, in this case, of several sets of trios designed to combat psychology, an overly predictable use of theatrical space, and causal, linear narrative.

In embracing Perry's use of the word "polyphony" (rather than Bakhtin's use, which describes drama rather than performance),[136] I remind the reader of Hoffmann's description of the inner creative world of the artist, for whom "hearing is an internal seeing" and "sight becomes an inner hearing"[137] (see introduction) and of Meyerhold's description of music and the movement of the actor together as a "distinctive kind of polyphony"[138] (see chapter 1). Meyerhold in particular understood that there can be simultaneous lines of autonomous meaning in the theater—some visual, others aural, spatial, or structural—and that accumulated meanings are generated by the collisions and interweavings of these multiple expressive voices.

Columbine's Garter does not contain dialectics of contrasting elements, as Tairov's productions do, but a complex polyphonic layering of lines of meaning comprised of individual attractions. What Eisenstein later wrote of *Old and New* (*The General Line*, 1929) holds true here: *Columbine's Garter* is based on "a *simultaneous advance* of a multiple series of lines, each maintaining an independent compositional course and each contributing to the total compositional course of the sequence."[139] The pantomime features multiple sets of contrasting trios: *fabula*, *siuzhet*, and soundscape; Pierrot, Columbine, and Harlequin; imperial Russia, Soviet NEP Russia, and the West; circus, music hall, and film;

and, in terms of space, upper horizontal plane, lower horizontal plane, and vertical plane. The analysis of the libretto that follows focuses on the pantomime's character collages, innovative use of spatial planes, and organization into events and attractions. The full libretto is translated in appendix D.

Character Montage

Eisenstein was fascinated by the idea of coexisting selves, perhaps one reason why he never settled on a single pseudonym. In *Columbine's Garter*, each character is structured not through cumulatively developed psychology but around unexpected shifts between or combinations of disparate selves. Significantly, a full quarter of the libretto is dedicated to descriptions of its dramatis personae. In these descriptions, Eisenstein and Yutkevich conflate several individuals into one, merge humans with objects, and prompt transformations from one self into another. Through this grafting of selves, a character's unapologetically conflicting aspects often come to light. By analyzing Columbine's parents, who are created through simultaneous juxtaposition, and Pierrot's four friends, who are developed via successive juxtaposition, I will show how the pantomime's authors use both techniques to construct the libretto's main love triangle.

The designs for Columbine's parents collide the grotesque with constructivism. Columbine has rented "Ma-Pa," a single character split into two, for the wedding as one rents a banquet hall: they themselves replace the wedding buffet. They are assemblages of various parts, some human, most not. Ma, a restaurant-automaton, handles input: her breasts distribute sparkling water and condensed milk (coffee in a late design variant); one thigh is marked "roast," and the other "soup." Between her legs is a coin slot that allows customers to pay for their meal (figure 41); in one design variant, this cash box is "modestly concealed from view" with a fig leaf. Pa handles output. He is a human water closet, comprised of a tank (marked "Moscow Art Theatre" in one design variant), a phallic pull-chain with which he is flushed, a body that merges toilet with tailcoat, and a bulbous car horn between his posterior tails that toots flatulently at opportune moments (*Columbine's Garter,* 4–5) (figure 42). Ma-Pa also contains a variety of human elements, mainly satirical bits and pieces of "Russia no. 2," the Russian émigré community in France: "She is a former baroness with a German surname. *Fräulein* in the court of H[er] F[ormer] I[mperial] [Majesty]. He is a *Kammerjunker*, a cavalier of the Order of the Garter" (*Columbine's Garter,* 4). What otherwise would have been discrete elements of either Ma *or* Pa become deliciously merged, via this she-he structure, into a single satirical collage.[140]

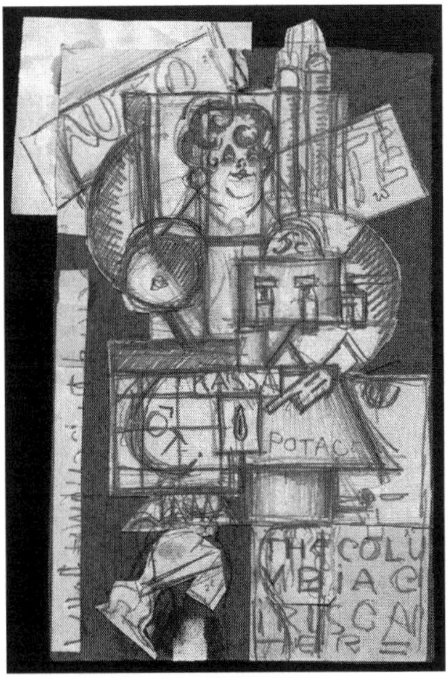

Figure 41. Sergei Eisenstein, costume/scene design sketch for Ma in Eisenstein and Yutkevich's *Columbine's Garter* (1922). Russian State Archive of Literature and Art, f. 1923, op. 1, ed. khr. 817: 2.

Pierrot's four friends, whose plural selves develop sequentially, illustrate Eisenstein and Yutkevich's use of successive juxtaposition. Eisenstein's early notes described them as an ambiguous combination of doctors, who work with life, and funeral parlor agents, who work with death. In the final libretto, they are "from the types of Félix Vallotton. Spherical, in top hats. Square beefsteak faces. Starched linens . . . Played by three men and one 'lady' in a male costume" (*Columbine's Garter,* 5). In act 1 they are comic doctor-friends; in act 2 they become the jazz band. In the third act, they are police officers who accompany the American detective Ned Rocker, but, after Columbine's death, their trick wigs stand on end in surprise, revealing red linings, the traditional Russian hair color for clowns. They then transform into the bearers of funeral torches (by setting off Roman candles hidden in their nightsticks), into question marks (by turning their backs with question marks on them to the audience—a detective film reference), and finally into sandwich-board advertisements for garters.

The pantomime's three main characters use both simultaneous and successive juxtaposition: each is a visual mosaic of disparate elements; each also undergoes a major transformation over the course of the action. Eisenstein and Yutkevich's Columbine openly revolted against Koonen's graceful,

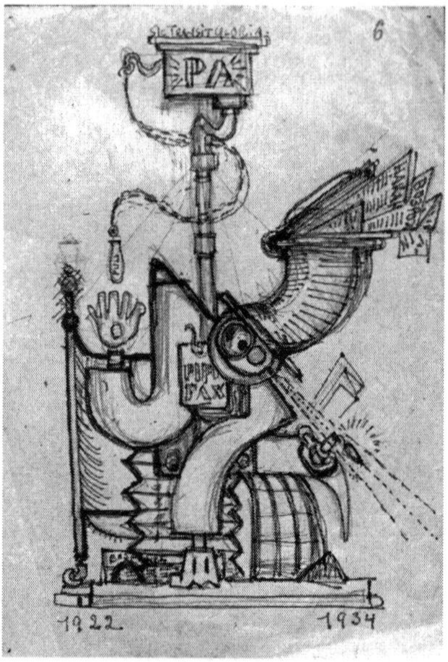

Figure 42. Sergei Eisenstein, costume/scene design sketch for Pa, *Columbine's Garter* (late design variant, 1934). Russian State Archive of Literature and Art, f. 1923, op. 1, ed. khr. 817: 6.

white-clad Pierrette (see figure 25). In their refraction, Columbine becomes a femme fatale and *café-chantant* star (*étoile*) masquerading as someone "on her way" to becoming "an honest woman" through her marriage to Harlequin. Three different languages describe Columbine's assemblage of personalities and costume parts.[141] She first is described in French and English: "*Étoile*—'The Columbian Girl,' *En train de devenir honnête femme par alliance à Sir Archibald Harlequin*, Straps and Garter Manufacturer U.S.A. 60 High St. Boston" (*Columbine's Garter*, 2). Her costume descriptions are in Russian, with the occasional French word inserted. Eisenstein and Yutkevich use languages to construct Columbine as they had Ma-Pa. Elsewhere in the pantomime, French parodies French pornography[142]—likely the intention here—but it also satirizes the White Russian émigré community in France. They use English to recall detective films and to parody Soviet obsessions with America. Disparate locations—NEP-era Moscow, Boston, Paris, and Colombia—become an accumulated, generalized West.

Columbine's constructed self is also fragmented in various ways. In act 1, her body is displayed through the sequential projection of its parts onto a screen. An image of her leg in a flame-red steel garter is an exclamation point of visual punctuation that first appears here and recurs throughout the pantomime. In act 2, she wears a sequined gala dress (a deliberate departure from wedding white), but hints of her other selves remain: her vivid red-orange underthings are visible to the audience, and a long circus whip, the kind used by a ringmaster for equestrian acts, replaces her act 1 riding crop.

Columbine's major transformation takes place in act 1. Her erotic projected image is juxtaposed with her physical entrance in modest clothing immediately after. While making love to Pierrot, she reveals her femme fatale self suddenly by effecting a quick-change transformation via "a play of clasps" (*Columbine's Garter*, 2). We see the *café-chantant* Columbine for the remainder of the pantomime, until her final transformation: her death at the hands of Pierrot. Visual traces of act 1 remain throughout in the form of a stocking that droops as she walks—a constant reminder of her missing garter.

Eisenstein and Yutkevich's Pierrot is no longer the wistful youth celebrated in prerevolutionary Russian commedia. He is old, toothless, bald, and played by a woman, a declaration that the heyday of the romanticized, sentimental Pierrot had passed. He is an amalgam of several Pierrots: Russian cabaret singer Alexander Vertinsky's famous "Black Pierrot," Meyerhold's *Balaganchik* Pierrot, and any number of French and Russian traditional Pierrots—all grafted here with a bohemian, monocle-wearing morphine addict. The cumulative result is a series of unstable binaries—male and female, youth and age, life and death—in a single being.

Pierrot has two major successive transformations: in act 1 he progresses from age to youth to age to death, while in act 3 he moves from death to electric reanimation. That he is old is a surprise reveal in the first act, its own mini-attraction. Only after this does he apply the makeup, costume, and youthful physicality of Pierrot—in full view of the audience, metaphorically conveying that his outward appearance masks internal decay. When Columbine transforms into an *étoile*, Pierrot reverts to an old man, allowing her to end his life with ease. Pierrot's act 3 transformation is Ned Rocker's reanimation of him by electric chair. Thus Pierrot's life and death are merged into a single being: the flow of blood is simply replaced with the flow of electricity. Meyerhold's version of the pantomime had ended with Pierrot's friends dancing around Pierrot and Columbine, whom they thought to be alive, contrasted with the horrific discovery that they were not. Eisenstein and Yutkevich's Pierrot also provokes an uncanny sensation by being simultaneously alive and dead.

Each of the three major Russian refractions of Schnitzler's pantomime focused its sympathy on a different character: Meyerhold on Pierrot, Tairov on Pierrette—and Eisenstein and Yutkevich on Harlequin. Of *Columbine Garter's* main trio, Harlequin is the most jubilantly fragmented: he is a commedia mask, a straps-and-garter manufacturer, a high-wire circus performer, and a constructivist human-machine, with added hints of Fantômas (a popular French serial film character) and even Foregger. This composition demands successive transformations the virtuosity of which recalls the central pantomime in Tairov's *Brambilla*, in which Harlequin reassembled himself from pieces, except that in *Columbine's Garter* character itself is assembled. Unsurprisingly, Harlequin was written to be played by a circus acrobat, the noted tightrope performer Fedor Knorre, husband to Maria Babanova (Stella in *Magnanimous Cuckold*).[143]

Harlequin also has a surprise alternate identity. In the libretto's character descriptions, the true identity of Ned Rocker, reanimator of Pierrot and agent of revenge upon Columbine, is masked by the letter X:

> XXX *Ned Rocker, detective* . . . The king of detectives in a flared overcoat of immense proportions. Energetic profile, half-comprised of automobile goggles and pipe. Topped with a cap. A Browning. (*Columbine's Garter*, 7)

The deliberately masked link between Ned Rocker and Harlequin, who emerges out from under the detective's cape at the pantomime's end, was likely borrowed from *Fantômas* films, adverts for which also obscured the actor's identity.

Space = Meaning

Columbine's Garter took the framing of the audience's attention and experience to a new extreme by fragmenting the stage into aggressively colliding horizontal and vertical planes. In acts 1 and 3, the Kamerny's romanticized version of Pierrot's room is replaced with constructivist crossbars that evoke an enormous, arched garret window that spans the entire proscenium opening. Its crossbars "are used for crossing and as a playing space for the actors. The outer frame of the window forms an arched bridge (making it possible to cross from one side of the proscenium opening to the other)" (*Columbine's Garter*, 9). In Yutkevich's explanation, "the huge attic window that took up the entire stage space was the stage itself. The characters were to move only on the vertical plane, holding on to the crossbars."[144] In keeping with other contemporary constructivist experiments, Pierrot's window became a playground on which to physicalize emotions.

Pierrot's entire world is this vertical plane. He expresses excitement by climbing about its bars, and he readies himself for Columbine's arrival by hanging upside down from them to peer into an inverted mirror. While Tairov's garret window looked out onto "carnival fires" beyond it, Pierrot's world looked out onto "a modern, capitalist, American city comprised of electric and neon advertisements."[145] This vertical window also functioned as a living film screen. Near the end of his life, Eisenstein looked back on the vertical world in *Columbine's Garter*, identifying it as a "potential film screen" that was spatially and philosophically opposed to "the orchestra of theatrical action": Columbine's horizontal wedding-ball world in act 2.[146]

In act 2, Eisenstein and Yutkevich prompted a disorienting spatial perspective shift: they tilted Pierrot's window all the way back to form a raked, semicircular floor that recalls both a circus ring and a theater in the half round. The libretto adds, "Windowpanes made of frosted glass and lit from below form a luminous floor" (14). Because Pierrot's tilted window is illuminated, it feels as if act 2 takes place, in defiance of gravity, on the side of a building. This new horizontal playing space becomes the lower of two parallel planes. A network of trapezes and tightrope cables overhead builds the expectation that action will also take place on the upper plane over the heads of spectators and actors:

> Above the floor at a considerable height is a static trapeze, which has four extensions (steel cables) for tightrope walking . . . A circus rope, hung from the cupola and reaching to the floor, vertically transects the trapeze. (*Columbine's Garter*, 14)

Each of the three spatial planes—the window-floor on the lower horizontal plane, the tightrope cables on the upper horizontal plane, and the vertical window (in act 1) and rope (in act 2)—is associated with one of the pantomime's main characters: Pierrot's domain is the window. Columbine's is the luminous floor. As Harlequin undergoes the most radical character shifts, his use of space is the most varied: he performs where the vertical and horizontal intersect. His first act 2 entrance is a rapid descent from the flies to the horizontal cables overhead, but he also frequently transects the upper and lower horizontal planes by gliding up or down the rope. His position overhead, climbing in and out of the flies, allows him to physically frame parts of the theater building that are not typically used as playing spaces. His location also allows his actions and emotions to contrast violently with the action on the floor below, essentially creating in a theatrical setting what the split frame does in film. Spatially, then, Columbine, Pierrot, and Harlequin create a vertical montage, where each character's domain is an independent visual line that interweaves with the others.

Events +/– Attractions

While composing the story for *Columbine's Garter*, Eisenstein and Yutkevich also fully designed its images, mise-en-scène, and sounds. Eisenstein, a trained engineer, had an extraordinary ability to think on multiple planes simultaneously in a way that was visually and architecturally ordered. *Columbine's Garter* is laid out on the libretto pages so that the contributions of each theatrical artist—costume designer, scenic designer, playwright, director, and sound designer (all of whom were, of course, Eisenstein and Yutkevich)—remain entirely distinct. This gave the two Sergeis the opportunity to view the pantomime through the prisms of all its production artists while celebrating the autonomy and equity of each.

When working on the text for *Inspector General*, Meyerhold and his laboratory assistants cut apart and pasted together the script, adding in handwritten notes as they went. In many of his promptbooks, Tairov wrote liberally in margins and on the verso sides of script pages, but sometimes abandoned the play entirely when working with actors on physical improvisations or pantomime sequences. As Eisenstein and Yutkevich composed *Columbine's Garter*, they wrote the parts of each artist in response to one another. The play was not written first, but together with the costume designs, scenic designs, and mise-en-scène. Though many Russian theatricalist directors believed that theater should synthesize multiple arts, *Columbine's Garter* is the most genuinely synthetic dramatic text I have encountered: it synthesizes literature, music, art, architecture, and performance while embracing each line of artistic meaning as distinct.

These through-lines of authorship are preserved with astonishing clarity via their layout on the libretto's pages. Costume design descriptions appear at the start of the scenario, organized by role, and include a constructivist character description and costume details for each of the acts. Scenic design descriptions come at the beginning of each act and outline the unusual use of space and specific technical needs. Sound effects, costume transformations, and other cue-specific production notes appear as footnotes.

The layout of the pantomime's action is far more unusual: plot events and mise-en-scène appear on each page as two parallel columns that force the reader's eye to zigzag back and forth across the page from one column to another while reading. The left relates the sequence of events (Eisenstein does not yet use the word "montage"), which can be read straight through for sense without needing to refer to the column on the right. The right column frames how or where each event is to be staged. This latter column does not simply fulfill or respond to the events on the left. It is not marginalia written in after the fact, but a distinct line of meaning in a polyphonic whole. If we think of the libretto as a split screen, the left side communicates the events, and the right the attractions. The left column is the realm of the playwright, while the right is the domain of the director.

Columbine's Garter features a wide variety of attractions. Some are design attractions: the strikingly vivid red of Columbine's steel garter and the comically wheezing horn on Pa's posterior. Others are more clearly directorial: the use of film on surprising projection surfaces and Harlequin's abrupt plunge through the air on a circus rope. The pantomime's right column makes it clear, however, that Eisenstein and Yutkevich viewed the director's contribution to a production, the *how* of each theatrical sequence, as uniquely valuable for attractions that develop through space and time. Since coming to Moscow, Eisenstein had designed many productions, sometimes contributing directorial ideas through design, but he had yet to direct a production of his own. Even *Columbine's Garter* was to have been directed by Foregger, one reason Eisenstein eventually cooled toward the project. In *Columbine's Garter*, Eisenstein and Yutkevich developed the attraction while also learning as directors how to viscerally and cognitively engage the viewer. Becoming a director became synonymous, for them, with generating the most effective montage of attractions.

The discussion that follows analyzes the attractions (the right column) for each of the pantomime's three acts in the context of the events (the left column) that connect them. These attractions fall into three main categories. The first is the spatial expression of emotion, often prompted by an unusual use of space. In these attractions, mise-en-scène becomes a metaphor for emotion rather than an outgrowth of psychological motivation. The second category consists of self-contained acts that prompt connotative meaning—typically acrobatic circus acts that require physical daring, virtuosic skill, or both, emphasizing in each case the "actual-materialistic" element of theater that Eisenstein discovered with *The Mexican*'s boxing match. The third is inverted expectation, emotional culmination, surprise, and other emphatic directorial punctuation that shapes the viewer's experience.

Act 1: "In the Clutches of the Beauty-Adventuress"

In act 1, the attraction column establishes the vertical use of space and the emotions that are to be expressed physically on it. At the start of the pantomime, Pierrot is seated in an armchair pushed against the window frame, his back to the audience (event column). He remains here until the pantomime's third scene. Most of his body is obscured by the chair and rings of cigar smoke. The attraction column presents Pierrot's body geometrically: his legs rest on the window frame "in the shape of an unfolded mathematical compass" (*Columbine's Garter*, 9).

In the second scene, the event-attraction structure unfolds more explicitly. The action is fairly straightforward: Pierrot's four friends pay him a doctor's visit, take his pulse, try to cheer him up, and leave, all the while behaving as one person fragmented into four. It is from the attraction column that we learn they make a surprise entrance through a trapdoor, introduce themselves to the audience with an acrobatic circus act, and establish, through movement, the exciting potential of the vertical playing space:

They enter, left, from a trapdoor. They ascend and cross, one after another, along the window bridge. They descend to the floor and perform an entrée.

They greet him. A doctor's examination; they simultaneously take out watches

after they have climbed onto the window crossbars above Pierrot. All four sit on the horizontal crossbeam. (*Columbine's Garter*, 9)

The circus term "entrée"—literally entrance—is often translated as "turn" or "act," though it also has much in common with the commedia *lazzo*. In *Columbine's Garter*, the entrée is most often used at first entrance to introduce characters, thus serving the same structural function as Meyerhold's parade or as the establishing shot in film. A libretto footnote informs the reader that the friends' entrée is "the traditional circus entrance" (9) of a well-known contemporary acrobatic troupe.

After the friends comically take Pierrot's pulse, they attempt unsuccessfully to cheer him with music:

They sit,

legs dangling down. In turn they take out a box (flat), a handle, a gramophone horn, and a record. They assemble and

wind up a gramophone. The gramophone plays

"Tipperary." (*Columbine's Garter*, 9–10)

Their onstage construction of a gramophone hints at the constructivist characters and actions to come. "Tipperary," a 1912 British music hall hit, is the reader's first written indication that popular music has replaced Dohnányi's score.

The scene after the departure of Pierrot's friends is structured around two events: a short film that displays Columbine's scantily clad body and the deconstruction of the traditional Pierrot. After Columbine telegraphs Pierrot that she is coming over (event column), Pierrot clambers around the window-stage in excitement (attraction column). An intertitle with Pierrot's response (event column) is projected on a "radioscope" screen: "*Venez sans céremonies et telle que vous étes!*"—"Come without ceremony, just as you are!" (*Columbine's Garter*, 10). The "radioscope" here is a made-up device that serves as a film screen, an echo in miniature of Pierrot's vertical window, as it provides a projection surface for Pierrot's thoughts. The attraction column describes this film: "A narrow section of screen moves vertically, sequentially revealing parts of Columbine's figure" (10). It comes to a stop on an image of Columbine's leg in a huge scarlet garter, an image that Noussinova calls the pantomime's "semiotic center" due to the frequency and timing of its recurrence.[147]

As Pierrot's ecstasy culminates, he turns to face the audience for the first time, revealing that he is old, toothless, and played by a woman (event column). This surprise reveal is echoed in the mise-en-scène: his movements across the window crossbars are now enfeebled by age (attraction column). Thus a seemingly fixed commedia character is destabilized through inverted expectations of age and gender.[148] Pierrot then transforms himself into "the traditional Pierrot" (event column) by applying the makeup of Vertinsky's Black Pierrot (*Columbine's Garter*, 11), but he does so upside down, hanging loosely from the window transom by his legs (attraction column)—before injecting morphine and tossing aside his journal, the latest issue of *Notes of Dreamers*, no. 6. This intertextual reference is a topical mini-attraction: issue 6 was dedicated to the recently deceased Alexander Blok.

Columbine's first entrance is in an elevator (event column) that comes through the trap door and lets her off atop the window frame (attraction column). She and Pierrot descend to the floor (attraction column) and dance—the first time action takes place on the horizontal plane. As they make love across the window frame, her dress transforms into a *café-chantant* costume. She tears off Pierrot's wig and slaps his bald head (event column), an action that transforms him back into an old man (attraction column). She then strangles him by snapping her steel garter around his neck (event column), linking sexuality with death, the *femme* with the *fatale*. His earlier excitement at her arrival and their lovemaking on the window-stage is echoed in his frantic spasms around the same space as the garter strangles him, culminating in his death in an inverted crucifix (attraction column).

A swiftly moving elevator zooms upward, containing a mysterious male silhouette and an intertitle in English: "*Ned Rocker, detective, 231–233 West Monroe St., New York, USA*, with a loaded Browning" (*Columbine's Garter*, 12). In response, the neon advertisements of a capitalist city light up and "begin to rotate at a furious pace," while a footnote adds cacophonous city sounds. The focus shifts to Columbine, who dons a half-mask and saunters along the footlights (event column), unaware that the stocking on her ungartered leg is drooping (attraction column), Eisenstein and Yutkevich's ironic substitute for Pierrette's forgotten wedding veil (12).

The act 1 finale (attraction column) positions Pierrot's inverted corpse in silhouette against a vivid electric city comprised of "a background flooded with light" (*Columbine's Garter*, 12), illuminated neon legs in garters, and neon advertisements—including one for Foregger's theater—that descend from the flies. These juxtapositions create a dense visual layering of sexual decadence, gaudy advertisements, and American and Soviet NEP capitalism. The blazing light also points to the electrification of the theater, which the Eccentrics celebrated in their manifestos. That this finale and the one in act 2 are both in the attraction column points to the value Eisenstein and Yutkevich placed on end-of-act audience jolts.

Act 2: "Night at the Metropolitan Hotel, or, The Garter-Exposer"

Act 2 fragments Harlequin and Columbine's wedding celebration into brief sequences, as Meyerhold's *Columbine* ball scene had done, thus retaining a sense of Dohnányi's musical juxtapositions without the music itself.[149] The twelve act 2 scenes contrast topical music hall numbers (event column) with daring circus acts (attraction column). It is in this act that the pantomime's composition on multiple planes is most vividly apparent. Columbine, the Dance Master, Ma-Pa, and the jazz band perform on the lower horizontal stage, while Harlequin's world is above theirs on tightropes and trapezes, transected by a rope. The contrast between Columbine's and Harlequin's incompatible worlds is reinforced by the popular entertainments from which they draw: the world of the wedding party participants is one of variety, music hall, tap, and jazz, while Harlequin's is comprised of aerial acts that invade the space below.

Two sets of intertitles punctuate Eisenstein and Yutkevich's music-hall wedding ball. The Dance Master's head is replaced with "a signaling apparatus with flashing, illuminated names of the dances;" the appearance of these titles is accompanied by the sound of a railway bell that is rung with a long lever "between a pair of legs in yellow checked trousers ending in enormous American shoes with double, tap-dancing soles" (*Columbine's Garter*, 6). Thus each dance is announced with an intertitle, a ringing bell, and an obscene gesture, an impertinent refraction of the tinkling bells and pistol shots with which Meyerhold announced scene changes and intermissions. The second intertitle appears on the doors of two "WCs" (marked "Men" and "Women"), to which the guests retreat between dances (scenes 2 and 4) and in which they remain during several of the acts.

The first six scenes of act 2 introduce one new character at a time via kinetic, constructivist entrées. Scene 1 introduces the Dance Master and his song callboard, after which he sings and tap dances about NEP Moscow's "universal obsession with America" (*Columbine's Garter*, 14). In scene 3, Ma-Pa perform a comic entrée that demonstrates how their costumes function, followed by a ditty about Russia no. 2, the émigré community abroad. Scene 5 calls for Eisenstein and Yutkevich, the pantomime's authors, to perform as Pipifax, its clown ringmasters. Yutkevich, "*Pip-heroico*," was to be dressed in "white satin with green and pink roosters, an entirely white face, a wig *à trois cornes*: pale pink, blue, yellow." Eisenstein, "*Fax-Buffo*," was to have "a fanned out red beard, orange part, little top hat with a green plume in the shape of a question mark on one side. Short jacket, spherical checked trousers (*blanc et noire*); coquettish little bow on a bare neck, monocle on a black ribbon. A watch on the leg; on it a *kukish*" (6–7). Eisenstein repeated this *kukish*—a vulgar gesture that places the thumb between the first two fingers—in his film "Glumov's Diary" the following year. Pipifax's self-referential nod from within the work to the creators outside the work parallels Eisenstein's later filmed insertion of himself into *Wiseman*, the production of which "Glumov" was a part.

For the whole of act 2, Pierrot's four friends are a constructivist "jazz band that extends to the proscenium opening in a kinetic structure of human body and musical instruments" (*Columbine's Garter*, 14). Eisenstein and Yutkevich viewed jazz itself as an attraction. Yutkevich later noted that jazz was "all the rage"[150] then, though it wasn't until American jazz performers toured the Soviet Union a few years later that most Russians learned what jazz looked and sounded like. Valentin Parnakh, who first introduced jazz to the Soviet Union in the fall of 1922—albeit in a much-altered form—viewed it as "a physically liberating rhythm that could make the common man an artist and, in the process, drive decadent classical ballet from the stage."[151] Earlier that year Parnakh argued that American dances such as the fox-trot and the shimmy were "the expression of . . . a music of dissonances, syncopations, crashes, soaring brass, shrieking ratchets, whistles, howls, and alarm sirens all sounding like an alternating current of electricity."[152] For Eisenstein and Yutkevich, Parnakh's version of jazz promised an appealing opportunity to replace the Kamerny's graceful *Pierrette* with a modern, liberating physicality.

In scene 6, the jazz banders perform a song about "the latest theatrical rage" (*Columbine's Garter*, 15), followed by a collective dance of all the onstage human and human-machine constructions, marking a mini-finale to the first half of the act. The only descriptions to appear in the libretto's attraction column for the first half of the act were the introduction of the Dance Master's callboard, the guests' bathroom visits, and this collective constructivist dance.

Harlequin's first entrance is above this chaotic mechanical dance: his lithe figure—in the black leotard and half-mask of Fantômas—descends on the rope from the cupola to perch on the trapeze and scan the crowd for his bride. In *Columbine's Veil*, Meyerhold generated a rhythmical grotesque by staging frenzied movement and eerie stillness in abrupt, alternating patterns. Because the stage space of *Columbine's Garter* is fractured into parallel planes, Eisenstein and Yutkevich could provoke the same kind of contrast through simultaneous staging.

When he can wait no longer, Harlequin ruptures the action below by plummeting into it along the rope. His rage is translated into attractions, each one a concretized metaphor:

Harlequin's rage. Stamps his feet.	
	Tap dance.
Irritated, he asks Columbine's parents, demanding that they explain her absence.	
	Boxing. Beats Pa-Ma. . . .
He runs up to the orchestra, breaks the musical instruments.	
	Three drum cascade: he leaps into the left one, flies out of the right one,
and disappears	
	with a crash into the middle one. (*Columbine's Garter*, 15–16)

Thus rage becomes a tap dance, interrogation a boxing match, and the breaking of musical instruments, an act with trick drums.

Only now does Columbine enter (event column) to perform an "equestrian" act with Pip and Fax (attraction column), now dressed as riders. During the dance that follows (attraction column), two guests on trapezes lower two marionette versions of Pierrot (attraction column), Eisenstein's and Yutkevich's refraction of Pierrot's ghost. These marionettes gave Columbine the opportunity to heighten her emotional response by running from one Pierrot only to encounter another. In Meyerhold's and Tairov's productions, Columbine/Pierrette flees the ball in horror after seeing Pierrot's ghost; here Eisenstein and Yutkevich gave Harlequin an additional opportunity for revenge. When she inadvertently reveals her ungartered leg (event column), he admonishes her physically by performing a trapeze act, then gliding down the rope to advance on her before disappearing back into the flies (attraction column).

The aftermath of Harlequin's wrath plays out physically on the other characters. Amidst "commotion, noise, and whistles," the Dance Master is toppled into the jazz band and the ladies along the edges of the stage lie with their legs "thrown into the air," provoking a scene of complete, meticulously choreographed bedlam (*Columbine's Garter*, 17). The act's final sound is that of Pa's horn. Once again, the visceral effect of this finale is emphasized by its placement in the attraction column.

Act 3: "Ned Rocker Acts, or, Death in the Embrace of the Electric Lover"

More of act 3 takes place in the event column than in the other two acts, probably because its audience jolts are generated by the rapidity of its quick-fire juxtapositions rather than by the entrées that were a defining structural feature of act 2 in particular. The act 3 attraction column deals almost entirely with the use of space.

In act 1, electricity was used to project erotic images and illuminate the advertisements of a capitalistic city. In act 3, electricity is a means of revenge. Detective Ned Rocker enters through the audience in total darkness pierced only by the beam of his flashlight, which comes to a stop on Pierrot in his death pose on the once-again vertical window. Next:

Ned pulls out an electric chair	
	with a shiny metal seat. (*Columbine's Garter*, 19)

He removes Pierrot from the window, places him on the chair, lays a cable, and waits. After Columbine enters and inadvertently flips Pierrot's switch, he advances on her with "automaton-like steps" (19). This reanimation by electrification inverts the electric chair's expected function by returning a semblance of life. The action that follows is a gristly refraction of Koonen's romanticized dance of death in Tairov's *Pierrette's Veil*:

The electric corpse pursues Columbine, who is out of her mind with horror. In a final dance	
	on the window crossbars,
Columbine dies in the steel embrace of her electric lover. (*Columbine's Garter*, 19–20)	

Rocker whistles for Pierrot's friends, now policemen, and a rapid series of shocks and transformations ensues. The event column describes Harlequin's final transformation: "Rocker throws off his detective's garb, under it is *Harlequin*" (*Columbine's Garter*, 20). The attraction column relates the responses of the four policemen to the pantomime's final scene. First, "their smooth black wigs stand on end, revealing their redheaded essence." Next, "Roman candles melancholically shoot out from the white nightsticks of the policemen." They turn to reveal question marks on their backs, and, finally, unroll sandwich board posters from their nightsticks, "with posters that depict four pink legs in garters" (20). This rhythmically escalating, quick-fire sequence, what in film would be a series of increasingly rapid cuts, generates the same kind of astonishment as the fireworks the policemen ignite.

In the scenario's finale, Columbine and Pierrot come down to the footlights and present a final song and dance with the four friends. The pantomime's final image is of a garter advertisement. As with the finale in circus, the intention is not to bring the action to a logical close (Columbine and Pierrot are dead, after all) but to present reprises of spectacular moments in a kaleidoscopic look back at what the audience has experienced.

Eisenstein and Yutkevich's *Columbine* organizes wildly disparate references—vampire films, Buffalo Bill, Cocteau's *Parade*, the electric chair, French pornography, and the Moscow Art Theatre—into patterns of interrelations. Additional categories that cumulatively generate through-lines of meaning include class markers (monocles, top hats, gaiters, spherical bodies), new technologies and inventions (neon advertisements, the electric chair, light bulbs, American padlocks, the cinematograph, elevators), sexual and scatological references (lovemaking, Ma's coin slot, the lever between the Dance Master's legs, the pull-chain on Pa's flushable self, the *kukish*), and the varied soundscape of a "silent" pantomime (music-hall songs, jazz, urban cacophony, circus drum rolls, crackling film strips, car horns, and a smattering of Dohnányi).

Columbine's Garter also cites a wide range of popular entertainments: boxing, music hall, *café-chantant*, variety, circus, film, figure skating, and detective novels. Eisenstein's understanding and love of the circus deeply informs the pantomime's structural elements, most notably its entrées, which establish characters and scenes, and its finales, which reframe the viewer's memory of what has been seen. Although it would be easy to view Eisenstein and Yutkevich's use of film in *Columbine's Garter* as a first step in an inevitable transition to cinema, and although their *Columbine* is replete with references to films its creators had recently seen—*Les Mystères de New York*, *The Laughing Mask*, *The Mask with the White Teeth*,[153] *Fantômas*, and a Buffalo Bill documentary—film was not only a source of thematic inspiration: it was a medium for formal innovation. *Columbine's Garter* creates a visual landscape of intertitles on many surfaces—a screen, a callboard, adverts, and sandwich boards—as a structuring device for theme, variation, and punctuation. Most importantly, Eisenstein reveled in the lowness of film as a form during an era when many viewed it as the "illegitimate child of photography and fairground sideshows."[154] In this sense, film, garters, and Eisenstein's obscene *kukish* were not that different in their intended effect.

Columbine's Fate

In November 1922 newspapers began to announce that *Columbine's Garter* had begun rehearsals. One periodical added enthusiastically, "The production will be the first experience of 'advertising-theater' in the forms of the modern tragic balagan and will be the first 'blow to the externally-utilitarian theater.'"[155] Another announced soon after, however, that "due to lack of funds . . . the staging of *Garter* has been delayed." Yutkevich adds: "Even before then it became clear to us that nothing was going to come of it. Eisenstein, disappointed in Foregger, agreed to be an assistant to Meyerhold, who was staging . . . *Tarelkin's Death*. And I, having the position of Head of the Artistic-Design division, continued . . . to design productions."[156]

Years later Eisenstein provided additional context for why *Columbine's Garter* never premiered. As the project moved forward, he became increasingly concerned that Foregger would take credit for the pantomime's staging ideas. Eisenstein added, "Having received a most flattering approbation by Evreinov, to whom all these concerns were presented, I decided to use the 'far-fetched' in my own household. And I applied some things from [*Columbine's Garter*] in what was already my own independent work as a director: . . . Ostrovsky's *Wiseman*."[157] During this brief but intense period of theatrical experimentation, Eisenstein recycled ideas in multiple places and regularly incorporated notes and plans into other productions. Within Eisenstein's "imagined theater"[158]—his hundreds of pages of theory, designs, and production plans—*Columbine's Garter* was a particularly valuable fermentation chamber from which his artistic credo could be clarified and its formal elements reimagined elsewhere.

EPILOGUE: THROUGH THEATER TO FILM

Wiseman (1923)

Eisenstein borrowed copiously from *Columbine* in *Enough Stupidity in Every Wiseman* (*Wiseman* for short), Sergei Tretiakov's 1923 refraction of Ostrovsky's play, which Eisenstein directed with the Proletkult First Workers' Theatre. In Eisenstein's first "independent work as a director,"[159] he encouraged his actors to "clown it up" as much as they liked—something he was not able to do freely in *Tarelkin*.[160] *Wiseman*, which opened in April 1923, and "The Montage of

Attractions for *Enough Stupidity in Every Wiseman*," the theoretical manifesto that Eisenstein published in the journal *Lef* (*Left*) that May, constitute Eisenstein's first and most famous public articulation of how he aimed to reinvent the theatrical experience.

In "Montage of Attractions," as in *Columbine's Garter*, Eisenstein reveals how he creatively refracted FEKS, Meyerhold, and the theater of his day. While drawing from theatrical innovations in the zeitgeist, he creates his own version of them, often using a new vocabulary to do so. Like Meyerhold, Eisenstein rejects honoring "the playwright's intention" or creating a "true reflection of the period" in favor of a theater that "transfer[s] the center of attention to what . . . was previously considered secondary and ornamental."[161] Meyerhold had called for the interlude, the aside, and the frame to be recognized as central to the audience's experience instead of prioritizing faithfulness to daily life or a dramatic text. What differs here is the language Eisenstein uses and how he applies his ideas in practice. Eisenstein's theater relies on accumulated collisions of attractions, self-contained "unit[s] of effectiveness" (entrées, for instance) designed for affective, emotional (but not psychological), and cognitive impact on the viewer.[162] The fact that he sought to provoke several kinds of response simultaneously illuminates why he was so fascinated with polyphonic construction.

Eisenstein directly transferred several attractions from *Garter* to *Wiseman*, one example being a circus entrée with "three as a horse" in which a star "cracks her whip" and other characters "scamper about the ring."[163] Both productions have fireworks at the end, a shock–delight technique Meyerhold and Eisenstein used in *Tarelkin*. A famous film segment from *Wiseman* shows Eisenstein bowing in front of a promotional poster that advertises *Wiseman* and his "Montage of Attractions," thus self-referencing himself, the production, and his theories. Like Meyerhold's Dapertutto, this cellulose self allowed Eisenstein to present his actual and artistically refracted selves simultaneously (figure 43).

More significant than individual borrowings, however, are the works' similar approaches to character and space. Like *Garter, Wiseman* fragmented and reassembled characters in various destabilizations of the linear, psychologically developed self. As Gerould describes it, "Kurchaev expanded into three hussars; Glumov was George the clown at one and the same time; and the clown in the red wig, who first appeared in the prologue . . . subsequently turned into Glumov's mother. Two other women's parts . . . were played by men, and all the servants were played by one actor."[164] *Wiseman*, too, reframes theatrical space with the revolutionary idea that any and every part of the theater can be a place to perform. In frequently reproduced images from *Wiseman*, though they have not typically been read this way, ladders and a balance beam form an inner proscenium, a theater within a theater

Figure 43. Sergei Eisenstein, still from the film "Glumov's Diary" in Tretiakov's *Enough Stupidity in Every Wiseman*, after Ostrovsky, dir. Sergei Eisenstein, Proletkult First Workers' Theatre (1923). © A. A. Bakhrushin State Central Theatre Museum, Moscow.

upon which performers play and frame the action below (figure 44). Glumov and Harlequin also vertically transect space, ascending a rope to the flies and using their descent to "shower" another character "with curses."[165] As Yutkevich recalls of *Columbine's Garter*, "Harlequin, in Eisenstein's concept, was to appear out of the audience as a tightrope walker, something that was later transferred to . . . *Wiseman*."[166]

In *Wiseman's* short internal film, "Glumov's Diary," in which Glumov chases a thief who has stolen his diary through Moscow, characters chase one another atop the mansion that housed the performance. This mansion had once belonged to Savva Morozov, one of the primary financial backers of the Moscow Art Theatre in its early years. The implications of this, that Eisenstein's theatrical revolution not only repurposed a site of former wealth but also did so in insolent rejection of the MAT, would not have been missed on its audience. Yet Eisenstein's new use of space goes beyond this. If *Columbine's Garter* exploded the possibilities for where one might perform *within* the theater, "Glumov" expanded this to include the building's exterior. Eisenstein not only disrupted the "fourth wall" through which Meyerhold had broken, but also penetrated what Smith has called the "fifth wall," the

Figure 44. Parodic action (satirizing Hoover's American Relief Administration) within and downstage of the inner proscenium in *Wiseman*, Proletkult First Workers' Theatre (1923). Russian State Archive of Literature and Art, f. 1923, op. 1, ed. khr. 805: 16.

wall that separates the theater from the world outside.[167] This impulse—to take theater beyond the fifth wall—was one of the things that drew Eisenstein to film.

Strike (1925) and *The Glass House* (1927–47)

Eisenstein repeatedly rediscovered theater while in the process of working on something else: he was entranced by Meyerhold's *Masquerade* while studying to be an engineer; he received a position as a designer for Proletkult after coming to Moscow to learn Japanese.[168] It therefore seems appropriate that he should have discovered film while designing and directing theater. Eisenstein's transition from theater to film is more complex, though, than one common view, repeated by Perry, would indicate: that the theater was too restrictive a medium for him. In relation to Glumov's leaps in *Wiseman* from one spatial plane to another, Perry argues, "the obvious awkwardness of having such events follow one another in rapid succession points up the reason why Eisenstein became convinced that it was not the theater but the cinema which most effectively could represent this notion of simultaneity, multiple attractions, or polyphony."[169] Theater was restrictive for Eisenstein in a different way, however. Most likely the primary reason for Eisenstein's change of medium, especially in the context of his fraught experience with Meyerhold, was that Meyerhold's revolution in theatrical form was so far underway that it was difficult for Eisenstein's voice to stand out as unique. This uniqueness, Eisenstein's fervent desire to create "*my* meaning in refracted form,"[170] was of vital importance to him. Literature had proved a useful tool for provoking a revolution in theatrical form. Film was similarly fertile ground for a new revolution to which the lessons of theater could be applied.

When Eisenstein was in the United States in the 1930s, Prince Mirsky summed up the director's film innovations in an essay in the *Virginia Quarterly Review*: "What makes the new Soviet school important not only for the art of the cinema but for modern culture and philosophy in general is that it introduces *a new attitude towards the creative process itself,* a new way of producing imaginative values."[171] We have seen how Russian directors equated Hoffmann with the mental artistic freedom of the capriccio, with the autonomy of the individual perspective, with refracting rather than mirroring one's world, and with making creations about the process of creation. That these same impulses continued in Eisenstein's film work I will illustrate with a few examples from *Strike*, his first feature film, and *The Glass House*, an unrealized project he began in 1927 and returned to recurrently over the remainder of his life.

In *Strike*, which opened in early 1925, Eisenstein developed images and devices that appeared in earlier work: A character who opposes the workers becomes a human seesaw, recalling the seesaws in Meyerhold's *Tarelkin* (see figure 30) and *The Forest* (1924). Again, too, Eisenstein constructs multiple spatial planes and frames individual attractions. In one scene, workers sit above the ceiling of the factory on a structure of crossbars that recalls Pierrot's window, while near the end, during the police repression of the workers' strike, apartment balconies on multiple tiers are framed in a single image. Characters also appear in literal frames before performing brief entrées: when the camera shows a close-up of photos of four secret police agents in a photo album, each framed photo comes to life, allowing its inhabitant to perform a tiny scene.

Strike has many examples of Eisenstein's continued fascination with uncomfortable graftings of humans, animals, and machines. "Throughout *Strike*," Nesbet observes, "people are subjected to an uncomfortable oscillation between their role as mechanized, automatized (and oppressed) lineworkers and the even more unsatisfactory identification with animals."[172] After workers refuse to continue to be treated like machines (a conclusion the viewer reaches via a series of "associational" juxtapositions[173] between the workers and the machines they operate), they are slaughtered in the

Figure 45. The Owl, one of four spies juxtaposed with animals, in Eisenstein's film *Strike* (1925).

film's most famous sequence: a successive juxtaposition between the massacre of the strikers and the actual slaughter of a bull. Animal-human collisions are used in many other ways, too. In an example that evokes both Callot's etchings and *The Golden Pot*'s fire salamander–archivist, four spies are each paired with an animal: a fox, a monkey, an owl, and a bulldog. After the animal cross-fades to the corresponding human (figure 45), the human retains some of the animal's characteristics.

In 1927 Eisenstein made copious production notes for a film, *The Glass House*. He returned to this project in 1930 with the hope of developing it for Paramount Pictures and again in 1947. It was to have been set in a building made entirely of glass with transparent walls, floors, and ceilings that allowed for simultaneous juxtapositions of its apartment dwellers. The inhabitants were to have a fundamental "indifference to each other . . . established by showing that the characters do not see each other through the glass doors and walls because they do not *look*—a developed 'non-seeing.' . . . All live *as though there are real walls*."[174] The structure of the film was to "be built on the gradual growth of 'seeing' by the inhabitants" of what is through those transparent walls. This is followed first by a series of crimes, then by a tragic event in one of the apartments, the horror of which is accentuated by its having been watched by the other inhabitants: "the walls, floor, and ceiling seem to be made of faces" looking on. Eventually the inhabitants smash and destroy the glass house.[175]

Eisenstein's notes for *Glass House* reveal a continued interest in several formal innovations from *Columbine's Garter*. Structurally, according to Eisenstein, the film was to

> Take the most ordinary actions and change the point of view.
>
> Take the most traditional types and psychological collisions and change the point of view. For the first—polishing the floors—rolling up carpets—cleaning and placing furniture.
>
> Do it as a farce, as grotesque, as nightmarish tragedy.[176]

The building itself allowed Eisenstein to work with a seemingly infinite number of contrasting spatial planes—a significant expansion from the three in *Columbine's Garter*. There is an unusually direct parallel between Eisenstein and Yutkevich's contrast between the dead Pierrot on his giant window and the whirling neon advertisements of the city beyond and a similar scene here: individuals in one of the glass rooms are above "a whirling town" and "a moving street"[177] that again allowed Eisenstein to position the static against the frenetic.

Formal devices from Eisenstein's theater work echoed in his films for the remainder of his career. The disorienting perspective shifts of *Columbine's Garter* lay behind unusual camera angles and temporally and visually fragmented shots in *Battleship Potemkin*'s famous scene on the Odessa steps. The San Francisco docks for Eisenstein's unrealized *Sutter's Gold* recall the simultaneous settings in notes from his Tyss period. The side balconies from *Master Martin* recur in Eisenstein's drawings for an unrealized stage production of Prokofiev's *War and Peace* (1942).[178] The tsar's looming profile in *Ivan the Terrible* has ties to *Columbine*'s juxtapositions of planes, and, as Clayton observes, to "Pantalone as depicted by Jacques Callot."[179] These point to a larger poetics of form that values simultaneity, collision, shifted perspective, and theater itself as a framing and refracting device.

Eisenstein did not move *from* theater to film, but *through* theater to film. Without his theater thinking, we would not have had his film thinking. One might argue that he refracted the theater in a different medium—film—or that he viewed film through the prism of theater. In either case, he used film to reinvent theater beyond the fifth wall, and, in the process, reinvented film.

Another echo that Eisenstein returned to recurrently—in his private writings—was that of Meyerhold. In August 1941 Meyerhold's stepdaughter Tatiana Esenina contacted Eisenstein, asking him to come take and preserve Meyerhold's archive, hidden at the latter's former dacha near Moscow. In a 1944 diary entry titled "The Treasure," Eisenstein looks back on this swelteringly hot day.[180] As he wandered into Meyerhold's dacha through a scene of chaos and disrepair—abandoned cottages, broken teacups, scattered toys—he recalled Meyerhold's *wayang golek* puppet (see figure 38), the same puppet about which he later wrote in "Wie sag' ich's meinem Kinde?"

> Among the household rubbish I do not see the slim waist of a Javanese puppet.
> White and gold. It should have been here . . .
> O, princess of the fairy-tale *wayang* . . .
> When I saw you for the first time, behind you was the sparkle of . . .
> The simple tile of a simple house on Novinsky Boulevard . . .
> He is now before us. With almost imperceptible finger movements, he pours his soul into the animated gold and white body of the fairy-tale princess.
> And she lives with his breath . . .
> She drowsily raises her hands and floats, it seems, before the spellbound eyes of the proselytes of the great master.
> Somewhere here, in the dust and junk.
> Some kind of bashful shyness keeps me from asking the young woman with the blue circles under her eyes about it.
> Maybe it is the same kind of shyness that is afraid to destroy the long-held dream of an unexpected touch.[181]

In contrast with Eisenstein's intangible memory of a Meyerhold who might still reappear (Eisenstein did not yet know of Meyerhold's 1940 death), his description of the archive itself is dissonantly quotidian, enveloped as it was in heat and dust:

> Part of it is under a canopy over the back porch.
> Part of it is in the space between the slope of the roof and the pantry ceiling.
> That which I came for at the call of the young woman with the circles under her eyes.
> Hot as an oven in that semi-attic . . .
> Red dust lazily rolling on the blue, dead folders.
> Rays of light through chinks, only flies playing over these stacks of paper.[182]

Many have wondered why Eisenstein would agree to risk his life to preserve Meyerhold's archive, why he would risk taking part of this archive with him to Alma Ata, to which he was evacuated during World War II,[183] using it to continue trying to decipher the "true recipe" of Meyerhold's creative work, a process begun in his student days.[184] Eisenstein may physically have left

Meyerhold's workshops after their stormy collaboration on *Tarelkin's Death*, but the two directors were indelibly linked by common creative blood and by a common need "to make *my* meaning in refracted form."[185]

Unlike Meyerhold, Eisenstein was not arrested, nor was he steadily suffocated in precisely the way Tairov was. But in the ten years leading up to Meyerhold's arrest, only one of Eisenstein's films was permitted to be shown to the public: *Alexander Nevsky* (premiered December 1938). His pro-collectivization film *Bezhin Meadow* (1937) was fiercely denounced as "formalism, formalism and once again formalism."[186] When several Moscow film studios and organizations took three days in March 1937 to discuss this film's "lessons,"[187] Eisenstein's response to his critics contained the typical apology, the admission of the prolonged error of his ways, but he also articulated with sharp precision what formalism in a 1930s Stalinist context really meant, noting of his film *October* that he had thought

> that talent and glory gave me the right to have an original vision of the October Revolution. In *The Old and the New* I once again attempted to give my own special, as it were independent views of the world, instead of carefully studying the statements of the Party and expressing them. I thought I had the right, but it turned out I did not.[188]

During a time when so many individualities were erased in so many ways, Eisenstein, who generated hundreds of drawings, sketches, and plans for projects that never saw the light of stage or screen, yet deeply informed his entire life's work, understood the value of preserving the traces of the making of an artist.

Epilogue

The Afterlife of a Death Jubilee

HOFFMANN'S JUBILEE

By 1922, the centenary of Hoffmann's death, Russian theatrical Hoffmaniana had manifested in three distinct, though often overlapping ways: Hoffmannian plots, themes, and forms. Productions in the first category included stagings of Hoffmann's works—or of ballet and opera adaptations of them: Yosef Lapitsky's *Tales of Hoffmann*, Fedor Komissarzhevsky's *The Bride Choosing* and *Tales of Hoffmann*, the Kamerny's *Brambilla* and *Formica*, and others. Russian theater was also deeply infused with Hoffmannian themes: humans controlled by fate, marionettes as ideal actors, commedia as the theater's salvation, the truer invisible world of the artist, the nightmarish, and the hallucinatory. Meyerhold, Eisenstein, and Yutkevich each adopted Hoffmannian pseudonyms, but doppelgängers more generally were yet another recurrent theme in Russian theater, literature, and art.

It was Hoffmannian form, however, in conjunction with the creative freedom of the capriccio that proved most revolutionary to theater and film. The self-referentiality and grotesque collisions of romantic irony provided provocative new ways to engage the spectator imaginatively. Meyerhold, Ignatov, and Eisenstein used framing devices and multiple spatial planes to bare the theater's inherent real/fictional collisions. Tairov staged pantomimes within plays and blurred the lines between vivid spectacle and provocative manifesto. Hoffmann's objects and people that miraculously transform at a second glance became, for Meyerhold and Eisenstein, collisions of tempos, moods, styles, and attractions.

In the early 1920s there was a considerable degree of artistic pluralism in Soviet Russia. Even so, given the burgeoning quantity of productions that rejected prerevolutionary subject matter and embraced political agitprop, the last major staging of a Hoffmann tale might perhaps have been *Princess Brambilla* had it not been for the Hoffmann jubilee. The official date of the centenary of Hoffmann's death was June 25, 1922, but articles were published and productions staged in his honor over the course of most of that year. Several new translations of Hoffmann tales appeared, including Morozov's edition of *The Musical Novellas* and Viacheslav Ivanov's of "The Doubles." The Serapion Brotherhood held a special literary event in

Hoffmann's honor. In the theater, the opening of *Signor Formica* and the hundredth performance of *Princess Brambilla* coincided with the jubilee. Several theaters besides the Kamerny also marked the event with productions; the Maly Opera Theatre presented three: *Tales of Hoffmann*, *Coppélia*, and Tchaikovsky's *Nutcracker*. Eisenstein attempted unsuccessfully to stage *The Golden Pot* and *Master Martin*. Lapitsky remounted the production of *Tales of Hoffmann* that Eisenstein so heavily criticized. Mikhail Kuzmin dedicated the central section of his performance-poem *The Little Grove* (pub. 1923) to Hoffmann and launched a new journal, *The Green Bird*, which included the first Russian translation of this Gozzi *fiaba*.

Three productions staged the year of Hoffmann's death jubilee illustrate the German writer's Soviet fate: Sokolov's *Nutcracker and the Mouse King*, which dramatized a specific tale, was accused of aestheticism and escapism. Derzhavin's *Strange Adventure of E. T. A. Hoffmann* (*Neobyknovennoe prikliuchenie E. T. A. Gofmana*),[1] which explored Hoffmannian themes, made Hoffmann a central character in a parallel revolution. Lastly, Vakhtangov's *Princess Turandot*, which refracted Hoffmannian forms without referring to Hoffmann's tales, celebrated defiant joy in the face of revolution and famine. Although these productions marked the "death" of direct Hoffmann stagings in the Soviet Union for many years, they marked the beginning of the afterlife of Hoffmaniana in Russian and beyond: a vital theatricalist poetics of form and a new attitude toward the creative process.

The Nutcracker and the Mouse King (1922)

The Nutcracker and the Mouse King opened on September 26, 1922, at the RSFSR State Children's Theatre, one of Russia's first theaters for youth. Its director was Vladimir Sokolov—Chiari in the Kamerny's *Brambilla* and author of the Kamerny's *Formica*. This *Nutcracker* marked two new directions in Hoffmannian theatrical experiments: its actors were puppets and its spectators were children.

Sokolov's *Nutcracker* reflected the agenda of the director of the State Children's Theatre, Henriette Pascar, who believed that children who had lived through war and famine were best served by productions that create "a festive corner of comfort and beauty, a world of bright colors, and happy sounds, a world of fairy tale heroes."[2] Ignatov's production review was complementary of Sokolov's correspondingly child-centric interpretation. Despite one criticism that "Drosselmeier's appearance next to the clock is too terrifying for children,"[3] Ignatov concluded that Sokolov "conveyed Hoffmann very accurately and subtly, moreover not the chimerical Hoffmann, as he is for adults, but he managed to find in him true children's characters."[4]

Other reviews harshly criticized *Nutcracker* on ideological grounds, condemning it as an inappropriate Soviet children's theater prototype. A *Pravda* critic argued:

> Instead of a healthy tale with a strong heroic element (in the person of "Nutcracker"), it turned out to be a horrific monodrama of a little girl tortured by nightmares. A spectacle hardly suitable for a child. All these hysterics are embodied in forms completely contradictory to a healthy and competently constructed theater.[5]

This same reviewer, Lvov, charged the production in a second article with faults ranging from "theatrical illiteracy" to "hysterics and mysticism."[6] Another critic condemned the prerevolutionary Russian intelligentsia's continued use of Hoffmann in postrevolutionary Russia:

> Most have been inclined to see in him a pure phantast, the magician of an imagined world . . . And this entailed the presentation of Hoffmann's works exclusively in the manner of aestheticism, sometimes even of the mysticism and sinister symbolism characteristic of the art of the era of decadence.[7]

The danger, this critic added, was that the decadents had used Hoffmann's "'inspirational' narcotic of fantasy" to avoid dealing with a difficult, though necessary reality and Hoffmann's artist/philistine divide to create an art-weapon that was "opposed to the influence of the ideas of Socialist materialism and the new proletarian culture."[8] In his view, if Hoffmann was to be used at all, he should be made "soundly educational" for children. His interpretation of Hoffmann bears little resemblance to how the writer had been understood since his works first crossed the Russian border: "Everywhere Hoffmann defends labor, work, a simple and healthy life, and a sound moral in the best and most sensitive approach . . . He always combines beauty with labor and a hidden, upright moral."[9] To emphasize Hoffmann's nightmarish qualities could only result in "damaging healthy, sweet children."[10] Lvov similarly concluded: "Artistic education in a renewed nation should be built not on sentimental aestheticism, but on the healthy and sound foundations of physical education, industrialism, and the genuine skill of the artist."[11]

These criticisms were symptomatic of larger changes in children's theater that were soon to occur. In 1923 a resolution was passed at the Twelfth Party Congress urging "the use of [all] theatre for the systematic mass propaganda of ideas related to the struggle of communism."[12] Pascar was fired that same year and fled the Soviet Union. Her successor, Yuri Bondy, a student of Meyerhold, wrote, "I affirm, that the one and only form of theatre necessary for children at the present time is the theatre of agitation."[13] Traditional fairy tales were replaced by fairy tales with a socialist message, then abandoned altogether in the mid-1920s in favor of direct propaganda plays. As Sofia Lunacharskaia wrote in 1931:

> Art as an amusement, a diversion of attention away from life is not for [the Soviet child]. . . . The theatre . . . must give him sustenance for the struggle, an optimistic attitude toward the surmounting of all difficulties and obstacles, and a faith in the strength of the collective and in the glorious life of emerging socialism.[14]

Hoffmann's joy of creation, freeing perspectival shifts, and primacy of the fantasy were replaced with education, hygiene, and the collective betterment of the Soviet child, an agenda that was formally extended to all generations when socialist realism was mandated in 1934, though the process began well before. As Lidia Ginsburg wrote in 1927, "The merry times of laying bare the device have passed . . . Now is the time when one has to hide the device as far as one can."[15]

The Strange Adventure of E. T. A. Hoffmann (1922)

The Strange Adventure of E. T. A. Hoffmann, written and directed by Konstantin Nikolaevich Derzhavin (1903–1956), a former Meyerhold student, combined Hoffmannian subject matter with a story about a parallel revolutionary period: 1793 Paris at the height of the Reign of Terror. A loose conflation of Alexandre Dumas père's *The Woman with the Velvet Choker* (*La Femme au collier de velours*) and Washington Irving's "The Adventure of the German Student," Derzhavin's play, which opened at Petrograd's New Drama Theatre in December 1922, featured Hoffmann as a German student in revolutionary France. In the tales upon which the play was based,[16] he descends into madness after he realizes he has been conversing with a decapitated woman, her head held in place only by the velvet choker around her neck.

Derzhavin's recasting of Hoffmann as a revolutionary was generally well received. One reviewer described it as "an interesting and uncommon show . . . that cannot be brushed aside with a stock evaluation."[17] Another added:

> I welcome this attempt, not to stage Hoffmann directly, which is not such a great service, for anyone can achieve this, even the least experienced theatrical hack, but to walk in the footsteps of Hoffmann's muse, to use . . . her whimsical combination of the everyday with the most intricate fantasy, her

> propensity for nightmares, her love for the strange, incomprehensible phenomena that await us at every turn.[18]

In a description of the adaptation process, Derzhavin wrote that in borrowing from Dumas and Irving, he changed their work significantly, mixing historical French Revolution figures with characters from Hoffmann's tales. Above all, however, he attempted "to translate the literary stylistic devices of Hoffmann the novelist into the language of dramatic-theatrical devices."[19] For instance, he conceived the work in three stylistic planes, "the realistic, fantastical, and abstract," adding, "The real and fantastical in my play flow naturally one out of the other; they represent, as it were, two sides of one and the same object."[20] Derzhavin's audience understood, of course, that the French Revolution was meant as a parallel to the Russian one. In this context, Hoffmann's colliding planes could be reinterpreted as the shifting and chaotic reality of another nation undergoing a major, but necessary overthrow of power.[21]

Derzhavin facilitated transitions between planes by presenting "*silhouettes* of theatrical figures, not delving into a detailed analysis of their day-to-day psychology." [22] This allowed for identities that shifted, both literally and figuratively:

> Our relatively small troupe depicts a whole kaleidoscope of characters . . . The actors' incessant changing of their appearances and masks from one to another . . . creates a particular kind of atmosphere backstage, saturated with a kind of Hoffmannian nervousness and unusualness.[23]

Costume designs by Vladimir Dmitriev used a Callot-infused chiaroscuro to reinforce Derzhavin's interpretation of the characters as silhouettes.[24]

Despite the topical content of *Strange Adventure*, in Sergei Yutkevich's assessment, Derzhavin imitated Meyerhold's past work rather than developing it in new directions. Yutkevich recalls sitting in the "empty house" at the New Drama, where his mounting frustration made him want to rush backstage and tell Derzhavin (aged 19) and Dmitriev (aged 22):

> You are young, damn you, you are the young students of the most creative master of our era! . . . What is it to me that the play is competently . . . staged when I crack my jaw from yawning in the gaps (if you can call them interludes) between your endless scenes? . . . Learn theatrical montage from the cinematograph. Why would you let loose a greenhorn lass, forcing her to move "not like in life," but like, in your opinion, one ought to in Hoffmann? . . . Finally, why this forced, disharmonious music reeking of Henri Forterre in his earliest period?[25] Throw out all that rancid romanticism, leave behind

> the "pure" art of "AKAM [academic theaters]," sell the elephants; it's time to build a new theater of modern times!
>
> I wanted to go and tell them this, but . . . I didn't. I already knew the answer. They would look at me with pity and say . . . that it is not "what" that is important, but "how," and they would talk about . . . "presentational theater." They would ask whether I know the great Carlo Gozzi and his *Love of Three Oranges*, and [say] that I have bad taste, as Hoffmann is a wonderful writer and very much in tune with modern times.[26]

For Yutkevich, Eisenstein, and many of their generation, the time had come for the Russian theater not to repeat itself, not to mirror its own innovations, but to refract its refractions.

Princess Turandot (1922)

Another production that premiered during Hoffmann's jubilee year did not identify itself as Hoffmannian. Nor was it part of the Hoffmann celebrations. *Princess Turandot* opened at the tiny MAT Third Studio in February 1922, four months before Hoffmann's death jubilee and three months before the death of Evgeny Bagrationovich Vakhtangov (1883–1922), *Turandot*'s director. Rarely in his private or public writings did Vakhtangov mention Hoffmann. Although Meyerhold and others used Hoffmann as a foundational source to develop new theatrical devices, once they were in common use there was no need to return repeatedly to their origins. In many cases, to do so was to dilute further innovation. This is not to say that Vakhtangov was unaware of his artistic milieu. His repeated experiments with the grotesque at the various studios at which he worked culminated in one of his most famous productions, *The Dybbuk* (1922) at Habima (The Stage). His interest in marionettes, emphasis on "fantastical realism," and experiments with irony also demonstrate his profound creative responsiveness to the theatricalist experiments that surrounded him.[27]

Vakhtangov's *Turandot* refracted Meyerhold's sharp contrasts, Stanislavsky's attention to the actor's spontaneous truthfulness, and Tairov's love of play. *Turandot* was full of a celebratory spirit that recalled Tairov's *Brambilla*, though in somewhat more direct response to the Revolution. As Zhezhelenko declared, "Vakhtangov asserted that theatre in a country that had won a revolution should be celebratory, joyful, openly theatrical."[28] Rather than reproducing Andrei Malaev-Babel's excellent analysis of *Turandot* and what he calls its "thresholds of creativity,"[29] I will briefly nod to a few theatricalist conventions that Vakhtangov refracted in *Turandot* to illustrate how Hoffmaniana spread to much broader contexts.

Vakhtangov was concerned that a postrevolutionary audience would not find contemporary relevance in a straightforward presentation of Gozzi's eighteenth-century fairy-tale play unless the production also commented on it. He therefore developed three distinct planes for the actors to negotiate: their real selves, a fictional company of Italian strolling players, and Gozzi's characters, thereby creating both a play-within-a-play and actors-within-actors. Drawing from his MAT First Studio training, Vakhtangov encouraged actors to develop complete biographies for their fictional actor selves. The aim was twofold: to give them a logical basis for their self-awareness and overt commentary and to reframe Gozzi's play through the prism of the contemporary actor.

Turandot framed character in other ways as well. Vakhtangov, after Meyerhold, termed the play's commedia masks "forestage servants." These servants performed initially improvised (and eventually set) *lazzi* interludes, drew back the curtain, and changed the scenery. The month after *Turandot* opened, Meyerhold's *Magnanimous Cuckold* had its actors place individual costume pieces over otherwise identical, utilitarian uniforms. Vakhtangov's take on *prozodezhda* was concert dress: tuxedos for the men and evening gowns for the women.

Turandot began with what Vakhtangov, again refracting Meyerhold, called a "parade": the actors came out onto the forestage in their evening wear and faced the audience (figure 46) before tossing light fabrics and props into the air in a playful, virtuosic dance of materials. Eventually they put these objects on over their evening dress, using them to transform "*into characters* before the audience's eyes."[30] Many objects were deliberately improbable: a lampshade for a hat, a towel for a beard, a tennis racket for a scepter. Thus Vakhtangov, in Malaev-Babel's analysis, "boldly unmasked the machinery of the stage in the audience's eyes, and—most importantly—he demystified the sacred act of the actors' transformation."[31]

In Vakhtangov's *Turandot*, the hope for artistic and societal rejuvenation that followed the Revolution was created afresh each night: the actors' visible love of play and transformation demonstrated not only versatility and skill, but also adaptability in the face of adversity. *Turandot* also was infused with defiant life in the face of death—Vakhtangov's own from cancer, which was so advanced by the time of *Turandot*'s general rehearsal that Vakhtangov was unable to attend it.[32]

THE AFTERLIFE OF REFRACTED LIGHT

The death of direct stagings of Hoffmann's tales in the mid-1920s was followed by a significant afterlife in which directors creatively engaged—and

Figure 46. Opening parade for Gozzi's *Princess Turandot*, dir. Evgeny Vakhtangov, Moscow Art Theatre Third Studio (1922). Photo courtesy of Andrei Malaev-Babel.

continue to engage—with a theatricalist poetics. Tairov's Kamerny Theatre became the international face of the Soviet avant-garde through its widely acclaimed European tours (1923, 1925, 1930), South American tour (1930), and the 1923 German translation of *Notes of a Director*. Russian film, perhaps most notably that of Andrei Tarkovsky,[33] has continued to draw from a poetics of juxtaposition with origins in both Meyerhold and Eisenstein. Tennessee Williams and other playwrights were deeply inspired by Eisenstein's film form, though the wider international effect of his film thinking is truly incalculable. Meyerholdiana spread so widely by the 1930s that there were few Soviet theaters that did not bear its traces. Living newspaper and Blue Blouse troupes adopted Meyerholdian modes of audience engagement, forming an agitprop vocabulary that was refracted in 1930s U.S. theater and again in the political theater of the 1960s. The Moscow State Yiddish Theatre brilliantly fused the theatrical grotesque with avant-garde art and nostalgia for a lost Jewish world. Vakhtangov's *Turandot* and *The Dybbuk* became founding productions for the Vakhtangov Theatre and Israel's Habima respectively. Brecht refracted Meyerhold and Eisenstein (as well as the "verbal montage" of his teacher Sergei Tretiakov), especially with regard to episodic structure, interruptions, real/fictional collisions, theater that celebrates its own making, and audience mental engagement, though many innovations refracted by Brecht have since come to be attributed to him. Grotowski claimed Meyerhold as a major inspiration; Peter Brook adopted Meyerhold's view of the creative process in *Midsummer Night's Dream* (1970) and *The Empty Space* (1971). And the rehabilitation of Meyerhold in the decades after Stalin's death fueled U.S. and European experimental theater in the 1960s, '70s, and beyond.

While it is important to note this extensive afterlife, to trace each of its subsequent paths would be impossible. Fantasy unleashed is like the winds set loose from Aeolus's bag. This book's concluding thoughts will therefore explore something broader (and perhaps a little more abstract) than direct lineages. I suggest that innovations become absorbed into how theater is practiced in two major ways: One is through direct, traceable contact. The other, much more far-reaching, is through the transmission of "theatregrams." In her analysis of Shakespeare's use of commedia, Louise George Clubb contests the common assumption that the transmission of plots, characters, and formal devices must be directly traceable via personal contact or written documentation, using the term "theatregram" to describe the process of dissemination via oral, visual, and other largely non-traceable means. Her definition of theatregrams as "units of structure (characters, situations, actions/words, thematic patterns)"[34] that together form a repertoire provides a valuable way to ponder more broadly how the structural "units" of theater are spread and absorbed.

Like commedia, the visual, aural, and corporeal aspects of live performance are transmitted and adopted in many ways: through thrilling production moments, startling formal devices, artist collaborations, research brought into rehearsal rooms, memories of earlier productions, and lectures and exercises passed on by teachers. When Emma Rice and Kneehigh Theatre use framing characters to engage the audience, Tectonic Theatre Project's Moisés Kaufman discusses the "copulation of form and content," and Dmitry Krymov and his actor-designers prompt astonishing perspective shifts, these are, to varying degrees, indirect refractions of Russian directorial theatregrams.[35]

However, because of the violent erasure of Meyerhold, the systematic discrediting of Tairov, and the periodic creative silencing of Eisenstein, there remain gaps and distortions in our understanding of their legacies. Stalin was brilliantly and brutally adept at staging a variety of erasures, but the process of silencing, as we have seen, began before his rise to power. Plays and productions were banned, authors and composers unpublished, films unscreened, theaters closed, diaries mutilated, artists exiled, individuals discredited in show trials (and show reviews), audiences coerced into staying away, accidental deaths staged, suicides provoked, and artists suffocated under a weighty burden of mundane hackwork. Even canonized figures—

Stanislavsky, Eisenstein, and others—experienced erasures in plain sight, their individual traits, experimentation, and variety eclipsed in favor of a unified and carefully maintained public image.

To erase artists, even if creative work is never fully repressible, is to sever connections that often are never fully repaired. One of these is common knowledge of where and with whom particular theatregrams originated. Another is a comprehensive understanding of the artistic philosophy that inspired their creation. In such instances, conventions that once were part of a cohesive aesthetic system sometimes are subsumed even into philosophically opposing definitions of theater, in which, for instance, actors invade the audience not to draw them in but to alarm them, stagehands shift scenery in semidarkness between otherwise naturalistic scenes, or asides and prologues return to being a "negligible" rupture of the fictional frame.[36]

In her book *Stanislavski in Focus*, Sharon Carnicke analyzes the "pervasive veil of assumptions" that continues to cloud understandings of Stanislavsky and his actor training system.[37] Meyerhold, Tairov, and Eisenstein are equally subject to lingering veils of assumptions, often despite excellent scholarship to the contrary. The purpose of this book has been to recover some of their continued newness and relevance by providing a new perspective on them. What has determined the book's underlying logic is the belief that veils of assumptions can partially be lifted by returning to the archives, by analyzing productions, and by viewing these directors through the sources that they themselves refracted.[38]

This book has not, however, attempted to condense their innovations into a method. The glory of the capriccio is that it is idiosyncratic, both in terms of how it is composed and how it is received. Creative thought does not move in a straight line. It loops, veers in unexpected directions, trails off, and picks up again. It zigzags. Yet it does not lack structure. These directors paired the capriccio's freedom with rigorous engagement with literature, art, music, popular entertainment, and theater. Each challenged the assumption that fidelity to one's sources or to daily life must be the theater's starting point. Each used form, the visible presence of the artist in the work, *as* meaning. And each created theater that celebrates jarring collisions without nihilism, theater in which joy is embraced as a valid and necessary outcome of creation.

Just a few of the interconnected innovations this book has explored include theatrical irony, commentary on (rather than reflection of) reality, framed character and space, musical mise-en-scène, polyphonic compositions of multiple art forms, plays-within-plays, emphasis on masks and other theatrical objects, and the jarring collisions of the grotesque. Meyerhold is to be credited with "the invention of mise-en-scène,"[39] Tairov with mimedrama in which movement replaces words, and Eisenstein with montages of self-contained attractions that provoke rather than deliver meaning.

Not coincidentally, these innovations have much in common with what Hans-Thies Lehmann terms "postdramatic theatre," defined in part as "a theatre that feels bound to operate beyond drama."[40] It is namely because so vital a strain of contemporary theater tends toward the postdramatic that reexamining the real and imagined theater of these Russian directors is so valuable.[41] While this book, like Lehmann's, has aimed to "develop an aesthetic logic" that gives spectators "the tools to articulate their perception" of theatrical meanings found outside spoken words,[42] it has been my contention that this can be accomplished by looking back at the theatricalist innovations of the past through the director's prism.

Looking forward, it is my hope that others will create refractions of this book's refractions, working "in the manner" of a Meyerhold, a Tairov, or an Eisenstein to disrupt assumptions of how form, space, character, color, sound, and story *ought* to be used and to make new theatrical capriccios sparked by their poetics of joy, thus becoming part of these artistic constellations that do not build upon one another in linear trajectories of accumulated meaning, but in complex and unpredictable patterns of refracted creative light.

What Prince Mirsky observed of Eisenstein, that his work "reveals a new attitude towards the creative process itself, a new way of producing imaginative values"[43] is true of all this book's directors. Their greatest legacy is this insight into the creative process. Vakhtangov's *Princess Turandot* at the MAT Third Studio was a product of his lifelong concern with the nature and origins of creative thought. In November 1917, just a few days after the Revolution, he wrote in a notebook:

> The conscious doesn't ever create anything—the unconscious creates. . . . Each rehearsal of a play is only productive when material is either sought or assigned for the next rehearsal; in the gap between rehearsals the creative work of mulling over the given material takes place in the unconscious. Nothing can be created from nothing—this is why one can't play a role . . . "by inspiration."
>
> Inspiration is the moment when the unconscious combines with material from the mulled-over work without the participation of the conscious . . . The flame that accompanies this moment is a natural state, as it is naturally warm during the fusion of several chemical elements into one form . . .
>
> Everything that is thought up consciously does not bear the signs of fire. Everything that is created in the unconscious and formulated unconsciously is accompanied by a release of this energy.[44]

Vakhtangov's musings on the nature of inspiration recall Meyerhold's thoughts on fantasy and artistic creation, penned a decade before. Meyerhold wrote:

> Having put into practice the director's creative work, the actor is *alone*, face to face with the spectator, and out of the friction of two pure elements, the creative work of the actor and the creative fantasy of the spectator, a real flame is kindled.[45]

It seems appropriate to conclude this study of Russian directorial Hoffmaniana with these two ideas of what refraction does: it prompts a chemical reaction between consciously "mulled-over" sources and unconscious inspiration by them, and it ignites a flame between the fantasy of the actor and the fantasy of the audience. The former articulates how creativity is sparked and the second how it is shared. Both give off heat. Both generate energy. Whether articulated as Meyerhold's flame, Tairov's joy, Eisenstein's electricity, or Vakhtangov's chemical fusion, for these directors—and for the many kindred artists in their wake—creation itself, the mental independence of artmaking, is the lifeblood of human existence. Theater refracted through this prism does not reflect an unchanging reality; it provides a new definition of reality, one that we ourselves create. In the words of Valery Briusov, with whose essay this book began, "the creative urge is the only reality that exists on earth."[46]

Appendix A

Three Essays from *Love for Three Oranges*: *The Journal of Doctor Dapertutto*

HOFFMANIANA

O incomparable Maestro! Ernst Theodor, who out of love for another immortal being took another name—Amadeus, glorious Hoffmann! Russian literature has honored You[1] no less than Balzac and the French did from the first day of their acquaintance with You. Your complete works, 19 volumes in French translation (*Oeuvres complètes*, Paris: 1830–1833), stood in Pushkin's library. Dostoevsky was intoxicated by You. You were an interpreter of art in Stankevich's circle; and the fiery Belinsky and incomparable Herzen paid the very same homage to You. The mad Apollon Grigoriev and the tranquil Count Odoevsky were enamored of You. Through Vl[adimir] Soloviev, You connected the past with our present. The green *Moscow Observer* from the [18]30s and the coffee-colored *Reading Library* smile at us from the shelves. Yes, we once again remember You, having forgotten only briefly.

In Germany You are being published again: both by Müller in Munich and in the publication *Golden Library of Classics*, edited by George Ellinger, who wrote a conscientious German book about You roughly twenty years ago. Here for now they are not considering this. And just as well. You are too exceptional, You do not need a throng; we are going to read You either in the original or in the old translations of the [18]30s and 40s.

Even without reprintings, we nevertheless study Your creative work. In the past year You have been written about a great deal. First and foremost, [the publisher] Alcyone published *The Golden Pot* in Vl[adimir] S. Soloviev's translation along with his valuable foreword (first published 34 years ago).[2] How long it had been: between 1913 and January 1839, when this tale was printed in the *Moscow Observer*!

S[ergei] S. Ignatov has published an entire book (*E. T. A. Hoffmann. Man and Works*. M[oscow]: 1914) about you, devoted mainly to an explication of the technical devices of Your works and to the role that all forms of art have played in Your life and works, and, apropos of this, of Your relation to the theater.

M. A. Petrovsky gave a lecture about Your influence on Russian literature and published a wonderful article in the third issue of *History of Western Literature* (M[oscow]: Mir).

In the second half of the first volume of P. N. Sakulin's dissertation ("On the History of Russian Idealism: Count V. F. Odoevsky," Moscow: 1913), twenty pages in the fifth chapter are dedicated to Your influence, which otherwise would seem not to have existed, on the works of Count Odoevsky.

Perhaps this is not very much, but remember that since 1901 no one has concerned himself with You in independent research. But now in every issue of the journal *Love for Three Oranges*, we will, in one way or another, remind artists, musicians, and writers about You.

Vladimir Kniazhnin[3]

OPEN LETTER FROM THE AUTHORS OF THE DIVERTISSEMENT *LOVE FOR THREE ORANGES* TO A. A. GVOZDEV

Highly esteemed Alexei Alexandrovich!

We were very pleased that the only attentive and thoughtful review of our divertissement emerged from Your pen.[4] Who else but You, an expert on old Venice, the author of interesting investigations of the adventurer Casanova, can judge people who resolve to continue the interrupted thread of Count Carlo Gozzi's theatrical activity?

We are very pleased, but permit us to indicate to You, however, the fact that in the almost hundred and fifty lines' length of Your note, in six places You name our divertissement a translation, despite the fact that in the subtitle You yourself called our work an adaptation, and in the text You (of course, unwittingly) constantly interchange the words "translation" and "adaptation."

Meanwhile, for us it is very important to declare absolutely firmly and definitely that we presented for the public's judgment not a translation of the fairy tale *Love of Three Oranges*, but a reworking. Then all Your observations, Your pointing out of the "translation's" inaccuracies quickly vanish. So for example:

1. We intentionally did not call the King of Cups and Knight of Cups by the names King of Clubs and Jack of Clubs, in part because the suits of old Italian card decks do not entirely coincide with the suits of the contemporary deck, and in part because we did not want to provoke in the contemporary spectator associations that are needlessly divorced from the pictorial traditions of the Italian comedy of masks.

2. We had absolutely no need [of the translations] *infermo* = sick, *spezzante* = ruinous, or "secret death," because *inferno* = hell, *sprezzante* = contemptuous, and "occult death" in the corresponding places are precisely what we need in this exaggerated parody to which we are so committed.
3. You hold it against us that "in places Gozzi's observations about the performance end up in the text of the play itself." Deliberately so, because Gozzi doesn't have a "play text"; there is only a reflective record of the scenario. The truly improvised text, for reasons that are entirely obvious, is absolutely unknown.
4. With regard to Your words about the incorrectness of the translation of the expression *maledizione chiaresca* [attacks on Chiari], on this occasion we would like to embark upon a more detailed explanation.

It seems to You—and You consistently draw upon this viewpoint not only in Your note about our divertissement but also in the lecture about Carlo Gozzi and his "Useless Memoirs" You gave this year—that Count Carlo Gozzi's reflective analysis of the fairy tale *Love of Three Oranges* is noteworthy only for its element of polemical parody. You absolutely ignore its specifically theatrical aesthetic aims, which in our view, are the most valuable part of this scenario and of *fiabe dramatiche* [*sic*] in general. It would be very sad if, by deliberately permitting ourselves to remove Gozzi's polemical element, the theatrical element was not made prominent enough to act strongly and suddenly upon the mind and senses of the audience of our day. The essence of this element, from our point of view, consists in contrasting improvised comedy with scripted comedy, the theater of masks with the theater of character.

In the divertissement we composed (after Gozzi), we, not predetermining what the new manifestation of the basic formula of the four eternal masks of improvised Italian comedy would be, entirely consciously removed Gozzi's polemical satire about Signor Goldoni and Abbot Chiari simply because Gozzi's technical methods of scenario composition are much more important than their transient combative meaning.

This relationship to Gozzi's polemics and the aesthetic element contained in his *fiabe* show that the transformation of Gozzi's satire into lavish theatrical spectacle ("divertissement" and "balagan") based on the old comedy of masks does not at all lead to the belittling of Gozzi's literary glory. On the contrary, the theatrical techniques of the commedia dell'arte become more clear and more distinctly valuable to us as they resonate in the scenarios of Count Carlo Gozzi.

In closing, we permit ourselves to note also that even if we may have some affinities with the undertakings of Gordon Craig, it is hardly possibly to consider us his followers, and certainly, in any case, it is impossible to simultaneously call us followers of Gordon Craig and "worshippers of the commedia dell'arte."

Konstantin A. Vogak
Vsevolod Meyerhold
Vladimir Soloviev
November 17, 1914[5]

COMEDY OF PURE JOY: LUDWIG TIECK'S *PUSS IN BOOTS* (1797)

The German romantics created the worldwide renown of Count Carlo Gozzi. It was they who first "discovered" his dramatic fairy tales, imbued a dead literary monument with a living spirit, made vital and contemporary something that could have seemed like the accidental and outdated caprice of a "strange talent," a cultural "reactionary," an enthusiast of beautiful but lifeless days of yore. Perhaps the romantic understanding of Gozzi is a re-creation, new work made from old materials, but it issues from a living feeling of love, from spontaneous artistic experience; and truth of some kind must lie behind this interpretation, one that remains profound and persuasive to the present day.

For the romantics, Gozzi represented "comedy of pure joy." In his works, laughter arises not as a mockery of human failings or of imperfections in human souls and lives, but out of a spiritual fullness, out of a creative overabundance of living joy. "Our basic state is joy," says Novalis. "Joy is beautiful in and of itself," teaches Fr[iedrich] Schlegel. "Beautiful joy is the highest aim of the science of beauty." In order for comedy to provoke in us a feeling of beautiful joy, we must cleanse artistic pleasure from the true-to-life residue of a moral approach to things—indignation, denunciation, censure—that violate the purity of our enjoyment of the beautiful. The classical French comedy of the 17th-century comedy of manners and comedy of characters, which set for itself a social-moral task ("to correct manners with mockery," in the words of an old Russian poet)—was opposed by the romantics with cheerful and harmless comic play that is reminiscent of improvised folk comedy. Let art be like play—light, cheerful, fantastical, not like everyday, all-too-ordinary life! For the romantics the dramatic fairy tales of C[arlo] Gozzi represented just this sort of merry and joyful play.

First and foremost, Gozzi's fairy tales transport the spectator to a marvelous fantastical land—even their names put one in a poetic mood—where wondrous things happen that don't resemble real life, where things become possible that don't happen in the real world. The characters in his comedies are seized by elevated lyrical passions; they live with beautiful feelings, noble moods, and generous fantasies, in the face of which spectators feel themselves transported to a world of another order, one that is more sublime, joyful, and light than this world that surrounds us. And along with the lyrical strivings that elevate the soul, the merry masks of improvised comedy are introduced into the action of the fantastical fairy tales—like irony, which inevitably accompanies poetic illusion and delight. With their self-conscious comic play, with their reflections on the fairy-tale heroes, they provide accompaniment to all their words and deeds. They are spectators, ideal comic mirrors with various distorting curves, reflecting in their own particular distortions the development of the poetic action. With their commentary on the action, their direct addresses from the stage to the *parterre*, with their references to everyday—not theatrical—reality, they destroy the scenic illusion of the primary, lyrically significant action; more precisely, they reveal the *illusoriness* of everything happening on the stage. What the spectator sitting in the *parterre* encounters is not life as it is really lived; what appears on the stage is not firm material reality, but only a merry game, only a show put on for the amusement of an audience. Thus the German romantics sketched out the characteristics of the comedy of pure joy embodied in C. Gozzi's dramatic fairy tales.

Puss in Boots, a comedy by L[udwig] Tieck (1773–1853), one of the most interesting poets of the romantic era, was written, to a certain extent, as an expression of the kind of comic performance ideal that was envisioned by the founders of this artistic movement. Therefore positive reviews of that era paid less attention to the satirical element of the young poet's new work than they did to the fundamental mood embodied in it: that of cheerful, lighthearted comic play. "This comedy is of the air," Tieck himself says of his favorite composition, "all woven out of froth and light jokes that one should not take more seriously than the author intended," something very merry and strange, reminiscent of Gherardi's *The Italian Theater*,* in which, in my opinion, jokes make the whole world seem like the object of an elegant parody. His enthusiastic critic August Schlegel perceives the work no differently: "This is a joke, an impudent and lighthearted joke, in which the author every minute interrupts himself, seemingly destroying his own work, sending out jibe after jibe in all directions like light darts." And Hoffmann, in *Fantasy Pieces*, talks about the theater's task to evoke in the spectator a poetic joy that liberates him from the bonds of ordinary reality and elevates him to a poetic, ideal point of view on the world—and he recalls, moreover, the dramatic fairy tales of Gozzi and Tieck, who with his *Puss in Boots* "pro-

* E. Gherardi, *Théatre Italien*, 1701. Collection of scenarios and comedies that formed the repertoire of the Italian theater in Paris. [Zhirmunsky's note.]

voked a true revolution in the minds of all those who are poetically inclined and interested in theater."

Upon comparing the dramatic fairy tales of Gozzi and Tieck's *Puss*, one notices, first and foremost, the extraordinary development of a comic element in the poet-romantic's work. Already in Gozzi the masks move in the direction of separating from the action and often play the role of spectators, bearers of comic reflection on the poetic events. Tieck replaces these masks with real spectators. The stage of his comedy represents a stage with a *parterre* in front of it. On the inner stage a young author, obviously a romantic, has mounted his new work, an adaptation of the well-known children's fairy tale about *Puss* (from the anthology by Perrault); spectators sit in the *parterre* and watch this fairy tale; during the intermissions they exchange remarks; they interrupt the action of the play with their own critical commentary; they applaud and hiss; conversations in the *parterre* serve as an introduction to the play and a theatrical departure from it. Thus the *parterre*'s participation in the action gives Tieck the ability to develop an element of comic reflection, the bearer of which in Gozzi had been the masks; this element is treated here as a special kind of action—"action in the *parterre*"—the characters of which appear as "spectators;" one might have titled it "An Account of How an Enlightened Public Received a Romantic Comedy-Fairy Tale." In conjunction with this, the destruction of the stage illusion also assumes entirely new and exceptional forms. The presence of the audience on the stage, the participation of the author and the theatrical machinist, who exchange remarks with the spectators—all this adds to the fairy-tale action a somehow illusory, unreal quality, the merry play of fairground entertainments, rather than serious reality. Tieck wields, moreover, an even more distinct means of suddenly destroying theatrical illusion. He compels the actor to break character, thereby revealing the actor standing behind the guise of the play's character. At the beginning of act III the curtain rises too early, and the public is witness to a conversation between the author and the machinist that is unrelated to the action and would have taken place behind the wings, had it not been so crowded there. It can be said that in romantic comedy this sudden destruction of the illusion of reality, or to put it differently, *the revelation of the illusory nature of theatrical play*, is the most important element in the creation of the impression of "pure joy." Tieck develops this element even more deeply and deliberately in an interesting dramatic fairy tale written the following year: *Topsy-Turvy World* (1798).

Under the influence of comic elements that have been developed to their extremes, the fairy-tale part of the action also undergoes, by comparison to Gozzi, a fundamental change. The poetic content of the children's fairy tale is essentially swallowed up here by comedy of artistic form. The characters of *Puss in Boots* appear, in Tieck, as a kind of contemporary and trivial—in an emphasized way—travesty. In the fairy-tale action everything is reminiscent of our times and our everyday life, so that what is lost is the fairy-tale viewpoint, the temporal and spatial distance from us of the fairy-tale's content—necessary elements in sympathizing with fantastical and wondrous characters and events. The king in Tieck's comedy, on one hand, seems like a real fairy-tale king who never goes walking without his crown and scepter; because he is a fairy-tale king his gluttony and bad manners can still be forgiven; but in the conversations with his daughter he clearly displays his other side: the sentimental and somewhat coarse father of the household in so-called "petit-bourgeois drama." It is the same with his daughter—she is a fairy-tale princess, but she composes sentimental poetry, is interested in science, and hence refuses all her suitors—a parody of the refined *Turandot* transferred into the era of enlightenment and bourgeois-sentimental ideals. Finally, Puss himself, despite his feline ways, which humorously seep through into his human character, is made into a rationalist and philanthropist: he speaks about love for humankind and about struggling with the passions—a juxtaposition that subsequently was used very successfully by Hoffmann in *The Life and Opinions of the Tomcat Murr*.

In general, the characters of [Tieck's] comedy have a schematized-generalized quality. The poet borrowed these simplified comic types from the children's fairy tale: the lucky fool Gottlieb, his cat, the king, his daughter, the court scholar, and the jester. In their movements and words, these characters are reminiscent somehow of the marionette theater. Even the action of the comedy, in Tieck's treatment, takes on a marionette quality. The lack of lyrical and emotional content that had existed in Gozzi, the lack of psychological motivation and intensification in the action's development gives the action a tinge of something superficial, mechanical. It develops from fact to fact, from movement to movement; it does not seem to us animated or alive—it clearly bears a pronounced marionette quality. But is not the puppet theater truly the best stage for theatrical performance that wishes to be only a performance, only a merry show, only an amusing play of shadows that appear for a moment and are gone? It is no accident that Hoffmann said that the best theater for Gozzi's comedies is the theater of marionettes.

Yet there is also another side to Tieck's comedies that is no less interesting for the contemporary reader: the satirical representation of the "enlightened public," the spectators and critics of *Puss in Boots*. Its context is the end of the 18th century, the era of enlightenment and sentimentality, but even so it reminds us of the recent past and of years we remember. They demand that the dramatic presentation have verisimilitude, rational plausibility and probability ("realism"); they demand family scenes and domestic portraits ("the quotidian"); and finally, they demand moral benefit, a didactic tone and a moral spirit ("the denunciatory tradition"). One of the spectators even takes a sociopolitical point of view—he impatiently awaits a "revolutionary play." Of course, in the judgment of an audience such as this, one that is so very enlightened and serious, there is no leeway for anything poetic or fantastical, the young poet-romantic's fairy-tale comedy is an utter failure, and his words remain uncomprehended: "I have tried to return you to the world of the distant feelings of your childhood years."

In this sense, it is no coincidence that I have pointed out a likeness to the present. Readers of *Puss* probably are reminded of much from contemporary literature. They recall the "author" and other examples of ruptured illusion in Alexander Blok's *Balaganchik*; it is no coincidence that Blok, in the preface to *Lyrical Dramas*, uses the romantic term "transcendental irony." F. Sologub also talks about "irony" and "the lyrical," and his word usage is very close to the romantic meaning. These congruencies, which can be explained clumsily only as "influences" and "borrowings," confirm the idea that we expressed and developed long ago in a book about German romanticism, that not only in their general attitude to life, but also in many of the particulars of the development of artistic forms, modern-day symbolism (or neo-romanticism) bears an astonishing similarity to the romanticism of the late 18th and early 19th centuries.

Viktor Zhirmunsky
1916[6]

Appendix B

Columbine's Veil

A PANTOMIME IN THREE ACTS[1] AFTER ARTHUR SCHNITZLER, BY DOCTOR DAPERTUTTO (VS. E. MEYERHOLD).

MUSIC BY DOHNÁNYI

"HOUSE OF INTERLUDES," SAINT PETERSBURG (1910)[2]

Act One (Pierrot's Room)

Scene 1. In love with Columbine but jilted by her, Pierrot weeps.

Pierrot's servant enters. Seeing Pierrot lying on the bed, the servant thinks he is sleeping and cautiously leaves the room.

Pierrot broods over memories of his beloved, looks through letters, admires a portrait of Columbine and a rose that he once received from her, and, overcome by tears, falls asleep in a dark corner of his garret.

Scene 2. The servant enters again, but Pierrot's friends and their sweethearts arrive unexpectedly. Having convinced the new arrivals that Pierrot is sleeping, the servant leads the guests to Pierrot's bed and is perplexed: Pierrot is not there. The servant runs to fetch a candle. The merry guests look for Pierrot. The servant returns with the candle. The guests see that Pierrot is asleep in the corner. They laugh at him, want to wake him up. One of the friends remembers the Pianist,[3] who stayed behind in the entryway and who was dragged along by them everywhere they went, and recommends waking Pierrot up with raucous dances; he calls the Pianist. The Pianist enters. The merry couples ask him to play on the harpsichord. The Pianist plays a waltz. Pierrot's friends dance, snickering at Pierrot, who does not wake up either from the sounds of the waltz or from the jostling of the dancers. At last Pierrot wakes up. The friends reproach him: how can he sleep when there are such charming ladies nearby? Pierrot is out of sorts. The friends are offended by the inhospitable Pierrot. One of the friends seizes the portrait of Columbine and is ready to fling it to the ceiling. Pierrot leaps up, wants to snatch Columbine's portrait, but he is surrounded by noses on all sides. Pierrot suffers. The friends signal to the Pianist; he plays a waltz while the merry couples, dancing, mock the poses of the suffering Pierrot. Finally the friends grow tired of Pierrot and run off. The Pianist, not noticing their departure, continues to play the waltz. The sounds of the waltz irritate Pierrot; slamming down the lid of the harpsichord, he abruptly stops the Pianist's playing. The Pianist is indignant. He is about to give Pierrot a thrashing, but Pierrot's friends' sweethearts rush in and forcibly drag the Pianist away.

Scene 3. Pierrot is alone. He decides to end his life in suicide. Having locked the door with a key, he tears up letters and flowers, kisses Columbine's shoes, which he has decorated, and goes into the other room for poison. He returns with a goblet and a bottle of some kind of potion. Just when he is filling the goblet with the deadly drink, someone knocks at the door. Pierrot hurriedly places the poison on the harpsichord, unlocks the door and, in horror, sees Columbine in a wedding dress. Pierrot tears off her wedding veil.

Columbine begs him not to be angry and to listen to her explanation. But Pierrot, pointing at the wedding ring (meaning the marriage ceremony has already been performed), thinks it pointless to talk. Now his resolve to end his own life becomes inevitable. Columbine is prepared not to stop him; she is ready to die with him. Pierrot is enraptured; he thanks her. Columbine asks to wait just a little while: "First we will be merry, drink, dance, and after that: death."

Columbine hopes that Pierrot, drunk on wine and love, will forget about the poison. But Pierrot, just when their merrymaking is at its height, remembers the poison. He resolutely takes the goblet with the poison and invites Columbine to take a sip. Columbine hesitates. Pierrot laughs maliciously, drinks, and again offers her the goblet. She doesn't drink, and Pierrot, after drinking again, dies. Columbine flees in horror.

Act Two (At Columbine's Parents' House)

Scene 1. A wedding ball in full swing at Columbine's parents' house. The waltz ends. The Dance Master announces a quadrille.

Scene 2. They wait for Harlequin and Columbine, but Harlequin enters alone. The Dance Master at first doesn't notice this, but later, having given the orchestra a downbeat at the beginning of the quadrille, suddenly notices that Harlequin has no partner. Having stopped the orchestra with difficulty, the Dance Master calls to Columbine's parents and informs them that Columbine is missing.

Scene 3. The mother explains that her daughter is probably arranging her gown, and goes to call her. The father asks Harlequin to forgive Columbine.

Scene 4. The Dance Master, in order to avoid scandal, invites the dancers to promenade in the garden to the music of a minuet.

Scene 5. Columbine's father and Harlequin wait. The mother returns. She announces that Columbine is nowhere to be found. Harlequin flies into a rage. He pulls the Pianist, whose music even further underscores the horror of the deceived Harlequin, down off the stage; he beats the Pianist and his musicians.

Scene 6. The guests rush over; they want to calm the out-of-control Harlequin, but he himself collapses out of exhaustion.

Scene 7. Columbine enters. Harlequin hurls himself at her: "Where were you?" "I was fixing my dress." "That's a lie." Columbine begs Harlequin not to be angry and the guests to continue dancing. But Harlequin demands an explanation.

Scene 8. In order to quell the buzz of scandal, the quick-witted Dance Master gives the Pianist the signal to play a furious galop, while inciting the guests to begin a wild dance. At the very moment when everyone, even Harlequin, is ready to collapse from exhaustion from the wild dance, a little moor appears to offer the guests a refreshing drink.

Scene 9. Columbine reaches out her hand to take a glass; the little moor vanishes, and in his place Pierrot's ghost appears with the veil in his hands. Columbine tries to catch hold of the veil, but Pierrot vanishes. The phantom taunts her, appearing first in one doorway, then in another. Columbine runs after Pierrot's ghost. Harlequin rushes after her.

Act Three (Pierrot's Room)

Scene 1. The candles burn out. Onstage is the dead Pierrot. Columbine runs in. In the doorway Harlequin comes to a halt, watching her. She doesn't see him. Columbine, seizing the veil, rushes out of the room. Harlequin stops her. Harlequin looks all around but does not notice the prostrate Pierrot. Harlequin runs into the adjoining room and returns immediately. He is dumbfounded—he hasn't found anyone. As he is mounting an assault on Columbine, Harlequin stumbles over Pierrot's corpse. He thinks that Pierrot is drunk. Everything becomes clear to Harlequin: Columbine ran away from the ball to a rendezvous with Pierrot. Harlequin is furious—he is ready to kill Columbine, but this would be too contemptible a revenge. Harlequin has an idea. He tries to wake Pierrot, takes hold of him and shakes him, but Pierrot's body slips and just keeps falling. Harlequin realizes that Pierrot is dead. He is first stunned, then glad. Now he knows how to exact revenge on the perfidious Columbine. Harlequin sets up Pierrot's corpse at the table with Columbine, half-dead with fear, next to him, and, locking the door with the key, runs away. Columbine, locked in with the corpse, drinks the poison out of despair. The pre-death agony grows into a dance. Dancing, Columbine falls dead at Pierrot's feet.

Scene 2. Pierrot's friends and their sweethearts enter. It seems to them that Pierrot and Columbine are merged in a passionate kiss. The Pianist enters. The merry couples wish to wake up the spellbound lovers with a dance. Sprinkling them with flowers, the couples dance, but Pierrot and Columbine are motionless. One friend pushes Pierrot. The latter falls, as does Columbine. The friends see two corpses; they are paralyzed by horror. The Pianist nearly goes out of his mind.

Appendix C

Pierrette's Veil

A PANTOMIME IN THREE ACTS BY ARTHUR SCHNITZLER WITH MUSIC BY E. DOHNÁNYI AND PROLOGUE BY IU. BALTRUSHAITIS.

DIRECTED BY ALEXANDER TAIROV AT THE SVOBODNY THEATRE, MOSCOW (1913)[1]

The jilted Pierrot is helplessly overcome by his memories . . . Pierrette is gone, happiness is impossible, and life has gone away . . . Pierrot's weighty spiritual agitation is replaced by a dull torpor, out of which the entrance of his friends brings him with a rude jolt. Powerless to help him, unable to understand him, his friends leave. Pierrot is alone again. Pierrette appears. Stunned by the unexpectedness of her arrival, but not yet admitting the possibility of her presence, Pierrot throws himself down before Pierrette. But Pierrette has brought not an impassioned message of joy, but poison. Together with her lover, she raises a poisoned goblet, but Pierrot drinks it alone and dies alone.

The wedding feast in the house of Pierrette's father. The sullen, anxious figure of Harlequin is fleetingly glimpsed in the motley crowd of guests. The festivities began long ago, but Pierrette is missing. But lo, she comes, barely concealing the horror she has experienced; still with the sight of death in her eyes, she returns to the sober, humdrum world, where she must live by Harlequin's side. With difficulty she manages to mollify her groom's anger and draw him into the whirlwind of dance. But before Pierrette's stunned soul rises the shade of the dead Pierrot. Perplexed by her alarm and fear, Harlequin suddenly notices that she is not wearing a veil. In a new burst of rage, he showers Pierrette with reproaches, questions, and threats. In the now whirling crowd, the shade of Pierrot again appears to her.

Pierrot's room. Burning candles, some spent, some nearly burnt out. In the gloom only the dead Pierrot and a white strip of veil can be made out. The majestic silence of death is broken by the arrival of Pierrette. She frantically picks up the veil and wants to take it back to Harlequin, but, meeting him at the door, is forced to stop. Stunned by the sight of the surroundings, Harlequin notices the dead Pierrot, rushes to him, and little by little comprehends the horror that has taken place. A feeling of revenge possesses him. He seats Pierrot in a chair, leads Pierrette to him, and makes her clink glasses with the dead and embrace him. But stunned with mortal fear, crushed beneath an inhuman burden of pain, the soul of Pierrette is overstrained, and she dies at the feet of Pierrot.

Appendix D

Columbine's Garter

THE COLUMBIAN GIRL'S GARTER

A PANTOMIME IN 3 ACTS.

SCENARIO BY S. M. EISENSTEIN AND S. I. YUTKEVICH[1]

Act 1: "In the Clutches of the Beauty-Adventuress"
Act 2: "Night at the *Metropolitan Hotel*, or, The Garter-Exposer"
Act 3: "Ned Rocker Acts, or, Death in the Embrace of the Electric Lover"

Dramatis Personae

1. Columbine (The Columbian Girl) . . . . *S. E. Savitskaia.*[2]
2. Pierrot . . . . *L. I. Semenova*
3. Harlequin. . . . . *F. F. Knorre*[3]
4. Ma and Pa . . . . *Columbine's parents*
5. Dance Master
6. Pip & Fax. . . . . *Comic entrée*[4]
7. Guest-dancers of the "Metropolitan-Hotel" . . . . *students of Volmas-for*[5]
8. Jazz band of the "Metropolitan-Hotel"
9. XXX . . . . *Ned Rocker, detective*
New-York. U.S.A.
West Monroe Street, 231–233.[6]
10. Four friends of Pierrot

Descriptions of the *Dramatis Personae*

COLUMBINE.—*Étoile*[7]—*"The Columbian Girl," En train de devenir honnête femme par alliance à Sir Archibald Harlequin,*[8] *Straps and Garter Manufacturer U.S.A 60 High St. Boston.*

Act 1. Modest urban outfit; with a play of clasps it becomes a semi-*café-chantant*-style costume. Bowler hat. Short veil. Yellow kid gloves. Little purse. Lorgnette. Riding crop. At the end of the act—a black satin half mask.

Act 2. A cascading *gala* costume. Red-orange *dessous*.[9] Skirt covered in sequins. Black satin bodice. Black above-elbow-length gloves. Bare shoulders. Flame-red wig. Top hat. In her hands a *chambrière*.[10]

Act 3. The same and a little mantilla.

PIERROT. Viscount. Aesthete. Ramolli[11] at 34. Wig. False teeth. Morphine addict. About ten years ago, around the time of the much-talked-about duel with Major V., he launched Columbine, a youthful reader in the house of the aged Duchess W., [into society]. Member of the "House of Literati."

Act 1. Before the "dressing scene:" pajamas (purple and white). Narrow trousers. Patent leather pumps. *Serre-tête*.[12] Turned-down collar with a large, cut-out neck. Monocle on a black ribbon. Blue socks. On his right leg a bracelet with a watch. Makeup: old-man face, slack mouth, bags under the eyes. Total lack of teeth.

He changes into: an exaggerated version of the traditional costume of Pierrot. Smock. Bare neck. Lacquered wig with a part. Whitened face. Asymmetrical makeup of Vertinsky. Scarlet triangle of lips. Amber rosary.

HARLEQUIN. Industrialist *Archibald Harlequin, Straps and Garter Manufacturer 60 High N. Boston U.S.A.* Irma Vapp's* *bastard* by Buffalo Bill.† At the age of twenty, he found himself at the head of a straps, corset, and garter atelier. Ever since, he has been the "Garter King." Roughly ten minutes ago, he saw Columbine for the first time and offered to replace her title "*Café-Chantant* Queen" with the more stable one of "Garter Queen." His wedding present—the newest garter model, made of steel—is on Columbine's left leg.

Act 2. black leotard of Fantômas.‡ Starched dickey, collar and cuffs. High white spats. Hair parted in the middle. Black velvet half mask.

* Popular female-criminal from the famous detective film *Vampires*. 2 parts. Goumant, Paris. Passage Soliel, St. Petersbourg [*sic*]. [Translator's note: Unless otherwise indicated with square brackets, all footnotes are by Eisenstein and Yutkevich. The correct spelling of Irma Vapp is Irma Vep, the main character in Louis Feuillade's 1915 serial film *Les Vampires* and an anagram for the word "vampire." Passage Soleil may be the name of the movie theater at which the film played in Saint Petersburg. O. M. Fel'dman, ed., *Meierkhol'd i drugie: Dokumenty i materialy*. vol. 2 of *Meierkhol'dovskii sbornik* (Moscow: OGI, 2000), 564.]

† See *Buffalo Bill—Hero*. Third edition I-50.

‡ Pierre Souvestre & Marcel Allain. *Fantomas*. Grand Roman Cinédit, vol. 1. Paris: Asthème Fayard & Compaigne. Éditeurs du livre populaire. 1913.

Act 3. Finale. Master of ceremonies/publicity agent of the firm *Archibald Harlequin*. Black American suit. Monocle. Shoelace ends are hidden. Constructivist. Resembles Greifenturn.[13]

MA—PA. High-society émigrés. Russia no. 2.[14] [She is] a former baroness with a German surname. *Fräulein* in the court of H[er] F[ormer] I[mperial] [Majesty]. [He is] a *Kammerjunker*,[15] a cavalier of the Order of the Garter.

[She is] the proprietress of an automatic-restaurant (grand rooms) by the chef of the Winter Palace. [He is] a shareholder of the firm "*Tanglefoot* and Son"[16] and of the pleasure establishment "Le Pavillon d'Armide," one of the "Scythians."

Side job: act as double and single parents for hire. (Respectable references from the best houses: *Winter-Garten, Folies-Bergères, Moulin-Rouge*, etc.) At present serving in this capacity for Columbine.

MA—[Her] costume is constructed from elements of the restaurant: the left breast is a sparkling water tap with different colored syrups (three faucets); the right one is a tank of "*Condensed Milk*." Through the glass walls of a case labeled "*Rotis*" is seen a well-nourished right thigh tightly covered in pink *tricot*.[17] From the case down to the knee, the leg is covered in frilly pantaloon lace. The right thigh is a tank with the inscription "*potage*."[18] Between the case and the tank the slot of a cash box is modestly concealed from view. Heavily painted cheeks, canary-yellow wig, day-old gloves that extend above the elbow, and a serpent-like klaxon[19] encircling her figure* complete the construction.

PA—Constructed commode tailcoat.[20] From the rear, choked by massive carcasses of protruding tails, sticks out a klaxon that is going hoarse. Out of the heap of shoulders pokes a billiard ball of a mangy head with a bewilderedly bulging eye. The nose is a blinking red "*Osram*."[21] From the tailcoat rise three metallic pipes; a box with the inscription: Aktteo[22] crowns it like a sarcophagus. On the metallic (imitation gold) chain that comes out of the box and passes through the cardboard of the shoulders hangs a phallic-looking white charm with the inscription "*pull!*" Atop the klaxon is perched a lone copper candlestick with a yellow wax candle. In his hands is a roll of "*Tanglefoot*." Under his kneecap dangles an order star on a bright ribbon.

4 Friends of Pierrot: From the types of Félix Vallotton.[23] Spherical, in top hats. Square beefsteak faces. Starched linens. Matchstick legs in American

* For more detail, see Interpretative Panopticon: "Dying Queen Cleopatra with a serpent" (horrors every 1.5 minutes.) [Translator's note: For a description of the Saint Petersburg Panopticon, see Fel'dman, *Meierkhol'd i drugie*, 565.]

sleepers,[24] ginger *Walk-Overs*.[25] Played by three men and one "lady" in a male costume (3 friends). For the finale of act 1: four chrysanthemums in their buttonholes.[26] In act 2 they play in the *jazz band*. A collection of stars and ribbons of exotic orders. On the sides of the top hats are little round multicolored rosettes.

Act 3: Policemen. Police *capotes*[27] thrown over their tailcoats. Police helmets of the "*bobby*" type cover black wigs with hair on end, over a redheaded lining. Four white nightsticks (they are Roman candles). Finale: sandwich boards; on their chests are posters of legs in garters.

Dance Master–Subscriber to *La vie parisienne* and director of the Advanced School for Choreographic Knowledge in Paris and London, for information on details and address see the *Reklam-Diptichon*[28] of the checked jacket of the constructed costume. The percussive element (of his costume): replacing the Dance Master's calls is a signaling apparatus with the flashing, illuminated names of the dances.* Placed atop the starched collar, capped with a top hat. The necktie is replaced by a vertically elevated (higher than the top hat) treble clef of thick brass wire. To the left of the apparatus is hung an actual railway bell; it rings before each signboard change on the apparatus; this (the ringing) is effected by a lever like an automobile brake (nickel plated, with mahogany handles.) The mechanism that sets it in motion is between a pair of legs in yellow checked trousers ending in enormous American shoes with double, tap-dancing soles. Packets from a system of pink discs cut into the main cylinder of the figure (of white iron). Out of them juts a pink cardboard ballerina leg.

***Pip and Fax*. Eccentrics (scorn all fakes!)**

1st entrée:

Pip-heroico, white satin with green and pink roosters, an entirely white face, a wig *à trois cornes*: pale pink, blue, yellow.

Fax-Buffo: fanned-out red beard, orange part, little top hat with a green plume in the shape of a question mark on one side. Short jacket, spherical looking checked trousers (*blanc et noire*); coquettish little bow on a bare neck, monocle on a black ribbon. A watch on the leg; on it a *kukish*. Inscription "ARA" on his rear end.[29] Striped socks. Bedroom slippers in an enormous size.

2nd entrée: ("Trio with *chambrière*" with Columbine) in the riding habits of the "Advanced Equestrian School." Bowler hats, jackets, gray jodhpurs. High boots with yellow linings. White waistcoats. Gray gloves.

* [Based on] the principle of the light commands of *Skeitings*. [Translator's note: *sic*: figure skating]

Guests:

Cavaliers: yacht club jerseys, striped trunks ending above the knee. Ankle socks. Bare legs in black rubber men's garters. Brown cleats. Triangles of sewn-on stars on their chests. Instead of headgear, giant yellow visors. All are blond, Anglo-Saxons.

Ladies: male sailor costumes. Flared trousers. Light and dark blue berets with a red pompom. All are brunettes. From Montmartre.

XXX *Ned Rocker, detective. 16 West Monroe St., N.Y. USA 232–237.* The king of detectives in a flared overcoat of immense proportions. Energetic profile, half-comprised of automobile goggles and pipe. Topped with a cap. A Browning.

ACT 1: "IN THE CLUTCHES OF THE BEAUTY-ADVENTURESS"

Pierrot's Boudoir

The stage is constructed vertically in the form of a semicircular window (the size of the proscenium opening), the crossbars of which are used for crossing and as a playing space for the actors. The outer frame of the window forms an arched bridge (making it possible to cross from one side of the proscenium opening to the other). On the right (from the audience): a loveseat is suspended above the window; over it there is an intimate light. Below is an electric meter with a fuse board. Above it is a lever. On the lower left is the cube shape of an armchair (back to the audience) pushed into the window. Further left is a telegraph machine with a radioscope screen. Higher on the window frame is an oval mirror.* Beyond the window to the left is an elevator. In the dark upstage area is a construction of narrow light beams.

Scene 1

PIERROT in the armchair. He sits, resting his legs on the window crossbars.

His right leg vertically and left leg horizontally are in the shape of an unfolded mathematical compass. His right arm is horizontal on the arm of the chair.

* Silvered side to the audience.

His head and body are hidden by the back of the armchair. Part of a magazine. Rings of cigar smoke.

Play with the extremities.

Scene 2
The Four Friends of Pierrot pay Pierrot a doctor's visit.

They enter, left, from a trapdoor. They ascend and cross, one after another, along the window bridge. They descend to the floor and perform an entrée.°

They greet him. A doctor's examination; they simultaneously take out watches

after they have climbed onto the window crossbars above Pierrot. All four sit on the horizontal crossbeam.

They take his pulse

on both legs, one arm, and head.

Simultaneously they shake their heads. They put away their watches,

turn their backs, and climb on top of the window frame.

They sit,

legs dangling down. In turn they take out a box (flat), a handle, a gramophone horn, and a record. They assemble and

wind up a gramophone. The gramophone plays

"*Tipperary*."[30]

The 4 Friends take ocarinas[31] out of their side pockets and accompany it. When it ends, they move closer to Pierrot,

climbing down the interior side of the window crossbars (facing the spectator),

° Traditional circus entrance of the renowned *7 Leotaris 7*.

and for the second time take his pulse. Disapproving shake of the head. Exit. Pierrot is motionless.

Scene 3

Radioscope signal. Pierrot leaps up and

with his back to the audience, rushes back and forth about the window crossbars. He descends [and]

runs up to the radioscope. He puts receivers over his ears. Rapping sound of the radioscope. A mimed conversation. (Columbine announces her arrival; Pierrot rejoices and rushes.)
He flips the lever. On the screen:
Venez sans céremonies et telle que vous étes! . . .[32]
He flips the lever. On the screen: an image of Columbine in *dessous*.

A narrow section of screen moves vertically, sequentially revealing parts of Columbine's figure. Flash. It stops.

On the screen is one leg in a black stocking with a huge scarlet garter. Pierrot is in erotic ecstasy.
For the first time he turns his face to the audience.
Pierrot is an old man.
The screen goes black. Pierrot heads to his dressing room,

clambering along the window to the mirror with enfeebled movements.

Pierrot's dressing scene.
He takes off his *serre-tête*.
Underneath is a bald skull with remnants of hair. He pulls on a black lacquered wig with an impeccable center part. He applies the traditional makeup of *Pierrot*.

Pierrot conducts the entire scene hanging by his legs, with the dressing mirror below him. Due to this, his movements are exaggeratedly languorous.

He moves onto the loveseat. Perfumes himself. Injects morphine. Buffs his nails. Offhandedly leafs through *Notes of Dreamers*, no. 6,[33] tosses it aside.
Descends to the meter and counts the seconds.

Scene 4

Columbine appears in the elevator,[*]

arriving from the trap door and coming to a stop by the summit of the window.

Columbine exits the elevator—onto the window frame.

She descends halfway.

Pierrot darts from his place and rushes towards her,

freezing in a spread-eagle pose on the window.

Encounter of Pierrot and Columbine.

They step down onto the floor.

Dance

between the armchair and the meter.

Love on the armchair.
They move to the loveseat. They continue. Columbine demands a breakup. She returns his letters and demands hers.
The intoxicated Pierrot continues, paying no attention.[†]
Columbine tears his wig off[‡] and cynically slaps him on his bald pate.

This prompts Pierrot's transition to *ramolli*.

* Bravura music. Ovations, applause (claque).
† Trick with her bodice. See costume descriptions.
‡ A cry.

Pierrot, having lost strength, collapses back into the corner of the loveseat. Columbine lifts her dress and places her leg with a flame-red garter onto his lap.
Pierrot latches onto her leg with a kiss.
Columbine cold-bloodedly throws her other leg up, takes off the second steel garter and snaps it around Pierrot's neck.
In spasms, Pierrot convulsively clambers*

about the entire window frame.

Columbine, wearing a lorgnette, watches him with curiosity from the loveseat. Pierrot dies

in the center of the window, upside down, hanging from one leg, facing the audience.

Beyond the window, over the city, neon light advertisements light up.
Swiftly, the elevator rushes past,

headed upwards.

On its closed doors is a sharp, immobile silhouette. On the screen: *Ned Rocker, detective, 16 West Monroe Street, New York, USA, 291–233.* with a loaded Browning.
The electric advertisements begin to rotate at a furious pace.†
Columbine indifferently smoothes her dress.‡

She descends. The footlights light up.

Columbine in a black satin mask.

The ungartered stocking droops halfway down.

She walks along the row of footlights,

* The orchestra falls silent. Circus drum roll.

† The drum roll segues into the clamor of a city (a system of honks, klaxons, sirens, rings, whistles, radio drones, etc.).

‡ The clamor finally abruptly transitions into music hall music.

Suggestive play of the hips.
Second cross to center.
A shout: "*Holla*! [*sic*]"

Scene 5
The 4 FRIENDS* enter in pairs from both sides. They dance with Columbine. Song verses.
Finale: the gentlemen carry Columbine off on their arms.

The effect of Scene 5: Columbine and the 4 gentlemen are lit from below along the footlights; a black window silhouette with Pierrot spread out against a background flooded with light.
Description of the lighting backdrop of Acts 1 and 3.
A large rotating clock dial.
The clock hand is a leg wearing a garter. It rotates counter-clockwise. A luminous corset of exaggerated proportions. Descending from the borders are dancing electric legs in male garters. Multicolored transformers and the illuminated letters of an advertisement for Volmas-for. The rest will be based on the quantity of electric advertisement orders that come in from Moscow firms.

Act 2: "Night at the *Metropolitan Hotel*, or, The Garter-Exposer"

Hall at the Metropolitan Hotel.
Reception on the wedding day of Harlequin.

Raked semicircular section of floor, formed by tilting back the window frame from the first act. Windowpanes made of frosted glass and lit from below form a luminous floor. Upstage is set up as an amphitheater bordering the semi-

* Four chrysanthemums in their buttonholes.

circle of floor, a hyperbolical orchestra. Center: a jazz band that extends to the proscenium opening in a kinetic structure of human body and musical instruments. Above the floor at a considerable height is a static trapeze, which has four extensions (steel cables) for tightrope walking. At the junction points of trapeze and cables on both sides there is a small circular platform. A circus rope,[34] hung from the cupola[35] and reaching to the floor, vertically transects the trapeze. Two trapezes are attached to the proscenium opening stage right and left, temporarily hoisted up to its edges with ropes. On two doors, which symmetrically cut into the orchestra—in the breaks between dances—lit up in red:

For Men *For Women*.

In addition to the floor, the hall is lit by two *Luxes*.

Scene 1

The Dance Master at the center of the luminous floor, alone.

On the signal board of the costume of the Dance Master suddenly blazes the inscription:
1* (played by the *jazz band*).

Song verses and tap dance by the Dance Master. The theme of the song: a mockery of the universal obsession with America. The final verse: "Only we, here, have the real America! . . ."

Scene 2

Four pairs of guests, entrance and dance.
When the dance ends they exit

into the corresponding *W.C.*

Scene 3

Entrée of Pa–Ma. Song verses in duet. Refrain with the Dance Master.
Theme of the song:
Russia no. 2.

* As the scenario is futher developed, the order (1) of the appearance on the signal board of new names of musical numbers, and (2) of those played by the *jazz band* will be indicated in the text with the corresponding name.

Scene 4

The guests enter

from their corresponding *W.C.s*.

Dance.

When it ends

they exit into the corresponding *W.C.s*.

Scene 5

Comic entrée of *Pip and Fax*.

Scene 6

The guests enter and sit along the outer edge of the semicircular floor, make small talk.*

Song verses by the four *jazz banders*.

Song about the latest theatrical rage.

Performed by the 4 friends of Pierrot, who, for the duration of the second act, play in the *jazz band*.

Collective dance.

Animated stage; all participants and the mechanical orchestra dance.

Scene 7

The dance continues.

Harlequin, unnoticed by anyone, descends

from above, along the rope from the cupola,

and sits on the trapeze.

He searches for Columbine in the crowd of dancers with his eyes, with growing agitation.

He darts away from his place and begins to run about the cables. With lightning speed he descends along the rope to the floor.†

* Women only, with their backsides to the audience.

† Having temporarily disappeared into the flies. The effect of Harlequin's plunge along the entire vertical length of the rope.

Harlequin's rage. Stamps his feet.

Tap dance.

Irritated, he asks Columbine's parents, demanding that they explain her absence.

Boxing. Beats Pa-Ma.[*]

Confusion among the guests. Harlequin scatters
the Guests

with roundoffs along the disc-shaped floor and the footlights.

He runs up to the orchestra, breaks the musical instruments.

Three drum cascade:[†] he leaps into the left one, flies out of the right one,

and disappears

with a crash into the middle one.

The guests, in horror, scatter.

Scene 8
Entrance of Columbine with a *chambrière*.

Ovations, applause. Columbine bows.

Scene 9
Two of the guests enter and set props.

They untie the trapezes and position the trampolines for

the next number.

Scene 10
Trio with a *chambrière* performed by Columbine, *Pip and Fax*.

Pip and Fax, in the riding outfits of the "Advanced Equestrian School," enter from opposite sides. Mimetic play following the parade.[36] A dance,

[*] Due to the blows, Pa's top hat flattens and expands again, on his nose the electric bulb glows, and the klaxon hoarsely honks between the tails of the tuxedo.

[†] Each cascade is accented with cymbal clashes by the 4 gentlemen, who have stood up.

constructed on the raked semi-circular floor; here and there, the figures of the cavaliers on trapezes.* During one of these

two Pierrot figures appear

as marionettes, lowered from the flies and animated from the trapezes by the cavaliers.†

Columbine's horror.

Dance in trio on the floor.[37]

Scene 11

Harlequin appears

with a leap from out of the *jazz band* onto the trapeze.

Pip and Fax, unnoticed, disappear.

(Variant: when Harlequin appears—they fall off the trapeze.)

Columbine rushes about in a paroxysm of horror; she breaks off the dance in the center of the stage, falling onto the floor and revealing an ungartered leg.

Harlequin in fury rushes at her.

assailing her with a "mill of death"‡ to the muffled rumble of the drums. Upon finishing, he glides along the rope to the floor.

and advances on her, crowding her with progressively smaller circles toward the center exit.

Columbine slips away.

Harlequin swiftly climbs upward

along the rope, disappearing into the flies.

* The trampolines allow the cavaliers to shift from floor to trapeze at the crack of the *chambrière*.

† During the number, the stage fills with Guests who take positions along the outer circumference of the floor.

‡ "The mill of death" is an acrobatic trapeze act.

Scene 12. Finale

Scandal at the *Metropolitan Hotel.*

Commotion, noise, whistles.
The stunned dance-master is toppled into the *jazz band.*
Pa-Ma: on the sides toward the proscenium opening.

Finale.

Guests: on the periphery of the floor, ladies, lying on their backs with legs thrown into the air; cavaliers, upstage, with despair on their faces.
The four gentlemen listlessly droop over the *jazz band* barrier.*

Act Three: "Ned Rocker Acts, or, Death in the Embrace of the Electric Lover"

Scene 1

Total darkness.

From the back of the auditorium, a narrow light beam from a policeman's flashlight. It comes to a stop on the frozen grimace of the strangled Pierrot. The beam moves from the auditorium onto the stage and draws along with it the trailing figure† of
Ned Rocker
with a Browning. The stage dimly lights up,

revealing the set from the first act.‡
The advertisements are extinguished.

With quick, confident movements,
Ned pulls out
an electric chair

with a shiny metal seat.

He lifts up the inert Pierrot,

* In the tense silence, the lonely klaxon (of Pa) hoarsely sobs.

† *Ned Rocker, detective. New York West Monroe St. 231–233 U. S. A.*

‡ [Dohnányi's] music begins at this moment.

taking him off the window crossbars. (See the end of the first act.)

He sits him down on the apparatus. With an abrupt movement he shifts the levers.
The electrification of Pierrot.
Rocker hoists the corpse onto his back and carries him off right,

backstage.

He returns, lays

across the entire stage

a signal wire to the electric switch.
He hides the chair,*

putting it down in the cube-shaped armchair.

He disappears,

diving into the same armchair.

Pause.

Scene 2

Columbine stealthily creeps in from the left. She walks to the right toward the switch. She flips it.† From the left, with automaton-like steps, appears the corpse of Pierrot and stops by the armchair

(on the left side).

Columbine walks up to the armchair, from the right. She stops; having noticed someone's shadow, she leans forward. Pierrot automatically repeats her movement.
A pale light appears in the armchair, illuminating their faces.‡
The mask of Pierrot bares its teeth.
Pause.

* Variant: the detective pulls out (and puts away) the apparatus from his enormous overcoat.
† Dohnányi's music stops.
‡ Characteristic crackle of moving-picture reels.

The light goes out.* Columbine hurls herself toward the elevator platform

along the window frame, toward the location of her entrance in Act One.

The corpse of Pierrot blocks her path, spreads out its arms and freezes, copying in inverted form his death pose.
The sound of American locks clicking.[38]
Pause. She recoils unsteadily.
The electric corpse pursues Columbine, who is out of her mind with horror. In a final dance

on the window crossbars

Columbine dies in the steel embrace of her electric lover.

Scene 3
Leap of Ned Rocker from the flies.
With a quick glance he confirms that Columbine, his criminal bride, is dead.
He lets out a piercing whistle.

Reply whistles in all corners of the theater.

Scene 4
The Four Policemen appear from the right.

The Four Friends of Pierrot, re-costumed accordingly.

They look with surprise at Ned Rocker.
Rocker points at the corpse.
Astonishment of the policemen. They take off their helmets.

Their smooth black wigs stand on end, revealing their redheaded essence.

* The sound stops.

They look questioningly at the
detective.
Ned Rocker takes out an enormous
dark blue card:
Ned Rocker, detective
U.S.A. New York. 16 West Monroe St.

Roman candles melancholically
shoot out from the white nightsticks
of the policemen.

Rocker throws off his detective's garb,
under it is
Harlequin
in the costume of the master of
ceremonies, with a monocle.
The policemen turn their backs:
on them are four question marks.
Harlequin fires into the air.
The advertisements light up.
Columbine and
Pierrot come down to the footlights.
The policemen transform into
sandwich boards*

with posters that depict four pink legs
in garters.

Finale

Harlequin's shouts. Pierrot and
Columbine's dance.
Song verses and dances by the four
gentlemen.
Collective dance.
Garter advertisement.

To V. E. Meyerhold
Au patriarche de l'Echarpe
les novices de la "Jarretière."[39]

* The "sandwiches" with posters are on the chest only. Until the scene where they turn their backs, they are rolled up on the policemen's nightsticks. They use their turn away to unroll them.

Notes

PREFACE

1. Presentational and representational, now common terms, were used originally in the context of Russian modernist theater. See Alexander Bakshy, *The Path of the Modern Russian Stage and Other Essays* (Boston, Mass.: John W. Luce, 1918).

2. Tracy C. Davis and Thomas Postlewait, *Theatricality* (Cambridge: Cambridge University Press, 2003).

INTRODUCTION. HOFFMANN'S PRISM

1. Valery Briusov, "Against Naturalism in the Theatre (from 'Unnecessary Truth')," in *Theatre in Theory 1900–2000: An Anthology*, ed. David Krasner (Malden, Mass.: Blackwell, 2008), 57.

2. Ibid.

3. Ibid., 57–58.

4. Ibid., 58.

5. Ibid., 60.

6. Vsevolod Meyerhold, "Naturalistic Theatre and the Theatre of Mood" (1906), in Vsevolod Meyerhold, *Meyerhold on Theatre*, ed. and trans. Edward Braun (London: Bloomsbury Methuen Drama, 1998), 23–33. First published in *Teatr: Kniga o novom teatre* (Saint Petersburg: Shipovnik, 1908). Reprinted in Vsevolod Meierkhol'd, *O Teatre* (Saint Petersburg: Prosveshchenie, 1913).

7. Briusov, "Against Naturalism," 57.

8. Ibid., 59.

9. Meyerhold, *Meyerhold on Theatre*, 49; Marjorie L. Hoover, *Meyerhold: The Art of Conscious Theater* (Amherst: University of Massachusetts Press, 1974).

10. Briusov, "Against Naturalism," 60.

11. Jeremy Adler, introduction to E. T. A. Hoffmann, *The Life and Opinions of the Tomcat Murr: Together with a Fragmentary Biography of Kapellmeister*

Johannes Kreisler on Random Sheets of Waste Paper, trans. Anthea Bell (London: Penguin, 1999), vii.

12. E. T. A. Hoffmann, "The Compleat Stage Manager," in *Fantasy Pieces in Callot's Manner: Pages from the Diary of a Traveling Romantic*, trans. Joseph M. Hayse (Schenectady, N.Y.: Union College, 1996), 47.

13. Johann Wolfgang von Goethe, *Gedenkausgabe der Werke, Briefe, und Gespräche*, ed. Ernst Beutler (Zurich: Artemis, 1949), 928. Quoted in Birgit Röder, *A Study of the Major Novellas of E. T. A. Hoffmann* (Rochester, N.Y.: Camden House, 2003), 8n2.

14. Like Meyerhold, playwright/poet/composer Mikhail Alexeevich Kuzmin (1872–1936) had an intense interest in Hoffmann. According to Bowlt, Hoffmann "prompted a veritable cult with Yurii Degen, Mikhail Kuzmin, and other members of the Marseilles Sailors," a homosexual literary salon. Kuzmin's short story "Tibertius Penzel" featured Hoffmann as its hero; his adaptation of Tieck's *Puss in Boots* was staged with marionettes in 1919; and he dedicated the middle third of his 1923 play-poem *The Little Grove* (*Lesok*) to Hoffmann. See John Bowlt, ed., *The Salon Album of Vera Sudeikin-Stravinsky* (Princeton, N.J.: Princeton University Press, 1995), 64; Mikhail A. Kuzmin: "Mirok ironii, fantastiki i satiry: Kukol'nyi teatr," in *Uslovnosti: Stat'i ob isskustve* (Petrograd: Poliarnaia zvezda, 1923); Kuzmin, "Lesok," *Sobranie stikhov/Gesammelte Gedichte II: Gedichtbände nach der Revolution* 12 (1977–78); and A. Timofeev, Vladimir Markov, and George Cheron, eds., *Teatr v chetyrex tomakh (v dvukh knigakh)* (Oakland, Calif.: Berkeley Slavic Specialties, 1994).

15. *Obozrenie teatrov* 3076 (April 20, 1916): 12. Quoted in A. M. Konechnyi et al., "Artisticheskoe kabare 'Prival komediantov,'" in *Pamiatniki kul'tury, Novye otkrytiia: Pis'mennost', iskusstvo, arkheologiia. Ezhegodnik 1988* (Moscow: Nauka, 1989), 113–14.

16. Pronin wrote: "We are preparing a pantomime about 'the man who lost his reflection.' Erasmus, Dr. Dapertutto in red and steel-blue buttons, and Giulietta. Anselmus, the two snakes, Pietro Belcampo, the traveling enthusiast, councilors and devils, and, finally, Kreisler himself—all this, plus a black cat and a 'tiled stove' should fill the cellar, bring it to life." Letter from Boris Pronin to V. A. Podgornyi, September 21, 1915, quoted in Dora Kogan, *Sergei Iurevich Sudeikin, 1884–1946* (Moscow: Iskusstvo, 1974), 190. The pantomime was never performed, as the delay of the cabaret's opening to spring rendered the pantomime's New Year's Eve theme moot.

17. Valentina P. Verigina, *Vospominaniia. Teatral'nye memuary* (Leningrad: Iskusstvo, 1974), 216.

18. Count Carlo Gozzi (1720–1806): Italian playwright best known for his attempts to revive commedia dell'arte in his ten *fiabe teatrali* (theatrical fairy tales), in which he celebrated commedia's fantastical qualities by mixing traditional masks with fairy-tale content. These *fiabe* (1761–65), of which *Love of*

Three Oranges (L'amore delle tre melarance) was the first, doubled as fierce polemical attacks on the domesticized commedia plays of Carlo Goldoni (1707–1793), who soon wearied of the theater wars and moved to France in 1762, and the tragedies of Pietro Chiari (1712–1785), who eventually stopped writing for the stage.

19. These figures were inspired by the paintings of Pietro Longhi. The Venetian *tabàro* and *baùta* is a cape and mantle typically worn with a beaked white carnevale mask. James H. Johnson, *Venice Incognito: Masks in the Serene Republic* (Berkeley: University of California Press, 2011), 17, 49.

20. Verigina, *Vospominaniia*, 215.

21. N. I. Lopatin and D. V. Fomin, eds., *Russkii krug Gofmana* (Moscow: Tsentr knigi VGBIL, 2009), 7.

22. Charles Passage categorizes Hoffmannian devices used by Russian authors according to recurring topoi: the artist-hero in opposition to the philistine-villain; the beautiful world opposed to the ordinary world; madness, possession, and hallucinatory dreams; automata, puppets, and toys coming to life; the doppelgänger; hypnotism; talking animals; and recurrent types such as the youthful artist-hero, the femme fatale heroine, and the mage. Charles E. Passage, *The Russian Hoffmannists* (The Hague: Mouton, 1963).

23. Lopatin and Fomin, *Russkii krug Gofmana*, 9.

24. Z. V. Zhitomirskaia, *E. T. A. Gofman: Bibliografia russkikh perevodov i kriticheskoi literatury* (Moscow: Kniga, 1964), 19.

25. Ibid., 19–20. Most notable in this latter vein were *Genial'nyi fantast* by P. N. Krasnov (1900), E. Degen's "Ernst-Teodor-Amadei Gofman" in the journal *Mir bozhii* (1901), and *K istorii russkogo romantizma* by S. I. Rodzevich (1917). Zhitomirskaia notes that German Hoffmann scholarship also contributed to the revived Russian interest.

26. Although individual tales such as "Don Juan" (trans. 1840), *Princess Brambilla* (trans. 1844), and *The Golden Pot* (trans. 1880) were translated beginning at mid-century, sporadic translations increased to a flurry in the 1890s. New translations of "The Nutcracker and the Mouse King" appeared around the 1892 premiere of Tchaikovsky's ballet; there were also new translations of *The Life and Opinions of the Tomcat Murr* by Konstantin Balmont in 1893 and by Maria Beketova, Alexander Blok's aunt, in 1894. This growing interest prompted Panteleev of *The Foreign Literature Herald* to publish Hoffmann's collected works (1896–99). Hoffmann's only previous Russian collected works, a modest, four-volume set from the 1870s, had received scant attention compared to this eight-volume edition. Long out of print by the 1910s, Panteleev's collection was the edition owned by Blok and Meyerhold. See E. T. A. Hoffmann, *Sobranie sochinenii*, ed. F. I. Bulgakov, 8 vols. (Saint Peterburg: Tipografiia brat'ev Panteleevykh, 1896–1899).

27. Sergei Sergeevich Ignatov (1887–1959) and Meyerhold were childhood friends who became colleagues through a mutual interest in Hoffmann

and in theatrical reform. (Vsevolod E. Meierkhol'd, *Perepiska: 1896–1939*, ed. V. P. Korshunova, M. M. Sitkovetskaia, intro. Iu. A. Zavadskii [Moscow: Iskusstvo, 1976], 385.) Ignatov reviewed most of the Hoffmann-influenced productions of the day, and his prolific research on Hoffmann complemented Meyerhold's theatrical experiments: Meyerhold wrote to Ignatov that his students knew the latter's book "from cover to cover." Letter from Meierkhol'd to Ignatov, November 7, 1913, ibid., 159. Ignatov went on to become a member of Tairov's Kamerny Theatre literary board (1921–25), a teacher for Meyerhold (1921–), and a GITIS professor beginning in the mid-1930s. ("Ignatov, Sergei Sergeevich," in *Teatral'naia entsiklopediia*, ed. P. A. Markov, vol. 2 [Moscow: Sovetskaia entsiklopediia, 1961–67], 842.)

28. S. S. Ignatov, *E.T.A. Goffman: Lichnost' i tvorchestvo* (Moscow: Tipografiia O. L. Somovoi, 1914), 183.

29. Zhitomirskaia, *E. T. A. Gofman*, 18.

30. Bowlt, *Salon Album*, 19; Konechnyi et al., "Artisticheskoe kabare," 102.

31. Jacques Callot (1592–1635): prolific French artist whose etchings and engravings depict grotesque and whimsical commedia dell'arte masks, fêtes of the Medici court, and *Les Misères et les malheurs de la guerre* (1633), a series of engravings that captured the horrors of the Thirty Years' War.

32. Ludwig Tieck (1773–1853): German romantic playwright, dramaturg, and translator especially known for his fascination with Shakespeare and for his wildly metatheatrical comic plays, including *Puss in Boots* (*Der gestiefelte Kater*, 1797) and *Topsy-Turvy World* (*Die verkehrte Welt*, 1797). See Ludwig Tieck, *Ludwig Tieck's Puss-in-Boots and the Theater of the Absurd: A Commentated Bilingual Edition*, trans. and ed. Gerald Ernest Paul Gillespie (Brussels: Peter Lang, 2013); and Tieck, *The Land of Upside Down*, trans. Oskar Mandel in coll. with Maria Kelsen Feder (London: Associated University Press, 1978).

33. Silvija Jestrovic, *Theatre of Estrangement: Theory, Practice, Ideology* (Toronto: University of Toronto Press, 2006), 43.

34. Adler, introduction to Hoffmann, *Tomcat Murr*, ix.

35. M. M. Raraty, "E. T. A. Hoffmann and His Theatre," *Hermathena* 98 (1964): 54.

36. Ibid., 53.

37. E. T. A. Hoffmann, *Contes fantastiques de E.-T.-A. Hoffmann*, ed. E. Renduel (Paris: E. Renduel, 1830–32).

38. Hayse, introduction to Hoffmann, *Fantasy Pieces*, vii.

39. Andrew Wachtel, *Plays of Expectations: Intertextual Relations in Russian Twentieth-Century Drama* (Seattle: University of Washington Press, 2006), 90–96.

40. Joseph M. Hayse, Notes to "Kreisleriana," in Hoffmann, *Fantasy Pieces*, 298–99.

41. Ronald Taylor, *Berlin and Its Culture: A Historical Portrait* (New Haven, Conn.: Yale University Press, 1997), 101.

42. E. T. A. Hoffmann, "Kapellmeister Kreisler's Musical Sufferings," in *E.T.A. Hoffmann's Musical Writings: Kreisleriana, The Poet and the Composer, Music Criticism*, ed. David Charlton, trans. Martyn Clarke (Cambridge: Cambridge University Press, 2003), 81–82.

43. E. T. A. Hoffmann, "Kreisleriana. Nos. 1–6," in Hoffmann, *Fantasy Pieces*, 15.

44. Alessandra Comini, *The Changing Image of Beethoven: A Study in Mythmaking* (Santa Fe, N.Mex.: Sunstone, 2008), 83.

45. Ibid.

46. Hayse, Notes to "Johannes Kreisler's Apprentice Letter," in Hoffmann, *Fantasy Pieces*, 326.

47. Inspired by States's term "binocular vision." See Bert O. States, *Great Reckonings in Little Rooms: On the Phenomenology of Theater* (Berkeley: University of California Press, 1985), 8.

48. *Pocket Fowler's Modern English Usage*, s.v. "Fantasy," Oxford Reference Online, accessed 16 Jan. 2016, http://www.oxfordreference.com.turing.library.northwestern.edu/view/10.1093/acref/9780199232581.001.0001/acref-9780199232581-e-1359.

49. *Tolkovyi slovar' zhivogo velikorusskogo iazyka*, s.v. "Fantaziia," by Vladimir Ivanovich Dal' (Moscow: Gosudarstvennoe izdatel'stvo inostrannykh i natsional'nykh slovarei, 1956), vol. 4, R-Ia: 532.

50. Somewhat counterintuitively, the word fantasy, as understood in Russian modernist culture and, hence, as used in this book, aligns with Samuel T. Coleridge's well-known definition of imagination rather than of fancy.

51. Hoffmann, "Jacques Callot," in *Fantasy Pieces*, 3–4.

52. Grove Art Online, s.v. "Callot, Jacques," by H. Diane Russell, Oxford Art Online, accessed January 16, 2016, http://www.oxfordartonline.com.turing.library.northwestern.edu/subscriber/article/grove/art/T013207.

53. More recent scholarship has convincingly challenged this long-held view. See Kyna Hamill, "Schiaminossi, Callot and Fencing," *Print Quarterly* 26, no. 4 (2009): 361; and Donald Posner, "Jacques Callot and the Dances Called Sfessania," *The Art Bulletin* 59, no. 2 (1977): 203–16.

54. Hoffmann, *Fantasy Pieces*, 3–4.

55. In the introduction to his translation of *Princess Blandina*, Ignatov comments on Hoffmann's theatrical use of a literary term: "Romantic irony on the stage . . . takes shape under the influence of purely theatrical irony and the theatrical methods of the comedy of masks. This permits us to transfer questions about romantic theater from the realm of the purely literary . . . to the realm of the theatrical." Sergei Ignatov, introduction to *Printsessa Blandina*, ed. S. S. Ignatov (Moscow: Izdatel'stvo vserossiskogo soiuza poetov, 1925), 4.

56. *Crystal Reference Encyclopedia*, s.v. "Romantik," xreferplus, accessed November 15, 2005, http://80-www-xreferplus-com.ezproxy.library.tufts.edu/entry/953583.

57. Chris Baldick, "Romantic Irony," *The Oxford Dictionary of Literary Terms*, Oxford Reference Online, accessed May 7, 2015, http://www.oxfordreference.com/view/10.1093/acref/9780199208272.001.0001/acref-9780199208272-e-1002.

58. Allen Speight, "Friedrich Schlegel," *The Stanford Encyclopedia of Philosophy* (Winter 2011 Edition), ed. Edward N. Zalta, accessed January 16, 2016, http://plato.stanford.edu/archives/win2011/entries/schlegel/.

59. Georgia Albert, "Understanding Irony: Three *Essais* on Friedrich Schlegel," *MLN* 108, no. 5 (December 1993): 841. See pp. 840–43 in the same essay for a useful discussion of permanent parabasis.

60. Jestrovic, *Theatre of Estrangement*, 34.

61. Ibid., 45–46.

62. J. Douglas Clayton, *Pierrot in Petrograd: The Commedia dell'Arte/Balagan in Twentieth-Century Russian Theatre and Drama* (Montreal: McGill-Queen's University Press, 1993), 5.

63. Wolfgang Kayser, *The Grotesque in Art and Literature*, trans. Ulrich Weisstein (New York: McGraw-Hill, 1966), 39.

64. Sergei Eizenshtein, "Iz lektsii v VGIKe: 31 December 1935," in *Eisenshtein o Meierkhol'de, 1919–1948*, ed. Vladimir Zabrodin (Moscow: Novoe izdatel'stvo, 2005), 230–31.

65. Samuil Vermel', "Ironiia i teatral'nost'," *LTA* 2 (1914): 44.

66. Ibid., 45. For a valuable study of Meyerhold's relation to cubism (that came out afer this book was in production), see Amy Skinner, *Meyerhold and the Cubists: Perspectives on Painting and Performance* (Bristol, U.K.: Intellect, 2015).

67. G., "Novye puti (Beseda s Vs. E. Meierkhol'dom)," *Rampa i zhizn'*, no. 34 (1911): 2.

68. Taylor, *Berlin and Its Culture*, 101.

69. Hoffmann, *Tomcat Murr*, 3.

70. Ibid., 3–4.

71. Laurence Sterne, *The Life and Opinions of Tristram Shandy, Gentleman* (Ware, U. K.: Wordsworth Editions, 1996), 109.

72. Gerhard R. Kaiser, *E. T. A. Hoffmann* (Stuttgart: J.B. Metzler, 1988), 139.

73. Jeremy Adler, introduction to Hoffmann, *Tomcat Murr*, xix.

74. E. T. A. Hoffmann, "Don Juan," in Hoffmann, *Fantasy Pieces*, 60.

75. Taylor, *Berlin and Its Culture*, 101.

76. Abigail Chantler, *E.T.A. Hoffmann's Musical Aesthetics* (Burlington, Vt.: Ashgate, 2006), 20.

77. E. T. A. Hoffmann, "Johannes Kreisler's Apprentice Letter," in Hoffmann, *Fantasy Pieces*, 293.

78. Schumann composed *Fantasiestücke* of his own and called himself *Johannes Kreisler Jun.* well into adulthood. Johannes Brahms, *Johannes Brahms: Life and Letters*, selected and annotated by Styra Avins; trans. Josef Eisinger and Styra Avins (Oxford: Oxford University Press, 1997), 13.

79. Modest Ivanovich Pisarev (1844–1905) was known for his psychological acting style, critical essays, and influence on Ostrovsky's creative development. See "Pisarev, Modest Ivanovich," in Markov, *Teatral'naia entsiklopediia*, 4:364.

80. M. V. Pisarev, introduction to *Neobychainyia mucheniia odnogo teatral'nogo direktora*, by E. T. A. Hoffmann, ed. M. I. Pisarev, trans. M. V. Karneev (Saint Petersburg: Lederle, 1894), 3–4.

81. In Hoffmann's version, Fata Morgana brings on Prince Tartaglia's "melancholy" by chopping up "tragedies of fate" and putting them in his chocolate; the Smeraldina plot line is absent altogether; and, most significantly, Truffaldino is replaced with the German Kasper. The reader will note that Gozzi's *fiaba* is translated *Love of Three Oranges* and Meyerhold's journal and divertissement *Love for Three Oranges* throughout this book, as the Italian and Russian titles differ slightly.

82. Antonio Sacchi [also Sacco] (1708–1788): Italian commedia actor-manager, "probably the leading Italian player of the century." His famous Truffaldino was featured (nearly twenty years apart) in both Goldoni's *Servant of Two Masters* and in Gozzi's *Love of Three Oranges*. Martin Banham, *The Cambridge Guide to Theatre* (Cambridge, Mass.: Cambridge University Press, 1995), 548.

83. Keith Owen Tribble, "European Symbolist Theater: Conventions and Innovations" (Ph.D. diss., University of Washington, 1990), 201. Mikhail Kuzmin proposed that Gozzi's *fiabe* would make ideal material for the early Soviet puppet repertoire. (Mikhail A. Kuzmin, "Mirok ironii, fantastiki i satiry: Kukol'nyi teatr," in *Uslovnosti: Stat'i ob isskustve* [Petrograd: Poliarnaia zvezda, 1923], 39.) Liubov' Iakovleva and N. Petrov attempted unsuccessfully to stage Gozzi's *Green Bird* with puppets. (I. N. Solomonik, "Domashnye i studiinye spektakli," in *Kukly vykhodiat na stsenu: Kniga dlia uchitelia* [Moscow: Prosveshchenie, 1993], 141.) In 1937 Sergei Obraztsov staged Gozzi's *King Stag*, claiming that "Gozzi's play was being presented for the first time as its author had intended—by marionettes." (N. I. Smirnova, *Teatr Sergeia Obraztsova* [Moscow: Nauka, 1971], 132, 319.)

84. Hoffmann, *Neobychainyia mucheniia*, 60–61, 130.

85. Ibid., 133.

86. Raraty, "E. T. A. Hoffmann," 64.

87. Tribble, "European Symbolist Theater," 225.

88. Ibid., 177.

89. Ibid., 224. Additional instigators of the Russian fascination with puppets were the plays of Maurice Maeterlinck (also an admirer of Hoffmann), nostalgic reminiscences of the Russian fairground, western European puppetry experiments, and Craig's "The Actor and the Übermarionette," first published in Russian translation in 1911.

90. In 1908 Fedor Sologub and Valery Briusov each wrote about the place of the marionette in the new theater. For Sologub, the marionette represented man

as a neutral stage actor for monodramas and as the ultimate victim of Fate, while Briusov viewed puppets as mechanical beings impossible to infuse with creative life. See Sologub's "The Theatre of a Single Will" and Briusov's "Realism and Convention on the Stage" in *Russian Dramatic Theory from Pushkin to the Symbolists: An Anthology*, trans. and ed. Laurence Senelick (Austin: University of Texas Press, 1981).

91. Vsevolod Meierkhol'd, "The Fairground Booth [Balagan]," in Meyerhold, *Meyerhold on Theatre*, 128. I have followed Clayton's lead in retaining—rather than translating—the word *balagan* throughout this book in order to preserve the word's associations with fairground booth theaters, chaos, scandal, popular entertainment, and theatricalist theater. See Clayton, *Pierrot in Petrograd*, 54–55.

92. Meierkhol'd, "The Fairground Booth," 129.

93. Ibid., 130.

94. L. S. Oves, ed., *Nauchno-issledovatel'skii proekt po tvorcheskomu naslediiu V. E. Meierkhol'da "Liubov' k trem apel'sinam," 1914–1916*, 2 vols. (Saint Petersburg: RIII, 2014), 2:364. Hereafter *Liubov' k trem apel'sinam.*

95. Also translated *The Land of Upside Down*.

96. Oskar Mandel, introduction to Ludwig Tieck, *The Land of Upside Down*, 18.

97. Tieck, *The Land of Upside Down*, 20.

98. Mandel, introduction to Tieck, *The Land of Upside Down*, 13.

99. Sergei S. Ignatov, "Hoffmaniana I (E. T. A. Gofman na stsene)," *LTA* 4–7 (1915): 180.

100. E. T. A. Hoffmann, *Printsessa Blandina*, trans. Sergei Ignatov (Moscow: Izdatel'stvo vserossiiskogo soiuza poetov, 1925), 14, 16.

101. W. Harich, ed., *E. T. A. Hoffmann: Dichtungen und Schriften sowie Briefe und Tagebucher* (Weimar: Lichtenstein, 1924), 368. Trans. in Raraty, "E. T. A. Hoffmann," 65.

102. Ignatov, *E. T. A. Goffman*, 44. Although Ignatov's *Blandina* translation was not published until 1925, Ignatov wrote to Meyerhold in 1912 that he had already translated *Blandina* as the intended appendix for his Hoffmann monograph. Letter from Ignatov to Meierkhol'd, April 4, 1912, 1–2. Russian State Archive of Literature and Art, Moscow (hereafter RGALI), f. 998, op. 1, ed. khr. 1634.

103. Ignatov asked that his staging plan be published in *LTA* in advance of a proposed production, writing, "I would with great pleasure stage *Princess Blandina* at your Studio next season according to the plan indicated in my notes, under your leadership." Letter from Ignatov to Meyerhold, March 25, 1914. RGALI f. 998, op. 1, ed. khr. 1634. Meyerhold apparently responded enthusiastically, as Ignatov wrote back, "I thank you for the invitation to stage *Blandina*." Letter from Ignatov to Meyerhold, June 2, 1914. The production never took

place, perhaps because the studio ended its public performances after World War I curtailed its 1915–1916 season.

104. Ignatov, "Hoffmaniana I: E. T. A. Gofman na stsene," 180.

105. Ibid., 180–81.

106. Ibid., 181.

107. Ibid.

108. Ibid., 181–82.

109. Tony Pearson, "Evreinov and Pirandello: Twin Apostles of Theatricality," *Theatre Research International* 12, no. 2 (1987): 147–67. Nikolai Nikolaevich Evreinov (1879–1953) was a brilliantly innovative director, playwright, and theorist known for his plays, theoretical writings, productions at the Distorting Mirror cabaret, and the mass spectacle *Storming of the Winter Palace* (1920). He never staged Hoffmann (preferring to be identified with the ever-changing Harlequin), but he admired Tieck's irony and framing devices. In his essay "The Commission of the Understanding (A Dream as Improbable as It Is Instructive)," he uses the ghost of Tieck to make the polemical point, aimed at Meyerhold, that Tieck's innovations preceded Hoffmann's. Nikolai Evreinov, *Teatr dlia sebia* (Saint Petersburg: Sovremennoe iskusstvo, 1917), 64–65. Excellent Evreinov studies in English include Sharon M. Carnicke, *The Theatrical Instinct: Nikolai Evreinov and the Russian Theatre of the Early Twentieth Century* (New York: Peter Lang, 1989); and Spencer Golub, *Evreinov, the Theatre of Paradox and Transformation* (Ann Arbor, Mich.: UMI Research Press, 1984).

110. Playwright Sergei Mikhailovich Tretiakov (1892–1939) pioneered "verbal montage" in his script for *Wiseman* (1923, dir. Eisenstein) and several other plays, including *I Want a Baby* (1926–28, dir. Meyerhold but banned before opening). Tretiakov was arrested in 1939 and never returned from the gulag. Brecht wrote of Tretiakov as "my teacher" in "Is the People Infallible?" a poem dedicated to Tretiakov, though Tretiakov's name "was expunged from all editions of the poem" until after Brecht's death. Robert Leach, introduction to *I Want a Baby*, trans. Stephen Holland, ed. Robert Leach (Birmingham, U.K.: University of Birmingham Press, 1995), vi.

111. The *Brambilla* illustrations are also mirror images of the Callot etchings. Alexander Schultz, "The Mirror of Laughter: Mediation, Self-Reflection, and Healing in E.T.A. Hoffmann's *Princess Brambilla*," *European Romantic Review* 22, no. 3 (June 2011): 418, 421. For additional analysis of the changes to these images, see E. T. A. Hoffmann, *Three Märchen of E. T. A. Hoffmann*, trans. Charles E. Passage (Columbia: University of South Carolina Press, 1971), xix.

112. For more on Gozzi's theater wars, see the discussion of *Love for Three Oranges* in chapter 1.

113. Ignatov, *E. T. A. Goffman*, 40.

114. Reinhold Grimm, "From Callot to Butor: E. T. A. Hoffmann and the Tradition of the Capriccio," *MLN* 93, no. 3 (April l978): 401.

115. Michael Kennedy and Joyce Bourne Kennedy, "Capriccio," in *Oxford Dictionary of Music*, ed. Tim Rutherford, Oxford Reference Online, accessed 9 May 2014, http://www.oxfordreference.com.turing.library.northwestern.edu/view/10.1093/acref/9780199578108.001.0001/acref-9780199578108-e-1599.

116. Grimm, "From Callot to Butor," 400.

117. Morton Gurewitch, *The Comedy of Romantic Irony* (Lanham, Md.: University Press of America, 2002), 91.

118. E. T. A. Hoffmann, preface to "Princess Brambilla: A Capriccio after Jacques Callot," in *The Golden Pot and Other Tales*, by E. T. A. Hoffmann, trans. and ed. Ritchie Robertson (Oxford: Oxford University Press, 2000), 119.

119. The following discussion of refraction is developed from my article "Baring the Frame: Meyerhold's Refraction of Gozzi's *Love of Three Oranges*," published in *Theatre Survey* 56, no. 3 (September 2015). Copyright © 2015, The American Society for Theatre Research, Inc. Reprinted with the permission of Cambridge University Press.

120. My emphasis. Vsevolod Meierkhol'd, "K istorii i tekhnike teatra" (1907), in Vsevolod Meierkhol'd, *Stat'i, pis'ma, rechi, besedy*, ed. A. V. Fevral'skii, vol. 1 (Moscow: Iskusstvo, 1968), 132.

121. Meierkhol'd, "K istorii i tekhnike teatra," 129–30, 139.

122. My emphasis. Aleksandr Ia. Tairov, *O teatre: Zapiski rezhissera. Stat'i, besedy, rechi, pis'ma* (Moscow: VTO, 1970), 148.

123. Sergei Eizenshtein, "'Vse velikoe prosto': S. M. Eizenshtein o teatre, 1919–1923," ed. V. V. Zabrodin, in *Mnemozina: Dokumenty i fakty iz istorii otechestvennogo teatra XX veka*, ed. Vladislav V. Ivanov, vol. 4 (Moscow: Indrik, 2009), 439. Reproduced from RGALI f. 1923, op. 1, ed. khr. 888: 122–25 verso.

124. Meierkhol'd, "K istorii i tekhnike teatra," 109.

125. Braun translates Meyerhold thus: "The art of the director is the art not of an executant, but of an author—so long as one has earned the right." Edward Braun, *Meyerhold: A Revolution in Theatre* (London: Methuen Drama, 1998), 221. Though subsequent readers have sometimes misinterpreted this to mean that Meyerhold wished to usurp the place of the playwright, in its original context Meyerhold argues simply that playwriting and directing were originally "a single profession" that was artificially split due to the specific, virtuosic skills required of each. He adds, "But their nature is one and the same! Therefore the art of the director is not the art of an executant, but that of an author. But one must have the right." Vsevolod Meierkhol'd, "Meierkhol'd govorit: Zapisi vyskazyvanii Vsevoloda Emil'evicha na repetitsiiakh i v besedakh," ed. A. K. Gladkov, in *Tarusskie stranitsy*, ed. V. Koblikov, N. Otten, N. Panchenko, K. Paustovskii, and A. Shteinburg (Kaluga: Kaluzhskoe knizhnoe izdatel'stvo, 1961), 306.

126. Bert O. States, *Great Reckonings in Little Rooms: On the Phenomenology of Theater* (Berkeley: University of California Press, 1985), 8.

127. Excellent transposition studies include Caryl Emerson, *Boris Godunov: Transpositions of a Russian Theme* (Bloomington: Indiana University Press, 1986); and Alexander Burry, *Multi-Mediated Dostoevsky: Transposing Novels into Opera, Film, and Drama* (Evanston, Ill.: Northwestern University Press, 2011). A key work on adaptation is Linda Hutcheon and Siobhan O'Flynn's *A Theory of Adaptation.* Its authors observe, interestingly, that "it is the (post-) Romantic valuing of the original creation and of the originating creative genius that is clearly one source of the denigrators of adapters and adaptation." (Linda Hutcheon, with Siobhan O'Flynn, *A Theory of Adaptation,* 2nd ed. [London: Routledge, 2013], 3–4.) Indeed, in the two centuries since romanticism's heyday, common views of the creative process have been impoverished by binary thinking that does not recognize artistic creation as *both* a response *and* something original. This aspect of romanticism is often misunderstood: for Hoffmann and like-minded contemporaries, the point was not that creation be wholly original, but that it have the freedom to be. As the reader will recall, Hoffmann's *Princess Brambilla* is a capriccio (something original) written in Callot's manner (a response).

128. Hoffmann, "Jacques Callot," 3.

129. Adler, introduction to Hoffmann, *Tomcat Murr,* viii.

CHAPTER ONE. MEYERHOLD-DAPERTUTTO: FRAMING THE GROTESQUE

1. Directed by Boris Sushkevich (1887–1946).

2. Doktor Dapertutto [Vsevolod Meierkhol'd], "Sverchok na pechi, ili, u zamochnoi skvazhiny," *Liubov' k trem apel'sinam: Zhurnal Doktora Dapertutto* 1–3 (1915): 90–93.

3. Doktor Dapertutto [Vsevolod Meierkhol'd], "Glossy Doktora Dapertutto k 'Otritsaniiu teatra' Iu. Aikhenval'da," *LTA* 4–5 (1914): 77.

4. Ibid., 75.

5. Robert Leach, *Vsevolod Meyerhold* (Cambridge: Cambridge University Press, 1993), 51.

6. Bert O. States, *Great Reckonings in Little Rooms: On the Phenomenology of Theater* (Berkeley: University of California Press, 1985), 8.

7. Vsevolod Meierkhol'd, "Amplua aktera" (Moscow: GVYRM, 1922), in *Meierkhol'd: K istorii tvorcheskogo metoda: Publikatsii. Stat'i* (Saint Petersburg: Kul'tInformPress, 1998), 43.

8. See T. A. Green and W. J. Pepicello, "Semiotic Interrelationships in the Puppet Play," *Semiotica* 47 (1983): 157. Mandel refers to "oscillations between levels of fiction" in Tieck's plays. Oscar Mandel, "Introduction" to *The Land of Upside Down,* by Ludwig Tieck; trans. Oskar Mandel in coll. with Maria Kelsen Feder (Rutherford, N.J.: Fairleigh Dickinson University Press, 1978), 21.

9. Andrei Bely, *Simvolizm* (Moscow, 1910), section 2, "Formy iskusstva." (Meierkhol'd's note.) Vsevolod Meyerhold, *Meyerhold on Theatre*, trans. Edward Braun (London: Bloomsbury Methuen Drama, 1998), 137.

10. Edward Braun, *Meyerhold: A Revolution in Theatre* (London: Methuen Drama, 1998), 125.

11. Lionel Abel, *Metatheatre: A New View of Dramatic Form* (New York: Hill and Wang), 1963.

12. Italics in original. Kevin Newmark, *Irony on Occasion: From Schlegel and Kierkegaard to Derrida and de Man* (New York: Fordham, 2012), 20.

13. J. Douglas Clayton, "From Gozzi to Hoffmann: German Sources for *Commedia dell'Arte* in Russian Avant-Garde Theatre," in *The Science of Buffoonery: Theory and History of the Commedia dell'Arte*, ed. Domenico Pietropaolo (Ottawa: Dovehouse Editions, 1989), 117–31.

14. Braun, *Meyerhold: A Revolution in Theatre*, 101.

15. E. T. A. Hoffmann, *Fantasy Pieces in Callot's Manner: Pages from the Diary of a Traveling Romantic*, trans. Joseph M. Hayse (Schenectady, N.Y.: Union College, 1996), 242.

16. A. A. Mgebrov, *Zhizn' v teatre*, 2 vols. (Moscow; Leningrad: Academia, 1929–32), 2:155.

17. A character from "The Nutcracker and the Mouse King."

18. Valentina P. Verigina, "Po dorogam iskanii," in *Russkii krug Gofmana*, ed. Lopatin and Fomin, 263.

19. Maria M. Tatar, "E.T.A. Hoffmann's 'Der Sandmann': Reflection and Romantic Irony," *MLN* 95, no. 3 (1980): 590.

20. Braun, *Meyerhold: A Revolution in Theatre*, 101.

21. Ibid., 6, 64.

22. Vsevolod Meierkhol'd, "V. E. Meierkhol'd—A. P. Chekhovu, May 8, 1904: Chaadaievka," in *Perepiska: 1896–1939*, by Vsevolod E. Meierkhol'd, ed. M. M. Sitkovetskaia and V. P. Korshunova (Moscow: Iskusstvo, 1976), 45.

23. Also translated as *The Puppet Show*. As with the word *balagan*, I retain Blok's Russian title, *Balaganchik*, the diminutive of *balagan* (fairground booth), for its connotations of merry, raucous, festive, subversive disorder. See J. Douglas Clayton, *Pierrot in Petrograd: The Commedia dell'Arte/Balagan in Twentieth-Century Russian Theatre and Drama* (Montreal: McGill-Queen's University Press, 1993), 13–14, 54–55.

24. Alexander Blok, *The Puppet Show*, trans. Mary Kriger and Gleb Struve, *Slavonic and East European Review* 28, no. 71 (1950): 309.

25. Braun, *Meyerhold: A Revolution in Theatre*, 67.

26. Vsevolod Meierkhol'd, *Stat'i, Pis'ma, Rechi, Besedy*, ed. A. V. Fevral'skii, vol. 1: 1891–1917 (Moscow: Iskusstvo, 1968), 251. Translated in Meyerhold, *Meyerhold on Theatre*, 70.

27. Alla Mikhailova, ed., *Meierkhol'd i khudozhniki* (Moscow: Galart, 1995), 20.

28. Vsevolod Meierkhol'd, prologue to *O Teatre* (Saint Petersburg: Prosveshchenie, 1913), in Meierkhol'd, *Stat'i*, 1:103–4.

29. Leach, *Vsevolod Meyerhold*, 38.

30. Valentina Verigina, "Po dorogam iskanii," in *Vstrechi s Meierkhol'dom: Sbornik vospominanii*, ed. L. D. Vendrovskaia and M. A. Valentei, et al. (Moscow: VTO, 1967), 41. Quoted in Braun, *Meyerhold: A Revolution in Theatre*, 65.

31. Braun, *Meyerhold: A Revolution in Theatre*, 67.

32. The discussion of *Columbine's Veil* that follows is developed from my article "A Theatrical Zigzag: Doctor Dappertutto, *Columbine's Veil*, and the Grotesque," published in *Slavic and East European Performance* 29, no. 3 (November 2009). Reprinted by permission of *European Stages*.

33. The first, the Strand, folded after only three days. Its late-night counterpart, the Distorted Mirror, founded by Zinaida Kholmskaia and Alexander Kugel, was far more enduring; in 1910 it moved to a 750-seat theater and Nikolai Evreinov took over as artistic director. Laurence Senelick, "Nikolay Evreinov's 'Inspector General,'" *Performing Arts Journal* 8, no. 1 (1984): 113.

34. Konstantin Rudnitskii, *Russkoe rezhisserskoe iskusstvo: 1908–1917* (Moscow: Nauka, 1990), 33. The word parade as used throughout this book does not indicate a simple procession, as contemporary usage might suggest. Rather Meyerhold was experimenting with the presentational style and direct audience contact made possible by the French and Russian fairground parade, a "sketch performed outside a fairground booth to attract spectators." W. D. Howarth, ed. *French Theatre in the Neo-classical Era, 1550–1791* (Cambridge: Cambridge University Press, 1997), xxxix.

35. The House of Interludes folded in 1911 after a financially unsuccessful tour to Moscow.

36. Literally *Columbine's Scarf*. I follow Marjorie Hoover's lead in translating the title as *Columbine's Veil*. For an English translation of Schnitzler's pantomime, see Lawrence Sullivan, "Arthur Schnitzler's *The Veil of Pierrette*," *Europa Orientalis* 14, no. 2 (1995): 184–205. The triple bill at the House of Interludes also included Kuzmin's *The Dutch Girl Liza* (based on the medieval play *Robin et Marion*) and Potemkin and Gibshman's *Black and White*.

37. S. Auslender, "Dom intermedii," *Apollon* 12 (1910): 27.

38. Vsevolod Meierkhol'd, "Avtobiografiia V. E. Meierkhol'd," ed. and intro. N. N. Panfilova and O. M. Fel'dman, in *Pamiatniki kul'tury: Novye otkrytiia. Ezhegodnik 1992* (Moscow: Nauka, 1993): 111.

39. Meyerhold, *Meyerhold on Theatre*, 140.

40. [Vsevolod Meierkhol'd], "Sharf Kolombiny." Pantomime libretto (Saint Petersburg: Tipografiia Siriius, 1910), RGALI, f. 998, op. 1, ed. khr. 70.

41. Quoted in Vadim Shcherbakov, "Po obe storony maski," *Teatr* 1 (1990): 63.

42. Eizenshtein, "Iz lektsii v VGIKe: 31 December 1935," 230–31.

43. Andrei Bely, *Simvolizm* (Moscow, 1910), section 2, 'Formy iskusstva." Meyerhold's note. In Meyerhold, *Meyerhold on Theatre*, 137.

44. *Der Schleier der Pierrette* is based on Schnitzler's full-length play *Der Schleier der Beatrice* (1898–99).

45. The Russian word *tapeur*, derived from French for "to tap," is a piano plunker, a musician for hire; the same word is used for the accompanist in silent film. The libretto refers to this character as the *tapeur*; reviews also describe him as a Kapellmeister; and Sapunov's costume design (figure 12) states "*tapeur* and Kapellmeister."

46. Liudmila Tikhvinskaia, *Povsednevnaia zhizn' teatral'noi bogemy Serebrianogo veka: Kabare i teatry miniatiur v Rossii, 1908–1911* (Moscow: Molodaia Gvardiia, 2005), 99.

47. Rudnitskii, *Russkoe rezhisserskoe iskusstvo*, 37.

48. Meyerhold, *Meyerhold on Theatre*, 140.

49. "Los Caprichos" is a set of eighty etchings, first published as an album in 1799, by Francisco Goya (1746–1828).

50. Aleksandr Matskin, *Portrety i nabliudeniia* (Moscow: Iskusstvo, 1973), 285. Quoted in Clayton, *Pierrot in Petrograd*, 85.

51. Vsevolod Meyerhold, "The Fairground Booth," in Meyerhold, *Meyerhold on Theatre*, 140.

52. Rudnitskii, *Russkoe rezhisserskoe iskusstvo*, 35.

53. Ibid.

54. All act 2 libretto citations are from [Meierkhol'd], "Sharf Kolombiny," 3.

55. Despite the fact that Meyerhold initially condemned film as too photographic to be considered art, much of his work is structured similarly to film as we now understand it, partly because of cross-pollination with Kuleshov, Eisenstein, and others. His views also changed when he directed a film, no longer extant, of Oscar Wilde's *The Picture of Dorian Gray* (1916). Meyerhold muses on the reader's experience of juxtaposition in one phantasmagorical scene in which the portrait is carried into an opium den:

> Here the concentration of light on the figures is such that it reminds us of the creations of Hoffmann, in whom, on certain pages, everyday events suddenly cease to be as they are and seem fantastical. The reader stops for an instant, astonished by the change of mood that bursts in, the onset of fantastical associations, and so he rereads the page, wanting to ascertain at which line the change took place—the interweaving of the real and the fantastical. (Vsevolod Meierkhol'd, "Vs. Meierkhol'd. 'Portret Doriana Greia,'" ed. and intro. S. Ginzberg, *Iz istorii kino* 6 [1965]: 20.)

56. M. M. Bonch-Tomashevskii, "Pantomima A. Shnitslera v Svobodnom teatre," *Maski* 2, no. 22 (1913–14): 52. Quoted in Clayton, *Pierrot in Petrograd*, 83.

57. Bonch-Tomashevskii, "Pantomima Shnitslera," 52. Quoted in Clayton, *Pierrot in Petrograd*, 83.

58. Braun, *Meyerhold: A Revolution in Theatre*, 99, 101. Braun inadvertently misidentifies this as being from Shcherbakov, "Po obe storony maski," 64. The source is Konstantin Rudnitskii, *Rezhisser Meierkhol'd* (Moscow: Nauka, 1969), 38–40.

59. [Meierkhol'd], "Sharf Kolombiny," act 2, scene 9: 3.

60. [Meierkhol'd], "Sharf Kolombiny," act 3, scene 2: 4.

61. Bonch-Tomashevskii, "Pantomima Shnitslera," 53.

62. Ernst Jentsch's famous 1906 essay on the uncanny notes, using Hoffmann's *The Sandman* as an example, that one of the most disturbing forms of perceptual dissonance is the inability to distinguish an inanimate object from a living one. Whether or not Meyerhold knew Jentsch's essay, he, too, reveled in this kind of juxtaposition. Ernst Jentsch, "On the Psychology of the Uncanny (1906)," *Angelaki* 2, no. 1 (1996): 7–17.

63. Gertsen, "Znamenitye sovremenniki: Goffman," *Teleskop*, 1836. Quoted in "Hoffmaniana III (Russkie pisateli o Gofmane)," *LTA* 3 (1914): 85.

64. Clayton, *Pierrot in Petrograd*, 85.

65. RGALI, f. 998, op. 1, ed. khr. 70.

66. John E. Malmstad, "Mixail Kuzmin: A Chronicle of His Life and Times," *Centrifuga: Russian Reprintings and Printings* 12, no. 3 (1977): 203.

67. Mikhail Kuzmin, *Obozrenie teatrov* 3076 (April 20, 1916): 12. Quoted in A. M. Konechnyi et al., "Artisticheskoe kabare 'Prival komediantov,'" in *Pamiatniki kul'tury: Novye otkrytiia. Ezhegodnik 1988* (Moscow: "Nauka," 1989), 112–13.

68. Evgenii Znosko-Borovskii, "Bashennyi teatr," *Apollon* 8 (1910): 32, in *Meierkhol'd v russkoi teatral'noi kritike: 1898–1918*, ed. Nikolai V. Pesochinskii, E. A. Kukhta, and N. A. Tarshis (Moscow: Artist. Rezhisser. Teatr, 1997), 194.

69. Vsevolod Meyerhold, "Iz lektsii na teatral'nom seminare 'Inturista'" (May 21, 1934), in Meierkhol'd, *Stat'i*, 2:294.

70. The use of blackface in Russian theatre remains a largely neglected area of research. Blackface was used variously in the first part of the twentieth century, ranging from would-be positive depictions in *Uncle Tom's Cabin* to demeaning racial stereotypes in works like Stravinsky/Fokine/Benois's ballet *Petrushka,* which features a moor still sometimes played in blackface today, both in and outside of Russia. Most imperial-era Russians had few, if any, direct encounters with Africans or African Americans. Each of this book's directors used blackface at one point or another—Meyerhold with the forestage servants, Eisenstein in Jack London's *The Mexican* (1920), and Tairov in Eugene O'Neill's *All God's Chillun Got Wings* (1929), retitled *The Negro*. Tairov's production illustrates a broad Soviet attempt in the late 1920s to shift toward positive images of African Americans that highlighted historical similarities with the Russian proletariat, such as slavery and serfdom. Context for this latter provided by Christina Hilleboe

Kiaer in her lecture "An Aesthetics of Anti-Racism: African-Americans in Soviet Visual Culture," October 28, 2015, Kaplan Institute for the Humanities, Northwestern University.

71. Thanks to Tracy Davis for drawing my attention to this painting tradition.

72. David Bindman and Henry Louis Gates Jr., eds., *The Image of the Black in Western Art*, vol. 2, part 2 (Cambridge, Mass: Belknap, 2011), xi–xii.

73. David Bindman, Bruce Boucher, and Helen Weston, "The Theater of Court and Church: Blacks as Figures of Fantasy," in Bindman and Gates, eds., *The Image of the Black in Western Art*, vol. 3, part 3, 58.

74. Ibid., 58.

75. Ibid.

76. Ibid., 56.

77. Ibid., 59.

78. Meyerhold, *Meyerhold on Theatre*, 102.

79. Sergei Auslender, "Vpechatleniia sezona: S. Peterburg, Aleksandrinskii teatr, Don Zhuan," *Ezhegodnik imperatorskikh teatrov*, vol. 7 (1910), in Pesochinskii et al., *Meierkhol'd v Russkoi teatral'noi kritike: 1898–1918*, 200.

80. Sergei Volkonskii, "*Don Zhuan* i *Mokroie*: Po povodu dvukh postanovok," in *Chelovek na stsene* (Saint Petersburg, 1912), in Pesochinskii et al., *Meierkhol'd v Russkoi teatral'noi kritike: 1898–1918*, 216.

81. Volkonsky wrote, "Give us the curtain! But there is no curtain. . . . Oh, holy veil that separates art from life, close before us and give us faith, false though it may be, in the mystery and fullness of what lies hidden behind you!" Volkonskii, "*Don Zhuan*," in Pesochinskii et al., *Meierkhol'd v Russkoi teatral'noi kritike: 1898–1918*, 217.

82. Braun, *Meyerhold: A Revolution in Theatre*, 141.

83. Valentina P. Verigina, *Vospominaniia: Teatral'nye memuary* (Leningrad: Iskusstvo, 1974), 206.

84. Meyerhold, *Meyerhold on Theatre*, 116–17.

85. Letter from Sergei Ignatov to Vsevolod Meierkhol'd, late February 1914. RGALI f. 998, op. 1, ed. khr. 1634.

86. Called the Troitskaia Street Studio before it changed locations to Borodinskaia Street in 1914.

87. Ignatov most likely introduced Meyerhold to Gozzi's plays. In a December 1911 letter Ignatov offered to send Meyerhold a volume of Gozzi's complete *fiabe* from his university library, also mentioning Hoffmann's interest in Gozzi. Ignatov to Meyerhold, December 2, 1911, RGALI f. 998, op. 1, ed. khr. 1634. In the same letter he informed Meyerhold that Fedor Komissarzhevsky was planning a production of Schiller's adaptation of Gozzi's *Turandot*. Meyerhold responded: "I am very grateful to you for having sent me this wonderful little volume. O, how much it has given me!" Meyerhold to Ignatov, March 14, 1912, in Meierkhol'd, *Perepiska,* 143.

88. A note from the editor indicates that one issue was delayed because several journal employees were summoned into active military duty. "Ot redaktora," *LTA* 4–5 (1914): 3.

89. Oves, ed., *Nauchno-issledovatel'skii proekt po tvorcheskomu nalediiu V. E. Meierkhol'da "Liubov' k trem apel'sinam," 1914–1916*, 2:13. Hereafter *Liubov' k trem apel'sinam.*

90. Clayton, "From Gozzi to Hoffmann," 118.

91. Many of the journal's employees and authors, including Viktor Maksimovich Zhirmunsky (1891–1971), studied at the Department of Romance and Germanic Studies at the University of Saint Petersburg, "where the formalists Eikhenbaum and V. Shklovsky were shaped." Raissa Raskina, *Mejerchol'd e il Dottor Dappertutto: Lo studio e la rivista "L'amore delle tre melarance"* (Rome: Bulzoni, 2010), 21–22.

92. Viktor M. Zhirmunskii, "Komediia chistoi radosti. (*Kot v sapogakh,* Liudviga Tika. 1797 g.)," *LTA* 1 (1916): 85.

93. The following discussion of *Love for Three Oranges* is developed from my article "Baring the Frame: Meyerhold's Refraction of Gozzi's *Love of Three Oranges*," published in *Theatre Survey* 56, no. 3 (September 2015). Copyright © 2015, The American Society for Theatre Research, Inc. Reprinted with the permission of Cambridge University Press.

94. Konstantin Andreevich Vogak (1887–1938): writer, translator, director, and collaborator at Meyerhold's studio (1913–15). After fighting in World War I, he emigrated to western Europe. Vladimir Nikolaevich Solov'ev (1888–1941): director, teacher, playwright, critic, Borodinskaia Street Studio co-leader and contributor to *LTA*. After 1922, he taught directing at the present-day Saint Petersburg State Academy of Theatre Arts. Oves, *Liubov' k trem apel'sinam,* 1:46–47.

95. For an analysis of the relation between Meyerhold/Soloviev/Vogak's scenario and Prokofiev's opera, see Harlow Robinson, "Love for Three Operas: The Collaboration of Vsevolod Meyerhold and Sergei Prokofiev," *The Russian Review* 45, no. 3 (July 1986): 290.

96. For example, Carlo Gozzi, *Translations of The Love of Three Oranges, Turandot, and The Snake Lady*, trans. and adapt. John Louis DiGaetani (New York: Greenwood, 1988). For a closer translation, see Carlo Gozzi, *Carlo Gozzi's Reflective Analysis of His Fable Entitled "The Love of the Three Oranges,"* trans. John Addington Symonds (Boston, Mass.: Chrysalis, 1959).

97. Martellian verse is a fourteen-syllable adaptation of Alexandrine verse developed by Pier Iacopo Martello (1665–1727).

98. Gozzi, *Carlo Gozzi's Reflective Analysis*, 10.

99. As Bermel and Emery note, this conventionalization of wind doubled as a gibe at Chiari's "violations of the . . . unities of place and time." Carlo Gozzi, *Five Tales for the Theatre*, ed. and trans. Albert Bermel and Ted Emery (Chicago: University of Chicago Press, 1989), 307n17.

100. Clayton, *Pierrot in Petrograd*, 29.

101. Vsevolod Meierkhol'd, Vladimir Solov'ev, and Konstantin Vogak, "Otkrytoe pis'mo avtorov divertismenta 'Liubov' k trem apel'sinam' A. A. Gvozdevu," *LTA* 4–5 (1914): 87–88. The trio also defended themselves against Gvozdev's accusations of translation errors by noting that their divertissement was a "reworking" of Gozzi's *fiaba*, not a translation of it. Years later, however, Soloviev admitted, "In all honesty, A. A. Gvozdev . . . was very right . . . At the time we knew Italian very badly . . . So those words with which I polemicized nineteen or so years ago, I take back." Saint Petersburg State Museum of Theatre and Music, КП7730/44. ОРУ 3405: 10. Quoted in Oves, *Liubov' k trem apel'sinam*, 1:329.

102. See Ludwig Tieck, *The Land of Upside Down* and *Ludwig Tieck's Puss-in-Boots and the Theater of the Absurd: A Commentated Bilingual Edition*, trans. and ed. Gerald Ernest Paul Gillespie (Brussels: Peter Lang, 2013).

103. In addition to Meyerhold's prolonged interest in works that allowed for theatrical interruption and audience interaction, Oves suggests that small forms like divertissements allowed Meyerhold to circumvent censorship. Oves, *Liubov' k trem apel'sinam* 1:75n1.

104. Howarth, *French Theatre in the Neo-classical Era*, xxxix.

105. Meyerhold, "The Fairground Booth," 127.

106. Vsevolod Meierkhol'd, Vladimir Solov'ev, and Konstantin Vogak, "Liubov' k trem apel'sinam: Divertisment, Dvenadtsat' stsen, prolog, epilog i tri intermedii," *LTA* 1 (1914): 19–20. Page numbers from the *Three Oranges* divertissement are hereafter provided as in-text citations.

107. Oves, *Liubov' k trem apel'sinam*, 1:76n2.

108. Prokofiev's opera doubled the number of warring choruses, adding "Lyrics" and "Empty Heads"; he also gave the Eccentrics a more active role in shaping the unfolding action.

109. "Argument" in the commedia sense of plot summary.

110. Literally "twofold tragedy" and "daily-life comedy."

111. According to the scenario's authors, this scene is drawn from "an anonymous pamphlet: *Four Masks of the Italian Comedy.*" Meierkhol'd, Solov'ev, and Vogak, "Liubov' k trem apel'sinam," 34.

112. Marvin Carlson, *The Haunted Stage: The Theatre as Memory Machine* (Ann Arbor: University of Michigan Press, 2003), 7.

113. Meyerhold, "The Fairground Booth," 131.

114. Julia Vaingurt, *Wonderlands of the Avant-Garde: Technology and the Arts in Russia of the 1920s* (Evanston, Ill.: Northwestern University Press, 2013), 64.

115. Braun, *Meyerhold: A Revolution in Theatre*, 173. Quoted (with a useful framing discussion) in Vaingurt, *Wonderlands*, 65.

116. Syssoyeva draws a useful connection between Meyerhold's understanding of actors as generators of their own material and today's collective creation. See Kathryn Mederos Syssoyeva, "Revolution in the Theatre I: Meyerhold,

Stanislavsky, and Collective Creation. Russia, 1905," in *A History of Collective Creation*, ed. Kathryn Mederos Syssoyeva and Scott Proufit (New York: Palgrave Macmillan, 2013), 37–57.

117. Zhirmunskii, "Komediia chistoi radosti," 88.

118. Ibid.

119. See Kyna Hamill, "Schiaminossi, Callot and Fencing," *Print Quarterly* 26, no. 4 (2009): 354–63; and Donald Posner, "Jacques Callot and the Dances Called Sfessania," *The Art Bulletin* 59, no. 2 (1977): 203–16.

120. Thanks to Kyna Hamill for bringing Callot's background planes to my attention.

121. Sergei S. Ignatov, "Hoffmaniana I (E. T. A. Gofman na stsene)," *LTA* 4–7 (1915): 181.

122. Hans-Thies Lehmann, *Postdramatic Theatre* (London: Routledge, 2006), 100.

123. Meyerhold, "The Fairground Booth," 127.

124. Zhirmunskii, "Komediia chistoi radosti," 85–86.

125. My emphasis. Tatar, "E.T.A. Hoffmann's 'Der Sandmann': Reflection and Romantic Irony," 607.

126. Ibid., 608.

127. Andrew Wachtel, *Plays of Expectations: Intertextual Relations in Russian Twentieth-Century Drama* (Seattle: Herbert J. Ellison Center, University of Washington, 2006), 71.

128. Viktor Shklovsky, "The Making of *Don Quixote*," in *Theory of Prose*, trans. Benjamin Sher, intro. Gerald L. Bruns (Normal, Ill: Dalkey Archive, 1990), 94.

129. Marc Silberman, Steve Giles, and Tom Kuhn, eds., *Brecht on Theatre*, 3rd ed. (London: Bloomsbury Methuen, 2015), 72.

130. Meyerhold rehearsed *Three Oranges* for an intended 1915 staging but ultimately replaced it with a journal-sponsored production of Blok's *Balaganchik* and *Incognita*, during the intermission of which Chinese jugglers tossed real oranges to the audience. Oves, *Liubov' k trem apel'sinam*, 1:74.

131. Marjorie L. Hoover, "A Mejerxol'd Method," 26.

132. [Vsevolod Meierkhol'd], "Studiia: Klass Meierkhol'da: Tekhnika stsenicheskikh dvizhenii," *LTA* 4–5 (1914): 97.

133. Ibid., 96–97.

134. Ibid., 97.

135. Leach, *Vsevolod Meyerhold*, 30.

136. Vsevolod Meierkhol'd, "Uslovnyi teatr," in Meierkhol'd, *Stat'i*, 1:164.

137. [Vladimir Solov'ev], "Studiia: Klass Vl. N. Solov'eva, Osnovnye printsipy stsenicheskoi tekhniki improvizovannyi ital'ianskoi komedii," *LTA* 4–5 (1914): 93.

138. Ibid.

139. [Vladimir Solov'ev], "Studiia: Klass Vl. N. Solov'eva," *LTA* 1 (1914): 60.

140. Signed by Soloviev's alter ego, Volmar Luscinius.

141. [Solov'ev], "Studiia: Klass Vl. N. Solov'eva," 60–61.

142. Ibid., 61.

143. Hoover, "A Mejerxol'd Method," 27.

144. "Studiia: Programma: Tri apel'sina, astrologicheskaia truba, ili do chego mozhet dovesti liubov' k metram stseny," *LTA* 6–7 (1914): 113.

145. [Vsevolod Meierkhol'd], "Studiia: Klass Vs. E. Meierkhol'da," *LTA* 1 (1914): 62.

146. [Meierkhol'd], "Studiia: Klass Vs: E. Meierkhol'da, Tekhnika stsenicheskikh dvizheniia," 95.

147. This is an early reference to a term that became central to Meyerhold's biomechanics, which uses a sequential trio of gestures: the *otkaz*, an initial movement in the opposite direction of the main movement, the movement itself, and the *tochka*, the movement's concluding punctuation.

148. [Vsevolod Meierkhol'd and Vladimir Solov'ev], "Studiia: Klass Vs: E. Meierkhol'd i Vl. N. Solov'eva," *LTA* 4–5 (1914): 92.

149. Leach, *Vsevolod Meyerhold*, 30.

150. [Vsevolod Meierkhol'd], "Studiia Vs. Meierkhol'da (1916–1917)," *LTA* 2–3 (1916): 144.

151. Students were expected to develop an expansive knowledge base as creative fodder for their work. Topics of study included "The Role of the Balagan in the Fate of Theatrical Regeneration (Molière, Shakespeare, Hoffmann, Tieck, Pushkin, Gogol, Remizov, and Blok)"; dramatic works from the 1830s and 40s; circus; Gozzi; Spanish theater; Indian, Japanese, and Chinese staging conventions; new theatrical theories (Craig, Meyerhold, Evreinov, Komissarzhevsky, Gnesin, Dalcroze); the director and the designer in the theater; and the programs of contemporary theater schools. [Meierkhol'd], "Studiia Vs. Meierkhol'da," 145–46.

152. [Meierkhol'd], "Studiia Vs. Meierkhol'da (1916–1917)," 144.

153. Some studio actors performed in non-studio events, such as Meyerhold's 1915 productions of Blok's *Balaganchik* and *Incognita*—a journal rather than Studio event—the revival of *Columbine's Veil* at the Players' Rest, and Meyerhold's 1917 *Masquerade* at the Alexandrinsky.

154. Part 1: Cervantes's *The Cave of Salamanca*

Part 2: Études and Pantomimes

1. The Street Conjurers
2. The Story of the Page Who Was Loyal to His Master and of Other Events Suitable for Presentation
3. Two Smeraldinas
4. Tragedy of *Hamlet, Prince of Denmark*
    a. The Mousetrap
    b. Ophelia

5. Harlequin, Dealer of Slapstick Blows

Part 3: Études and Pantomimes

1. Three Oranges, An Astrological Telescope, or the Lengths to Which Love for the *Metteur en Scène* Can Go
2. Colin-Maillard
3. Two Baskets and Uncertainty over Who Hoodwinked Whom
4. Fragment of a Chinese Play "The Woman, the Cat, The Bird, and the Snake"

Titles are drawn from longer descriptions of each scene in *LTA* 6–7 (1914): 105–15.

155. "Studiia. Programma," *LTA* 6–7 (1914): 106.

156. Ibid., 113.

157. Ibid., 107.

158. Ibid., 112.

159. "'Komedianty': Vecher studii V. E. Meierkhol'da," *Petrogradskaia gazeta*, February 13, 1915. Reprinted in "Studiia," *LTA* 1–3 (1915): 148.

160. "Studiia: Programma," *LTA* 6–7 (1914): 109.

161. Sergei Iutkevich, "Doctor Dapertutto, ili sorok let spustia," in Vendrovskaia and Valentei, *Vstrechi*, 214.

162. Vickie L. Ziegler, *Bending the Frame in the German Cyclical Narrative: Achim von Arnim's "Der Wintergarten" & E. T. A. Hoffmann's "Die Serapionsbrüder"* (Washington, D.C.: Catholic University of America Press, 1991), 2.

163. There has yet to be a comprehensive study of Meyerhold's journal in English. Marjorie Hoover attempted in an article to reclaim Meyerhold's studio training as a theatricalist "Method" equal in importance to Stanislavsky's System in "A Mejerxol'd Method," 23–41. Excellent studies in other languages include L. S. Oves's annotated *Liubov' k trem apel'sinam* and Raissa Raskina's *Mejerchol'd e il Dottor Dappertutto.*

164. Some of the journal's most active participants were Meyerhold, Ignatov, Soloviev, Yakov Blokh, Konstantin Miklashevsky, Vladimir Piast, and Alexander Briansky. Znosko-Borovsky helped to edit the issue in which his play *The Steadfast Prince* appeared, and Alexander Blok briefly edited the poetry section. L. S. Oves, "Khronika zhizni zhurnala v perepiske, vospominaniiakh i arkhivnykh materialakh," in Oves, *Liubov' k trem apel'sinam*, 2:6.

165. These include Viktor and Miron Zhirmunsky, Vasily Gippius, Konstantin Vogak, Konstantin Mochulsky, Vladimir Piast, and Alexander Levinson. Raskina, *Mejerchol'd e il Dottor Dappertutto*, 21–22.

166. Ziegler, *Bending the Frame*, 3.

167. "Editorial," *LTA* 1 (1914): 3.

168. Hoover, "A Mejerxol'd Method," 25; Sergei Eizenshtein, "Iz pis'ma k Iu. I. Eizenshtein, Oktiabria 1921," in *Eizenshtein o Meierkhol'de: 1919–1948*, ed. V. V. Zabrodin (Moscow: Novoe izdatel'stvo, 2005), 85.

169. Samuil Vermel', "Moment formy v iskusstve," *LTA* 1 (1914): 15–17.

170. A planned volume of Gozzi's fiabe in Russian was advertised in the journal but never materialized, perhaps due to the paper shortage. Kuzmin revived the project in 1922 with a new journal, *The Green Bird*, which published a translation of the related fiaba. A volume of six Gozzi fiabe finally appeared in 1923. Ia. N. Blokh, M. A. Kuzmin, and A. A. Gvozdev, eds., *Zelenaia ptichka* ([Petrograd]: Petropolis, 1922); Carlo Gozzi, *Skazki dlia teatra*, trans. Ia. and R. Blokh and M. Lozinskii, intro. and ed. Ia. N. Blokh (Petrograd: Tipografiia kominterna, 1923).

171. Konstantin Miklashevskii, *La commedia dell'arte, ili teatr ital'ianskikh komediantov XVI, XVII, i XVIII stoletii* (Saint Petersburg: Sirius', 1914–17).

172. Vladimir Kniazhnin, "Hoffmaniana," *LTA* 1 (1914): 58.

173. "Khronika," *LTA* 1–3 (1915): 160.

174. Elizabeth Cheauré, *E. T. A. Hoffmann: Inszenierungen seiner Werke auf russischen Bühnen: Ein Beitrag zur Rezeptionsgeschichte* (Heidelberg: Carl Winter, 1979), 25.

175. Vladimir Kniazhnin, "Hoffmaniana II," *LTA* 2 (1914): 54.

176. Raskina, *Mejerchol'd e il Dottor Dappertutto*, 21.

177. Ibid.

178. These included a medieval season (1907–08) and a Spanish Golden Age season (1911–12). A planned commedia season never materialized. Evgenii Znosko-Borovskii, *Russkii teatr nachala XX veka* (Prague: Plamia, 1925), 333.

179. D. Filosofov, "Hoffmaniana IV: Printsessa Brambilla," *LTA* 4–7 (1915): 191–92.

180. John Bowlt, "Conjuring with Nostalgia: Alexandre Benois and the Culture of History." Plenary paper presented at the Wiggins Symposium "Dreamer and Showman: The Magical Reality of Alexandre Benois," Boston Public Library, January 28, 2006.

181. Aleksandr Benois, "Gofman na stsene," *Rech'*, May 20, 1916, 2.

182. Filosofov, "Hoffmaniana IV: Brambilla," 192.

183. Ibid.

184. Ibid., 193.

185. Ibid.

186. "Popravka," *Rech'*, November 9, 1915, 3.

187. Aleksandr Viktorovich Rykov, "Moi vstrechi s Meierkhol'dom," in Lopatin and Fomin, *Russkii krug Gofmana*, 258.

188. Vladimir Solov'ev, "Pis'mo v redaktsiiu (otvet na stat'iu G. D. Filosofova 'Printsessa Brambilla')," *Birzhevye vedomosti*, November 12, 1915, 5. Reprinted in "Hoffmaniana IV: Printsessa Brambilla." *LTA* 4–7 (1915): 196.

189. There are two reasons why Komissarzhevsky, despite this pioneering work, is not discussed in more detail in this book. While a substantial archive

of his post-emigration productions in Europe and the United States exists (at the Harvard Theatre Collection), aside from published works I have found few primary sources on his pre-1919 Hoffmaniana in Russia. More importantly, Komissarzhevsky used Hoffmann very differently than Meyerhold, Tairov, and Eisenstein did: like the World of Art group, he viewed Hoffmann as stylistically and thematically resonant, but not as a source for reinventing theatrical form—the focus of this book. Komissarzhevsky used dramatic literature or opera as the starting point for each new production and accused Meyerhold of "giving a single face to all the authors of the entire world." (F. F. Kommissarzhevskii, *Teatral'nyia prediudy* [Moscow, 1916], 8–9.) He was similarly opposed to Hoffmann's and Meyerhold's interest in metaphorical marionettes, which he viewed as autocratic and creatively limiting for actors (ibid., 15).

190. See Theodore Komisarjevsky, *Myself and the Theatre* (New York: E. P. Dutton, 1930).

191. Igor' Il'inskii, *Sam o sebe* (Moscow: Iskusstvo, 1973), 157.

192. Sergei Eizenshtein, letter to Iu. I. Eizenshtein, October 8, 1920, "Enfin m'y voici," in Zabrodin, *Eisenshtein o Meierkhol'de*, 76; Sergei Eisenstein, "Through Theater to Cinema (1934)." *Film Form: Essays in Film Theory*, ed. and trans. Jay Leyda (San Diego: Harcourt Inc., 1977), 3.

193. Clayton, *Pierrot in Petrograd*, 93.

194. Ibid., 95.

195. Vasilii Sakhnovskii, "Assambleia i Printsessa Turandot," *Maski* 2 (1912): 55. Quoted ibid., 93.

196. The brother of Vera Komissarzhevskaia, Komissarzhevsky worked under Meyerhold when the latter was a director at his sister's theater, and, after she fired Meyerhold (partly at Komissarzhevsky's suggestion), replaced him.

197. Vladimir Solov'ev, "*Turandot* Grafa Karlo Gotstsi na russkoi stsene," *LTA* 2 (1914): 48. Quoted in Clayton, *Pierrot in Petrograd*, 95.

198. Solov'ev, "*Turandot*," 48. Quoted ibid.

199. Solov'ev, "*Turandot*," 47. Quoted ibid., 94.

200. Clayton, *Pierrot in Petrograd*, 95.

201. Solov'ev, "*Turandot*," 49.

202. Raskina, *Mejerchol'd e il Dottor Dappertutto*, 20.

203. Ibid., 19.

204. S. I. Iutkevich, "Molodost'," in Lopatin and Fomin, *Russkii krug Gofmana*, 261.

205. Braun, *Meyerhold: A Revolution in Theatre*, 213.

206. See, for example, Sergei Radlov, *Desiat' let v teatre* (Leningrad: Priboi, 1929), 148.

207. V. Shershenevich, "Urozhai isteriki," *Teatral'naia Moskva* 46 (1922): 5.

208. A. A. Gvozdev, *Teatr imeni Vs. Meierkhol'da: (1920–1926)* (Leningrad: Academia, 1927), 52.

209. Codirected with Gennadi Trostianetski; coproduced with Nikolai Pesochinsky.

210. David Chambers, "The Master of Praxis," *Theater* 28, no. 2 (1998): 52.

211. Newsclipping from *Zhizn' i iskusstva*, October 5, 1926, RGALI f. 963, op. 1, ed. khr. 514: 9.

212. Mikhail Chekhov, "Postanovka 'Revizora' v Teatre imeni Meierkhol'da," in *Gogol' i Meierkhol'd: Sbornik,* ed. E. F. Nikitina (Moscow: Nikitinskie subbotniki, 1927), 84.

213. M. M. Sitkovetskaia, ed., *Meierkhol'd repetiruet*, 2 vols., vol. 1: *Spektakli 20-kh godov*, intro. M. M. Sitkovetskaia and O. M. Fel'dman (Moscow: Artist. Rezhisser. Teatr, 1993), 26.

214. Ibid., 27.

215. Leach, *Vsevolod Meyerhold*, 46.

216. Sitkovetskaia, *Meierkhol'd repetiruet*, 40.

217. Meyerhold, "Meyerhold and Music," in *Meyerhold at Work*, ed. Paul Schmidt (Manchester: Carcanet New Press, 1981), 154. Quoted in Robinson, "Love for Three Operas," 290.

218. Sitkovetskaia, *Meierkhol'd repetiruet*, 50.

219. Ibid., 29.

220. Ibid., 53.

221. At this time "general rehearsals," invited final dress rehearsals, were attended by the censor, who passed or banned the production before opening.

222. According to Meyerhold's chronometrage (run-time) reports, he combined episodes 1 and 2 and episodes 3 and 5 and inverted the order of episodes 10 and 11. See RGALI f. 963, op. 1, ed. khr. 513.

223. Sitkovetskaia, *Meierkhol'd repetiruet*, 28.

224. Nick Worrall, "Meyerhold Directs Gogol's 'Government Inspector,'" *Theatre Quarterly* 2, no. 7 (1972): 78. The translations of the *Inspector General* episode titles in my analysis draw from Worrall's invaluable essay.

225. The total depth of the mobile stage was just under 12 feet (5 *arshins*). RGALI f. 963, op. 1, ed. khr. 494: 12.

226. Sitkovetskaia, *Meierkhol'd repetiruet*, 34.

227. Ibid., 43.

228. Ibid., 34.

229. Ibid., 100.

230. Emmanual Kaplan, "Rezhisser i muzyka," Vendrovskaia and Valentei, *Vstrechi*, 337. In Meyerhold, *Meyerhold on Theatre*, 218.

231. Sitkovetskaia, *Meierkhol'd repetiruet*, 137.

232. Ibid., 33–34.

233. Ibid., 35.

234. Meyerhold's initial impulse was to mark this contrast by having the platform containing the set for the inn rise from a trap. Ibid., 42.

235. V. Piast, "'Revizor' v episodakh (Vpechatleniia s montirovochnoi repetitsii u Meierkhol'da)," *Krasnaia gazeta*, December 7, 1926, in *Meierkhol'd v russkoi teatral'noi kritike: 1920–1938*, ed. Tatiana Lanina (Moscow: Artist. Rezhisser. Teatr, 2000), 207.

236. David L. Tal'nikov, *Novaia reviziia "Revizora": Opyt literaturno-stsenicheskogo izucheniia tealtral'noi postanovki* (Moscow: Gosudarstvennoe izdatel'stvo, 1927), 40.

237. My emphasis. Zabrodin, *Eisenshtein o Meierkhol'de*, 238.

238. Sitkovetskaia, *Meierkhol'd repetiruet*, 27.

239. Ibid. For a useful description of Khlestakov's transformations, see Julia Listengarten, *Russian Tragifarce: Its Cultural and Political Roots* (Cranbury, N.J.: Associated University Presses, 2000), 37–39.

240. Meyerhold was accused of inventing this scene to showcase his spouse, yet he conceived the changing scene as early as October 1925 and cast Raikh in the role only in September 1926, nearly a year later. Ibid., 37.

241. Ibid.

242. V. Piast, "'Revizor' v episodakh," in Lanina, *Meierkhol'd v russkoi teatral'noi kritike: 1920–1938*, 206.

243. S. Vishnevetskaia, "Vsevolod Meierkhol'd i Vsevolod Vishnevskii," in Vendrovskaia and Valentei, *Vstrechi*, 401.

244. Erast Pavlovich Garin, *S Meierkhol'dom: Vospominaniia* (Moscow: Iskusstvo, 1974), 138.

245. Worrall, "Meyerhold Directs Gogol's 'Government Inspector,'" 88.

246. Sitkovetskaia, *Meierkhol'd repetiruet*, 71–72.

247. Letter from Ol'ga Bokshanskaia to Nemirovich-Danchenko, December 8, 1926, in *Pis'ma O. S. Bokshanskaia Vl. I. Nemirovichu-Danchenko*, ed. I. N. Solov'eva (Moscow: Izdatel'stvo moskoskogo Khudozhestvennogo teatra, 2005), 1:520–21, translated in *The Soviet Theater: A Documentary History*, ed. and trans. Laurence Senelick and Sergei Ostrovsky (New Haven, Conn.: Yale University Press, 2014), 263–64.

248. Sitkovetskaia, *Meierkhol'd repetiruet*, 46.

249. Ibid., 38. This interpretation was possibly inspired by Vasily Rozanov, who argued in a prerevolutionary essay that Gogol's "characters were not living people, but 'wax figures' . . . created out of a 'waxen mass of words.'" Vasilii Rozanov, "Gogol' i Pushkin," in *Legenda o velikom inkvisitore F. M. Dostoevskogo, s prilozheniem dvukh etudov o Gogole* (Saint Petersburg, 1906), 261–62, 265. Quoted in Robert A. Maguire, "Introduction: The Legacy of Criticism," in *Gogol from the Twentieth Century: Eleven Essays*, ed. Robert A. Maguire (Princeton, N.J.: Princeton University Press, 1974), 17.

250. Although the panopticon later came to be a common prison design, the first panopticon, designed in Russia in the early nineteenth century, was a factory.

On Meyerhold and cubism, see Amy Skinner, *Meyerhold and the Cubists: Perspectives on Painting and Performance* (Bristol, U.K.: Intellect, 2015).

251. Walter Benjamin, "Moscow Diary, December 19, 1926," 11, 56–58, translated in Senelick and Ostrovsky, *The Soviet Theater*, 264.

252. Walter Benjamin, "Disputation bei Meyerhold," (January 3, 1927), *Die literarische Welt*, February 11, 1927, 3. Walter Benjamin, *Gesammelte Werke*, ed. Tillman Rexroth (Frankfurt am Main: Suhrkamp Verlag, 1972) 4:481–83, translated in Senelick and Ostrovsky, *The Soviet Theater*, 268.

253. Vladimir Ivanovich Blium (1877–1941, known by the pseudonyms "Sadko" and "Tyss") is perhaps best remembered as the censor parodied in the Kamerny Theatre's production of Bulgakov's *The Crimson Island* (1928). Bulgakov's play-within-a-play satirized Soviet censorship with a barbed pen and featured a censor called "Savva Lukich," transparently Blium. Steven Richmond, "'And Who Are the Judges?' Mikhail Bulgakov versus Soviet Censorship, 1926–1936," *Russian History / Histoire Russe* 33, no. 1 (2006): 83–107.

254. This was not the only time Soviet authorities condemned theaters by purporting that their public had abandoned them. Stalin used the same argument to close the Moscow State Yiddish Theatre in 1949; the liquidation of all Soviet Yiddish theaters soon followed.

255. V. Blium, "Diskusiia o 'Revizore,'" *Zhizn' iskusstva* 4 (1927), in Lanina, *Meierkhol'd v russkoi teatral'noi kritike: 1920–1938*, 218–19.

256. Blium, "Diskusiia o 'Revizore,'" in Lanina, *Meierkhol'd v russkoi teatral'noi kritike: 1920–1938*, 221.

257. Leach, *Vsevolod Meyerhold*, 37.

258. Ibid., 40.

259. See ibid., 44 and RGALI f. 963, op. 1, ed. khr. 356.

260. Blium's emphasis. Blium, "Diskusiia o 'Revizore,'" in Lanina, *Meierkhol'd v russkoi teatral'noi kritike: 1920–1938*, 224.

261. Senelick and Ostrovsky call formalism "a catchall term, its very lack of definition enabling it to be used to scapegoat surviving left-wing artists of the 1920s." Senelick and Ostrovsky, *The Soviet Theater*, 351.

262. Actor/director/teacher Mikhail Alexandrovich Chekhov (1891–1955), who played Khlestakov in the MAT's 1921 *Inspector General*, was midway through his stint as the artistic director (1924–28) of the second Moscow Art Theatre when Meyerhold's *Inspector General* opened. Like Meyerhold, he fell under attack in the 1920s for "alien and reactionary" experiments. In 1928 he emigrated, never to return to Russia. Mel Gordon, *The Stanislavsky Technique: Russia: A Workbook for Actors* (New York: Applause Theatre and Cinema Books, 1987), 132.

263. Chekhov, "Postanovka 'Revizora,'" in Lanina, *Meierkhol'd v russkoi teatral'noi kritike: 1920–1938*, 240–42.

264. “Resolution on the Liquidation of the Vs. Meyerhold Theatre,” *Teatr* 1 (1938); *TASS* and *Pravda* (January 8, 1938); repr. in *Teatr* 1 (1990): 142, translated in Senelick and Ostrovsky, *The Soviet Theater*, 402.

265. Meyerhold, letter from prison to Soviet Premier Molotov, January 2 and 13, 1940. *Sovetskaia kultura*, February 16, 1989, 5 and *Teatral'naia zhizn'* 5 (1989): 1–3. Quoted in Edward Braun, “Vsevolod Meyerhold: The Final Act,” in *Enemies of the People: The Destruction of Soviet Literary, Theater, and Film Arts in the 1930s*, ed. Katherine Bliss Eaton (Evanston, Ill.: Northwestern University Press, 2002), 153.

266. Meyerhold's conviction was overturned on November 26, 1955, after which the “lengthy and hazardous process of artistic rehabilitation” began. Braun, *Meyerhold: A Revolution in Theatre*, 307.

CHAPTER TWO. TAIROV-CELIONATI: MIME-DRAMA AND KALEIDOSCOPIC COMMEDIA

1. Aleksandr Tairov, “Sumerki Zor,” January 17, 1921, RGALI f. 2328, op. 1, ed. khr. 22. Quoted in A. Z. Iufit, ed., *Russkii sovetskii teatr 1917–1921*, vol. 1 of *Sovetskii teatr: Dokumenty i materialy* (Leningrad: Iskusstvo, 1968), 161.

2. For a detailed account of this collaboration, see Keith Owen Tribble, “The Russian Premiere of Claudel's L'Échange,” *Paul Claudel Papers* 3, no. 1 (2005): 81–98.

3. Sheila Fitzpatrick, *The Commissariat of Enlightenment: Soviet Organization of Education and the Arts under Lunacharsky, October 1917–1921* (Cambridge: Cambridge University Press, 1970), 151.

4. From a public debate reported in *Vestnik teatra* 78–79 (1920): 16; quoted in Edward Braun, *Meyerhold: A Revolution in Theatre* (London: Methuen Drama, 1998), 161.

5. Like many in the early Soviet period, Koonen's and Tairov's was a de facto marriage.

6. Alisa G. Koonen, *Stranitsy zhizni*, 2nd ed. (Moscow: Iskusstvo, 1985), 239.

7. Tairov, “Sumerki Zor,” 9, in Iufit, *Russkii sovetskii teatr 1917–1921*, 161.

8. Aleksandr Ia. Tairov, *Proklamatsiia khudozhnika* (Moscow, 1917), 21. Private collection of Sasha Khmelnitskaia and Sergei Korobkov.

9. Fitzpatrick, *The Commissariat of Enlightenment*, 146.

10. Abram Efros, introduction to *Kamerny teatr i ego khudozhniki*, ed. Mikhail A. Zelikson (Moscow: VTO, 1934), xxx.

11. The vast archives of Tairov, Koonen, and the Kamerny Theatre at the Russian State Archive of Literature and Art have received scant attention from English-language scholars. A notable exception is Caryl Emerson's translation of the Kamerny's unrealized *Eugene Onegin* and her work on fiction writer

and Kamerny dramaturg Sigizmund Krzhizhanovsky. See Caryl Emerson, "The Krzhizhanovsky–Prokofiev Collaboration on Eugene Onegin, 1936 (A Lesser-Known Casualty of the Pushkin Death Jubilee)," in *Sergey Prokofiev and His World*, ed. Simon Morrison (Princeton, N.J.: Princeton University Press, 2008), 60–114. For Italian, German, and French studies that use these archives, see Aurora Egidio, *Aleksandr Tairov e il Kamernyj Teatr di Mosca, 1907–1922* (Rome: Bulzoni, 2005); Elizabeth Cheauré, *E. T. A. Hoffmann: Inszenierungen seiner Werke auf russischen Bühnen: Ein Beitrag zur Rezeptionsgeschichte. Beiträge zur neueren Literaturgeschichte* (Heidelberg: Carl Winter, 1979); and Claudine Amiard-Chevrel, "'Princesse Brambilla' d'après E. T. A. Hoffmann: Mise en scène de Tairov," in *Mises en scène années 20 et 30: Les voiles de la création théatrale*, ed. Denis Bablet (Paris: Centre National de la Recherche Scientifique, 1979), 127–53.

12. Nick Worrall, *Modernism to Realism on the Soviet Stage: Tairov, Vakhtangov, Okhlopkov* (Cambridge: Cambridge University Press, 1989), 19.

13. Ibid., 20.

14. Ibid., 21.

15. Pavel Markov, "O Tairove," in Aleksandr Ia. Tairov, *O teatre: Zapiski rezhissera: Stat'i, besedy, rechi, pis'ma* (Moscow: VTO, 1970), 12–13.

16. See Laurence Senelick, *Gordon Craig's Moscow Hamlet: A Reconstruction* (Westport, Conn.: Greenwood, 1982).

17. Many of Alisa Georgievna Koonen's (1889–1974) most memorable performances were in tragic roles—Salomé, Phaedre, Antigone, Joan of Arc in *St. Joan*, Abbie in *Desire under the Elms*, the Young Woman in *Machinal*—but she was equally adept in playful roles such as the Doll in Debussy's *La Boîte à joujoux* and as both twins in Charles Lecocq's comic operetta *Giroflé–Girofla*.

18. Aleksandr Tairov, "Beseda o mimodrame v Svobodnom teatre." Stat'ia o postanovke pantomimy 'Pokryvalo P'eretty' [libretto A Shnitzlera, muzyka Donani] v Svobodnom teatre, 1913. RGALI f. 2328, op. 1, ed. khr. 309: 1.

19. Ibid., 1–2.

20. Tairov, "Beseda o mimodrame," 2 verso.

21. Aleksandr Tairov, "Pis'mo v redaktsiiu *Teatral'noi gazety*," RGALI f. 2328, op. 1, ed. khr. 5: 3–4. Quoted in Vadim Shcherbakov, "Pokryvalo P'eretty," in *Rezhisserskoe iskusstvo A. Ia. Tairova*, ed. Konstantin Rudnitskii (Moscow: VTO, 1987), 86.

22. "Pantomima 'Pokryvalo P'eretty,'" v 3-kh deistviiax, libretto A. Shnitslera, muzuka E. Donani. Klavir i libretto v russkom perevode. Postavlena A. Ia. Tairovym v Svobodnom teatre, khudozhnik A. A. Arapov. RGALI f. 2328, op. 1, ed. khr. 311. The libretto and score are under the same call number. Handwritten in Russian on the first page of the score: "Alisa Koonen, November 4, 1913 (1st performance); April 16, 1914 (45th performance).

23. Tairov, "Pis'mo v redaktsiiu." Quoted in Shcherbakov, "Pokryvalo P'eretty," 86.

24. Koonen, *Stranitsy zhizni*, 177.

25. Ibid., 178.

26. Ibid., 177.

27. Ibid., 179.

28. See Alisa Koonen, "Tetradi s zapisiami mizanstsen spektaklia Svobodnogo teatra 'Pokryvalo P'eretty,'" RGALI f. 2768, op. 1, ed. khr. 108: 1–14.

29. The recent publication of several of Koonen's diaries, many pages of which she mutilated, makes it clear that her memoirs also suffer from substantial self-censorship. Even so, her production descriptions remain a uniquely invaluable source of information. See Alisa G. Koonen, *Tri tetradki Alisy Koonen*, ed. V P. Nechaev, A. S. Shulenina, and A. Zaslavskaia (Moscow: Navona, 2013); and Alisa Koonen, "'Ia—ne Ermolova, ne Rashel': Ia, pozhalui–sovremennaia Adrienna Lekuvrer.' Dnevniki A. G. Koonen 1914–1925," in *Mnemozina: Dokumenty i fakty otechestvennogo teatra XX veka*, ed. Vladislav V. Ivanov, vol. 5 (Moscow: Indrik, 2014).

30. Koonen, *Stranitsy zhizni*, 180.

31. Ibid., 180–81.

32. Ibid., 176–77.

33. Ibid., 182.

34. Ibid., 175.

35. Iu. C. V., "V mire masok (Na vcherashnei general'noi repetitsii v Svobodnom teatre)," *Rul'* (n. d.), RGALI f. 2328, op. 1, ed. khr. 313: 4–6. Page numbers in the following few endnotes correspond to RGALI's handwritten notations on *Pierrette's Veil* newsclippings collected in a scrapbook rather than to page numbers in the original periodicals.

36. A. A. Ch., "Pokryvalo P'eretty (Na general'noi)," *Moskovskaia gazeta* (n. d.), RGALI f. 2328, op. 1, ed. khr. 313: 1–3.

37. Sergei Mamontov, "Pokryvalo P'eretty," *Russkoe slovo* (n. d.), RGALI f. 2328, op. 1, ed. khr. 313: 52–56.

38. "Pokryvalo P'eretty: Pantomima v 3 deistv: Artura Schnitzlera s muzyk. E. Donani i prologom Iu. Baltrushaitisa," *Teatr: Gazeta s programmami i libretto vsekh moskovskikh teatrov* 1379 (1913): 38. National Library of Russia: RU\NLR\DRG\5615 РНБ: Газ.1-М/1–131.

39. Aleks. Struve, "'Pokryvalo P'eretty' v Svobodnom teatre" (periodical unknown. n. d.), RGALI f. 2328, op. 1, ed. khr. 313: 46–47.

40. Iu. Engel, "Pokryvalo P'eretty (Svobodnyi teatr)," *Russkiya vedomosti* (n. d.), RGALI f. 2328, op. 1, ed. khr. 313: 11–18.

41. Mamontov, "Pokryvalo P'eretty."

42. V., "V mire masok."

43. Ibid.

44. M. M. Bonch-Tomashevskii, "Pantomima A. Shnitslera v Svobodnom teatre," *Maski* 2, no. 22 (1913–14): 50.

45. J. Douglas Clayton, *Pierrot in Petrograd: The Commedia dell'Arte/Balagan in Twentieth-Century Russian Theatre and Drama* (Montreal: McGill-Queen's University Press, 1993), 98.

46. Engel, "Pokryvalo P'eretty."

47. Bornyi, "'Pokryvalo P'eretty' v "Svobodnom teatre,'" *Akter* (n. d.), RGALI f. 2328, op. 1, ed. khr. 313: 89–100.

48. M. Nir., "Pokryvalo P'eretty: Na general'noi repetitsii v Svobodnom teatre" (periodical unknown, n. d.), RGALI f. 2328, op. 1, ed. khr. 313: 19–20.

49. Bonch-Tomashevsky's article also notes that Fedor Komissarzhevsky staged Schnitzler's pantomime in the Russian provinces.

50. Bonch-Tomashevskii, "Pantomima Shnitslera," 56.

51. Ibid., 55.

52. Ibid., 56.

53. Ibid., 49.

54. Koonen, *Stranitsy zhizni*, 228.

55. Ibid.

56. Worrall, *Modernism to Realism*, 23.

57. Ibid., 24.

58. Ibid.

59. Koonen, *Stranitsy zhizni*, 203.

60. Alexander Tairov, *Notes of a Director* (Coral Gables, Fla.: University of Miami Press, 1969), 64.

61. Worrall, *Modernism to Realism*, 25.

62. Ibid.

63. Many directors of Tairov's day used stage architecture to complement the actors' movement. One famous example is Adolphe Appia's "Rhythmic Spaces," a series of twenty designs Appia created for Émile Jaques-Dalcroze to investigate the relationship between space, time, music, and movement. See Mahmoud Hammam Abdel-Latif, "Rhythmic Space and Rhythmic Movement: The Adolphe Appia/ Jaques-Dalcroze Collaboration" (Ph.D. diss., Ohio State University, 1988).

64. Worrall, *Modernism to Realism*, 15.

65. Koonen worked with Craig on *Hamlet* at the Moscow Art Theatre; Craig called her "my ideal Ophelia," though, to Craig's disappointment, she did not play Ophelia in the final production. (Senelick, *Gordon Craig's Moscow Hamlet,* 22n31.) While Koonen and Tairov were sympathetic to Craig's innovations, Tairov felt that Craig's approach limited actors' freedom instead of providing them with creative skills.

66. Meyerhold wrote, "Only an amateur, desiring to become an acrobat, is able to achieve the techniques of the balletic arts in his acting. With an acro-

bat, juggler, boxer, or fencer, how is it possible for such false, affected poses to arise . . . or the endless rushing about, and the wrists tracing circles and ellipses along planes which are invisible, but imagined by these 'Kamerniks' in their 'atmosphere.' And . . . the flits about the stage by these forever elegant . . . dandies . . . even when it seemed that what would be appropriate would be the crudest acting techniques of American eccentrics." Vsevolod E. Meierkhol'd, "Vs. Meierkhol'd o Tairove," *Teatral'naia Moskva* 33 (1922): 14.

67. Aleksandr Ia. Tairov, "*Printsessa Brambilla.*" Stenograph of A. Ia. Tairov's lecture on the production delivered at the Kamerny, May 31, 1920, RGALI, f. 2328, op. 1, ed. khr. 375, 1–26, in *Russkii sovetskii teatr 1917–1921*, ed. A. Z. Iufit, vol. 1 of *Sovetskii teatr: Dokumenty i materialy* (Leningrad: Iskusstvo, 1968), 173. Hereafter, "*Princess Brambilla* stenograph."

68. Koonen, *Stranitsy zhizni*, 236.

69. Emerson, "The Krzhizhanovsky–Prokofiev Collaboration," 109.

70. The following discussion of *Princess Brambilla* is developed from my article "Performance as Polemic: Tairov's 1920 *Princess Brambilla* at the Moscow Kamerny Theatre," published in *Theatre Survey* 51, no. 1 (May 2010). Copyright © 2010, The American Society for Theatre Research, Inc. Reprinted with the permission of Cambridge University Press.

71. Tairov, "*Printsessa Brambilla* stenograph," 168–69.

72. Ibid., 169.

73. Ibid.

74. Worrall, *Modernism to Realism*, 3.

75. Tairov, *Notes of a Director*, 65. Tairov's emphasis.

76. Sergei S. Ignatov, "Kaprichio E. T. A. Gofmana," *Kul'tura teatra* 4 (1921): 54. Celionati is misspelled in Ignatov's original.

77. "Kamernyi teatr: *Printsessa Brambilla*," *Vestnik teatra* 64 (1920): 10.

78. Thomas Joseph Torda, "Tairov's *Princess Brambilla*: A Fantastic, Phantasmagoric 'Capriccio' at the Moscow Kamerny Theatre," *Theatre Journal* 32 (1980): 488–98; Worrall, *Modernism to Realism*; Clayton, *Pierrot in Petrograd*.

79. Tairov, *Notes of a Director*, 97. Tairov's emphasis.

80. Aleksandr Tairov, *Zapiski rezhissera* (Moscow: Izdatel'stvo Kamernogo teatra, Pervaaia Obraztsovaia tipografiia MSNKh, Piatnitskaia 71, 1921), 148, quoted in Torda, "Tairov's *Princess Brambilla*," 490.

81. The Kamerny's stage versions of *The Man Who Was Thursday*, *Egyptian Nights*, and *Eugene Onegin* were written by Sigizmund Dominikovich Krzhizhanovsky (1887–1950), the Kamerny's dramaturg, more widely known now as the brilliant writer of phantasmagorical fiction whose works began to be published in 1989.

82. Tairov, *O teatre: Zapiski rezhissera*, 148.

83. K. P., "Kamernyi teatr i Gofman," *Zritel'*, March 6, 1923, 3.

84. Tairov, "*Printsessa Brambilla* stenograph," 172.

85. Koonen, *Stranitsy zhizni*, 249.

86. L. Krasovskii and P. Antokol'skii, "Printsessa Brambilla" (1920), typed libretto to the capriccio, RGALI f. 2030, op. 1, ed. khr. 250. It is likely that this was the composer's copy: there are handwritten musical cues, and portions of the dialogue have handwritten punctuation that emphasizes rhythmical speech. The VTO version, stamped 1945, was published later in a parallel Russian–German version by Elisabeth Cheauré. For the original of this latter, see L. Krasovskii and P. Antokol'skii, "'Printsessa Brambilla': Kaprichchio v 4 deistviakh; Tekst po Gofmanu Krasovskogo i Antokol'skogo" (1920), 71 pp., stamped 1945, call number III-H/П–76, Central Scientific Library of the Russian Theatre Workers' Union (STD, formerly VTO), Moscow.

87. Tairov, "*Printsessa Brambilla* stenograph," 172.

88. Act 2, tableau 1, scene 4, RGALI promptbook, 23. All quotations are from this version of the text. In a very few cases, if lines in the RGALI promptbook are illegible, and I am able to determine that these lines are identical in the VTO text, I substitute accordingly.

89. Act 2, tableau 1, scene 3, 19. In order to convey how the *Brambilla* promptbook text evolved, I indicate any handwritten changes to the typescript with angled brackets and stage directions with italics within parentheses.

90. Act 2, tableau 1, scene 3, 21.

91. Act 2, tableau 1, scene 3, 20.

92. Act 4, tableau 7, scene 10, 68.

93. Act 2, tableau 1, scene 8, 25. This description is crossed out in the RGALI promptbook but is very similar to photographic depictions of Giglio in the production.

94. This scene is cut in the VTO text. Act 3, tableau 5, scene 1, RGALI promptbook, 46.

95. Act 3, tableau 5, scene 3, 50.

96. Tairov, *Notes of a Director*, 124.

97. Ibid., 125.

98. Act 3, tableau 6, scene 5, 55–56.

99. Tairov, *Notes of a Director*, 68.

100. Tairov, "*Printsessa Brambilla* stenograph," 173.

101. Efros, introduction to *Kamernyi teatr i ego khudozhniki*, xxx.

102. Tairov, "*Printsessa Brambilla* stenograph," 173.

103. Ibid., 172.

104. Torda, "Tairov's *Princess Brambilla*," 493.

105. Konstantin Rudnitsky, *Russian and Soviet Theater 1905–1932*, ed. Lesley Milne, trans. Roxane Permar (New York: Harry N. Abrams, 1988), 47, 105.

106. "Iakulov," in *Teatral'naia entsiklopediia*, ed. P. A. Markov, vol. 5 (Moscow: Sovetskaia entsiklopediia, 1961–67), 1087.

107. S. S. Ignatov, "*Printsessa Brambilla* v moskovskom Kamernom teatre," typed manuscript with handwritten corrections, RGALI f. 2328, op. 1, ed. khr. 380: 13–14.

108. Georgii B. Iakulov, "Po povodu 'Printsessy Brambilly' (Beseda s G. B. Iakulovym)," *Vestnik teatra* 65 (1920): 12.

109. Efros, introduction to *Kamernyi teatr i ego khudozhniki*, xxxi. Yakulov avoided being associated with one artistic movement, but according to Bowlt, he "derived much of his strength" from cubism, futurism, and constructivism. John E. Bowlt, "The Construction of Caprice: The Russian Avant-Garde Onstage," in *Theatre in Revolution: Russian Avant-Garde Stage Design, 1913–1935*, ed. Nancy Van Norman Baer (New York: Thames and Hudson, 1991), 66.

110. Samiul Margolin, *Khudozhnik teatra za 15 let* (Moscow: OGIZ, Gosudarstvennoe Izdatel'stvo izobratitel'nykh iskusstv, 1933), 49; quoted in Torda, "Tairov's *Princess Brambilla*," 495.

111. Torda, "Tairov's *Princess Brambilla*," 492.

112. Florence Gilliam, "The Kamerny Theatre of Moscow," *Freeman* 7 (1923): 256.

113. Ibid.

114. Konstantin Derzhavin, *Kniga o Kamernom teatre 1914–1934* (Leningrad: Khudozhestvennaia literatura, 1934), 99.

115. Iufit, *Russkii sovetskii teatr 1917–1921*, 175. Quoted in Torda, "Tairov's *Princess Brambilla*," 493.

116. Nikolai Ivanovich Bykov, "Pervaia vstrecha s Kamernym teatrom," 17, A. A. Bakhrushin State Central Theatre Museum, Manuscript Division, f. 526, ed. khr. 135.

117. Vladimir Nikolaevich Sokolov (1889–1962, Sokoloff in emigration): actor and puppeteer who performed with Reinhardt and in Hollywood films after leaving Russia. He gave solo marionette performances on Kamerny tours, specializing in "short musical and *commedia dell'arte* items." Henryk Jurkowski, *The Twentieth Century*, ed. in collaboration with Penny Francis, vol. 2 of *A History of European Puppetry* (Lewiston, N.Y.: Edwin Mellen, 1998), 32.

118. Worrall, *Modernism to Realism*, 33.

119. Bykov, "Pervaia vstrecha," 13.

120. Ignatov, "*Printsessa Brambilla* v moskovskom Kamernom," 9.

121. Koonen also uses the word "grotesque" to describe the performance of Celionati and the tailor Bescapi. In Tairov's case, this refers more to an external heightening of character and emotion through exaggeration than to a Hoffmannian or Meyerholdian grotesque. See Alisa G. Koonen, "Vospominaniia: Kamernyi teatr v pervye gody revoliutsii," in Iufit, *Russkii sovetskii teatr 1917–1921*, 166.

122. Ignatov, "*Printsessa Brambilla* v moskovskom Kamernom," 15.

123. Derzhavin, *Kniga o Kamernom*, 99. Derzhavin likely uses the word *cabotinage* after Meyerhold's *cabotin* (histrion, strolling player). See Vsevolod Meyerhold, "The Fairground Booth," in *Meyerhold on Theatre*, ed. Edward Braun (London: Bloomsbury Methuen Drama, 1998), 119–42.

124. For a scene-by-scene summary (in French) of the RGALI *Brambilla* promptbook, see Amiard-Chevrel, "Princesse Brambilla," 132–36.

125. Bykov, "Pervaia vstrecha," 18.

126. Tairov, "*Printsessa Brambilla* stenograph," 171.

127. Act 2, tableau 2, scene 5, 36. In both the RGALI and VTO texts, Harlequin and Columbine are in love but are thwarted by Columbine's father, Pantalone, who has other suitors for her. After a series of adventures, the pantomime (in the written version) concludes with a pageant that features a magician in a tulip.

128. Summarized from Cheauré, *E. T. A. Hoffmann*, 67. Her source is A. A. Rumnev, *O pantomime, teatre, kino* (Moscow: Iskusstvo, 1964), 146ff.

129. Worrall, *Modernism to Realism*, 33.

130. Rumnev, *O pantomime*, 146. Quoted in Cheauré, *E. T. A. Hoffmann*, 68.

131. Tairov, "*Printsessa Brambilla* stenograph," 171.

132. Act 4, tableau 8, scene 2, 70.

133. Koonen, *Stranitsy zhizni*, 253.

134. Pavel Markov, "O Gofmane: K spektakle *Printsessa Brambilla*," in *O teatre*, vol. 4: *Dnevnik teatral'nogo kritika 1930–1976* (Moscow: Iskusstvo, 1977), 63.

135. Tairov, "*Printsessa Brambilla* stenograph," 173.

136. Viktor M. Zhirmunskii, "Komediia chistoi radosti (*Kot v sapogakh*, Liudviga Tika. 1797 g.)," *LTA* 1 (1916): 86. Quoted in Clayton, *Pierrot in Petrograd*, 60.

137. Tairov, "*Printsessa Brambilla* stenograph," 173.

138. Worrall, *Modernism to Realism*, 34.

139. J. N. Westwood, *Endurance and Endeavour: Russian History 1812–2001*, 5th ed. (Oxford: Oxford University Press, 2002), 280–81.

140. Bykov, "Pervaia vstrecha," 24–25.

141. "Prologue," RGALI promptbook, 2–3.

142. See Koonen, *Stranitsy zhizni*, 217.

143. Ibid.

144. Bykov, "Pervaia vstrecha," 20.

145. Fitzpatrick, *The Commissariat of Enlightenment*, 146.

146. Aleksandr Tairov, "Iz stenogrammy disputa o sovremennom teatre," November 16, 1924, RGALI f. 279, op. 1, ed. khr. 33, in *Russkii sovetskii teatr 1921–1926*, ed. A. Z. Iufit, vol. 2 of *Sovetskii teatr: Dokumenty i materialy* (Leningrad: Iskusstvo, 1975), 253.

147. Koonen, *Stranitsy zhizni*, 247.

148. Tairov, *Notes of a Director*, 143.

149. Vladimir Sokolov, "Signor Formica," director's copy, typed with corrections, 1922, 86 pp., RGALI, f. 2030, op. 1, ed. khr. 303.

150. O. Blium, "Kriticheskie zametki: *Sin'or Formica*," *Ermitazh* 6 (1922): 7.

151. V. Shershenevich, "Urozhai isteriki," *Teatral'naia Moskva* 46 (1922): 5.

152. Uriel', "Nazad ot Brambilly (Dnevnik retsenzenta)," *Teatral'naia Moskva* (1922): 12. The "House of Shchepkin" was a nickname for the Maly Theatre, where Mikhail Shchepkin (1788–1863) famously performed.

153. Efros, introduction to *Kamernyi teatr i ego khudozhniki*, xxxi.

154. Worrall, *Modernism to Realism*, 37.

155. Ibid., 40.

156. Ibid., 33.

157. Russian translation by Pavel Zenkovich and Natalia Krymova.

158. Alisa G. Koonen, "Stranitsy iz zhizni," *Teatr i muzika* 3 (1968): 91. Quoted in Thomas Joseph Torda, "Alexander Tairov and the Scenic Artists of the Moscow Kamerny Theater, 1914–1935" (Ph.D. diss., University of Denver, 1977), 481.

159. Pavel A. Markov, *The Soviet Theatre* (London: Victor Gollancz, 1934), 99–100.

160. Prikaz Komiteta po delam iskuustva pri Sovete Ministerov SSSR o proizvodstvennogo-tvorcheskoi rabote moskovskogo gosudarstvennogo Kamernogo teatra za no. 408, May 27, 1949, A. A. Bakhrushin State Central Theatre Museum, Manuscript Division f. 528, ed. khr. 195.

161. Tairov describes the sequence of events leading to their forced retirement in detail in a letter to Mikhail Andreevich Suslov, March 1950. Autograph and typescript RGALI f. 2328, op. 1, ed. khr. 741: 18–20. Excerpts from this letter are translated in *The Soviet Theater: A Documentary History*, trans. and ed. Laurence Senelick and Sergei Ostrovsky (New Haven, Conn.: Yale University Press, 2014), 502–6.

162. Torda, "Alexander Tairov and the Scenic Artists of the Moscow Kamerny Theater," 651–52.

163. See Egidio, *Aleksandr Tairov e il Kamernyj Teatr di Mosca, 1907–1922*; and Dasha Krijanskaia, "The Directing System of Alexander Tairov" (Ph.D. diss., Utrecht University, 2002).

164. Dasha Krijanskaia, "Alexander Tairov (1885–1950)," in *Fifty Key Theatre Directors*, ed. Shomit Mitter and Maria Shevtsova (London: Routledge, 2005), 37.

165. Worrall, *Modernism to Realism*, 16.

CHAPTER THREE. PEREGRINUS TYSS MEETS PIPIFAX: EISENSTEIN, THE GROTESQUE, AND THE ATTRACTION

1. Edward Braun, *Meyerhold: A Revolution in Theatre* (London: Methuen Drama, 1998), 185.

2. Mikhail Zharov, *Zhizn', teatr, kino: Vospominaniia* (Moscow: Iskusstvo, 1967), 174, in *Eizenshtein: Popytka teatra*, ed. Vladimir Zabrodin (Moscow: Eizenshtein-tsentr, 2005), 202.

3. Quoted from Raikh's original 1922 note to Eisenstein, RGALI f. 1923, op. 1, ed. khr. 2062: 1–2. For a slightly different version, see Sergei Eizenshtein, *Memuary*, vol. 1: *Wie sag' ich's meinen Kinde?!* (Moscow: Trud, Muzei kino, 1997), 391.

4. J. Douglas Clayton, *Pierrot in Petrograd: The Commedia dell'Arte/Balagan in Twentieth-Century Russian Theatre and Drama* (Montreal: McGill-Queen's University Press, 1993), 209.

5. David Bordwell, *The Cinema of Eisenstein* (London: Routledge, 2005), 4.

6. Naum Kleiman, "Arguments and Ancestors," in *Eisenstein Rediscovered*, ed. Ian Christie and Richard Taylor (London: Routledge, 1993), 35.

7. Grigorii Kozintsov [Kozintsev], "AB!" in *Ekstsentrizm*, by Grigorii Kozintsov, Georgii Kryzhitskii, Leonid Trauberg, and Sergei Iutkevich (Petrograd: Ekstsentropolis, 1922), 4.

8. Ted Perry, introduction to *Eisenstein at Work*, ed. Jay Ledya and Zina Voynow (New York: Pantheon Books, 1982), vii.

9. Jay Leyda and Zina Voynow, eds., *Eisenstein at Work* (New York: Pantheon Books, 1982), 35.

10. Perry, introduction to *Eisenstein at Work*, xiii.

11. For a notable exception, see Clayton, *Pierrot in Petrograd*, 205–28.

12. Sergei Eisenstein, "Through Theater to Cinema (1934)," in *Film Form: Essays in Film Theory*, ed. and trans. Jay Leyda (San Diego: Harcourt Inc., 1977), 3.

13. M. K. Ivanova and Vladislav V. Ivanov, introduction to "Teatral'nye tetradi S. M. Eizenshteina," in *Mnemozina: Dokumenty i fakty iz istorii otechestvennogo teatra XX veka*, ed. Vladislav V. Ivanov, vol. 2 (Moscow: URSS, 2006), 190.

14. Perry, introduction, vii.

15. See Vladimir Zabrodin, ed., *Eisenshtein o Meierkhol'de, 1919–1948* (Moscow: Novoe izdatel'stvo, 2005); Zabrodin, *Eizenshtein: Popytka teatra*; Ivanov, *Mnemozina*, vols. 2 and 4; Vadim Shcherbakov, "Eizenshtein i Iutkevich peresozdaiut shedevr mastera," in *Meierkhol'd i drugie: Dokumenty i materialy*, edited by O.M. Fel'dman. vol. 2 of *Meierkhol'dovskii sbornik* (Moscow: OGI, 2000). In English, Leach, Worrall, Gerould, and others have written case studies of Eisenstein stage productions, including *The Mexican, Tarelkin's Death, Wiseman, Do You Hear, Moscow?* and *Gas Masks*, but Eisenstein's theatrical ruminations extend well beyond this handful of shows. Ledya and Voynow provide a chronological list of over a hundred projects, most unrealized, in *Eisenstein at Work*.

16. Jean Narboni, "Introduction to *Poetika Kino*," trans. Rosamund Mulvey, in *Futurism / Formalism / FEKS: Eccentrism and Soviet Cinema, 1918–36*, ed. Ian Christie and John Gillett Christie (London: British Film Institute, 1978), 59.

17. Sergei Eizenshtein, ". . . Enfin m'y voici," in Zabrodin, *Eisenshtein o Meierkhol'de*, 78.

18. Pavel Muratov, *Obrazy Italii* (Moscow: Nauchnoe slovo, 1912).

19. Vernon Lee, *Studies of the Eighteenth Century in Italy* (London: T. Fisher Unwin, 1887).

20. Konstantin Miklashevskii, *La commedia dell'arte, ili teatr ital'ianskikh komediantov XVI, XVII, i XVIII stoletii* (Saint Petersburg: Sirius', 1914–17).

21. Vladimir N. Peretts, *Italianskiia komedii i intermedii predstavlennyia pri dvorie imperatritsy Anny Ioannovny v 1733–1735* (Petrograd: Imperatorskaia Akademiia Nauk, 1917).

22. Eizenshtein, ". . . Enfin m'y voici," in Zabrodin, *Eisenshtein o Meierkhol'de*, 78.

23. James Goodwin, *Eisenstein, Cinema and History* (Urbana: University of Illinois Press, 1993), 20.

24. RGALI f. 1923, op. 1, ed. khr. 696 and op. 2, ed. khr. 1588.

25. The full names of the individuals and works Eisenstein mentions are Edward Gordon Craig, Nikolai Evreinov's *Theatre for Oneself*, Ludwig Tieck, E. T. A. Hoffmann, Karl Immermann, and Robert Browning. Eizenshtein, ". . . Enfin m'y voici," in Zabrodin, *Eisenshtein o Meierkhol'de*, 78.

26. These playwrights include, among others, Gozzi, Molière, Hauptmann, Aristophanes, Maeterlinck, Ibsen, Cervantes, Johnson, Strindberg, Gogol, Terence, Sologub, Lunacharsky, Tolstoy, Lothar, Sheridan, Shakespeare, Ostrovsky, Andreev, Benavente, and Zola.

27. RGALI f. 1923, op. 1, ed. khr. 815 and f. 1923, op. 2 ed. khr. 1600.

28. Arkadii Timofeevich Avarchenko, *Dvoinik* (Petrograd: Novyi satirikon, 1916). The play's full text is available online: http://az.lib.ru/a/awerchenko_a_t/text_1916_dvoynik_oldorfo.shtml.

29. Zabrodin, *Eizenshtein: Popytka teatra*, 66. See also RGALI 1923, op. 1, ed. khr. 780: 2.

30. RGALI f. 1923, op. 1, ed. khr. 736.

31. Zabrodin, *Eisenshtein o Meierkhol'de*, 86.

32. Ibid., 289.

33. Zabrodin, *Eizenshtein: Popytka teatra*, 105.

34. E. T. A. Hoffmann, "Master Flea," in *The Golden Pot and Other Tales*, trans. and ed. Ritchie Robertson (Oxford: Oxford University Press, 2000), 246–47.

35. Ivanov, *Mnemozina*, 2:191.

36. Eisenstein's 1917–1919 drawings include designs for at least two other works from Peretts's *Italianskiia komedii* collection: *Zabavy na vode i na pole* (*Amusements on the Water and in a Field*) and *Chetyre Arlekina* (*Four Harlequins*).

37. All commedia drawings discussed here are from RGALI f. 1923, op. 1, ed. khr. 698.

38. It is possible that Eisenstein's design acknowledges the 1670 painting attributed to Verio, *Farceurs français et italiens du Théâtre-Royal*, which contains a balcony figure looking down on Molière and Comédie-Italienne players.

39. RGALI f. 1923, op. 2. ed. khr. 1098.

40. Sergei Eizenshtein, journal entry from September 5, 1919; in V. V. Zabrodin, ed., "'Vse velikoe prosto': S. M. Eizenshtein o teatre, 1919–1923," in Ivanov, *Mnemozina*, 4:439–40. See also RGALI f. 1923, op. 1, ed. khr. 888: 122–25 verso.

41. *Tales of Hoffmann,* staged by opera director Yosef Mikhailovich Lapitsky (1876–1944), opened March 21, 1916 (remounted 1922) at the Theatre of Musical Drama, Petrograd. Initially, Eisenstein only daydreamed of replacing Lapitsky's production. His interest in Offenbach's opera was likely rekindled by excitement that he was to study with Meyerhold: he completed the final costume designs for *Tales* in Moscow in September 1921 just after he began studying at Meyerhold's workshops.

42. Although the opera is written in three acts, a prologue, and an epilogue, it sometimes is referred to as having five acts. In such cases, the Olimpia act is act 2. Eisenstein refers to it as act 2 on his designs. For reviews of the production, see N. Malkov, "Skazki Gofmana Zh. Offenbakha," *Teatr i iskusstvo* 13 (1916), A. A. Bakhrushin State Central Theatre Museum, Manuscript Division. f. 384, ed. khr. 115, typescript, 3 pp.; and V. Bazilevskii, "Petrogradskie Etiudy," *Rampa i zhizn'* 14 (1916), A. A. Bakhrushin State Central Theatre Museum, Manuscript Division. f. 384, ed. khr. 116, typescript, 2 pp.

43. Sergei Eisenstein, "Iz 'Zametok kasatel'no teatra,' June 13, [1919], in Zabrodin, *Eisenshtein o Meierkhol'de*, 23.

44. I. Petrovskaia and V. Somina, *Teatral'nyi Peterburg: Nachalo XVIII veka–oktiabr' 1917 goda* (Saint Petersburg: Kulturnaia initsiativa, 1994), 319.

45. Some reviewers lauded Lapitsky's staging choice; one wrote: "Excellent scenery, stylish costumes, an interesting resolution of difficult directorial questions (for example, in *Tales of Hoffmann* the guests in the scene with Olimpia are all dolls like she is—this is very clever)." (Anatolii Konkarovich, "Pis'mo iz Petrograda," *Rampa i zhizn'*, 21 [May 21, 1917]: 11.) Alexandre Benois, however, saw the dolls as a cheap trick: "They say this was done to strengthen the nightmarish impression, and indeed, the whole administration of the Musical Drama will henceforth seem to me like a nightmarish assortment of people very far from art." (Aleksandr Benois, "Gofman na stsene," *Rech'*, May 20, 1916, 2.)

46. Zabrodin, *Eisenshtein o Meierkhol'de*, 24.

47. RGALI f. 1923, op. 1, ed. khr. 735: 14. Digital images of all twenty-five of Eisenstein's scene and costume designs for *Tales of Hoffmann* can be viewed on the Russian State Archive of Literature and Art website using the following durable URL: http://rgali.ru/object/201225249.

48. Eisenstein, "Iz 'Zametok,'" in Zabrodin, *Eisenshtein o Meierkhol'de*, 24.

49. Ibid.

50. Ibid. This idea may have been sparked by the MAT's 1907 production of Andreev's *Life of Man*, designed in black velvet with white outlines for contrast. See Nick Worrall, *The Moscow Art Theatre* (London: Routledge, 1996), 170.

51. Zabrodin, *Eizenshtein: Popytka teatra*, 84–85.

52. Ibid., 84.

53. Leyda and Voynow, *Eisenstein at Work*, 9.

54. Zabrodin, *Eizenshtein: Popytka teatra*, 101.

55. Sergei Eisenstein, "Through Theater to Cinema," *Film Form: Essays in Film Theory*, trans. and ed. Jay Leyda (San Diego: Harcourt, Brace, Jovanovich, 1977), 7.

56. Zabrodin, *Eizenshtein: Popytka teatra*, 101.

57. Ibid.

58. Sergei Cherkasskii, *Valentin Smyshliaev: Akter, rezhisser, pedagog* (Saint Petersburg: Sankt-Peterburgskaia gosudarstvennaia akademiia teatral'nogo iskusstva, 2004), 16.

59. RGALI f. 1923, op. 1, ed. khr. 1549: 71–72 verso; in Andrei Nikitin, *Moskovskii debiut Sergeia Eizenshteina (1920–1921)* (Moscow: Intergraf Servis, 1996), 94.

60. Zabrodin, *Eizenshtein: Popytka teatra*, 99.

61. Sergei Eizenshtein, director's remarks for the production of the comedy *Master Martin the Cooper*. RGALI f. 1923, op. 1, ed. khr. 796: 2 verso.

62. Ibid., 3 verso.

63. Ibid., 3.

64. Ibid., 2.

65. RGALI f. 1923, op. 1, ed. khr. 796. Digital images of Eisenstein's *Master Martin* sketches can be viewed on the Russian State Archive of Literature and Art website using the following durable URL: http://rgali.ru/object/201225740. See especially nos. 7 and 9.

66. Eizenshtein, director's remarks for *Master Martin*, 3.

67. Ibid., 1 verso.

68. Ibid., 1 verso.

69. Ibid., 3.

70. French: "from above."

71. Eizenshtein, director's remarks for *Master Martin*, 2 verso.

72. "Khronika: Teatr Proletkul'ta," in *Ekran: Vestnik teatra, iskusstva, kino, sporta* 12 (December 6–8, 1921): 12.

73. RGALI f. 1923, op. 2, ed. khr. 1611.

74. RGALI f. 1923, op. 1, ed. khr. 1549: 71–72 verso; in Nikitin, *Moskovskii debiut*, 94.

75. "Iz pisem S. M. Eizenshteina k Iu. I. Eizenshtein," December 31, 1920, in Lopatin and Fomin, *Russkii krug Gofmana*, 375.

76. Nikitin, *Moskovskii debiut*, 95.

77. Ibid., 202.

78. See Lopatin and Fomin, *Russkii krug Gofmana*, 379–81 for transcriptions of these petitions. For the originals, see RGALI f. 1990, op 1, ed. khr. 81: 15; ed. khr. 85: 24; ed. khr. 86: 37, 40; ed. khr. 59: 160.

79. Nikitin, *Moskovskii debiut*, 202.

80. Ibid., 95.

81. Sergei Eizenshtein, "From a Lecture at VGIKe, 31 December 1935," in Zabrodin, *Eisenshtein o Meierkhol'de*, 230–31.

82. Ibid., 231.

83. Sergei I. Iutkevich, "Nachalo puti," in *Eizenshtein v vospominaniakh sovremennikov*, ed. R. N. Iurnev (Moscow: Iskusstvo, 1974), 100.

84. This school, which housed multiple workshops, changed names several times, merged with or split off from other organizations, and finally "stabilized as GEKTEMAS ('State Experimental Theatre Workshop in the name of Meyerhold')" in the mid-1920s. (Robert Leach, *Makers of Modern Theatre* [London: Routledge, 2004], 63.) Meyerhold's workshops became the foundation for today's GITIS.

85. Erast Pavlovich Garin, *S Meierkhol'dom: Vospominaniia* (Moscow: Iskusstvo, 1974), 27.

86. Leach, *Vsevolod Meyerhold*, 121.

87. Garin, *S Meierkhol'dom*, 26.

88. Sergei Iosifovich Yutkevich (also Iutkevich, 1904–1985): Soviet director, one of the founders of the Factory of the Eccentric Actor. After studying with Meyerhold (1921–23), he became a filmmaker, known best for films about Lenin, for his work as head of the Soviet children's film agency, and for a short reconstruction of Eisenstein's banned film *Bezhin Meadow* (1968, with Naum Kleiman). Shortly after Stalin's death he directed stage productions of Mayakovsky's *Bathhouse* (1953, with N. Petrov and V. Pluchek) and *The Bedbug* (1955, with Pluchek); he also paid homage to Meyerhold with productions of Blok's *Balaganchik* and *Incognita* in the early 1980s.

89. Iutkevich, "Nachalo puti," 100–101.

90. Ibid., 102.

91. Ibid., 103.

92. Letter from Eisenstein to his mother, September 5, 1921, RGALI f. 1923, op. 1, ed. khr. 1549: 110–111; in Zabrodin, *Eizenshtein: Popytka teatra*, 103.

93. A "romance" is a sung ballad.

94. Sergei Eisenstein, "Wie sag' ich's meinem Kinde?" in *Beyond the Stars: The Memoirs of Sergei Eisenstein*, trans. William Powell (Calcutta, India: Seagull Books, 1995), 447–49.

95. See Fitzpatrick, *The Commissariat of Enlightenment*, 174–76.

96. Vsevolod E. Meierkhol'd, *Perepiska: 1896–1939*, ed. V. P. Korshunova, M. M. Sitkovetskaia., and intro. Iu. A. Zavadskii (Moscow: Iskusstvo, 1976), 213.

97. Ibid.

98. Vladimir Liutse was an actor/director/designer who played Brandahlystova's son in *Tarelkin's Death* (see figure 30) and who directed the world premiere of Mayakovsky's *Bathhouse*.

99. Iutkevich, "Nachalo puti," 105.

100. Letter from Eisenstein to his mother, January 7, 1922, RGALI f. 1923, op. 1, ed. khr. 1549: 117–118 verso; in Zabrodin, *Eizenshtein: Popytka teatra*, 108.

101. Vsevolod E. Meierkhol'd, "Iz vystupleniia na diskussii 'Tvorcheskaia metodologiia Teatra imeni Meierkhol'da,' December 25, 1930," in Vsevolod E. Meierkhol'd, *Stat'i, pis'ma, rechi, besedy*, ed. A. V. Fevral'skii, 2 vols., vol. 2: *(1917–1939)* (Moscow: Iskusstvo, 1968), 231–32.

102. Rezhisserskaia razrabotka P. Dement'eva postanovki L. Tika *Kot v sapogakh*, December 1, 1921, RGALI f. 963, op. 1, ed. khr. 1274:8 verso-9.

103. Translated in Leyda and Voynow, *Eisenstein at Work*, 10. Original punctuation. This note with accompanying drawing is held at RGALI, f. 998, op. 1, ed. khr. 856.

104. Fevralsky believed the drawing to have been Meyerhold's. See Meierkhol'd, *Stat'i*, 2: 553n401.

105. RGALI f. 1923, op. 1, ed. khr. 794: 6.

106. Iutkevich, "Nachalo puti," 106.

107. Ibid.

108. Meierkhol'd, *Stat'i*, 2: 553n401.

109. Sergei Iutkevich, letter to Sergei Eisenstein, January 15, 1922, RGALI f. 1923, op. 1, ed. khr. 2287; in Sergei I. Iutkevich, *Sobranie sochinenii v trekh tomakh: Molodost'*, 3 vols., vol. 1 (Moscow: Iskusstvo, 1990), 140.

110. Ibid., 143.

111. Ibid., 145.

112. Sincere thanks to Laurence Senelick for this information.

113. Sergei Eizenshtein, *Teatral'nye risunki* (Moscow: Sojuz Kinomatografistov SSSR. Bjuro propagandy sovetskogo kinoiskusstva, 1970), [n. p.]. In Russian with English translation.

114. Ibid.

115. Sergei Eizenshtein, journal entry from September 5, 1919; in V. V. Zabrodin, ed., "'Vse velikoe prosto': S. M. Eizenshtein o teatre, 1919–1923," in Ivanov, *Mnemozina*, 4:439–40. Original: RGALI f. 1923, op. 1, ed. khr. 888: 122–25 verso.

116. Iutkevich, *Molodost'*, 1:167.

117. Shcherbakov, "Eizenshtein i Iutkevich peresozdaiut shedevr mastera," 534.

118. Sergei Eizenshtein and Sergei I. Iutkevich, "Podviazka Kolombiny" (1922), RGALI f. 1923 op. 1, ed. khr. 816: 22. Page numbers from this version of the *Columbine's Garter* libretto are hereafter provided as in-text citations. Page numbers cited are those RGALI has written on each page.

119. Iutkevich, *Molodost'*, 1:167.

120. "Conversation with Trauberg (1968)," in Christie, *Futurism / Formalism / FEKS*, 28. Marinetti's 1913 manifesto "The Variety Theatre," translated into Russian in 1914, was another source the Eccentrics both acknowledged and rebelled against. In it, Marinetti calls for similar things: "One must completely destroy all logic in Variety Theatre performances . . . multiply contrasts and make the absurd and the unlifelike complete masters of the stage." Though the Eccentrics rejected suggestions that seemed naive ("spread a powerful glue on some of the seats" and "sell the same ticket to ten people"), Marinetti, like them, called for theater to "encourage the type of the eccentric American, the impression he gives of exciting grotesquerie, of frightening dynamism; his crude jokes, his enormous brutalities." Marinetti, "The Variety Theatre," ibid., 63–64.

121. Sergei Eizenshtein, "Fata Kolombiny," May 1, 1922, RGALI, f. 1923, op. 1, ed. khr. 815; in Fel'dman, *Meierkhol'd i drugie*, 552.

122. Meyerhold apparently asked his students to create multiple designs for a single play in contrasting styles or for different kinds of stages. Eisenstein developed two distinct sets of *Heartbreak House* designs.

123. For notes on *Columbine's Garter*'s topical and satirical references, see the translation of the pantomime libretto in Appendix D.

124. Grigorii Mikhailovich Kozintsev, "Eccentrism," *TDR* 19, no. 4 (December 1975): 96–98. For an alternate translation of Kozintsev's manifesto, see Christie, *Futurism / Formalism / FEKS*, 11–13.

125. Kozintsev, "Eccentrism," 97.

126. See Zabrodin, *Eisenshtein o Meierkhol'de*, 38–74 and "Grotesk i attraktsion," *Kinovedcheskie zapiski* 46 (2000), http://www.kinozapiski.ru/ru/print/sendvalues/585/.

127. Zabrodin, *Eisenshtein o Meierkhol'de*, 110.

128. The Imaginists were a group of Russian poets, founded in 1918, that believed that "a poem is an uninterrupted series of images." Victor Terras, *Handbook of Russian Literature* (New Haven, Conn.: Yale University Press), 200.

129. Zabrodin, *Eisenshtein o Meierkhol'de*, 109, reproduced from RGALI f. 1923, op. 2, ed. khr. 748: 11.

130. Vance Kepley, Jr., "Mr. Kuleshov in the Land of the Modernists," in *The Red Screen: Politics, Society, Art in Soviet Cinema*, ed. Anna Lawton (London: Routledge, 2005), 137.

131. Iutkevich, *Molodost'*, 1:172–73. This notation does not appear on the copy of the libretto held at RGALI, though the pantomime clearly is structured around this understanding of the attraction.

132. Samuil Vermel', "Ironiia i teatral'nost'," *LTA* 2 (1914): 44.

133. Perry, introduction to *Eisenstein at Work*, xi.

134. Ibid.

135. Ibid., xiii.

136. Caryl Emerson summarizes Bakhtin's argument: "Drama—even the great Shakespeare's—can contain only 'embryonic polyphony' . . . for although drama can be multileveled, it cannot contain multiple worlds." Caryl Emerson, *The First Hundred Years of Mikhail Bakhtin* (Princeton, N.J.: Princeton University Press, 1997), 77.

137. E. T. A. Hoffmann, "Johannes Kreisler's Apprentice Letter," in E. T. A. Hoffmann, *Fantasy Pieces in Callot's Manner: Pages from the Diary of a Traveling Romantic*, trans. Joseph M. Hayse (Schenectady, N.Y.: Union College Press, 1996), 293.

138. Vsevolod Meyerhold, "Studiia: Klass Vs: E. Meierkhol'da, Tekhnika stsenicheskikh dvizheniia," *LTA* 4–5 (1914): 97.

139. Perry, introduction to *Eisenstein at Work*, xii.

140. Yutkevich noted that other human-machine fusions in the pantomime, the Dance Master for instance, intentionally evoked Picasso's designs for Cocteau's *Parade*. Iutkevich, *Molodost'*, 1:172.

141. All italicized text appears in the original French or English.

142. Noussinova observes that the intertitles of this filmed version of *Columbine* were in French, "which leaves one to assume that it was perhaps a metaphor designating the 'Parisian genre,' the name given to pornographic films in Russia from 1900–1910." Natalia Noussinova, "Eisenstein excentrique," in *Eisenstein: L'Ancien et le nouveau*, ed. Dominique Chateau, Francois Jost, and Martin Lefebvre (Paris: Publications de la Sorbonne, 2001), 69. Translations from Noussinova by David Calder.

143. Shcherbakov, "Eizenshtein i Iutkevich peresozdaiut shedevr mastera," 564.

144. Iutkevich, *Molodost'*, 1:167, 172.

145. Ibid., 172.

146. Sergei Eizenshtein, *Metod*, vol. 1 (Moscow: Muzei kino, Eizenshtein-Tsentr, 2002), 126.

147. Noussinova, "Eisenstein excentrique," 69.

148. Eisenstein frequently prompted gender destabilizations: he designed costumes for *Be Kind to Horses* that were male on one side and female on the other, and several characters cross-dressed in *Wiseman*. Other examples of what he called "bi-sex," "the dialectical presence of male and female elements within a single image," abound in his work. Anne Nesbet, *Savage Junctures: Sergei Eisenstein and the Shape of Thinking* (London: I.B. Tauris, 2003), 15.

149. Dohnányi's music is used only once in the pantomime: immediately after Pierrot is electrically reanimated in act 3.

150. Iutkevich, *Molodost'*, 1:172.

151. S. F. Starr, *Red and Hot: The Fate of Jazz in the Soviet Union, 1917–1980* (New York: Limelight Editions, 1985), 43–44.

152. Valentin Parnakh, "Dzhaz-Band," *Veshch* 1–2 (1922): 25, quoted in Starr, *Red and Hot*, 44. Parnakh's first concerts in Moscow in the fall of 1922 and Meyerhold's subsequent integration of Parnakh and his band into *The Magnanimous Cuckold*, the first use of jazz on the Soviet theatrical stage (though Parnakh's interpretation little resembled actual jazz) did not take place until after Eisenstein and Yutkevich had written *Columbine's Garter*. It is likely, though, that Eisenstein read Parnakh's articles, which were published in prominent Russian émigré periodicals. Eisenstein saw Parnakh perform in December 1922 and convinced Parnakh to teach him the fox trot.

153. For additional information on these film references, see Noussinova, "Eisenstein excentrique," 72.

154. Narboni, "Introduction to *Poetika Kino*," in Christie, *Futurism / Formalism / FEKS*, 55.

155. The article adds, "Neon and electric advertisements developed by the student N. Arhiereev. In the lead roles are students: Savitskaia, Semenova, Gunger, Zelenaia, Deeva, Poslavsky, Ferry, Knorre, Senderov, Chuvelev." Iutkevich, *Molodost'*, 1:173.

156. Ibid.

157. Eizenshtein, *Metod*, 1:127.

158. M. K. Ivanova and Vladislav V. Ivanov, introduction to "Teatral'nye tetrad S. M. Eizenshteina," in Ivanov, *Mnemozina*, 2:190.

159. Eizenshtein, *Metod*, 1:127.

160. Mikhail Zharov. *Zhizn', teatr, kino: Vospominaniia* (Moscow: Iskusstvo, 1967), 174; in Zabrodin, *Eizenshtein: Popytka teatra*, 202.

161. Sergei Eisenstein, "Montage of Attractions for 'Enough Stupidity in Every Wiseman,'" trans. and ed. Dan Gerould, *TDR* 18, no. 1 (March 1974): 79.

162. Ibid., 78.

163. Ibid., 81.

164. Dan Gerould, "Eisenstein's *Wiseman*," *TDR* 18, no. 1 (March 1974): 74.

165. Eisenstein, "Montage of Attractions," 83.

166. Iutkevich, *Molodost'*, 1:172.

167. Steven K. Smith, "Activist Theatre: From Brecht through Boal," *The Brecht Yearbook* 30 (2005): 289.

168. Alma H. Law and Mel Gordon, *Meyerhold, Eisenstein, and Biomechanics: Actor Training in Revolutionary Russia* (Jefferson, N.C.: McFarland, 1996), 76.

169. Perry, introduction to *Eisenstein at Work*, xi.

170. Zabrodin, "'Vse velikoe prosto,'" in Ivanov, *Mnemozina*, 4:439.

171. My italics. D. S. Mirsky, "The Soviet Films," *The Virginia Quarterly Review* 7, no. 4 (October 1, 1931): 529. Quoted in Leyda and Voynow, *Eisenstein at Work*, 76.

172. Nesbet, *Savage Junctures*, 40.

173. Sergei Eisenstein, "The Montage of Film Attractions," in Leyda and Voynow, *Eisenstein at Work*, 18.

174. Leyda and Voynow, *Eisenstein at Work*, 36.

175. Ibid., 37.

176. Ibid., 36.

177. Ibid., 45.

178. Ibid., 146.

179. Clayton, *Pierrot in Petrograd*, 216.

180. Eisenstein writes at the end of "The Treasure" that Esenina gave him Meyerhold's archive because she was afraid the dacha (cottage) would be bombed during the German air raids in that region. According to Esenina, Eisenstein visited Meyerhold's dacha, northwest of Moscow on the former Gorenki estate, in August 1941, a month into the air raids. Though Esenina did not know Eisenstein personally, she had been advised that he would probably agree to take the archive and that he had a dacha at which to hide it. Esenina did not give Eisenstein Raikh's archive, which she had stored separately. Most unfortunately, Raikh's archive was later destroyed by squatters, one reason why scholars have not sufficiently explored her major contribution to Meyerhold's theater. Esenina never saw Eisenstein again; after Eisenstein died in 1948, she learned that Meyerhold's archive had gone to RGALI. She also learned that the Bakhrushin State Central Theatre Museum had secretly preserved a separate Meierkhol'd collection. Many of the sources used to write the Meyerhold chapter in this book come from these two secretly preserved archives. For Esenina's detailed account of the fate of Meierkhol'd and Raikh's archives, see Tat'iana S. Esenina, *T. S. Esenina o V. E. Meierkhol'de i Z. N. Raikh: Pis'ma K. L. Rudnitskomu*, compiled with commentary by N. N. Panfilova and O. M. Fel'dman (Moscow: Novoe izdatel'stvo, 2003), 51–61.

181. Sergei Eizenshtein, "Zakrovishche," in *Memuary*, vol. 1, compiled and with commentary by N. I. Kleiman, ed. V. V. Zabrodin (Moscow: Trud, Muzei Kino, 1997), 226–27.

182. Eizenshtein, "Zakrovishche," 227.

183. Zabrodin reproduces journal entries in which Eisenstein writes about reading Meyerhold's materials while in evacuation during World War II. See Zabrodin, *Eisenshtein o Meierkhol'de*, 272.

184. Iutkevich, "Nachalo puti," 103.

185. Sergei Eizenshtein, journal entry from September 5, 1919; in Zabrodin, "'Vse velikoe prosto,'" in Ivanov, *Mnemozina*, 4:439–40. For the original, see RGALI f. 1923, op. 1, ed. khr. 888: 122–25 verso.

186. Peter Kenez, "*Bezhin Lug (Bezhin Meadow)*," in *Enemies of the People: The Destruction of Soviet Literary, Theater, and Film Arts in the 1930s*, ed. Katherine Bliss Eaton (Evanston, Ill.: Northwestern University Press, 2002), 122.

187. Ibid., 121.

188. Ibid., 122.

CONCLUSION. THE AFTERLIFE OF A DEATH JUBILEE

1. A more literal translation is *The Unusual Adventure of E. T. A. Hoffmann*. My translation "strange" is to maintain Derzhavin's intended association with Hoffmann's *Strange Sorrows of a Theatre Manager*.

2. Leonora Shpet, *Sovetskii teatr dlia detei* (Moscow: Iskusstvo, 1971), 46–47. Quoted in Manon van de Water, *Moscow Theatres for Young People: A Cultural History of Ideological Coercion and Artistic Innovation, 1917–2000* (New York: Palgrave Macmillan, 2006), 45.

3. Sergei S. Ignatov, "Teatr dlia detei (Shchelkunchik i myshnyi tsar')," *Teatr* 3 (1922): 75.

4. Ibid., 76.

5. N. L'vov, "'Shchelkunchik' v detskom teatre," *Pravda*, September 29, 1922, 5.

6. N. L'vov, "Gos. detskii teatr: 'Shchelkunchik,'" *Zrelishcha: Ezhenedel'nik teatra, miuzik-kholla, tsirka, massovogo deistva, tefizkul'ta, balagana, kino* 6 (October 3–9, 1922): 19.

7. Kh. Khrisanf, "E. T. A. Gofman na stsene (Po povodu postanovki 'Shchelkunchika' v Gosud. detskom teatre)," *Izvestiia* 221 (1922): 5.

8. Ibid.

9. Ibid.

10. Ibid.

11. L'vov, "Gos. detskii teatr: 'Shchelkunchik,'" 19.

12. George E. Shail, "The Leningrad Theatre of Young Spectators" (Ph.D. diss., New York University, 1980), 683, quoted in van de Water, *Moscow Theatres*, 45.

13. Leonora Shpet, *Sovetskii teatr dlia detei* (Moscow: Iskusstvo, 1971), 54, quoted in van de Water, *Moscow Theatres*, 46.

14. Sofia Lunacharskaia, *Teatr dlia detei kak orudie kommunisticheskogo vospitaniia* (Moscow: Gosudarstvennoe izdatel'stvo khudozhestvennoi literatury), 21, quoted in van de Water, *Moscow Theatres*, 53.

15. Svetlana Boym, "Estrangement as a Lifestyle: Shklovsky and Brodsky," in *Exile and Creativity: Signposts, Travelers, Outsiders, Backward Glances*, ed. Susan Rubin Suleiman (Durham, N.C.: Duke University Press, 1998), 250.

16. Hoffmann is a character in Dumas only, though the plot of Irving's brief tale otherwise is similar.

17. A. Movshchenson, "Teatr Novoi dramy: Neobyknovennoe prikliuchenie Gofmana," *Zhizn' iskusstva* 49, no. 872 (December 12, 1922): 4.

18. Eduard Stark, "Neobyknovennoe prikliuchenie v teatre," *Zhizn' iskusstva* 50, no. 873 (December 19, 1922): 4. Stark was not a Bolshevik, one possible reason why he lauded the Hoffmannian qualities in Derzhavin's work.

19. Konstantin Derzhavin, "Neobyknovennoe prikliuchenie E. T. A. Gofmana (K postanovke v gosudarstvennom teatre Novoi dramy)," *Zhizn' iskusstva* 48, no. 871 (December 5, 1922): 1.

20. Ibid.

21. Derzhavin was a former member of TEO Narkompros (the Theatre Section of the Commissariat of Enlightenment) and was sympathetic to the Revolution, yet he avoided treating Dumas's material as direct propaganda. For Soviet views of the French Revolution, see Dmitry Shlapentokh, *The Counter-Revolution in Revolution: Images of Thermidor and Napoleon at the Time of Russian Revolution and Civil War* (New York: St. Martin's, 1999).

22. Derzhavin, "Neobyknovennoe prikliuchenie," 1.

23. Ibid.

24. Vladimir Vladimirovich Dmitriev (1900–1948) was a visual artist and stage designer. Meyerhold's designer for *The Dawns*, he also developed preliminary designs for *Inspector General*.

25. Henri Forterre (1882–1958) was the Kamerny Theatre's house composer.

26. Iutkevich, *Molodost'*, 1:176.

27. Poet/actor/playwright Pavel Grigor'evich Antokolsky (1896–1978), who created the prologue and epilogue for the Kamerny's *Brambilla*, suggested *Turandot* to Vakhtangov. Antokolsky was then a member of Vakhtangov's studio, where he performed and wrote several plays, including *Puss in Boots*, retitled *Betrothal in a Dream*, which opened at the studio, directed by Iurii Zavadsky, in the spring of 1919. Vakhtangov also considered staging *Brambilla*. See Vladislav V. Ivanov, ed., *Evgenii Vakhtangov: Dokumenty i svidetel'stva*, 2 vols., vol. 2 (Moscow: Indrik, 2011), 263, 292.

28. M. Zhezhelenko, "Akimov," in *Portrety rezhisserov: Kedrov, Akimov, Tovstonogov, Pluchek, Efremov*, ed. E. Ivanova (Moscow: Iskusstvo, 1972), 62. Soviet works on Vakhtangov amplified his support of the Revolution and softened his criticisms of other artists of his day, Stanislavsky in particular. The fullest collection of his writings (and the first to restore all Soviet cuts) is Ivanov, *Evgenii Vakhtangov*.

29. Andre Malaev-Babel, *Yevgeny Vakhtangov: A Critical Portrait* (London: Routledge, 2012), 215–35.

30. Ibid., 231.

31. Ibid., 230.

32. *Turandot* remained in the Vakhtangov Theatre's repertoire throughout the Soviet period; it eventually lost its vitality, not through repression, but repetition.

33. For a film scenario by Tarkovsky that engages with Hoffmann, see Andrei Tarkovsky, "Hoffmanniana," in *Collected Screenplays*, trans. Natasha Synessios (London: Faber, 1999), 323–72.

34. Louise George Club, "Italian Renaissance Theatre," in *The Oxford Illustrated History of Theatre*, ed. John Russell Brown (Oxford: Oxford University Press, 2001), 108. See also Louise George Clubb, *Italian Drama in Shakespeare's Time* (New Haven, Conn.: Yale University Press, 1989).

35. Rich Brown, "Moisés Kaufman: The Copulation of Form and Content," *Theatre Topics* 15, no. 1 (March 2005): 51–67.

36. Hans-Thies Lehmann, *Postdramatic Theatre* (London: Routledge, 2006), 100.

37. Sharon M. Carnicke, *Stanislavsky in Focus: An Acting Master for the Twenty-First Century*, 2nd ed. (London: Routledge, 2009), 7.

38. Tairov's only theoretical work to have been translated into English is *Notes of a Director* (trans. 1969). Among the copious English translations of Eisenstein's theory there are astonishingly few of his writings on theater. The most sizable body of Meyerhold's theoretical writings translated into English, Braun's 1969 *Meyerhold on Theatre*, still the gold standard for English-language Meyerhold translations, was first published nearly half a century ago, meaning that the abundant archival sources that have become available in years since, as well as more recent critical lenses that embrace theater's visual languages, no longer take fidelity to a dramatic text as a given, and more fully recognize the contributions of women collaborators have not been incorporated.

39. Gérard Abensour, *Vsévolod Meyerhold, ou, L'invention de la mise en scène* ([Paris]: Fayard, 1998).

40. Lehmann, *Postdramatic Theatre*, 27.

41. Curiously, in analyzing the "prehistory of postdramatic theatre," Lehmann focuses almost exclusively on written dramas and written theory, only nodding to places where the seeds of the postdramatic are to be found: commedia dell'arte, popular entertainments, pantomime, silent film—and the innovations of theatricalist directors. Meyerhold receives only three mentions in Lehmann's book, Tairov and Eisenstein only one each. No modernist director is analyzed in detail. Ibid., 47–67.

42. Ibid., 19.

43. D. S. Mirsky, "The Soviet Films," *The Virginia Quarterly Review* 7, no. 4 (October 1, 1931): 529. Quoted in *Eisenstein at Work*, ed. Jay Leyda and Zina Voynow (New York: Pantheon Books, 1982), 76.

44. From Vakhtangov's notebooks, November 3, 1917, in Ivanov, *Evgenii Vakhtangov*, 1:449.

45. Meierkhol'd, "Uslovnyi teatr," 141.

46. Valery Briusov, "Against Naturalism in the Theatre (from 'Unnecessary Truth')," in *Theatre in Theory 1900–2000: An Anthology*, ed. David Krasner (Malden, Mass.: Blackwell, 2008), 60.

APPENDIX A. THREE ESSAYS FROM LOVE FOR THREE ORANGES: THE JOURNAL OF DOCTOR DAPERTUTTO

1. The formal "you" in Russian usually is capitalized. Here, Kniazhnin's capitalization of the *informal* "you" in his ode to Hoffmann conveys an almost religious reverence.

2. Ernst Teodor Amadei Gofman, *Zolotoi gorshok (Skazka)*, trans. and intro. Vladimir S. Solov'ev (Moscow: Altsiona, 1913).

3. Vladimir Kniazhnin, "Hoffmaniana," *LTA* 1 (1914): 58–59.

4. *Rech'*, March 3, 1914. Meyerhold, Soloviev, and Vogak's note.

5. Vsevolod Meierkhol'd, Vladimir Solov'ev, and Konstantin Vogak, "Otkrytoe pis'mo avtorov divertismenta *Liubov' k trem apel'sinam* A. A. Gvozdevu," *LTA* 4–5 (1914): 86–88.

6. V. Zhirmunskii, "Komediia chistoi radosti (*Kot v sapogakh*, Liudviga Tika. 1797 g.)," *LTA* 1 (1916): 85–91.

APPENDIX B. COLUMBINE'S VEIL

1. Literally "pictures."

2. "Sharf Kolombiny," libretto pantomima (Saint Petersburg: Siriius, 1910), RGALI, f. 998, op. 1, ed. khr. 70.

3. In Meyerhold's pantomime, the Pianist in act 1 and the Kapellmeister in act 2 are the same person. See Chapter 1, note 45.

APPENDIX C. PIERRETTE'S VEIL

1. "Pokryvalo P'eretty: Pantomima v 3 deistv. Artura Schnitzlera s muzyk. E. Donani i prologom Iu. Baltrushaitisa," *Teatr: Gazeta s programmami i libretto vsekh moskovskikh teatrov* 1379 (1913): 38. National Library of Russia, RU\NLR\DRG\5615 РНБ: Газ.1-М/1–131.

APPENDIX D. COLUMBINE'S GARTER

1. Sergei Eizenshtein and Sergei I. Iutkevich, "Podviazka Kolombiny" (1922), RGALI f. 1923 op. 1, ed. khr. 816. All of Eisenstein and Yutkevich's original notes appear as footnotes in the pantomime text proper, as in the source text. My notes appear as endnotes or in square brackets at the end of the relevant footnote. Italicized text in the pantomime translation appears in its original language, usually French or English.

2. Sofia Erazimovna Savitskaia, an actress at Mastfor and Foregger's first wife. See O. M. Fel'dman, ed., *Meierkhol'd i drugie: Dokumenty i materialy*, vol. 2 of *Meierkhol'dovskii sbornik* (Moscow: OGI, 2000), 564.

3. Fedor Fedorovich Knorre, husband to Maria Babanova, noted for his skills as a tightrope walker. See ibid.

4. Entrée: "French, meaning entrance, entry, admission, beginning. This use of the word in connection with clowning may go back to the very early days of circus, when clowns stood at the entrance to the show, performing brief items from their acts." "Entrée," Geoff Stevens, *Circus Dictionary* (Buntingford, U.K.: Aardvark, 2004), 36.

5. Another name for Foregger's Theatre Workshop, Mastfor. See Fel'dman, *Meierkhol'd i drugie*, 555.

6. Harlequin under a different mask. Ibid., 564.

7. "Star."

8. "On her way to becoming an honest woman by marrying Sir Archibald Harlequin."

9. "Underclothes."

10. A traditional circus-ring whip. "Chambrière," Stevens, *Circus Dictionary*, 25.

11. "Daft, senile."

12. "Skullcap."

13. Nikolai Mikhailovich Foregger von Greifenturn.

14. That is, the Russian émigré community abroad that fled the Revolution and Civil War.

15. "Valet, chamberlain."

16. U.S. producer of flypaper: "Works of the O. & W. Thum Co.," *The Pharmaceutical Era* 11 (March 15, 1894): 279–80.

17. "Rôti:" Roasts or rotisserie. "Tricot": A ribbed fabric.

18. "Soup."

19. An old-fashioned car horn.

20. Commode: normally a chest of drawers, though Eisenstein and Yutkevich are playing with the additional meaning: a piece of furniture that conceals a chamber pot.

21. A German lightbulb manufacturing firm founded under this name in 1919.

22. A reference to the academic theaters of the Commissariat of Enlightenment. See Fel'dman, *Meierkhol'd i drugie*, 565.

23. Swiss-French artist and caricaturist.

24. "Slippers" [*sic*].

25. American shoe firm.

26. This could be a reference to the St. Louis club the Chrysanthemum (opened 1903) or to Scott Joplin's 1904 ragtime tune "Chrysanthemum: An Afro-American Intermezzo," especially in the context of Pierrot's four friends becoming jazz musicians in the next act. If so, it would be a typical early Soviet conflation of African American jazz with musical antecedents. See Edward A. Ber-

lin, *King of Ragtime: Scott Joplin and His Era* (Oxford: Oxford University Press, 1994), 135, 306.

27. Capes, usually hooded.

28. "Advertising diptych": a picture in two parts connected with a hinge.

29. "ARA": a satirical reference to Hoover's American Relief Administration, which provided food and medical care to millions of Russians during the famine years of 1921–23. See figure 44.

30. A 1912 British music hall hit by Jack Judge and Harry Williams.

31. A vessel flute, often made of clay, often goose-shaped.

32. "Come without ceremony, just as you are!"

33. The issue dedicated to Alexander Blok, who recently had died while the Soviet government deliberated over whether to grant him permission to travel abroad for medical treatment.

34. Rope or *corde lisse*: "A vertical rope, which may have a woven cotton-nylon cover . . . An aerialist . . . performs a routine of moves and poses near the top of the rope, which is suspended from the roof, usually concluding with a spectacular, slow headfirst descent . . . the rope wrapped around one leg as control." "*Corde lisse*," Stevens, *Circus Dictionary*, 29.

35. "[A] round structure at the top of a building . . . Early circus cupolas were . . . quite small and cup-shaped. A cupola provides an attachment point for aerialists' props or ropes." "Cupola." ibid., 30–31.

36. A conflation of Meyerhold's parades and circus parades.

37. Probably a dance between Columbine and the two Pierrot marionettes.

38. A U.S. company that began making padlocks in 1912.

39. "To the patriarch of the Veil from the novices of the 'Garter.'"

Works Cited

Full references for works not included in this bibliography (individual archival documents, production reviews, encyclopedia entries, internet links, and sources reproduced in other works) appear in the chapter endnotes.

ARCHIVES, LIBRARIES, AND MUSEUMS

Art Institute of Chicago
Bakhrushin State Central Theatre Museum, Moscow
  Fond 526: Alisa Georgievna Koonen and Aleksandr Iakovlevich Tairov (né Kornblit)
  Fond 529: Moscow Kamerny Theatre (MKT)
  Fond 688: Meyerhold Theatre (GosTIM)
Harvard Theatre Collection, Cambridge, Mass.
Laurence Senelick Collection, Medford, Mass.
National Library of Russia, Saint Petersburg
New York Public Library for the Performing Arts
Russian State Archive of Literature and Art (RGALI, formerly TsGALI), Moscow
  Fond 963: Meyerhold Theatre (GosTIM)
  Fond 998: Vsevolod Emil'evich Meierkhol'd
  Fond 1923: Sergei Mikhailovich Eizenshtein
  Fond 1990: Moscow Art Theatre 2 (MAT 2)
  Fond 2030: Moscow Kamerny Theatre (MKT)
  Fond 2328: Aleksandr Iakovlevich Tairov (né Kornblit)
  Fond 2768: Alisa Georgievna Koonen
Russian State Library, Moscow
Saint Petersburg Museum of Theatre and Music
Staatsbibliothek, Bamberg
Central Scientific Library of the Theatre Workers' Union (STD), Moscow

BOOKS AND ARTICLES

Abel, Lionel. *Metatheatre: A New View of Dramatic Form*. New York: Hill and Wang, 1963.

Amiard-Chevrel, Claudine. "'Princesse Brambilla' d'après E. T. A. Hoffmann: Mise en scène de Tairov." In *Mises en scène années 20 et 30: Les voiles de la création théatrale*, edited by Denis Bablet, 127–53. Paris: Centre National de la Recherche Scientifique, 1979.

Baer, Nancy Van Norman. *Theatre in Revolution: Russian Avant-Garde Stage Design, 1913–1935*. New York: Thames and Hudson, 1991.

Bindman, David, and Henry Louis Gates Jr., eds. *The Image of the Black in Western Art*. Cambridge, Mass.: Belknap, 2011.

Blok, Alexander. "The Puppet Show." *Slavonic and East European Review* 28, no. 71 (1950): 309–22.

Blokh, Ia. N., M. A. Kuzmin, and A. A. Gvozdev, eds. *Zelenaia ptichka*. [Petrograd]: Petropolis, 1922.

Bordwell, David. *The Cinema of Eisenstein*. London: Routledge, 2005.

Bowlt, John, ed. *The Salon Album of Vera Sudeikin-Stravinsky*. Princeton, N.J.: Princeton University Press, 1995.

Boym, Svetlana. "Estrangement as a Lifestyle: Shklovsky and Brodsky." In *Exile and Creativity: Signposts, Travelers, Outsiders, Backward Glances*, edited by Susan Rubin Suleiman, 241–62. Durham, N.C.: Duke University Press, 1998.

Brahms, Johannes. *Johannes Brahms: Life and Letters*. Translated by Josef Eisenger and Styra Avins. Oxford: Oxford University Press, 1997.

Braun, Edward. *Meyerhold: A Revolution in Theatre*. London: Methuen Drama, 1998.

———. "Vsevolod Meyerhold: The Final Act." In *Enemies of the People: The Destruction of Soviet Literary, Theater, and Film Arts in the 1930s*, edited by Katherine Bliss Eaton, 145–62. Evanston, Ill.: Northwestern University Press, 2002.

Briusov, Valery. "Against Naturalism in the Theatre (from 'Unnecessary Truth')." In *Theatre in Theory 1900–2000: An Anthology*, edited by David Krasner, 56–60. Malden, Mass.: Blackwell, 2008.

Brown, Rich. "Moisés Kaufman: The Copulation of Form and Content." *Theatre Topics* 15, no. 1 (March 2005): 51–67.

Burry, Alexander. *Multi-Mediated Dostoevsky: Transposing Novels into Opera, Film, and Drama*. Evanston, Ill.: Northwestern University Press, 2011.

Carlson, Marvin. *The Haunted Stage: The Theatre as Memory Machine*. Ann Arbor: University of Michigan Press, 2003.

Carnicke, Sharon M. *Stanislavsky in Focus: An Acting Master for the Twenty-First Century*, 2nd ed. London: Routledge, 2009.

———. *The Theatrical Instinct: Nikolai Evreinov and the Russian Theatre of the Early Twentieth Century*. New York: Peter Lang, 1989.

Chambers, David. "The Master of Praxis." *Theater* 28, no. 2 (1998): 50–55.
Chantler, Abigail. *E.T.A. Hoffmann's Musical Aesthetics*. Burlington, Vt.: Ashgate, 2006.
Cheauré, Elizabeth. *E. T. A. Hoffmann: Inszenierungen seiner Werke auf russischen Bühnen: Ein Beitrag zur Rezeptionsgeschichte*. Heidelberg: Carl Winter, 1979.
Cherkasskii, Sergei. *Valentin Smyshliaev: Akter, Rezhisser, Pedagog*. Saint Petersburg: Sankt-Peterburgskaia gosudarstvennaia akademiia teatral'nogo iskusstva, 2004.
Christie, Ian, and John Gillett. *Futurism / Formalism / Feks: Eccentrism and Soviet Cinema, 1918–36*. London: British Film Institute, 1978.
Clayton, J. Douglas. "From Gozzi to Hoffmann: German Sources for Commedia dell'Arte in Russian Avant-Garde Theatre." In *The Science of Buffoonery: Theory and History of the Commedia dell'Arte*, edited by Domenico Pietropaolo, 117–31. Ottawa: Dovehouse Editions, 1989.
———. *Pierrot in Petrograd: The Commedia dell'Arte/Balagan in Twentieth-Century Russian Theatre and Drama*. Montreal: McGill-Queen's University Press, 1993.
Clubb, Louise George. *Italian Drama in Shakespeare's Time*. New Haven, Conn.: Yale University Press, 1989.
———. "Italian Renaissance Theatre." In *The Oxford Illustrated History of Theatre*, edited by John Russell Brown, 107–41. Oxford: Oxford University Press, 2001.
Comini, Alessandra. *The Changing Image of Beethoven: A Study in Mythmaking*. Santa Fe, N.Mex.: Sunstone, 2008.
Derzhavin, Konstantin. *Kniga o Kamernom teatre 1914–1934*. Leningrad: Khudozhestvennaia literatura, 1934.
Egidio, Aurora. *Aleksandr Tairov e il Kamernyj Teatr di Mosca, 1907–1922*. Rome: Bulzoni, 2005.
Eizenshtein [Eisenstein], Sergei. *Beyond the Stars: The Memoirs of Sergei Eisenstein*. Translated by William Powell. Calcutta, India: Seagull Books, 1995.
———. *Film Form: Essays in Film Theory*. Translated by Jay Leyda. San Diego: Harcourt, Brace, Jovanovich, 1977.
———. *Memuary*. 2 vols. Compiled and with commentary by N. I. Kleiman, edited by V. V. Zabrodin. Moscow: Trud, Muzei Kino, 1997.
———. *Metod*. 2 vols. Edited by N. I. Kleiman. Moscow: Muzei kino, Eizenshtein-Tsentr, 2002.
———. "Montage of Attractions for 'Enough Stupidity in Every Wiseman.'" Translated and edited by Dan Gerould. *TDR* 18, no. 1 (March 1974): 77–85.
———. *Teatral'nye risunki*. Moscow: Soiuz kinomatografistov SSSR. Biuro propagandy sovetskogo kinoiskusstva, 1970.
Emerson, Caryl. *Boris Godunov: Transpositions of a Russian Theme*. Bloomington: Indiana University Press, 1986.

———. *The First Hundred Years of Mikhail Bakhtin*. Princeton, N.J.: Princeton University Press, 1997.

———. "The Krzhizhanovsky–Prokofiev Collaboration on Eugene Onegin, 1936 (A Lesser-Known Casualty of the Pushkin Death Jubilee)." In *Sergey Prokofiev and His World*, edited by Simon Morrison, 60–114. Princeton, N.J.: Princeton University Press, 2008.

Esenina, Tat'iana S., N. N. Panfilova, O. M. Fel'dman, and Konstantin Rudnitskii. *T. S. Esenina o V. E. Meierkhol'de i Z. N. Raikh: Pis'ma K. L. Rudnitskomu*. Moscow: Novoe izdatel'stvo, 2003.

Evreinov, Nikolai. *Teatr dlia sebia*. Saint Petersburg: Sovremennoe iskusstvo, 1917.

Fel'dman, O. M., ed. *Meierkhol'd i drugie: Dokumenty i materialy*. vol. 2 of *Meierkhol'dovskii sbornik*. Moscow: OGI, 2000.

Fevral'skii, A. V., ed. *V. E. Meierkhol'd: Stat'i, Pis'ma, Rechi, Besedy*. 2 vols. Moscow: Iskusstvo, 1968.

Filosofov, Dmitrii. "Hoffmaniana IV: Printsessa Brambilla." *LTA* 4–7 (1915): 189–98.

Fitzpatrick, Sheila. *The Commissariat of Enlightenment: Soviet Organization of Education and the Arts under Lunacharsky, October 1917–1921*. Cambridge: Cambridge University Press, 1970.

G. "Novye puti (Beseda s Vs. E. Meierkhol'dom)." *Rampa i zhizn'* 34 (1911): 2–3.

Garin, Erast Pavlovich. *S Meierkhol'dom: Vospominaniia*. Moscow: Iskusstvo, 1974.

Gerould, Dan. "Eisenstein's *Wiseman*." *TDR* 18, no. 1 (March 1974): 71–76.

Golub, Spencer. *Evreinov, The Theatre of Paradox and Transformation*. Ann Arbor, Mich.: UMI Research Press, 1984.

Goodwin, James. *Eisenstein, Cinema and History*. Urbana: University of Illinois Press, 1993.

Gordon, Mel. *The Stanislavsky Technique: Russia: A Workbook for Actors*. New York: Applause Theatre and Cinema Books, 1987.

Gozzi, Carlo. *Carlo Gozzi: Five Tales for the Theatre*. Translated and edited by Albert Bermel and Ted Emery. Chicago: University of Chicago Press, 1989.

———. *Carlo Gozzi: Translations of "The Love of Three Oranges," "Turandot," and "The Snake Lady."* Translated and edited by John Louis DiGaetani. New York: Greenwood, 1988.

———. *Carlo Gozzi's Reflective Analysis of His Fable Entitled "The Love of the Three Oranges."* Translated by John Addington Symonds. Boston: Chrysalis, 1956.

———. *Le fiabe di Carlo Gozzi*. 2 vols. Edited by Ernesto Masi. Bologna: Nicola Zanichelli, 1885.

———. *Skazki dlia teatra*. Edited and introduced by Ia. N. Blokh, translated by Ia. and R. Blokh and M. Lozinskii. Petrograd: Tipografiia Kominterna, 1923.

Green, T. A., and W. J. Pepicello. "Semiotic Interrelationships in the Puppet Play." *Semiotica* 47 (1983): 147.

Grimm, Reinhold. "From Callot to Butor: E. T. A. Hoffmann and the Tradition of the Capriccio." *MLN* 93, no. 3 (April 1978): 399–415.

Gurewitch, Morton. *The Comedy of Romantic Irony*. New York: University Press of America, 2002.

Gvozdev, A. A. *Teatr imeni Vs. Meierkhol'da: (1920–1926)*. Leningrad: Academia, 1927.

Hamill, Kyna. "Schianinossi, Callot and Fencing." *Print Quarterly* 26, no. 4 (2009): 354–63.

Hoffmann [Gofman], E. T. A. *E.T.A. Hoffmann's Musical Writings: Kreisleriana, the Poet and the Composer, Music Criticism*. Edited by David Charlton, translated by Martyn Clarke. Cambridge: Cambridge University Press, 2003.

———. *Fantasy Pieces in Callot's Manner: Pages from the Diary of a Traveling Romantic*. Translated and edited by Joseph M. Hayse. Schenectady, N.Y.: Union College Press, 1996.

———. *The Golden Pot and Other Tales*. Translated and edited by Ritchie Robertson. Oxford: Oxford University Press, 2000.

———. *The Life and Opinions of the Tomcat Murr: Together with a Fragmentary Biography of Kapellmeister Johannes Kreisler on Random Sheets of Waste Paper*. Translated by Anthea Bell. London: Penguin, 1999.

———. *Neobychainyia mucheniia odnogo teatral'nogo direktora*. Edited by M. I. Pisarev, translated by M. V. Karneev. Saint Petersburg: Lederle, 1894.

———. *Printsessa Blandina*. Translated and edited by Sergei Ignatov. Moscow: Izdatel'stvo Vserossiiskogo soiuza poetov, 1925.

———. *Sobranie sochinenii*. Edited by F. I. Bulgakov and C. C. Trubachev. 8 vols. St. Peterburg: Tipografiia br. Panteleevykh, 1896–99.

———. *Three Märchen of E. T. A. Hoffmann*. Translated by Charles E. Passage. Columbia: University of South Carolina Press, 1971.

"Hoffmaniana III (Russkie pisateli o Gofmane)." *LTA* 3 (1914): 85–87.

Hoover, Marjorie L. "A Mejerxol'd Method?: *Love for Three Oranges* (1914–1916)." *Slavic and East European Journal* 13, no. 1 (1969): 23–41.

———. *Meyerhold: The Art of Conscious Theater*. Amherst: University of Massachusetts Press, 1974.

Howarth, W. D., ed. *French Theatre in the Neo-classical Era, 1550–1791*. Cambridge: Cambridge University Press, 1997.

Hutcheon, Linda, with Siobhan O'Flynn. *A Theory of Adaptation*, 2nd ed. London: Routledge, 2013.

Iakulov, G. B. "Po povodu 'Printsessy Brambilly' (Beseda s G. B. Iakulovym)." *Vestnik teatra* 65 (May 18–23, 1920): 12.

Ignatov, Sergei S. *E.T.A. Goffman: Lichnost' i tvorchestvo*. Moscow: Tipografiia O. L. Somovoi, 1914.

———. "Hoffmaniana I (E. T. A. Gofman na stsene)." *LTA* 4–7 (1915): 179–82.

Il'inskii, Igor'. *Sam o sebe*. Moscow: Iskusstvo, 1973.

Iufit, A. Z., ed. *Russkii sovetskii teatr 1917–1921*. vol. 1 of *Sovetskii teatr: Dokumenty i materialy*. Leningrad: Iskusstvo, 1968.

———. *Russkii sovetskii teatr 1921–1926*. vol. 2 of *Sovetskii teatr: Dokumenty i materialy*. Leningrad: Iskusstvo, 1975.

Iutkevich, Sergei I. "Nachalo puti." In *Eizenshtein v vospominaniakh sovremennikov*, edited by R. N. Iurnev, 100–115. Moscow: Iskusstvo, 1974.

———. *Sobranie sochinenii v trekh tomakh*. Moscow: Iskusstvo, 1990.

Ivanov, Vladislav V., ed. *Mnemozina: Dokumenty i fakty iz istorii otechestvennogo teatra XX veka*. 6 vols. Moscow: Indrik, 1996–2014.

———. *Evgenii Vakhtangov: Dokumenty i svidetel'stva*, 2 vols. Moscow: Indrik, 2011.

Jentsch, Ernst. "On the Psychology of the Uncanny (1906)." *Angelaki: A New Journal in Philosophy, Literature, and the Social Sciences* 2, no. 1 (1996): 7–15.

Jestrovic, Silvija. *Theatre of Estrangement: Theory, Practice, Ideology*. Toronto: University of Toronto Press, 2006.

Johnson, James H. *Venice Incognito: Masks in the Serene Republic*. Berkeley: University of California Press, 2011.

Jurkowski, Henryk. *The Twentieth Century*, vol. 2 of *A History of European Puppetry*, 2 vols. Edited in collaboration with Penny Francis. Lewiston, N.Y.: Edwin Mellen, 1998.

Kaiser, Gerhard R. *E. T. A. Hoffmann*. Stuttgart: J.B. Metzler, 1988.

Kayser, Wolfgang. *The Grotesque in Art and Literature*. Translated by Ulrich Weisstein. New York: McGraw-Hill, 1966.

Kenez, Peter. "*Bezhin Lug (Bezhin Meadow)*." In *Enemies of the People: The Destruction of Soviet Literary, Theater, and Film Arts in the 1930s*, edited by Katherine Bliss Eaton, 113–26. Evanston, Ill.: Northwestern University Press, 2002.

Kepley, Vance, Jr. "Mr. Kuleshov in the Land of the Modernists." In *The Red Screen: Politics, Society, Art in Soviet Cinema*, edited by Anna Lawton, 131–46. London: Routledge, 2005.

"Khronika." *LTA* 1–3 (1915): 157–61.

Kleiman, Naum. "Arguments and Ancestors." In *Eisenstein Rediscovered*, edited by Ian Christie and Richard Taylor, 32–39. New York: London: Routledge, 1993.

Kniazhnin, Vladimir. "Hoffmaniana." *LTA* 1 (1914): 58–59.

———. "Hoffmaniana II." *LTA* 2 (1914): 54–55.

Kogan, D. *Sergei Iurevich Sudeikin, 1884–1946*. Moscow: Iskusstvo, 1974.

Konechnyi, A. M., et al. "Artisticheskoe kabare 'Prival komediantov.'" In *Pamiatniki kul'tury: Novye otkrytiia: Pis'mennost', iskusstvo, arkheologiia. Ezhegodnik 1988*, 96–154. Moscow: Nauka, 1989.

Koonen, Alisa G. *Stranitsy zhizni*. 2nd ed. Moscow: Iskusstvo, 1985.

———. "Stranitsy iz zhizni." *Teatr i muzika* 3 (1968): 97–115.

———. *Tri tetradki Alisy Koonen*. Edited by V. P. Nechaev, A. S. Shulenina and A. Zaslavskaia. Moscow: Navona, 2013.

Kozintsev [Kozintsov], Grigorii M. "Eccentrism." *TDR* 19, no. 4 (December 1975): 95–109.

Kozintsev [Kozintsov], Grigorii M., Georgii Kryzhitskii, Leonid Trauberg, and Sergei Iutkevich. *Ekstsentrizm*. Petrograd: Ekstsentropolis, 1922.

Krijanskaia, Dasha. "The Directing System of Alexander Tairov." Ph.D. diss., Utrecht University, 2002.

Kuzmin, Mikhail A. "Lesok." *Sobranie stikhov/Gesammelte Gedichte II: Gedichtbände nach der Revolution* 12 (1977–78): 535–63.

———. "Mirok ironii, fantastiki i satiry: Kukol'nyi teatr." In *Uslovnosti: Stat'i ob isskustve*, 38–39. Petrograd: Poliarnaia zvezda, 1923.

———. *Teatr v chetyrex tomakh (v dvukh knigakh)*. Edited by A. Timofeyev, Vladimir Markov, and George Cheron. 4 vols. in 2 bks. Oakland, Calif.: Berkeley Slavic Specialties, 1994.

Lanina, Tatiana, ed. *Meierkhol'd v russkoi teatral'noi kritike: 1920–1938*. Moscow: Artist. Rezhisser. Teatr, 2000.

Law, Alma H., and Mel Gordon. *Meyerhold, Eisenstein, and Biomechanics: Actor Training in Revolutionary Russia*. Jefferson, N.C.: McFarland, 1996.

Leach, Robert. "Eisenstein's Theatre Work." In *Eisenstein Rediscovered,* edited by Ian Christie and Richard Taylor. London: Routledge, 1993.

———. *Makers of Modern Theatre*. London: Routledge, 2004.

———. *Vsevolod Meyerhold*. Cambridge: Cambridge University Press, 1993.

Lee, Vernon. *Studies of the Eighteenth Century in Italy*. London: T. Fisher Unwin, 1887.

Lehmann, Hans-Thies. *Postdramatic Theatre*. London: Routledge, 2006.

Leyda, Jay, and Zina Voynow, eds. *Eisenstein at Work*. New York: Pantheon Books, 1982.

Listengarten, Julia. *Russian Tragifarce: Its Cultural and Political Roots*. Cranbury, N.J.: Associated University Presses, 2000.

Lopatin, N. I., and D. V. Fomin. *Russkii krug Gofmana*. Moscow: Tsentr Knigi VGBIL, 2009.

Maguire, Robert A., ed. *Gogol from the Twentieth Century: Eleven Essays*. Princeton, N.J.: Princeton University Press, 1974.

Malaev-Babel, Andrei. *Yevgeny Vakhtangov: A Critical Portrait*. London: Routledge, 2012.

Malmstad, John E. "Mixail Kuzmin: A Chronicle of His Life and Times." *Centrifuga: Russian Reprintings and Printings* 12, no. 3 (1977): 7–319.

Markov, P. A. *The Soviet Theatre*. London: Victor Gollancz, 1934.

Meierkhol'd [Meyerhold], Vsevolod E. "Amplua Aktera." Moscow: GVYRM, 1922. In *Meierkhol'd: K istorii tvorcheskogo metoda: Publikatsii, stat'i*, 41–43. Saint Petersburg: Kul'tInformPress, 1998.

———. [Doctor Dapertutto, pseud.]. "Glossy Doktora Dapertutto k 'Otritsaniiu teatra' Iu. Aikhenval'da." *LTA* 4–5 (1914): 67–80.

———. "Meierkhol'd govorit: Zapisi vyskazyvanii Vsevoloda Emil'evicha na repetitsiiakh i v besedakh," edited by A. K. Gladkov. In *Tarusskie stranitsy*, ed. V. Koblikov, N. Otten, N. Panchenko, K. Paustovskii, and A. Shteinburg. Kaluga: Kaluzhskoe knizhnoe izdatel'stvo, 1961.

———. *Meyerhold on Theatre*. Translated and edited by Edward Braun. London: Bloomsbury Methuen Drama, 1998.

———. *O Teatre*. Saint Petersburg: Prosveshchenie, 1913.

———. *Perepiska: 1896–1939*. Edited by V. P. Korshunova, M. M. Sitkovetskaia, introduced by Iu. A. Zavadskii. Moscow: Iskusstvo, 1976.

———. "Vs. Meierkhol'd: 'Portret Doriana Greia.'" Edited and introduced by S. Ginzberg. *Iz istorii kino* 6 (1965): 15–24.

———. *Stat'i, pis'ma, rechi, besedy*. Edited by A. V. Fevral'skii. 2 vols. (1891–1917; 1917–39). Moscow: Iskusstvo, 1968.

[———]. "Studiia: Klass Vs. E. Meierkhol'da." *LTA* 1 (1914): 61–62.

[———]. "Studiia: Klass Meierkhol'da: Tekhnika stsenicheskikh dvizhenii." *LTA* 4–5 (1914): 94–98.

[———]. "Studiia Vs. Meierkhol'da." *LTA* 2–3 (1916): 144–50.

———. [Doctor Dapertutto, pseud.]. "Sverchok na pechi, ili, u zamochnoi skvazhiny." *LTA* 1–3 (1915): 89–94.

———. "Vs. Meierkhol'd o Tairove." *Teatral'naia Moskva* 33 (1922): 14–15.

[Meierkhol'd (Meyerhold), Vsevolod E., and Vladimir Solov'ev]. "Studio: Klass Vs. E. Meierkhol'd i Vl. N. Solov'eva." *LTA* 4–5 (1914): 90–92.

Meierkhol'd [Meyerhold], Vsevolod E., Vladimir Solov'ev, and Konstantin Vogak. "Liubov' k trem apel'sinam: Divertisment: Dvenadtsat' stsen, prolog, epilog i tri intermedii." *LTA* 1 (1914): 18–47.

———. "Otkrytoe pis'mo avtorov divertismenta 'Liubov' k trem apel'sinam' A. A. Gvozdevu." *LTA* 4–5 (1914): 86–88.

Mgebrov, A. A. *Zhizn' v teatre*. 2 vols. Moscow: Academia, 1929–32.

Mikhailova, Alla, ed. *Meierkhol'd i khudozhniki*. Moscow: Galart, 1995.

Miklashevskii, Konstantin. *La commedia dell'arte, ili, Teatr ital'ianskikh komediantov XVI, XVII, i XVIII stoletii*. Saint Petersburg: Sirius, 1914–17.

Mitter, Shomit, and Maria Shevtsova. *Fifty Key Theatre Directors*. London: Routledge, 2005.

Muratov, Pavel. *Obrazy Italii*. Moscow: Nauchnoe slovo, 1912.

Nesbet, Anne. *Savage Junctures: Sergei Eisenstein and the Shape of Thinking*. London: I.B. Tauris, 2003.

Newmark, Kevin. *Irony on Occasion: From Schlegel and Kierkegaard to Derrida and De Man*. New York: Fordham University Press, 2012.

Nikitin, Andrei. *Moskovskii debiut Sergeia Eizenshteina (1920–1921)*. Moscow: Intergraf servis, 1996.

Nikitina, E. F. *Gogol' i Meierkhol'd: Sbornik*. Moscow: Nikitinskie subbotniki, 1964.

Noussinova, Natalia. "Eisenstein excentrique." In *Eisenstein: L'Ancien et le nouveau*, edited by Dominique Chateau, Francois Jost, and Martin Lefebvre, 67–75. Paris: Publications de la Sorbonne, 2001.

Oves, L. C., ed., *Nauchno-issledovatel'skii proekt po tvorcheskomu naslediiu V. E. Meierkhol'da "Liubov' k trem apel'sinam," 1914–1916*. 2 vols. Saint Petersburg: RIII, 2014.

Passage, Charles E. *The Russian Hoffmannists*. The Hague: Mouton, 1963.

Pearson, Tony. "Evreinov and Pirandello: Twin Apostles of Theatricality." *Theatre Research International* 12, no. 2 (1987): 147–67.

Peretts, V. N. *Italianskiia komedii i intermedii predstavlennyia pri dvorie Imperatritsy Anny Ioannovny v 1733–1735*. Petrograd: Imperatorskaia Akademiia Nauk, 1917.

Pesochinskii, N. V., E. A. Kukhta, and N. A. Tarshis, comp. and eds. *Meierkhol'd v russkoi teatral'noi kritike: 1898—1918*. Moscow: Artist. Rezhisser. Teatr, 1997.

Petrovskaia, I., and V. Somina. *Teatral'nyi Peterburg: Nachalo XVIII veka–oktiabr 1917 goda*. Saint Petersburg: Kul'turnaia initsiativa, 1994.

"Pokryvalo P'eretty: Pantomima v 3 deistv. Artura Schnitzlera s muzyk. E. Donani i prologom Iu. Baltrushaitisa." *Teatr: Gazeta s programmami i libretto vsekh moskovskikh teatrov* 1379 (1913): 38.

Posner, Dassia N. "Baring the Frame: Meyerhold's Refraction of Gozzi's *Love of Three Oranges*." *Theatre Survey* 56, no. 3 (September 2015): 362–88.

———. "Performance as Polemic: Tairov's 1920 *Princess Brambilla* at the Moscow Kamerny Theatre." *Theatre Survey* 51, no. 1 (May 2010): 33–64.

———. "A Theatrical Zigzag: Doctor Dapertutto, *Columbine's Veil*, and the Grotesque." *Slavic and East European Performance* 29, vol. 3 (November 2009): 43–57.

Posner, Dassia N., Claudia Orenstein, and John Bell, eds. *Routledge Companion to Puppetry and Material Performance*. New York: Routledge, 2014.

Posner, Donald. "Jacques Callot and the Dances Called Sfessania." *The Art Bulletin* 59, no. 2 (June 1977): 203–16.

Radlov, Sergei. *Desiat' let v teatre*. Leningrad: Priboi, 1929.

Raraty, M. M. "E. T. A. Hoffmann and His Theatre." *Hermathena* 98 (1964): 53–67.

Raskina, Raissa. *Mejerchol'd e il Dottor Dappertutto: Lo studio e la rivista "L'amore delle tre melarance."* Rome: Bulzoni, 2010.

Richmond, Steven. "'And Who Are the Judges?' Mikhail Bulgakov Versus Soviet Censorship, 1926–1936." *Russian History / Histoire Russe* 33, no. 1 (Spring 2006): 83–107.

Robinson, Harlow. "Love for Three Operas: The Collaboration of Vsevolod Meyerhold and Sergei Prokofiev." *The Russian Review* 45, no. 3 (July 1986): 287–304.

Röder, Birgit. *A Study of the Major Novellas of E. T. A. Hoffmann*. Rochester, N.Y.: Camden House, 2003.

Rozanov, Vasilii. *Legenda o velikom inkvisitore F. M. Dostoevskogo, s prilozheniem dvukh etudov o Gogole*. 3rd ed. Saint Petersburg: Izdanie M.V. Pirozhkova, 1906.

Rudnitskii, Konstantin. *Rezhisser Meierkhol'd*. Moscow: Nauka, 1969.

———. *Russian and Soviet Theater 1905–1932*. Edited by Lesley Milne, translated by Roxane Permar. New York: Harry N. Abrams, 1988.

———. *Russkoe rezhisserskoe iskusstvo: 1908–1917*. Moscow: Nauka, 1990.

Rumnev, A. A. *O pantomime, teatre, kino*. Moscow: Iskusstvo, 1964.

Schmidt, Paul, ed. *Meyerhold at Work*. Translated by Paul Schmidt, Ilya Levin, and Vern McGee. Manchester, U.K.: Carcanet New Press, 1981.

Schultz, Alexander. "The Mirror of Laughter: Mediation, Self-Reflection, and Healing in E. T. A. Hoffmann's *Princess Brambilla*." *European Romantic Review* 22, no. 3 (June 2011): 415–22.

Senelick, Laurence. *Gordon Craig's Moscow* Hamlet*: A Reconstruction*. Westport, Conn.: Greenwood, 1982.

———. *Historical Dictionary of Russian Theatre,* 2nd ed. London: Rowman and Littlefield, 2015.

———. "Nikolay Evreinov's 'Inspector General.'" *Performing Arts Journal* 8, no. 1 (1984): 113–18.

———, trans. and ed. *Russian Dramatic Theory from Pushkin to the Symbolists: An Anthology*. Austin: University of Texas Press, 1981.

Senelick, Laurence, and Sergei Ostrovsky, trans. and eds. *The Soviet Theater: A Documentary History*. New Haven, Conn.: Yale University Press, 2014.

Shcherbakov, Vadim. "Eizenshtein i Iutkevich peresozdaiut shedevr mastera." In *Meierkhol'd i drugie: Dokumenty i materialy*, edited by O.M. Fel'dman. vol. 2 of *Meierkhol'dovskii sbornik*. Moscow: OGI, 2000, 531–51. Moscow: OGI, 2000.

———. *Pantomimy Serebrianogo veka*. Saint Petersburg: Peterburgskii teatral'nyi zhurnal, 2014.

———. "Po obe storony maski." *Teatr* 1 (1990): 64.

———. "Pokryvalo P'eretty." In *Rezhisserskoe iskusstvo A. Ia. Tairova (K 100-letiiu so dnia rozhdeniia)*, edited by Konstantin Rudnitskii, 85–92. Moscow: VTO, 1987.

Shklovsky, Viktor. "The Making of *Don Quixote*." In *Theory of Prose*, translated by Benjamin Sher with an introduction by Gerald L. Bruns, 72–100. Normal, Ill.: Dalkey Archive, 1990.

Shlapentokh, Dmitry. *The Counter-Revolution in Revolution: Images of Thermidor and Napoleon at the Time of Russian Revolution and Civil War*. New York: St. Martin's, 1999.

Silberman, Marc, Steve Giles, and Tom Kuhn, eds. *Brecht on Theatre*. 3rd ed. London: Bloomsbury Methuen, 2015.

Sitkovetskaia, M. M., ed. *Meierkhol'd repetiruet*, vol. 1: *Spektakli 20-kh godov*. Moscow: Artist. Rezhisser. Teatr, 1993.

Skinner, Amy. *Meyerhold and the Cubists: Perspectives on Painting and Performance*. Bristol, U.K.: Intellect, 2015.

Smirnova, N. I. *Teatr Sergeia Obraztsova*. Moscow: Nauka, 1971.

Smith, Steven K. "Activist Theatre: From Brecht through Boal." *The Brecht Yearbook* 30 (2005): 289.

Solomonik, I. N. "Domashnye i studiinye spektakli." In *Kukly vykhodiat na stsenu: Kniga dlia uchitelia*, 136–51. Moscow: Prosveshchenie, 1993.

[Solov'ev, Vladimir], "Studiia: Klass Vl. N. Solov'eva." *LTA* 1 (1914): 60–61.

———. "Studiia: Klass Vl. N. Solov'eva: Osnovnye printsipy stsenicheskoi tekhniki improvizovannyi ital'ianskoi komedii." *LTA* 4–5 (1914): 93–94.

Starr, S. F. *Red and Hot: The Fate of Jazz in the Soviet Union, 1917–1980*. New York: Limelight Editions, 1985.

States, Bert O. *Great Reckonings in Little Rooms: On the Phenomenology of Theater*. Berkeley: University of California Press, 1985.

Sterne, Laurence. *Life and Opinions of Tristram Shandy, Gentleman*. Ware, U.K.: Wordsworth Editions, 1996.

Stevens, Geoff. *Circus Dictionary*. Buntingford, U.K.: Aardvark, 2004.

"Studiia: Programma." *LTA* 6–7 (1914): 105–15.

Sullivan, Lawrence. "Arthur Schnitzler's *The Veil of Pierrette*." *Europa Orientalis* 14, no. 2 (1995): 1–18.

Syssoyeva, Kathryn Mederos. "Meyerhold, Stanislavsky, and Collective Creation, Russia, 1905." In *A History of Collective Creation*, edited by Kathryn Mederos Syssoyeva and Scott Proufit, 37–57. New York: Palgrave, 2013.

Tairov, Aleksandr Ia. *Notes of a Director*. Coral Gables: University of Miami Press, 1969.

———. *O Teatre: Zapiski rezhissera. Stat'i, besedy, rechi, pis'ma*. Moscow: VTO, 1970.

———. *Proklamatsiia khudozhnika*. Moscow, 1917.

———. *Zapiski rezhissera*. Moscow: Izdatel'stvo Kamernogo teatra, Pervaia Obraztsovaia tipografiia MSNKh, 1921.

Tal'nikov, David L. *Novaia reviziia "Revizora": Opyt literaturno-stsenicheskogo izucheniia tealtral'noi postanovki*. Moscow: Gosudarstvennoe izdatel'stvo, 1927.

Tatar, Maria M. "E.T.A. Hoffmann's "Der Sandmann": Reflection and Romantic Irony." *MLN* 95, no. 3 (April 1980): 585–608.

Teatr: Kniga o novom teatre. Saint Petersburg: Shipovnik, 1908.

Taylor, Ronald. *Berlin and Its Culture: A Historical Portrait*. New Haven, Conn.: Yale University Press, 1997.

Tieck, Ludwig. *The Land of Upside Down*. Translated by Oskar Mandel in collaboration with Maria Kelsen Feder. London: Associated University Press, 1978.

———. *Ludwig Tieck's "Puss-in-Boots" and the Theater of the Absurd: A Commentated Bilingual Edition*. Translated and edited by Gerald Ernest Paul Gillespie. Brussels: Peter Lang, 2013.

Tikhvinskaia, Liudmila. *Povsednevnaia zhizn' teatral'noi bogemy Serebrianogo veka: Kabare i teatry miniatiur v Rossii, 1908–1911*. Moscow: Molodaia gvardiia, 2005.

Torda, Thomas Joseph. "Alexander Tairov and the Scenic Artists of the Moscow Kamerny Theater, 1914–1935." Ph.D. diss., University of Denver, 1977.

———. "Tairov's Princess Brambilla: A Fantastic, Phantasmagoric 'Capriccio' at the Moscow Kamerny Theatre." *Theatre Journal* 32 (December 1980): 488–98.

Tribble, Keith Owen. "European Symbolist Theater: Conventions and Innovations." Ph.D. diss., University of Washington, 1990.

———. "The Russian Premiere of Claudel's *L'Échange*." *Paul Claudel Papers* 3, no. 1 (2005): 81–98.

Vaingurt, Julia. *Wonderlands of the Avant-Garde: Technology and the Arts in Russia of the 1920s*. Evanston, Ill.: Northwestern University Press, 2013.

van de Water, Manon. *Moscow Theatres for Young People: A Cultural History of Ideological Coercion and Artistic Innovation, 1917–2000*. New York: Palgrave Macmillan, 2006.

Vendrovskaia, L. D., and M. A. Valentei et al., eds., *Vstrechi s Meierkhol'dom: Sbornik vospominanii*. Moscow: VTO, 1967.

Verigina, Valentina P. *Vospominaniia: Teatralnye memuary*. Leningrad: Iskusstvo, 1974.

Vermel', Samuil. "Ironiia i teatral'nost.'" *LTA* 2 (1914): 44–45.

Wachtel, Andrew. *Petrushka: Sources and Contexts*. Evanston, Ill.: Northwestern University Press, 1998.

———. *Plays of Expectations: Intertextual Relations in Russian Twentieth-Century Drama*. Seattle: Herbert J. Ellison Center, University of Washington, 2006.

Westwood, J. N. *Endurance and Endeavour: Russian History 1812–2001*. 5th ed. Oxford: Oxford University Press, 2002.

Worrall, Nick. "Meyerhold Directs Gogol's 'Government Inspector.'" *Theatre Quarterly* 2, no. 7 (1972): 75–95.

———. "Meyerhold and Eisenstein." In *Performance and Politics in Popular Drama: Aspects of Popular Entertainment in Theatre, Film, and Television, 1800–1976*, edited by David Bradby, Louis James, and Bernard Sharratt. Cambridge: Cambridge University Press, 1980.

———. *Modernism to Realism on the Soviet Stage: Tairov, Vakhtangov, Okhlopkov*. Cambridge: Cambridge University Press, 1989.

———. *The Moscow Art Theatre*. London: Routledge, 1996.

Zabrodin, Vladimir, ed. *Eisenshtein o Meierkhol'de, 1919–1948*. Moscow: Novoe izdatel'stvo, 2005.

———, ed. *Eizenshtein: Popytka teatra*. Moscow: Eizenshtein-tsentr, 2005.

Zelikson, Mikhail A., ed. *Kamerny teatr i ego khudozhniki*. Introduced by Abram Efros. Moscow: VTO, 1934.

Zhezhelenko, M. "Akimov." In *Portrety rezhisserov: Kedrov, Akimov, Tovstonogov, Pluchek, Efremov*. Edited by E. Ivanova, 55–96. Moscow: Iskusstvo, 1972.

Zhirmunskii, V. "Komediia chistoi radosti (*Kot v sapogakh*, Liudviga Tika. 1797 g.)." *LTA* 1 (1916): 85–91.

Zhitomirskaia, Z. V. *E. T. A. Gofman: Bibliografia russkikh perevodov i kriticheskoi literatury*. Moscow: Kniga, 1964.

Ziegler, Vickie L. *Bending the Frame in the German Cyclical Narrative: Achim von Arnim's "Der Wintergarten" & E.T.A. Hoffmann's "Die Serapionsbrüder."* Washington, D.C.: Catholic University of America Press, 1991.

Znosko-Borovskii, Evgenii. "Bashennyi teatr." *Apollon* 8 (1910): 31–36.

———. *Russkii teatr nachala XX veka*. Prague: Plamia, 1925.

Index

Page numbers in **boldface** refer to illustrations.